SECOND EDITION

IMPLEMENTING CHANGE

Patterns, Principles, and Potholes

GENE E. HALL

University of Nevada, Las Vegas

SHIRLEY M. HORD

Southwest Educational Development Laboratory

PEARSON

Boston   New York   San Francisco
Mexico City   Montreal   Toronto   London   Madrid   Munich   Paris
Hong Kong   Singapore   Tokyo   Cape Town   Sydney

Senior Editor: *Arnis E. Burvikovs*
Series Editorial Assistant: *Kelly Hopkins*
Marketing Manager: *Tara Whorf*
Production Editor: *Janet Domingo*
Editorial Production Service: *Lynda Griffiths*
Composition Buyer: *Andrew Turso*
Manufacturing Buyer: *Andrew Turso*
Electronic Composition: *Publishers' Design and Production Services, Inc.*
Cover Administrator: *Joel Gendron*

For related titles and support materials, visit our online catalog at
www.ablongman.com.

Between the time website information is gathered and then published, it is not unusual
for some sites to have closed. Also, the transcription of URLs can result in
typographical errors. The publisher would appreciate notification where these errors
occur so that they may be corrected in subsequent editions.

Library of Congress Cataloging-in-Publication Data

Hall, Gene E.
  Implementing change : patterns, principles, and potholes / Gene E. Hall, Shirley
M. Hord.—2nd ed.
    p. cm.
  Includes bibliographical references and index.
  ISBN 0-205-46721-0
    1. School improvement programs—United States.   2. Educational leadership—
United States.   I. Hord, Shirley M.   II. Title.
  LB2822.82.H355 2005
  371.2'00973—dc21

                                                                    2005049152

Printed in the United States of America

10 9 8 7 6 5 4 3 2 1   09 08 07 06 05

CONTENTS

CHAPTER FOUR

_____

Diffusion: Communication and Change Agents   **63**

CHAPTER FIVE

PART III   Tools and Techniques for Understanding the People Part of Change   108

CHAPTER SIX

CHAPTER TEN

▬▬▬

Defining Change Facilitator Style: Different Approaches Produce Different Results   207

PREFACE

We welcome you, the reader, to this book about understanding and facilitating the change process in organizational and educational settings. The ideas, research findings, and case examples presented here represent the cumulative understanding of researchers and those who have experienced change firsthand as leaders and participants. For some 35 years we and our colleagues have been contributing to this developing understanding through our own research, offering presentations and workshops, evaluating change efforts, and serving as coaches and mentors.

One clear conclusion is that we should be able to predict much more about what truly happens during this process than is typically the case. We also should be much better at attending to the needs of the people involved and preventing much that often goes wrong. Hopefully, our attempt to pass on some of what we have learned will be of help to you and the others with whom you are engaged during change.

The title of this book—*Implementing Change: Patterns, Principles, and Potholes*—is fittingly representative of its content. One of the problems in the field of change is that there is no agreement on the meaning of commonly used terms. For example, the word *change* itself can be a noun (e.g., the change that is being attempted) or a verb (e.g., changing the culture). The word also can be used to represent the whole of a change effort (e.g., "We have a big change underway!"). Having the term *implementing* as the first word in the tittle adds an important emphasis. Most changes require some time and effort to make them operational—in other words, implementation. As you will read throughout this book, we see that successful change begins and ends with understanding the importance of implementation constructs and dynamics.

The terms *patterns, principles*, and *potholes* have been carefully chosen as well. There are patterns in change processes, and most of this book is about describing and naming those patterns. In the study of change, as in the so-called hard sciences, there are a number of points, or principles, on which there is widespread agreement. We certainly do not know all that we should; however, some elements of change are understood and agreed on by many of us. All of us know full well that "potholes" may be encountered throughout a change process. While too often there is the inclination to give too much attention to these problems, it is foolish to ignore them.

We were very pleased with the positive reception and compliments received on the first edition of *Implementing Change*. Friends, colleagues, researchers, practitioners, and graduate students found the book useful. Still, there have been suggestions for improvements and we have learned more in the meantime. Therefore, in this second edition, we are making a few changes. We have dropped two chapters, made major changes in several others, and added three completely new chapters. **The major change is that we have broadened the change perspectives introduced. The primary emphasis continues to be on the concerns-based view. Other perspectives are introduced to add to your overall understanding of change.**

Part I opens by introducing one of the basic dilemmas of our time. What happens differently when change is initiated from outside versus inside? Over the last 40 years there has been a definite trend toward the impetus for change coming from outside the organization. This trend is easily charted in education. Many argue that ideally change should be initiated from within. However, this requires special conditions. Either way, there are a number of principles that hold. These are described in Chapter 1. Reading this chapter alone should lead to fewer surprises and more success in your change efforts. In Chapter 2 we describe characteristics of organizational culture that foster internal initiation of change. The chapter focuses heavily on the characteristics of professional learning communities, which represent an ideal for internal initiation, implementation, and maintenance of change.

The three chapters in Part II introduce three perspectives for understanding change that are classics. Each has an extensive history of research, model building, and applications. Each also offers a number of tools that can be used to facilitate, study, and evaluate change efforts. In Chapter 3 systems and systemic thinking are the topic. This approach became particularly important when the U.S. government needed a way to manage very large projects, such as construction of nuclear submarines and putting a man on the moon. Across the years of these massive undertakings, each piece had to be designed, fit together with the other pieces, and arrive at the assembly line at the right time. Chapter 4 introduces another of the classics: Diffusion. This perspective had its beginning early in the twentieth century with studies of the varying rates and willingness of farmers and others to adopt innovative practices. It very quickly became obvious that not everyone adopts an innovation at the same time. In Chapter 4 another perspective is introduced: Organization Development (OD). This approach focuses on group dynamics and the skills that can help teams be more effective. Organization Development offers a number of techniques and ways to facilitate change that can be useful. Chapters 6 through 10 deal with different patterns of the change process that we and our colleagues have studied.

Each chapter presents a basic pattern, construct names for the phenomenon, examples of what it looks like, descriptions of how to measure it, and implications for achieving change success. Each chapter also has a number of purpose-built features that are intended to help you draw connections between what you know now and what we would like you to understand when you have finished the chapters. To help ground the basic pattern being presented, every chapter begins with several quotes, which will probably be familiar to you. The ideas presented in the chapter illustrate how these quotes can be analyzed in terms of their meaning for change process success. To help you focus on some of the key topics in each chapter, a set of Focus Questions is offered near the beginning. Each chapter, except Chapter 12, also has a short case study, or vignette, that illustrates its pattern in action. To aid in remembering key points, a set of Guiding Principles is presenting following the Summary section in each chapter, except for Chapters 1 and 12. At the end of each chapter are a number of Discussion Questions and Fieldwork Activities designed to bring each of the patterns to life and to provide opportunities for you to test the constructs presented.

Based on recommendations from our reviewers, **we have added two new features in Chapters 2 through 11. One is "Implications for Leaders Facilitating Change."** The constructs presented in each chapter have direct implications for change facilitators. In this special section we offer key recommendations. **The second new feature is for those who are interested in research, evaluation, and assessing change processes. In "Using Constructs and Tools to Assess and Study Implementation," we offer ideas for using each chapter's constructs to design and conduct studies.**

As you will discover quickly, our particular perspective for viewing change, the Concerns Based Adoption Model or CBAM (pronounced "see-bam"), offers a number of important ways for understanding what change is about, especially as it relates to the people involved. There is a personal side to change, even when it is taking place in organizational settings. Our presentation of CBAM begins in Chapter 6 with the patterns and construct that explains this aspect of change. The chapters then build from the individual to the group to the whole organizational setting. In Chapters 9 and 10, change leadership is examined. In the last chapter, Chapter 12, we outline a systemic view of change along with examples of how a number of the constructs presented in the earlier chapters can be used simultaneously. We also use these constructs to examine the potential potholes in more depth. As we end the book, we explore some of our current enigmas as well, hoping to entice you into helping us learn by designing your own studies of change.

A large portion of this book was written with the assumption, and the expectation, that it is possible to be proactive in facilitating the change process. However, there are parts of the process that even the change leaders do not control. We call one key component of the uncontrollable "mushrooms," which is the topic of Chapter 11. Some change facilitators are skilled at detecting and addressing mushrooms, while others fail to see them at all. Although we think that this chapter will be of particular interest, an important caution is necessary. The chapter on mushrooms comes after ten other chapters, each of which presents a construct that needs to be understood *before* it is possible to explore the dynamics of mushrooms and what can be done about them.

So here it is. The new *Implementing Change* book! We hope that it will help you improve your understanding of the change process and how to facilitate change in ways that are responsible and beneficial. If you are interested in research, there are plenty of ideas scattered throughout that need to be systematically examined. Let us know what you are thinking of studying and what you learn.

We gratefully acknowledge the encouragement and support of our editor at Allyn and Bacon, Arnis Burvikovs. Arnis inherited us when we were completing the first edition. He has been steadfast in his efforts to see that we have a quality and substantively useful product. We also wish to thank the following reviewers: Patricia Cruzeiro, Chadron State College; Joyce Lieberman, Northern Illinois University; and Suzanne R. Painter, Arizona State University–West. We have considered and attempted to incorporate nearly all of their suggestions.

G. E. H.

S. M. H.

Dedication

We are indebted to the increasing number of teachers, school and district leaders, business leaders, and research colleagues who have generously shared with us their experiences with and befuddlements about change. Also, we continue to be indebted to our many CBAM colleagues around the world who have contributed to our learning about change and who have shared CBAM ideas with others.

We dedicate this edition to our departed colleagues Susan Loucks-Horsely and William L. Rutherford. Sue and Bill were caring colleagues and passionate professionals whose works contributed significantly to understanding and facilitating change. We, in addition to the profession, miss them enormously.

PART I

THE CONTEXT FOR IMPLEMENTING CHANGE

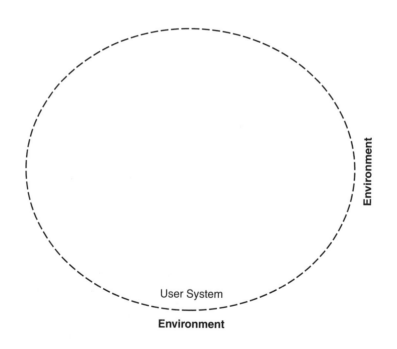

The graphic organizer on the opposite page is composed mainly of blank space. As constructs are introduced in each succeeding chapter, more information will be placed in this organizer. However, even this simple picture can be used to consider and learn about implementing change. As a beginning, there are only two words: *Environment* and *Culture*. The empty spaces that are outlined also symbolize important beginning ideas. The elliptical line identifies the boundary between the unit/organization that will implement change and the external environment within which it lives. This relatively simple drawing can be used to describe several of today's key understandings about change and several of the critical dilemmas.

One of the major dilemmas at this time has to do with the large number of change efforts that are being demanded by sources in the environment. Instead of organizations having the autonomy to consider, plan, and launch their own change initiatives, over the last several decades external forces such as state and federal policymakers, the courts, and various experts have set the change agenda. For example, high-stakes testing and the multiple mandates in No Child Left Behind (NCLB) are examples of external forces requiring change in schools. The Environmental Protection Agency (EPA) and the Occupational Safety and Health Administration (OSHA) are requiring businesses to implement changes. Rather than initiating change, organizations are having to respond to their environment and implement changes that were determined by outsiders.

Two important questions result from this tension between internal and external change forces:

1. How is implementing change different when the impetus for change comes from the environment versus being initiated internally?
2. What characteristics of an organization and the environment make it more likely to successfully initiate change from inside?

Addressing these questions are the topics in Chapters 1 and 2.

Chapter 1 describes 12 **principles of change** that most would agree apply regardless of whether the impetus for change is internal or external. Of course, there are some differences, and these will be noted. Still, this set of principles is important to successful change in both situations. Chapter 2 introduces constructs and research related to **organization culture.** There will be more, or less, implementation success depending on the condition and shape of the culture. Change success depends less on whether the source of the change is internal or external and significantly more on the degree to which the culture of the organization is open and ready to consider what is currently being done and is continually examining ways to improve. The ideal condition is to have a *professional learning community (PLC)*. Chapter 2 focuses on characteristics and the importance of facilitating the construction of a PLC-type organization culture.

■ ■ ■ ■ ■

CHAPTER 1

IMPLEMENTING CHANGE
Patterns, Themes, and Principles

Here we go again. You know how change is. It is like a pendulum, swinging back and forth.

We know from past experience that it is important to stay the course. It takes time to institutionalize new practices.

Learning means you are adjusting to change.
Art Linkletter on the *Larry King Show,* July 20, 2002

After all this research on classrooms, the inescapable conclusion is that building leadership makes a big difference.

Change has to hurt; it never is easy.

When everything comes together right, change is an energizing and very satisfying experience. Just think back to the times in your career that were the most fun.

There is an ancient Chinese curse that represents an excellent starting signal for our exploration of change. But before introducing this oft-quoted saying, take a minute to reflect about ancient times. We think of lives being simpler then. Most people lived on small plots of land, grew their own food, and had no education. All they knew about the world beyond the perimeter of their compound was what was told to them through myths, songs, and the occasional wanderer. In China, all of society was controlled by the emperor. There was stability, continuity, and predictability not only from year to year, but from generation to generation. In such a society, one of the worst things that you could say to someone was:

May you live in a time of change.

Now, think about life today. Change is everywhere. No one can escape change in his or her work or personal life. We are continuously bombarded with 18-second sound bytes about change: *the information age, downsizing, standards, diversity, substance abuse, violence, the economy, the environment, technology, change in schools.* It has gotten to the point where a popular saying is "The only person who likes change is a baby with a wet diaper!"

As inescapable as change is in today's world, we still tend to hope that change will avoid us personally and professionally. Further, when confronted with change, there is a natural tendency to focus on how to defend ourselves from it instead of how to use and succeed with it.

Comments such as those presented at the beginning of this chapter are typical of those heard when a new change initiative is proposed. Do they sound familiar? Of course they do. Every time we are engaged in change we have similar types of reactions and reflections about past experiences and perceptions of what the new will represent. The fact that all of us have heard such statements indicates that there are certain predictable themes and patterns to change. Perhaps, if we were to study such comments systematically, we could develop descriptions of what typically happens during change, which is the goal of this book.

For the past 35 years, the authors have been leaders of an international team of researchers studying the change process in schools, colleges, businesses, and government agencies. We have been systematically charting what happens to people and organizations when they are involved in change. Our research approach is different from that of others in a number of ways, including our primary focus on the people at the front lines who have to implement the expected change. Our secondary focus has been on how leaders can and do facilitate change.

The original team for these research efforts came together in the late 1960s at The University of Texas at Austin. From 1970 to 1986, this group studied the change process in schools and universities as part of the agenda of the Research and Development Center for Teacher Education. Along the way, researchers from around the United States, Belgium, the Netherlands, Australia, Canada, Taiwan, and several other countries joined in verifying the concepts and extending the research agenda. Now there is an international network of change process researchers who have conducted studies related to the concepts and principles presented here.

FOCUS QUESTIONS

1. Take a few minutes to think about change efforts that you have experienced. What three to five "principles" of change would you propose?
2. Which is better: required change from the outside or internally initiated?
3. Can teachers initiate and successfully implement change regardless of the amount of administrative support?
4. Does change have to hurt?

PRINCIPLES OF CHANGE

One important result of our long-term collaborative research agenda is that we now can draw some conclusions about what happens when people and organizations are engaged in change. A number of patterns have been observed repeatedly, and some have developed into major themes, or basic *principles,* and we do mean *principles.* As in the so-called hard sciences, there is now enough known about some aspects of the change process that we can state a series of principles that will hold true for all cases.

The change principles presented in this chapter are the givens underlying all that is presented in the subsequent chapters. From our point of view, these principles are no longer debatable points, for they summarize predictable aspects of change.

Before introducing selected principles about change, a caveat is needed: Each principle is not mutually exclusive, and at first reading some may seem inconsistent with others. Also, these principles do not cover all aspects of change. (Otherwise we would not need the other chapters in this book!) Instead, they address selected aspects of the change process in which the patterns are clear. Acknowledging that these principles are foundational to our way of thinking about change will save you time in trying to discover our implicit assumptions. In addition, understanding them should help you in predicting key aspects of change efforts with which you are engaged.

Also, we need to emphasize that at all levels—individual, organizational, and system—change is highly complex, multivariate, and dynamic. If it weren't so complicated, it would not be nearly as much fun to study, facilitate, and experience. So let's begin our journey of bringing order to change by introducing a set of principles about change that each of us has understood implicitly but probably not verbalized. Interestingly, we predict that you will be able to describe personal change experiences in which each of these principles has been ignored or violated. Certainly, your future change efforts can be more successful if these principles are acknowledged.

Change Principle 1: Change Is a Process, Not an Event

The very first assumption in our studies of change in the early 1970s was that change is a process, not an event (Hall, Wallace, & Dossett, 1973). In other words, change is not accomplished by having a one-time announcement by an executive leader, a two-day training workshop for teachers in August, and/or the delivery of the new curriculum/technology to the office. Instead, change is a process through which people and organizations move as they gradually come to understand and become skilled and competent in the use of new ways.

Our research and that of others documents that most changes in education take three to five years to be implemented at a high level (for example, see Hall & Loucks, 1977; Hall & Rutherford, 1976; George, Hall, & Uchiyama, 2000). Further, for each new unit (e.g., school, business, or state) that undertakes the change, the process will take three to five years. For each new adopting unit, the clock begins at the beginning. There are very few shortcuts. However, the use of the constructs and tools presented in this book will significantly reduce the time needed to achieve a higher level of implementation. Failure to address key aspects of the change process can either add years to, or even prevent, achieving successful implementation.

Unfortunately, too many policymakers at all levels refuse to accept the principle that change is a process, not an event, and continue to insist that *their* changes be implemented before their next election, which typically is within two years. This "event mentality" has serious consequences for participants in the change process. For example, the press to make change quickly means that there is no time to learn about and come to understand the new way, nor time to grieve the loss of the old way.

Have you ever realized that grief is a key part of change? Chances are that when people must change, they have to stop doing some things that they know how to do well and in fact like doing, which creates a sense of sadness. What many leaders see as resistance to change may in large part be grief over the loss of favorite and comfortable ways of acting. This personal side of change will be examined in depth in Chapter 7 on the Stages of Concerns about an innovation.

Although many other implications of this first principle will also be developed in subsequent chapters, one that is important to note here has to do with planning for change. The strategic plan for change will look very different depending on whether there is an assumption that change is a process or an event. If the assumption is that change is a process, then the plan for change will be strategic in nature. It will allow at least three to five years for implementation, and will budget the resources needed to support formal training and on-site coaching for the duration of this phase. There will be policies that address the need for multiyear implementation support, and data will be collected each year to inform the planners and further assist implementation in subsequent years.

If the assumption is that change is an event, the plan for implementation will be tactical in nature. It will have a short-term focus typically centering on one formal training session for teachers before school begins, no on-site coaching or follow-up, and perhaps a first-year evaluation to see if the new approach is making a significant difference. As will be described in later chapters, one usual consequence of not finding any significant differences in the first or second year of implementation is the mistaken conclusion that the new approach does not work, when in fact there was not enough time and support for implementation.

Examples of an event mentality can be seen also in the formal steps taken in the typical school improvement process. There will be several steps for developing the plan and then a single step for implementing it. If school improvement were being thought of as a process, instead of an event, it would be called school "improving." Such an event mentality was well expressed by one assistant superintendent who exclaimed in the spring of the first year of implementation, "What do you mean that teachers need more training!? We bought them the books. Can't they read?"

Change Principle 2: There Are Significant Differences in What Is Entailed in Development and Implementation of an Innovation

Development and implementation are two sides of the same coin. Development entails all of the activity related to creating an innovation, while implementation addresses establishing the use of the innovation in adopting sites. Development includes all of the steps and actions involved in creating, testing, and packaging an innovation, whereas implementation includes all of the steps and actions involved in learning how to use it. These two halves of the change process equation can be viewed as opposite ends of a balance. As illustrated in Figure 1.1, the typical pattern is to invest heavily, in terms of people, time, and resources, on the development side. This is true for both relatively simple innovations (such as new curriculum materials), complex innovation bundles, and large-scale policy changes (such as systemic reform). This creates an imbalance, since attention and investment are heavily loaded on the development side, and fails to acknowledge that implementation requires an equal investment of time and money.

However, there are some very important differences in how the development and implementation phases unfold. For example, the style of the change facilitators needs to be different. Change facilitators on the development side tend to be very visible and dynamic, whereas implementation facilitators need to have the patience to work daily with the front-line implementers who are attempting to figure out how to use the innovation.

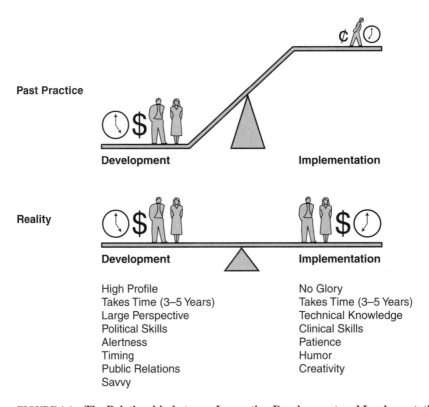

FIGURE 1.1 The Relationship between Innovation Development and Implementation

There are other differences between development and implementation. Leaders on the development side, such as policymakers, often lose interest once development is done and implementation begins. They are ready to move on to the next initiative, which frequently leads to loss of support for the implementation of the first initiative. By contrast, change facilitators on the implementation side have to have a great deal of patience and persistence. For example, they are frequently required to answer the same question from different individuals and to give each an appropriate response. Their patience is really tested when the same person asks the same question more than once! But to achieve implementation success, and to prevent small problems from turning into large ones, change facilitators must properly deal with each question.

Change Principle 3: An Organization Does Not Change until the Individuals within It Change

Although everyone wants to talk about such broad concepts as policy, systems, and organizational factors, successful change starts and ends at the individual level. An entire organization does not change until each member has changed. Another way to say this is that there is an individual aspect to organizational change. Even when the change is introduced to every member of the organization at the same time, the rate of making the change and of developing skill and competence in using it will vary individually. Some people will grasp the new way immediately, while most will need some additional time, and a few will avoid making the change for a very long time. Rogers (2003) has called this third group "laggards." Even when the change is mandated, some individuals will delay implementation. One implication of this principle is that leaders of organizational change processes need to devise ways to anticipate and facilitate change at the individual level.

This principle does not mean that all of the interventions (e.g., on-site coaching or a telephone hot line to address specific questions) in a change process must be addressed at the individual level. Nor does it mean that every individual will be at a different point in the process. People respond to and implement change in typical patterns which will be described in the following chapters. Change process leaders can and should anticipate many of these patterns. Many interventions should be targeted toward subgroups (e.g., principals training in what the change entails), and many others should be aimed at the organization as a whole. Still, since there is an individual element to how the change process unfolds, many of the interventions must be done with and for individuals.

Change Principle 4: Innovations Come in Different Sizes

As this chapter unfolds, we are gradually introducing key terms that will be used in the other chapters and that will add to your understanding of how the change process works. The concept of an *innovation* is one of these. When most people think or talk about change, they focus on what will be changed—in other words, the innovation.

But other than being aware that there is an innovation, most leaders do not seem to consider that there are ways to characterize innovations, and that they can vary in the amount of time, resources, and effort required for implementation.

For example, innovations can be either *products,* such as computers, curriculum texts, or assessment techniques, or *processes,* such as constructivist teaching techniques, principles of self-esteem in character education, or student teamwork. Depending on the type of innovation and its characteristics, the change process can require more time and be more resource consuming or relatively quick and simple to implement.

Another important implication of the innovation concept is that change initiatives are not typically centered on a single innovation but rather a *bundle* of innovations. In other words, several innovations will be frequently masquerading as one. Although a single name may be used—such as magnet schools, inclusion, literacy programs, restructured high schools, and integrated use of technology—each of these innovations in fact is a bundle of smaller innovations. For example, the integrated use of technology in reading and science instruction might entail the use of word processing, spreadsheets, e-mail, the World Wide Web, laptops, and video, each an innovation with its own requirements for implementation, training, and user supports.

Size is another important characteristic of innovations. Some are relatively small and simple, such as using a new edition of a standard curriculum text; others are enormous in terms of their complexities and demands on prospective users. Van Den Berg and Vandenberghe (1986) have proposed the concept of *large scale* to describe very complex school- and systemwide changes. Large-scale innovations require major changes in the roles of teachers, principals, and schools; take five to eight years to implement; and demand specialized training and ongoing consultation. In the United States, even larger innovations are implied in the term *systemic reform,* whose goal includes simultaneously changing all parts of curriculum and teaching in an entire state.

Change Principle 5: Interventions Are the Actions and Events That Are Key to the Success of the Change Process

As people plan and lead change processes, they tend to be preoccupied with the innovation and its use. They often do not think about the various actions and events that they and others take to influence the process, which are known as *interventions.* Training workshops are perhaps the most obvious type of intervention. Although workshops are important, the research studies cited in this book document that many other kinds of interventions are significant also, and that some are even more crucial to achieving change success!

Interventions come in different sizes. Interestingly, the most important interventions are the little ones, which most leaders forget to do or forget about having done. When change is successful, it is the quantity of the little things that makes the final difference. One of the major types of small interventions is what we call the "one-legged interview." One frequent opportunity for one-legged interviews occurs when a teacher and a principal meet in the corridor. If they do not talk or if they have a social chat, these do not count as innovation-related interventions. However, if the principal or teacher initiates a brief discussion about the innovation, then it is a one-legged interview type of intervention.

We use the name "one-legged" to indicate that these interventions are brief (most people can't stand on one leg very long), since both the teacher and the principal probably have to be somewhere else when the next bell rings. Yet a moment was taken to talk about the teacher's involvement with the innovation. The research reported in later chapters consistently indicates that teachers are more successful with change in schools where there are more one-legged interviews.

We will talk more about one-legged interviews in Chapter 9 on interventions. Here, the point is that it is critical to distinguish between the concepts of innovations and interventions. Change process leaders tend to think only about the innovation and not to think sufficiently about interventions in terms of an overall plan for and during the unfolding of the change process; and many fail to appreciate the value of the little interventions.

Change Principle 6: There Will Be No Change in Outcomes until New Practices Are Implemented

Organizations are under heavy pressure to increase performance. In business, the press is to increase productivity, quality, and sales. In schools, the bottom line is the expectation to have ever-increasing student scores on standardized tests. To improve performance, many policymakers and executives are placing heavy emphasis on evaluating the end results. For schools, this is seen in the widespread focus on high-stakes testing. Annual testing of students has been mandated, and by the No Child Left Behind Act there are negative consequences for schools that do not show adequate increases in test scores. An implicit assumption with this approach to change seems to be that schools will incorporate the necessary changes to make test scores go up. However, little support is being made available to schools to implement changes.

Figure 1.2 illustrates this problem. Imagine a setting where there is a very large and deep chasm with schools engaged in current practice located on the left cliff. On the right side of the chasm are the increases in student outcomes that are desired. Strategies that focus only on the right side fail to acknowledge several implementing change realities. First, if there are no changes in practice, there is little reason to expect a change in outcomes. As principals often observe, "If you always do what you have always done, you will continue to get what you always have gotten." The second failure is in relation to Change Principle 1: Change is a process, not an event. If it takes three to five years to implement new practices to a high level, then it is highly unlikely that there will be positive increases in outcomes during the first or second year of implementation. In the scene shown in Figure 1.2, practitioners are being asked to make a *Giant Leap*. They are being directed to improve outcomes without any support to improve or change their current practices.

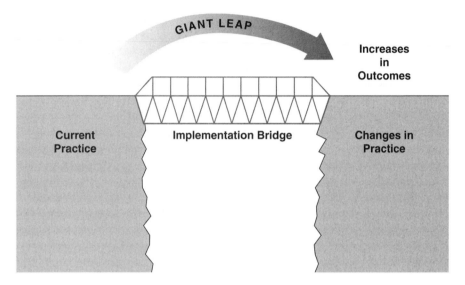

FIGURE 1.2   Implementation Bridge   Without an implementation bridge individuals and organizations must make a giant leap

In order for change to be successful, an *implementation bridge* is necessary. Each member of the organization (Change Principle 3) has to move across the implementation bridge. As they change their practices, there should be changes in outcomes. Without an implementation bridge, there is little reason to expect positive change in outcomes. Instead, there are likely to be casualties as attempts to make the giant leap fail. Individuals and whole organizations may fall into the chasm.

Each chapter in this book presents research-based constructs and tools that can be used to facilitate individuals and organizations in moving across the bridge. The constructs and tools also can be used to measure the extent to which they have moved across the bridge. These implementation assessment data can then be correlated with outcome measures. Ideally, outcomes should be higher for those individuals and organizations that have moved further across the bridge. This was the case in one large study that was done of implementation of standards-based teaching of mathematics (George, Hall, & Uchiyama, 2000). Students in classrooms with teachers who had moved further along with implementation had higher test scores.

Change Principle 7: Administrator Leadership Is Essential to Long-Term Change Success

A central theme of advocates for bottom-up change is that those nearest the action have the best ideas of how to accomplish the change. There are many implementers who believe that they do not need any involvement from or with those above them. But here again, the findings of research and experience argue for a different conclusion.

Many of us have had firsthand experience with trying to implement some sort of innovative effort from the bottom. A classic example for the authors of this book was when we first worked together as teacher education faculty members. We were hired to create and implement an experimental teacher education program based on the teacher concerns model of Frances Fuller (1969). We and several others formed a multidisciplinary faculty team that developed and operated an experimental teacher education program that was truly an innovation bundle, one that included innovations such as professor teaming, an all-day blocked schedule for students, early field experiences, and a partnership of principals and teachers. In short, it incorporated many of the innovations that are found in what are now called "professional development schools."

Although the teacher education program was very successful and became well known nationally and internationally, it died after five years. It did not become the regular teacher education program at our university, nor did it have much direct influence on the traditional teacher education program.

As faculty, we were at the proverbial bottom of the organization. As long as we had the energy, we were able to work collaboratively to develop and implement an innovation bundle. Although that bundle turned out to be successful, over time our faculty colleagues in the regular programs and the administration of the university did not actively support the continuation of the bundle nor the implementation of any of the specific innovations into the regular programs. Without their long-term support, the innovation withered and was forgotten.

The point here is not to analyze what we might have done to garner more administrator support (which we will do in other chapters). Rather, our goal is to use a firsthand experience to show that although the "bottom" may be able to launch and sustain an innovative effort for several years, if administrators do not engage in ongoing active support it is more than likely that the change effort will die.

In many ways Principle 7 is a corollary of Principle 6, since everyone along the Policy-to-Practice Continuum has a role to play if change is going to be successful. Yes, teachers and professors can create and implement new practices. Yes, administrators have to do things on a day-to-day basis that are supportive. (Remember those one-legged-interviews?) Administrators also have to secure the necessary infrastructure changes and long-term resource supports if use of an innovation is to continue indefinitely. And finally, yes, policymakers need to design polices that legitimize the infrastructure changes and innovative practices and encourage the continued use of the innovation.

Change Principle 8: Mandates Can Work

Change Principle 5 introduced the concept of interventions and gave special attention to a category of small interventions called one-legged interviews. Among the number of other types of interventions that will be described in later chapters, one of the more common is known as a *strategy*. A mandate is one kind of strategy that is used widely. Although mandates are continually criticized as being ineffective because of their top-down orientation, they can work quite well. With a mandate the priority is clear, and there is an expectation that the innovation will be implemented. The mandate strategy falls down when the only time that the change process is supported is at the initial announcement of the mandate. When a mandate is accompanied by continuing communication, ongoing training, on-site coaching, and time for implementation, it can work. As with most change strategies, the mandate has gotten a bad name, not because the strategy itself is flawed but because it is not supported with other necessary interventions.

Change Principle 9: The School Is the Primary Unit for Change

Although we have and will continue to emphasize the importance of understanding the dynamics of individuals in change, the key organizational unit for making change successful is the school. The school's staff and leaders will make or break any change effort, regardless of whether the change is initiated from the inside or outside. However, the school is not an island, but rather part of a district, state, and federal system of education. The school can and must do a lot by itself, but it also needs to move in concert with and be supported by the other components of the system.

Note the assertion that schools need outside support. Change is a complex, dynamic, and resource-consuming endeavor. No single organization, be it a school or a national corporation, is likely to have all the expertise and resources needed to succeed in change. As will be emphasized in later chapters, *external* change facilitators, as well as supports from other parts of the system, are necessary. This is why the concept of "local control" does a disservice to organizations such as schools. Change processes are easier and chances of sustained success are increased as the school staff understands more about how to use external resources and as those external to the school recognize the importance of their roles in facilitating each school in achieving change success.

Everyone, teachers and principals in a school and personnel in the district office, must consider and view how a school advances as a change process unfolds. Many of the same interventions, such as training teachers (and principals) in their roles with the innovation, can in fact be made throughout a district, especially during the first year of implementation. However, by the second year different schools will be moving at different rates and will have different change successes and challenges. Thus, at least some of the key interventions will need to be targeted specifically for each school.

Change Principle 10: Facilitating Change Is a Team Effort

In this book we will emphasize repeatedly the importance of facilitating the change process, which means that there must be ongoing leadership for change to be successful. In Chapter 10 we will describe different Change Facilitator Styles and the significance of each. Embedded in all of this and in many of the principles presented here is the core belief that change is a team effort. Just as in Change Principle 9 we stressed that no school is an island, we argue here that collaboration is also necessary among those responsible for leading change efforts.

Although in Change Principle 7 we described the crucial role of the school principal, we want to emphasize that many others also have a responsibility to help change processes become successful. Indeed, other administrators play important roles, as do front-line users and nonusers of the innovation. Teachers, for example, play a critical leadership role in whether or not change is successful. We really are in this phenomenon together, and all must help to facilitate the change process.

Team leadership for change extends far beyond the school site. In many ways all of the actors across the Policy-to-Practice Continuum (see Table 1.1) are contributors to change success. Each of these role groups has the potential to strongly influence what happens at the local site and with individual users. State and federal executives and policymakers obviously have the potential to affect change in schools. Each time there is an election, voters hear about the "education" governor/president. Administrators and staff in the school district office can make important contributions to efforts to move across the implementation bridge. Each of these "external" roles can, and do, make significant differences in the degree of success of change processes. Colleagues make a difference, too. Teachers and others inside the organization can help implementation efforts.

Change Principle 11: Appropriate Interventions Reduce Resistance to Change

One of the big questions about change has to do with dealing with resistance. In most change efforts some people will *appear* to be resisting and some may be actively sabotaging the effort. The first step is to determine the reason for the apparent resistance. Often what appears to be resistance is really working through the sense of loss for having to stop doing something that was comfortable. A second form of resistance is grounded in having serious questions about whether the change will really be an improvement. This questioning may be due to limited understanding about the new, or it may be based in solid reasoning and evidence. There is a third form of resistance that some see. Several contemporary writers have stated in one way or another that change is painful, and assert that this pain must be endured as a natural part of the

TABLE 1.1   The Policy-to-Practice Continuum

FEDERAL	STATE	DISTRICT	SCHOOL	CLASSROOM
President	Governor	Superintendent	Principal	Teacher
Secretary of Education	Commissioner of Education	Board of Education	Site Council	
Congress	Legislature			

change process. These authors might leave you feeling that only the masochist likes change. But this does not have to be the case.

Each of the three cases for apparent resistance have very different underlying reasons. To address these concerns requires very different interventions. In most situations, addressing the resistance requires attending to individual differences (Change Principle 3). *If* the process is facilitated well, change can be fun, and it certainly does not have to hurt or even be dreaded. Of course, there are moments of frustration and times of grieving over what is being lost. However, if there is major pain in change, chances are strong that the leadership for the change process has not understood what is entailed and required to facilitate the process. In each of the following chapters, basic constructs, measures, research findings, and case examples are introduced and used to describe ways of more effectively facilitating change. If these tools are understood and used well, there should be little resistance, or pain, and large gains.

Change Principle 12: The Context of the School Influences the Process of Change

In considering the school as the unit of change, we can think of it as having two important dimensions that affect individuals' and the organization's change efforts:

1. The *physical features,* such as the size and arrangement of the facility, and the resources, policies, structures and schedules that shape the staff's work
2. The *people factors,* which include the attitudes, beliefs, and values of the individuals involved as well as the relationships and norms that guide behavior

An increasing body of literature on the influence of workplace culture has evolved from both educational writers who study school improvement and from members of the corporate sector who are concerned with quality and its relationship to profits. Interestingly, these two rather disparate worlds share common views about desirable organizational conditions that result in effective staff performance and customer satisfaction/high-level learner outcomes.

In schools that have created such organizational conditions, the staff collectively reflects on its work with students and assesses its influence on student results. In this collegial inquiry, the staff may identify areas for improvement. Interestingly, addressing these improvement targets begins with the staff's identification of what *they* must learn in order to more effectively help students become more successful learners. This community of "professional learners" (Hord, 1997) embodies individuals who value change and who seek change in order to increase their efficacy as teachers. Having such a learning-oriented staff can contribute profoundly to how the change process unfolds and ultimately succeeds in a given school.

One attribute of these change-ready staffs is shared and supportive leadership. Such a community demands a sharing principal who is working participatively with the teachers in their quest for high-quality learning.

In Chapter 2, we review the literature and describe additional characteristics of these professional learning communities, whose culture embodies those conditions that are conducive to and supportive of change. The operationalization of these factors in a school makes a significant difference in the staff's concerns about change and in how the staff moves to higher-quality implementation of change. The following vignette presents a brief change story as a way to summarize what these change principles are like in action.

■ ■ ■ ■ ■ ▬▬▬▬▬▬▬▬▬▬▬▬▬▬▬▬▬▬▬▬▬▬▬▬▬▬

V I G N E T T E

A DISTRICTWIDE CHANGE INITIATIVE: PRINCIPLES ADDRESSED, PRINCIPLES MISSED

During the writing of this book, one of the authors was invited to conduct a CBAM training workshop for a medium-size school district. While the district leaders were facilitating change in ways that were consistent with most of the principles outlined in this chapter, several of the principles were being violated, with predictable results.

The district teachers had been engaged in implementing a well-known model of teaching for three years (Principle 1). This initiative was a districtwide mandate of the superintendent (Principles 7 and 8). The teachers, as well as the district office curriculum and staff development personnel, had received extensive training in the use of the teaching model (Principles 3 and 5).

As in most school districts, a number of other change initiatives and mandates were being advanced in the district at the same time. For example, each school was engaged with school improvement plans, annual standardized testing, inclusion, technology, and a new mathematics curriculum, and the elementary schools were engaged in restructuring the primary grades (Principle 4). Ironically, even with all of these change initiatives at work in the schools, the principals were allowed only to leave their schools for training in the teaching model; they had not received training in what any of the other innovations entailed. The change facilitation training was done with all the central office professionals, but no principals (Principles 7 and 10). The teachers received extensive training through workshops, but there were no specialized interventions to help teachers individually (Principles 5 and 11).

Further, although implementation of the teaching model had been underway for three years, there were no efforts by the district leadership to adjust change-facilitating interventions on a school-by-school basis. All schools were being treated in the same way (Principle 9).

As could be predicted, there was an undercurrent of talk about how too much attention had been given to the teaching model and not enough to a number of the other priorities. There also was dismay over the fact that principals were not permitted to leave their buildings for training in how to help teachers implement any of the other innovations (Principle 11).

Two principles were not supported in this situation: Principle 9, which argues that each school be seen as a unit of change; and Principle 10, which underlines the need for a

(continued)

■ ■ ■ ■ ■ ▬▬▬▬▬▬▬▬▬▬▬▬▬▬▬▬▬▬▬▬▬▬▬▬

V I G N E T T E   CONTINUED

team to facilitate change. As a result, the teaching model was being used well in some class-rooms and some schools but not in others.

What was needed next was a process that would help all of the system's profession-als—the district staff, principals, and teachers—realize that they were part of the same sys-tem and that they all had role responsibilities. The verticality of the superintendent's centralized directives was not allowing for a horizontal policy-to-practice perspective to de-velop. The need for each role group to do its own jobs well was being eroded. There was training of some, but the sense of a team effort was not being developed. The key to form-ing a horizontal/teaming approach was missed by prohibiting principals from participating in learning about what teachers were doing with the other innovations and about how to use change-facilitating concepts. An additional change leadership objective was missed by not assuring that all district change facilitators developed a common language about the change process and ways to facilitate it. A shared language gives those who have the opportunity to facilitate change a better understanding of how to do so, which means that teachers will have more success in implementing the various innovations that have been introduced.

VIGNETTE CRITIQUE QUESTIONS

1. If Principles 5, 9, 10, and 11 had been in place in this district, what specific differ-ences would they have made?
2. What should be done next in this district?
3. Think about a systemwide change process you have experienced. Which change principles were present and absent? Which, in your opinion, were key to its success and/or failure?

▬▬▬▬▬▬▬▬▬▬▬▬▬▬▬▬▬▬▬▬▬▬▬▬▬▬▬▬▬▬

SUMMARY

The main reason for writing this book is to describe what has been learned about fa-cilitating the change process. This knowledge, if used well, can reduce, if not avoid altogether, the apprehension and dread associated with change, and lead to success-ful results. Nearly all of the ideas and suggestions made are derived from research. In this chapter we have laid the foundation by summarizing a set of change principles that represent some of the predictable patterns about change in organizational set-tings. A very important next step is to develop an understanding and appreciation of the personal side of change, which we will address with the concept of *Stages of Con-cern*. The fact that leaders do make a difference will be addressed through our re-search on *Change Facilitator Style*. The leaders' actions, known as interventions, will be reviewed as well. Don't forget that the change process we are describing is taking place inside an organizational setting. The people in each organization have con-structed a culture based on values and norms that represent the beginning context for change. Consideration of this culture will be explored in Chapter 2.

We will constantly be asking you to think about situations that you are experiencing and about how you can facilitate change. This is done throughout to help you tie the various ideas together and to learn how to make them useful in your setting.

We are living in a time of change. But rather than viewing it as a painful curse, let's figure out how it works, how to facilitate the process, and how to learn from our experiences. To accomplish these outcomes, the following chapters are organized around key change process concepts. Each chapter includes research findings and examples of how the concepts can be used to facilitate change. Occasionally we point out areas where more research is needed. The primary purpose, though, is to introduce ways to understand how the change process works, and how to be most effective in influencing and facilitating that process.

DISCUSSION QUESTIONS

1. With which of the change principles presented in this chapter do you strongly agree? With which do you strongly disagree? Why?

2. Does change have to hurt? Explain your answer.

3. Change Principle 11 addresses resistance to change. Is resistance always necessary? When is resistance appropriate? What if the innovation is "bad"?

4. Describe a change process that you have had or are experiencing. Point out where the different principles fit. Do any of them explain why certain things have gone well and what is, or was, problematic?

FIELDWORK ACTIVITIES

1. Interview a person in a leadership role in a school district or other type of organization. Ask him or her to propose three to five principles they have learned about change. How do their principles compare with those presented in this chapter? How do they compare with yours?

2. Select a school or other type of organization and learn about the effort to implement a major innovation. Make a chart of the internal and external leaders of the change process. What types of facilitating interventions is each person making? To what extent are the individuals working as a Change Facilitator Team?

ADDITIONAL READINGS

Reigeluth, C. M., & Garfinkle, R. J. (1994). *Systemic change in education.* Englewood Cliffs, NJ: Educational Technology Publications.
Sarason, S. B. (1996). *Revisiting "The culture of the school and the problem of change."* New York: Teachers College Press.

CHAPTER 2

DEVELOPING PROFESSIONAL LEARNING COMMUNITIES AND UNDERSTANDING ORGANIZATIONAL CULTURE

Our principal expects us to work together on instruction, but provides no time in our schedule to do this; furthermore, he makes all the decisions about our classrooms anyway.

(Fifth-grade teacher)

Can you believe it? The school board added several days to our contract year, spread those days across the school year, so our middle school teachers meet to share and learn new instructional strategies.

Middle school principal

I am going to the state board of education to lobby for professional development resources so our high school departments can learn how to function collaboratively with each other.

High school mathematics department head

Did you know? The faculty and administrators in my children's schools get together regularly just like my medical doctors do to learn the latest and most effective ways to teach children. And, to review individual student learning problems. Are we lucky in this district, or what?

Parent in a local school district

I am so happy in my new job. I am part of the Cheese Department team for our largest market. Our team meets to decide on purchases, pricing, and such. We know that we are successful because of customers' satisfaction and the profit and loss sheet.

Staff person in a Whole Foods store

The culture in which organizations function, whether they are public sector schools, private corporate entities, or others, has a profound influence on the individual in the organization and on his or her individual and collective productivity. A growing literature has been developing as researchers and writers study to understand this phenomenon and its impact. What exactly is *culture?* A typical definition proposed by Marvin Harris (1968) states, "The culture concept comes down to behavior patterns associated with particular groups of people, that is to 'customs,' or to a people's 'way of life'" (p. 16). However, this definition ignores the distinction between the outsider's and insider's perspectives. Customs, behaviors, and patterns of conduct can be interpreted from multiple points of view. In response to this idea, Spradley (1979), an anthropologist, proposed that "culture . . . refers to the acquired knowledge that people use to interpret experience and generate social behavior" (p. 5). Both the conscious and subconscious minds are acquiring this knowledge from the individual's environment. It can be said, then, that a person becomes acculturated to a particular set of behaviors; behaviors represent the culture.

However, scholar/practitioner Edgar Schein (1992) maintains that "the culture of a group can now be defined as a pattern of shared basic assumptions that the group learned as it solved its problems . . . that has worked well enough to be considered valid and, therefore, to be taught to new members as the correct way to perceive, think, and feel in relation to those problems" (p. 12). Further, Schein analyzes levels of culture as "*artifacts,* the visible organizational structures and processes; espoused *values* . . . strategies, goals, philosophies . . . that are espoused justifications and generated by the conscious mind; and *basic underlying assumptions,* that are the unconscious, taken-for-granted beliefs, perceptions, thoughts and feelings" (p. 17) that come from the subconscious mind. In Schein's writing, the group has a common goal, vision, and mission that they work on as they do their work. The group's shared assumptions are influenced over time by their knowledge and experience.

Trice and Beyer (1993), sociologists, defined culture as "collective phenomena that embody people's responses to the uncertainties and chaos that are inevitable to human experience" (p. 2). These authors further identify two categories of these responses. One is the substance of a culture (shared belief systems); and the second is cultural forms (the observable actions by which the culture's members share and communicate the substance of their culture to each other). From these two categories, cultures develop and grow. "Cultures are a natural outgrowth of the social interactions that make up what we call organizations" (p. 2).

According to Trice and Beyer (1993), it is imperative for leaders of change efforts to be conscious of their organizations' cultures, to recognize dysfunctional elements, and to attempt to guide cultural evolution so that the organization can survive. Schein (1992) maintains that leaders must manage cultures or "the cultures will manage them. . . . Cultural understanding is essential to leaders if they are to lead" (p. 15). Guiding, leading, or managing culture is not yet well understood, but much attention is being given to it. More research in today's schools and businesses begs to be done, so that we might have better understanding of if and how culture can be "managed."

FOCUS QUESTIONS

1. What is organizational culture?
2. How does organizational culture influence the process of change in schools?
3. What is valued in a culture that is conducive to change?
4. How would the professionals, and all staff, interact in such a context?
5. What would a school be like where the focus is on the professional development of all, and the norm is continuous improvement in teaching and learning?
6. How would the change process work in the learning organization culture?

CONTEXT? CLIMATE? CULTURE?

For a long time, organizational culture has been a subject of corporate world inquiry, and although schools have been likewise interested, educators have given real attention to this area only fairly recently and have tended to look at climate. Despite the mandates in the last decades from state and district levels for schools to develop a climate that supports school improvement, little change in climate has occurred, due partly to lack of understanding about what climate is (James & Jones, 1974), what such a climate might look like, and how to achieve such a climate even if one knew what its characteristics might be.

To slice through this confusion and inconsistency about the use of the terms *context, climate,* and *culture,* we offer the following definitions:

1. *Climate* is the individuals' perceptions of a work setting in terms of *a priori* established concepts that can be measured empirically.
2. *Culture* is the individually and socially constructed values, norms, and beliefs about an organization and how it should behave that can be measured only by observation of the setting using qualitative methods.
3. *Context,* as defined in Boyd's (1992b) review of the corporate and school literature, is comprised of (a) culture (as defined above) and (b) ecological factors or situational variables.

Boyd (1992b) points out that the culture (people or human factors) and the situational variables (physical or structural factors) interact to make up the context, and that these two sets of vartiables are difficult to separate in terms of their individual and collective effects in a setting during the change process. Nonetheless, these concepts are important for understanding change in organizational settings. What may at first appear to be a semantic difference can in fact offer very important and useful additions to the change facilitator's portfolio of knowledge, skill, and understandings.

This chapter looks at the school organization's culture embedded in its context, and how it interacts with the individuals engaged in the organization's work. We know that institutions, or organizations, do not change; individuals do. We know also that, although the individuals change the organization, the organization has a profound influence on its people.

ORGANIZATIONAL CONTEXT

Obviously, organizational productivity is affected by its individual staff member's productivity. Currently, organizations are encouraged to remain open to the creative talents of its members and to innovation and improvement to best serve their clients. This is assessed to be true for schools as well as the corporate sector. Therefore, whether in the corporate sector or in schools, attending to the staff's work-related needs is imperative. Those studying workplace cultures of both schools and business have an important message for school improvers.

Five Disciplines

Senge (1990) was not the first to study and write about organizational culture, Argyris (1982), Deal and Kennedy (1982), Likert (1967), McGregor (1960), Schein (1985), and others have analyzed and commented (sometimes profusely) about the organizational culture of corporations and how people in particular settings can work more effectively. In addition. Deal and Peterson (1990), Boyd (1992b), and Boyd and Hord (1994) have identified factors that describe school organizational cultures that support the current, and likely the future, unprecedented demands on schools to change.

Senge's (1990) thinking about work in the corporate setting, reported in *The Fifth Discipline,* captured the attention of educational leaders who are struggling to persuade schools to become interested in change and improvement. Senge, looking to the work of Argyris (1982), identified factors that individuals and the organization collectively need to establish to become a "learning organization." Five disciplines, or ways of thinking and interacting in the organization, represent these factors. The

---

GUIDING PRINCIPLES OF ORGANIZATIONAL CULTURE

1. Organizations adopt change; individuals implement change.
2. The organizational culture influences the work of individuals.
3. Organizations must value and support individuals in change efforts.
4. There are identifiable factors that describe the context of learning organizations.
5. Leadership for change facilitation is shared among all participants of a professional learning community.
6. The unceasing quest for increased effectiveness drives the professional learning community.

first is *systems thinking,* a consideration of the whole system that also recognizes the parts and their patterns and interrelationships (see Chapter 3). The systems approach makes it possible to structure interrelationships more effectively. This discipline integrates the other four, fusing them into a coherent body.

Building a shared vision, the second discipline, is the construction of compelling images shared by the organization's members and focused on what the organization wants to create. These shared pictures of the future foster genuine commitment. *Personal mastery,* the third discipline, is the practice of continually clarifying and making personal vision more precise, identifying what each individual wants in his or her personal participation in the organization. Senge believes that unless all personal visions are included, there can be no shared vision.

The fourth discipline, the use of *mental models,* involves separating what has truly been observed from the assumptions and generalizations that people make based on their observations. Here, individuals reveal their assumptions for all to examine. The final discipline, *team learning,* is the activity of coming together to discuss and to learn with and from each other. Developing team learning skills involves each individual balancing his or her own goals and advocacy to achieve collaborative decision making that serves the well-being of all. This description of the interactive, collegial, vision- and decision-sharing "learning organization" can be found in the educational setting (Boyd & Hord, 1994)—and it is this new and infrequently found school culture that commands our attention and challenges our action.

Seventeen Factors

Boyd (1992a), reviewing a wide range of the literature on organizational context in the public and private sectors, identified 17 indicators that describe an educational context conducive to change. These 17 factors were clustered into four functional groupings by Boyd and Hord (1994): (1) reducing isolation, seeking to bring staff together into closer proximity so that interacting and working together is supported; (2) increasing staff capacity, which uses professional development to increase the staff's knowledge and skills to work together collaboratively; (3) providing a caring, productive environment that addresses not only the factors that support productive work but also the affective factors that contribute to the staff feeling valued and cared about; and (4) promoting increased quality, in which the staff continuously assesses their work in order to increase their own effectiveness and that of the school. How the 17 indicators relate to the functional groupings is portrayed in Figure 2.1.

These factors were found actively operating in the Driscoll Square School, which was being studied by the Leadership for Change (LFC) Project of the Southwest Educational Development Laboratory (Hord, 1992, 1993). The LFC staff was interested in understanding how schools and their leaders go about the work of school change. The Driscoll School strongly exemplified the descriptors of Senge's (1990) "learning organization" and Boyd's (1992a) 17 indicators of a context conducive to school change. The Driscoll School can be characterized as a *professional learning community (PLC)* (Boyd & Hord, 1994), which is one whose professional staff meets

FIGURE 2.1   Indicators of a Context Conducive to Change  *(Boyd + Hord)*

REDUCING ISOLATION

Schedules and structures that reduce isolation
Policies that foster collaboration
Policies that provide effective communication
Collegial relationships among teachers
A sense of community in the school

INCREASING STAFF CAPACITY

Policies that provide greater autonomy
Policies that provide staff development
Availability of resources
Norm of involvement in decision making

PROVIDING A CARING, PRODUCTIVE ENVIRONMENT

Positive teacher attitudes toward schooling, students, and change
Students' heightened interest and engagement with learning
Positive, caring student-teacher-administrator relationships
Supportive community attitudes
Parents and community members as partners and allies

PROMOTING INCREASED QUALITY

Norm of continuous critical inquiry
Norm of continuous improvement
Widely shared vision or sense of purpose

regularly and frequently to reflect on and inquire into its practices, and to learn together and take action on their learning for the benefit of students. The brief picture of this school's culture and other elements of its context presented in the vignette is illuminating.

■ ■ ■ ■ ■

VIGNETTE

THE DRISCOLL SQUARE SCHOOL DIFFERENCE

The Driscoll Square School, an elementary school built in 1923, is located in a large city on the fringe of the downtown industrial area. Like many schools in older urban cities, its population decreased as more and more people moved to the suburbs. Because of the decline in enrollment, the school was slated to be closed. However, a few tenacious parents prevailed, and it was saved—but as an open enrollment school, which meant that it had to generate an enrollment large enough to justify keeping the doors open.

A new principal brought the vision of a child-centered school and shared authority for those working with the children. The formerly ill-maintained school soon sparkled with

(continued)

children's art, music, singing, and dance. Each day now starts with Morning Meeting, when all children and staff meet in the basement to celebrate children's birthdays and accomplishments: a first-grader reading his first primer aloud to the audience, third-graders demonstrating a Native American dance; and fifth- and sixth-graders modeling how peer mediation helps to solve disagreements without fisticuffs.

Another regular event is Faculty Study, where all faculty meet on Thursdays, getting together as a total group some weeks and as grade groups on others. This two-hour block of time was gained by extending the instructional day four days a week and abbreviating it on Thursday, an arrangement that was reached after much lobbying and the signing of documents that declared that no teacher was coerced into accepting this agreement. These structures and schedules form the basis of the school's "learning community" in which all individuals refer to themselves as "family." They proclaim that the "Driscoll Difference" represents their essence. And what does this essence—their philosophy, values, and beliefs about children—look like operationally?

ANALYSIS

Morning Meeting has established a feeling that "we are all together in this enterprise," meaning that all adults and all children are involved. Further, since all teachers "own" all children, no teacher hesitates to take whatever kind of action seems appropriate with any of the children. Most of the faculty eat lunch in one room, where they share interests, concerns, and congratulations about all the children and themselves. Because the school is crowded, there was some consideration of using this area for a classroom. But after much soul searching, the faculty determined that their program and ways of operating would not be able to continue as effectively without this common meeting space.

Faculty Study makes it possible for the entire staff to be in one place at one time on a regular basis, with enough time to study and learn together, identify and solve problems, consider issues, and stay together on any and all matters. This has resulted in the development of the following important cultural norms:

1. A widely held vision of what the school should be
2. Broadly based decision making across the faculty that includes a management team that energetically represents the teachers' views
3. Widely distributed and inclusive leadership wherein everyone takes responsibility to bring new ideas, help each other implement the ideas, and share the leadership function, so that they operate differently from an organization with a "hero leader"
4. A pervasive attachment to critical inquiry that challenges faculty to regularly say to themselves:
   - What are we doing for our children?
   - Is there a better way?
   - Let's try it! (This is an expression of Little's [1982] "norms of collegiality and experimentation.")
5. A norm of continuous, seamless improvement

In this culture, there is no fear about introducing and implementing change. Change is valued and sought as a means of achieving improved effectiveness; change and im-

■ ■ ■ ■ ■ ▬▬▬▬▬▬▬▬▬▬▬▬▬▬▬▬▬▬▬▬▬▬▬▬▬▬▬▬▬

V I G N E T T E   CONTINUED

provement are introduced by everyone and are a way of life. However, adoption and implementation are not done frivolously. Much thought and study are given to changes and
whether their implementation will support and/or enhance the school's mission.

1. Do you know of a school that exemplifies the kind of culture described at Driscoll?
   How did this culture develop at the school?
2. What is the role of the principal and/or key teachers in the development and operation of a school that acts as collegially as Driscoll does?
3. Discuss the advantages and disadvantages, in terms of change process, for schools
   that operate as Driscoll does.

THE PLC CONTEXT AND CULTURE

Rosenholz (1989) first brought teachers' workplace factors into the discussion of
teaching quality by maintaining that teachers who felt supported in their own ongoing learning and classroom practice were more committed and effective than those
who were not supported. Such support was manifested as teachers worked together,
sharing their craft and wisdom, learning from each other, and collaborating on problems and issues of concern to them. This support increased teacher efficacy, which
meant that they gave more attention to students' needs and adopted new classroom
behaviors more readily.

Darling-Hammond (1996), Lieberman (1995), Little (1982), and McLaughlin
and Talbert (1993) agreed with Rosenholz, and have been increasingly clear and in-
sistent about the need to provide teachers with a context that supports their professional endeavors and nurtures their collaborative efforts. Their research has revealed
the influence of the workplace culture on teachers' practice and, consequently, on
outcomes for students. Darling-Hammond observed that workplaces that are supportive of teachers are few and far between, and that attention must be focused on rethinking the organizational arrangements of the work setting.

Typically, schoolwide change efforts have been short term and lacking in participation by the entire staff. Encouraging the staff's motivation to change so that improvement in the school is ongoing has been a formidable challenge to school change
leaders. If the context of the school affects teachers' ability and inclination to change,
what does the research tell us about such school settings?

Dimensions of a Professional Learning Community

The professional learning community (PLC) has become widely heralded as the way
for professional staff of schools to work for student benefits. The norms of collabo-

ration and democratic participation in decision making, as well as sharing power and authority, contribute to a culture in which the staff grows in professionalism and efficacy. This efficacy instills a confidence that each faculty member is influential in the learning process of his or her students, persuading faculty that each student can learn with the appropriate material and strategies. The PLC is one approach to a school's culture. In a review of the research on this topic, Hord (1997) identified the five dimensions of professional learning communities as follows: (1) shared values and vision, (2) collective learning and application, (3) supportive and shared leadership, (4) supportive conditions, and (5) shared personal practice (see Figure 2.2).

Shared Values and Vision.   In the schools where the professional staff—administrators and teachers—is organized in learning communities, they share an undeviating focus on student learning. The staff assumes that students are academically able and create visions of the learning environment that will enable each student to realize his or her potential. In this community, each individual member is responsible for his or her own actions, but the common good is uppermost. The relationships of the individuals are described as caring, and they are encouraged by open communication and trust. The vision of the PLC maintains a focus on quality, in the work of the staff and the students.

Collective Learning and Application.   In the PLC, people from across the organization work together collaboratively and continually. This approach is grounded in reflective dialogue in which the staff have conversations about students, learning, and teaching, citing related issues and concerns. The reflection is accompanied by inquiry that forces debate among the staff about what is important and provides them with opportunities for learning from and with each other. As a result of these learning conversations and interactions, decisions are made collectively, and new ideas and information are used in problem solving. The collective learning and widely shared decision making are in turn applied to action and new practice, thus expanding the

FIGURE 2.2   Dimensions of Professional Learning Communities

Shared values and vision: The staff's unswerving commitment to students' learning, which is referenced for the staff's work

Collective learning and application: The application of the learning to solutions that address students' needs

Supportive and shared leadership: Jointly held power and authority that involve the staff in decision making

Supportive conditions: Physical and human capacities that promote collaborative organizational arrangements and relationships

Shared personal practice: Feedback and assistance from peers that support individual and community improvement

---

repertoire of all. Schools where the staff is sharing, learning, and acting on their learning are labeled problem-solving schools, or centers of inquiry and improvement.

Supportive and Shared Leadership.   If a school staff is working collaboratively and making decisions, the role of the principal remains a highly significant one, with the principal participating with the staff as a learner and contributing democratically to decision making. This new relationship leads to a collegial leadership in which all staff members are growing and playing on the same team. Three factors are required of principals whose school staff is operating as PLCs: a need to share authority, the ability to facilitate the work of the staff, and the capacity to participate without dominating.

Supportive Conditions.   Supportive conditions provide the infrastructure and basic requirements of the when, where, and how the staff can collectively come together as a whole to learn, to make decisions, to do creative problem-solving, and to implement new practices—actions that are characteristic of the PLC. Two types of conditions are necessary: physical or structural conditions (James and Jones's [1974] situational variables), and the human qualities or capacities of the people involved. Examples of each type are provided next.

Physical Conditions.   These factors include the time to meet and interact, the size of the school and proximity of the staff to each other, communication procedures, and resources. Schedules and structures that reduce isolation of the staff are important so that they can come together. Policies that foster collaboration and provide for staff development should be in place. Time is a vital resource and the hardest to find. This factor is bedeviling and currently being explored so that more creative ways may be found to create time for staff to meet and do collaborative work.

People Capacities.   Positive teacher attitudes toward students, schooling, and change are found among staff in PLC arrangements. Staff's heightened interest in continuous learning and norms of critical inquiry and improvement are routinely in place. Staff's openness to feedback, which typically assumes trust among the individuals involved, must be developed for the PLC to operate optimally.

Shared Personal Practice.   In the PLC, teachers visit each other's classrooms to review their teaching behavior. This practice is in the spirit of peers supporting peers. In these visits, teachers observe, script notes, and discuss observations after the visit. Making time for these activities is difficult, but the process contributes to the individual's and the community's improvement. Mutual trust and respect are imperative. The staff must develop trust and caring relationships with each other. These relationships develop through both professional problem-solving activities and social interactions of the staff. As a result, the staff finds support for each other's triumphs and troubles.

In terms of the change process, when a school staff works collaboratively in a PLC culture, the outcomes for the staff are significant, as reported by Hord (1997) in the literature review. Not only do teachers express more satisfaction and higher morale (school climate factors) but they also make teaching adaptations for students, and these changes are done more quickly than in traditional schools. In such a context, teachers make a commitment to making significant and lasting changes, and they are more likely to undertake fundamental, systemic change.

Who Is the Professional Learning Community?

As noted earlier in the dimensions of a PLC, there is sharing of ideas and responsibilities. The bringing of ideas and taking responsibility are assumed by the community of professionals in schools at the campus setting, or at the district level. Essentially, all professional staff—administrators, teachers, counselors, and others— are involved in reflecting on their practice and its benefits for their clients—in this case, students. They assess what they do for students and whether their various instructional practices are or are not resulting in appropriate effects. If not, they identify what they need to learn to do differently in order to change, so that their students are successful learners. As noted in Figure 2.3, students are always at the heart of the community's conversation and efforts, but it is the campus professionals who have the responsibility and accountability to serve students well. In addition to the professional community, there are increasing circles of individuals who influence by their actions and policies (school board, parents, district office, community citizens) the work of the campus professionals. This structure is depicted in Figure 2.3.

Benefits of a Professional Learning Community

The research that has been conducted on professional learning communities reveals benefits that accrue to the staff and to students in a variety of settings and arrangements.

Schools.   Lee, Smith, and Croninger (1995) conducted an extensive study, sharing findings on 11,000 students enrolled in 820 secondary schools across the nation. In the schools characterized as PLC, the staff worked together and changed their classroom pedagogy. As a result, students were engaged in high intellectual learning tasks, and they achieved greater academic gains in math, science, history, and reading than those in traditionally organized schools. In addition, the achievement gaps between students from different family backgrounds were smaller in these schools, students learned more, and, in the smaller high schools, learning was distributed more equitably.

The schools in the study were communally organized and this arrangement promoted staff and students to commitment to the mission of the school; staff and students worked together to strengthen the mission. In these schools, teachers

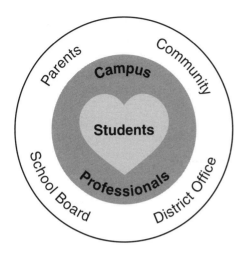

FIGURE 2.3   Who Is the Community?

Source: Achieving Learning Success for Each Student: Transforming Intentions into Reality. Northwest Regional Educational Laboratory for the Association Partnership including AASA, NAESP, and NASSP, Portland, Oregon.

envisioned themselves as responsible for the total development of the students and they shared a collective responsibility for the success of all students. In addition, the teachers and other staff expressed more satisfaction and higher morale, and students cut fewer classes and there was a lower drop out rate. Both staff and students contributed to lower rates of absenteeism.

In a study by Bobbett, Ellett, Teddlie, Olivier, and Rugutt (2002), the researchers found in a study of Louisiana schools that a strong positive relationship existed between teachers' professional commitment found in the professional culture of the schools and school performance of the students. The school's professional culture was the strongest predictor of school performance in the elementary schools in the study. After statistically controlling for the effects of poverty, teachers' professional commitment and collegial teaching and learning in the school culture accounted for a large amount of the variation (23 percent) among schools in school effectiveness and outcomes (on school test scores).

Leadership Teams.   In a recent evaluation study in Louisiana, the external evaluator and external facilitators noted that in Louisiana Alliance schools the principal, external facilitators, and leadership team supported the faculty's implementation of the Collaborative School Reform model. These leaders provided abundant guidance and assistance to the teachers in using the model. (Further discussion is included in the next section on leadership in the PLC.) In those schools where there was more support, and subsequently where more frequent meetings of the teachers in subgroups and the whole group engaging in community conversations occurred, the degree of implementation of the process was greater. This higher level of implementation was associated with increased student gains on the state accountability measures (Rood & Hinson, 2002).

University.   In yet a different setting, Gonzalez, Resta, and De Hoyos (2005) looked at the barriers and facilitators related to the implementation of policy initiatives to transform the teaching-learning process in higher education. The transformation required a different approach to classroom instruction, and this was mandated by the highest level of the university's administration. After several years of staff development to support the faculty in changing their instructional practices and an effort to develop professional learning communities of the faculty, a study showed that those faculty who perceived they were part of a PLC expressed concerns about their impact on students. Those teachers who did not view themselves as having membership in a PLC expressed concerns for managing their classrooms and other time and logistical management issues. If these outcomes can be attributed to the presence of a professional learning community culture, what roles can leaders play or what strategies do they employ to create and maintain a professional learning community?

LEADERSHIP IN A PROFESSIONAL
LEARNING COMMUNITY

Although Hargreaves (1997) does not use the term *professional learning community,* he suggests that "the central task in creating cultures of educational change is to develop more collaborative working relationships between principals and teachers and among teachers themselves" (p. 2). According to Schmoker (1997), school personnel are being asked, many of them for the first time, to be "thinking contributors who can generate solutions to emergent problems and obstacles. This is something new . . . [to be] brought together—regularly—to be asked for their suggestions, to develop real solutions to the most pressing concerns students face" (p. 143). Similarly, Zmuda, Kuklis, and Kline (2004) have maintained that a competent system necessitates several important changes that resonate here, "from an environment of isolation to one of collegiality . . . from individual autonomy to collective autonomy and collective accountability" (p. 1).

Collegial Learning

Collegial learning provides a means for enabling the culture of educational change. Thus, in their study of change, Caine and Caine (1997) quoted a teacher as saying that "actively processing in a social context is increasing my learning" (p. 197). And, in a poetic form, Wheatley and Kellner-Rogers (1996) exclaimed "that life leaps forward when it can share its learning" (p. 34). By supporting individual members, organizational learning can offer a very promising avenue to more successful change processes. This kind of organizational culture fosters mutual respect and regard, high levels of trust, and innovative solutions to problems. The faculty experiences the social and emotional support that these cultures produce. The staff is intellectually challenged by their peers and their work, and develop higher intellectual learning tasks for students. Teachers' conversations with other staff strengthens their content knowledge and broadens their repertoire of instructional strategies they bring to their students.

In schools where the staff exemplifies the learning organization, the principal is not "the sage on stage," as some have suggested, but "the guide on the side." The requirement to understand and consider the implementer's concerns and evolving use of new practices does not diminish. And the leadership actions and strategies necessary to support implementation remain de rigueur. It is how the leadership role plays out that differs.

Sharing Responsibilities

In the learning organization context, all members of the staff share the leadership role, although the nominal leader remains the point person. Ultimate responsibility must not be abandoned, and the positional leader (principal, superintendent, etc.) assumes and maintains this responsibility—but operationally in a less visible and more democratic way. Everyone on the staff contributes ideas for change, and everyone contributes to the interventions or strategies needed for high-quality implementation (discussed in Chapter 9). The staff participates with their peers in these strategies and facilitates implementation. These strategies are:

Developing a shared vision

Planning and providing resources

Investing in professional learning

Checking on progress

Providing continuous assistance

Creating a context conducive to change

With the sharing of tasks, the obligation of any one individual is lessened—and strengthened. Each individual has the opportunity to be involved in a highly active, committed way. Over time, the opportunities are accepted, and expectations and norms are established for continuing this kind of behavior. The staff values their role of involvement as decision makers and facilitators of improvement. They experience a new dimension of their efficacy as professionals. In this way, the entire staff develops facilitating leadership that supports change. The first step in making such a support structure possible is for school and district leaders to declare high-quality professional learning for all faculty as part of the daily work. They make it a priority goal within their settings.

Using Conversations

It has been suggested that the professional learning community is a network of conversations. This being the case, the role of leaders is to support the conversations with the physical conditions necessary for the staff to meet: time, a location, and policies that support the time that the staff invests in their community of conversations. Change leaders must also attend to the emotional and interpersonal needs and skills of the participants. Thus, developing the skills of the staff in active listening, setting aside assumptions while in the conversation, and trying to understand each other's comments and making meaning of them are all necessary skills to be developed.

Additional attention must be given by leaders to enabling the community to articulate a shared system of beliefs, explanations, and values, referred to as the *organizational culture,* which is continually sustained by further conversations (Capra, 1997). In a study that asked hundreds of executives and employees to describe the quality of conversations (as a Core Business Process) that had a powerful impact on them, Brown and Isaacs (1997, cited by Capra) reported about respondents' comments:

> There was a sense of mutual respect between us.
>
> We took the time to really talk and reflect about what we each thought was important.
>
> We listened to each other, even if there were differences.
>
> I was accepted and not judged by the others in the conversation.
>
> We explored questions that mattered.
>
> We developed a shared meaning that wasn't there when we began.

Types of Leadership

Capra (1997) clarified that two types of leadership are needed for conversation and community work. The first is the traditional idea of a leader—the person who is able to formulate the mission of the organization, to sustain it, and to communicate it well. The other kind of leadership is what facilitates the development and evolution of the community. This latter type is not limited to a single individual but is distributed, and its responsibility becomes a capacity of the whole. This means that there is the building up and nurturing of the conversations in a climate of warmth, mutual support, and trust, and where there is continual questioning and rewarding of innovation. Thus, leadership means creating conditions, rather than giving directions, and includes the freedom to make mistakes. Although there is the spirit of disagreement and debate, these communities are caring communities as well as learning communities.

IMPLICATIONS FOR LEADERS FACILITATING CHANGE

The local board of education must support, encourage, and persuade the school staff to engage in collaborative work. They do this by providing districtwide time across all schools for the staff to meet as a community. Further, the board communicates to the district community the purpose and benefits to be derived for their children when the professional staff meet and work in this way.

The superintendent of a district and the principal of a school are key to the creation and maintenance of any culture; most certainly this is true of professional learning communities. Therefore, these positional leaders must make certain that logistical and organizational arrangements are available to support the PLC.

Skills for operating as a professional learning community must be developed across the entire staff; otherwise, the PLC will not be productive. This suggests that the central office staff has roles to play in developing the capacity of campus-based administrators and teachers to work collaboratively.

An enduring focus should guide the professional learning community's work, and that focus is always on student results.

There should be accountability measures for the professional learning community's work (i.e., objectives that focus on outcomes for students, an agenda, activities to reach objectives, minutes of the meetings).

Other Ideas to Be Considered

Positional leaders model the democratic participation that they hope to engender in staff. They hire new staff that come with strong values of collaboration and collegiality, and they reward collaboration among teachers. They identify and support the acquisition of additional skills and models that focus on resolving conflict, using data for decision making, using criteria for making selection of new practices, and using criteria for selecting research results to be used by the group in improving its practice.

In collaborative school cultures, principals remain key to shaping the norms, values, and beliefs of the staff. Principals shape culture in the multiple daily interactions they have with the school community. Kent Peterson (Allen, 2003), who has studied and written about school culture for many years, has described the principal as a potter who builds culture through hiring, budget, and supervisory decisions; the principal is a poet whose written and oral messages can reinforce a healthy culture; the principal is an actor on all the stages of school events; and the principal is a healer who can help repair the culture when tragedy, conflict, or loss occurs. Such actions by the principal and other leaders produce schools that are anchored in relationships and intellectual tasks that stimulate and challenge each member of the community to be his or her very best.

NEEDED EVALUATION, RESEARCH, AND DEVELOPMENT ON ORGANIZATIONAL CULTURE

The literature on professional learning communities is relatively new. Not a lot has been written, and although there is a core of material that provides clear content, there are some reports that appear to be more focused on the typical school improvement process.

There is a need for additional rigorous research studies that will lead to understanding the contribution of the professional learning community or learning organization to the successful planning and implementation of change efforts. Some of the study questions related to PLC as an organizational arrangement in schools or other organizations are:

Does the PLC provide the most desirable context for the efficient, high-quality implementation of change?

Does it support staff in moving more quickly to resolve lower stages of concern (see Chapter 7) and then to progress to higher stages?

Does the collaborative nature of the individuals in this arrangement aid staff in their growth and development to higher levels of use (see Chapter 8)?

Just what interventions do the staff provide to their peers in their collective endeavors to change and increase their effectiveness (see Chapter 9)?

What configurations of the PLC might be discovered in such studies, and to what effect (see Chapter 6)?

There are skills that the community of professionals must learn in order to do this work together; in addition to these skills there are tools for continuously assessing where they are in providing the most effective strategies and the highest-quality instructional programs for students. What are the most effective means for developing these skills and becoming effective in using the tools in the PLC membership?

The ultimate and most important question for continued study is: How does the culture of a professional learning community affect student learning results, or the "bottom line" in other organizations?

STRATEGIES FOR FACILITATING A COLLABORATIVE CULTURE

We have seen a wide array of strategies and techniques that leaders may use to launch and develop a culture of collaboration. A final set of ideas, from Knapp, Copland, and Talbert (2003), contributes to the knowledge base of school leaders who build work cultures around learning:

Create structures for regular staff interaction about learning and teaching.

Set up cycles of schoolwide inquiry into learning and teaching performance.

Identify and address staff assumptions about norms, values, and beliefs related to learning.

Recruit teachers who work from a values base consistent with the culture that leaders seek to develop.

Create opportunities for staff to have a voice in decisions about issues related to teaching and learning.

Celebrate accomplishments in student and teacher learning.

Clearly, there is much to be done to build a collaborative culture—that is, a professional learning community—that is focused on continuous improvement.

OUR CLOSING PITCH

Joyce, Wolf, and Calhoun (1993) contend that the design and operation of the organization, rather than the staff, have been the major problem in improving schools. This idea can be inferred from our description of the professional learning community as a preferred arrangement. Further, they maintain that changing the organization will result in increased creativity and vitality of teachers and students. The challenge, then, is to create organizational settings (the school) that honor all individuals (children and adults) in a caring, productive environment that invites and sustains a continuous quest for improvement.

We, the authors, have lived and worked in a "learning organization" of the type that Senge (1990) has described; we have observed and studied a few schools that have the cultural attributes of a learning organization; and we profoundly believe that schools must develop this kind of context if real and continuous change and improvement are to occur. We see this as the educational challenge for the immediate future—and it is our own personal challenge as researchers and improvers. As Wheatley (1992) has suggested,

> We are beginning to look at the strong emotions that are part of being human, rather than . . . believing that we can confine workers into narrow roles, as though they were cogs in the machinery of production. . . . We are focusing on the deep longings we have for community, meaning, dignity, and love in our organizational lives. (p. 12)

SUMMARY

There is wide agreement that the professional culture described in this chapter—one with an efficacious and caring staff, whose *heart* and *mind* are focused on children—is what is needed in schools today. In this chapter we have shared commentary from a wide array of school and organizational theorists and reformers, all of whom extoll the virtues of paying attention to organizational culture in the workplace. We have promoted the concept of the professional learning community (PLC) as an ideal form of culture in any workplace and in any context. (We have seen such a culture operating in a context of authoratarian, hierarchical decision making, as a subculture that guided the norms and behviors of a small group of staff.)

We have described the professional learning community in terms of its five dimensions, or ways of operating, as identified from the literature. These dimensions are shared values and vision, collective learning and its application, supportive and shared leadership, supportive conditions (both physical structures and human capacities), and shared personal practice. We also reported the values and benefits to both the organization's staff and to its clients (in the case of schools and districts, the clients are the students); these reports came from research conducted across North America. Of prime importance, suggestions were made, based on the literature on this topic, about the role, strategies, and actions that leaders must take to initiate, develop, and maintain a professional learning community.

DISCUSSION QUESTIONS

1. Why would you want a school staff to be organized as a professional learning community?

2. What difference would it make to a school's change efforts if the school's culture were that of a professional community?

3. Discuss the "balance of power" in a staff organized as a learning community.

4. Describe key characteristics of the leadership for facilitating change in the learning organization school.

5. What functions does a context that supports change play? Explain why these functions are important.

FIELDWORK ACTIVITIES

1. Identify a school that appears to be developing a professional learning community culture. Make an instrument of the 17 Boyd and Hord (1994) indicators by adding rating scales to each one. Administer the instrument to the school's leadership or management team. Lead a discussion with them of their results, focusing on where the school is strong and where attention is needed.

2. In the district or region, identify a low-performing and a high-performing school and conduct a qualitative (ethnographic) study that identifies elements of the culture in the organizations. Or, conduct this study in your local fire department, tailor shop, or elsewhere, looking for descriptors or indicators of the culture of this workplace.

3. Find a school that has become a professional learning community. Interview long-time and new staff to solicit (a) current descriptions of the school, (b) descriptions of what the school was like before it changed, and (c) explanations of how it became a professional learning community.

4. Find a school that is amenable to becoming a professional learning community. Use interviews with several staff members to describe their vision of such an organization. Conduct a meeting with the school improvement council to plan strategies for recreating the school as a learning organization.

ADDITIONAL RESOURCES

Assessment Instrument

Of interest to many people who are working to maintain PLC in their organizations and to dissertation students who are studying the PLC in schools is the School Staff as Professional Learning Communities instrument. This brief instrument uses the five dimensions of the PLC described in this chapter and enables leaders to assess the degree to which the five dimensions are present in their organizations. For permission to use this copyrighted instrument, contact the Southwest Educational Development Laboratory, www.SEDL.org, 1-800-476-6861.

Recent Books on PLC

Hord, S. M. (Ed.). (2004). *Learning together, leading together: Changing schools through professional learning communities.* New York: Teacher College Press.

Huffman, J. B., & Hipp, K. K. with contributing authors A. M. Pankake, G. Moller, D. F. Olivier, & D. F. Cowan. (2004). *Reculturing schools as professional learning communities.* Lanham, MD: Scarecrow Education.

PART II

DIFFERENT PERSPECTIVES FOR UNDERSTANDING THE BIG PICTURE OF CHANGE

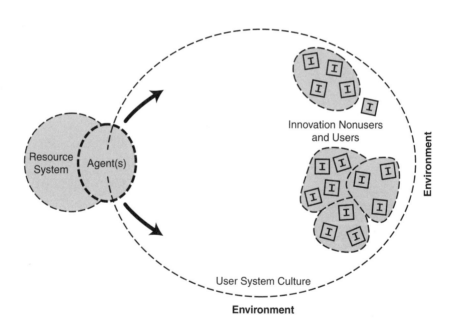

Innovation Nonusers and Users

Resource System

Agent(s)

Environment

User System Culture

Environment

Change can be viewed from many vantage points. For example, the "end-users" (teachers, staff, assembly line workers) who are expected to implement change have one view. They are close to the daily action and details of implementation. Leaders (executives and middle mangers such as superintendents and principals) will be aware of some of the details of implementation at the individual level, but have a broader view of what is happening across the whole organization. Students and customers have still another view, as do policymakers. Researchers and those who have developed models and theories have used one or more of these views as a frame of reference to describe and explain how change works. Each perspective emphasizes certain aspects and has reduced attention on other aspects. Each provides very useful constructs and tools for understanding, facilitating, and studying change.

There is a long and rich history to the study of change that has resulted in several very different perspectives becoming mainstays. Each of these has its own particular emphasis and view. Three of these perspectives with particularly useful constructs for those who are interested in facilitating change are described in Chapters 3, 4, and 5. Each of these perspectives is well established in the literature and widely applied. These perspectives make sense and each has more than 50 years of related research. They represent extremely different views and ways of thinking about change. Even when the same phenomenon is being addressed, it will have a perspective-specific interpretation or twist. The vocabulary used with each perspective is unique and has been carefully chosen to symbolize what is seen as most important within that view. The factors that are central to each perspective are unique, too. Although they are different in focus and construct definition, each perspective offers many useful suggestions for understanding, facilitating, and studying change.

Chapter 3 introduces the **Systems** perspective, which is based in having a large-scale, holistic view. The systems perspective begins by including all factors inside and outside the organization that in any way might be related to a particular change effort. A second important element in the systems view is interactions. Rather than seeing the whole as static, in the systems perspective all the elements and pieces are seen as composing subsystems that are, at least to some extent, interconnected. When something happens in one part of the system, it affects other parts. Leaders who can think *systematically* are much more effective in leading change efforts.

Chapter 4 introduces another long established, extensively researched and widely used perspective, **Diffusion.** In this perspective the central theme is *communication.* Keeping track of who talks to whom and the lines of communication are important diffusion constructs. Characteristics of individual innovation *adopters* have been examined and categorized according to how quickly they adopt an innovation. Another important component of the diffusion perspective is description of the innovation in terms of how it is perceived by adopters. In the diffusion perspective an important role is that of the change agent who introduces the innovation to members of the user system.

Organization Development (OD) is introduced in Chapter 5. This perspective emphasizes a different set of constructs. One focus is the *process skills* that various groups/teams and the whole organization possess, or may need to develop. Process skills for problem solving, decision making, and communicating are seen as essential for change success. Each individual also should develop a set of process skills in order to help the various groups/teams succeed. The OD perspective is guided by an external process consultant. A key assumption is that an organization that has well-developed process skills can better handle change.

Each of these perspectives has a rich history of research and application in business, government, schools, and developing countries. Each offers a number of constructs and tools that can help everyone to better understand, more effectively facilitate, and systematically study change.

The additional knowledge and constructs represented within these perspectives are summarized in the Part Two graphic. The large ellipse is now named the *User System Culture,* which symbolizes that the organization or community is engaging with a change process. Now there is a *Resource System* that represents external sources of expertise, support, and innovations. At the intersection of the two systems is a circle symbolizing the potential role of various *Agents* that can help in translation and communication between the two systems. The other addition is the various combinations and interconnections within and among the individuals and groups that make up the organization or social system.

CHAPTER 3

SYSTEMS THINKING

Interconnections of Parts That Make a Whole

Now that we've aligned our curriculum and instruction with assessment and the state's standards, we've seen positive gains in our students' achievement test scores.

Elementary school principal

Well, what we have not yet done a good job of is coordinating and aligning our advertising protocols with the legal department's recommendations.

Manager of a large chain of stores

Our board of directors is working on budget reallocation in order to provide training resources that support the corporation's work across all elements of management, the production line, and the payroll office.

CEO of a small manufacturing company

My child's school sent a letter to us explaining how the school is addressing our state's new curriculum standards, and how the administrators and teachers are learning to redesign their work with children to accommodate that. I don't quite understand all this, but I'm going to a meeting to learn how families can be part of this activity.

Parent of a middle school student

Sales are going well, but the increasing cost of fuel, along with the shortage of plywood (due to the hurricanes) and not enough carpenters could hurt things over the next six months.

Real estate agent

Change and improvement have been a goal of educators and the public for a very long time. Various approaches and strategies have been initiated but have not achieved broad scale change. Examining these efforts has engaged the attention of numerous researchers and writers. As an example, in 1992, Sashkin and Egermeier conducted an analysis of the history of policy approaches to school change and identified four strategies. The first was "fix the parts" approach that involved introducing and adopting specific innovations such as curricular programs and instructional practices. This approach was viewed as an exchange of new products (curriculum) or processes (instruction) for old. Sashkin and Egermeier termed the second approach "fix the people." In this approach, training and development were provided to educational personnel to change their practices/behaviors, attitudes, values, and beliefs.

In the third approach—"fix the school"—the school (rather than programs or people) was seen as the unit to change. A school improvement team would guide the school in needs analysis, solution identification, and plans for change. This approach was widely used throughout the 1990s and continues to be popular.

After analyzing these three approaches, Sashkin and Egermeier concluded that successful change had not been reached, but that a fourth approach, which they called "fix the system" could do it. This meant giving attention to all parts of the system simultaneously, since changing one part of the system influences other parts. These four approaches range in scope or magnitude from targeting selected parts in isolation to more recent holistic efforts. It is this whole system view that is the focus of this chapter.

FOCUS QUESTIONS

1. What is meant by "systems thinking" and using a "systems approach" for implementing change?
2. How are the critical pieces or parts of a system identified?
3. What is the value of a systems approach? Why consider working systemically?
4. How can the systems approach be applied to implementing change in education?

FAMILIAR NAMES IN SYSTEMS THINKING

Systemic change (not systematic change), *systems thinking, working systemically,* and a host of other similar labels have been bandied about for several decades. These labels have been sprinkled across the conversations of educators at the campus and district office levels. When asked what they mean in their use of such a term, many leaders tend to look askance, expressing puzzled, frowning looks and appear unable to provide a coherent response. Such reactions to the use of relatively new terms is not unusual. It seems that the nature of many executives and policymakers is to hear a new idea, refer to it before fully learning about and understanding it, and then try to use it as an uninformed novice.

A useful beginning point for examining systems thinking and theory is *Designing Social Systems in a Changing World* by Bela Banathy (1996). Throughout his career Banathy examined systems and was a student of the works of others. Banathy suggested that "people . . . cannot give direction to their lives, they cannot forge their destiny, they cannot take charge of their future unless they also develop competence to take part directly and authentically in the design of the systems in which they live and work, and reclaim their right to do so" (p. vii).

Banathy has further maintained that "this kind of empowerment when learned and exercised by families, groups, organizations, and social and societal systems of all kinds, is the only hope we have to give direction to our evolution, to create a democracy that truly represents the aspiration and will of people, and to create a society about which all of us can feel good" (1996, p. vii). Banathy expressed a grand challenge and a powerful goal.

Banathy's early work was followed much later by Peter Senge (1990), who used systems thinking to articulate how organizations should be created and operate. Senge's *The Fifth Discipline* found its way from the corporate world to education's school trustees' boardrooms and served as a wake-up call for educators who were considering how best to design their systems for improved student outcomes.

Another volume that has been most helpful in understanding the complexity and interdependence of the parts of systems is *Systemic Change: Touchstones for the Future School,* edited by Patrick Jenlink (1995). Jenlink brought together the intellect, expertise, and advice of a score of writers who help us "get a handle" on systems in education.

Whereas Banathy first penned a book in 1973 about a systems view of education and others like Jenlink have followed, the current work of researchers, administrators, and field practitioners in regional education laboratories and in higher education offer informative illustrations about the use of systems thinking in today's organizations. This chapter will briefly sketch what is known about systems from the literature and look intimately at applications in the field: how systems thinking is being used to define work, test its efficacy in practice, and make adaptations based on new learnings.

GOING DEEPER TO EXAMINE A SYSTEMS VIEW

In early work, Peter Checkland (1981) defined *human activity systems* as a "collection of structured sets of activities that make up the system, coupled with a collection of activities concerned with processing information, making plans, performing, monitoring performance . . . that express purposeful human activity that could be found in the real world" (cited in Banathy, 1996, p. 14). Similarly, Ackoff and Emery (1972) characterized social systems as purposeful systems whose members intentionally and collectively formulate objectives. These social organizations are such that the state of the parts can be assessed only by reference to the state of the whole system. Further, change in one part of the system is influenced by changes in the system as a whole.

Argyris and Schon (1978) maintained that a social group is an organization when it designs decision-making procedures for the collectivity, giving to individuals the authority to act for the collective group and setting boundaries. Laszlo (1972) suggested that social systems are guided by values; thus, social systems are not concerned with physical needs but with values that depend on the beliefs and values that the members have.

In 1995, Banathy explained a systems view of education. He noted that a systems view makes it possible to examine and describe the system and its setting, and also its components and parts. The systems view is a way of thinking that allows understanding and description of (p. 12):

> The qualities or descriptors of the amalgamated educational system operating at numerous interconnected levels (organizational, administrative, instructional)
>
> The relationships and interdependencies of the systems in operation at the levels
>
> The purposes and parameters of educational systems
>
> The relationships and activities that are undertaken between the systems and their environment

---

GUIDING PRINCIPLES OF SYSTEMIC WORK

1. All parts or components of an organization or system must be given attention when attempting systems work.
2. Any organization or system is made up of subsystems or components; these can be and should be identified.
3. Most systems are organized in levels; these should be recognized as well as the individuals within them.
4. For work in any system, there are competencies that are required; these should be identified and developed in the relevant individuals.
5. In systemic reform, as in any reform, there are actions and conditions that facilitate and others that impede; the wise leader will plan for the systems work with these in mind, and watch for new "arrivals."
6. Systems work is not without its shortcomings; be aware and plan accordingly.
7. Doing systems work is like being a juggler: Keep all plates in the air at one time and keep your eye on each of them.

The dynamics of the actions and relationships and designs of connectivity among the parts of the systems

The characteristics of the whole system and the qualities that characterize various levels of the system as a result of systemic interaction and synthesis

The behaviors and system changes and their environments that occur over time

Perhaps a more crisp articulation of systemic change by Jenlink, Reigeluth, Carr, and Nelson (1996, p. 2) is helpful: Systemic change is an approach that

1. Recognizes the interrelationships and interdependencies among the parts of the educational system, with the consequence that desired changes in one part of the system are accompanied by changes in other parts that are necessary to reach an idealized vision of the whole, and
2. Recognizes the interrelationships and interdependencies between the educational system and its community, including parents, employers, social service agencies, religious organizations, and much more, with the consequence that all stakeholders are given active ownership of the change effort

Obviously, a systems view examines the whole and its relationships to its parts. One could ask, What are the parts?

COMPONENTS OF THE EDUCATIONAL SYSTEM

The components or parts of the education system have been hinted at by several authors cited earlier. Other researchers and writers have further expanded identification of the parts or components of an education system, specifically in the reform context.

Components of Systems in Change

Anderson (1993) identified the components of a system in change as vision, public and political support, networking and partnerships, teaching and learning changes, administrative roles and responsibilities, and policy alignment. Danek, Calbert, and Chubin (1994) stated that the essential components of systems reform are national standards for content, skills, and attitudes; learning, teaching, and assessing standards; ambitious learning expectations and outcomes for all students connected to a rigorous academic core program; examination of policies, practices, and behaviors, and their modification to remove barriers and achieve the standards; broad-based involvement in designing an action plan with autonomy in implementing the plan; outcomes that measure systemic change; a system for monitoring and evaluating progress and adjusting programs accordingly; and a timeline for delivering the outcomes.

IMPLICATIONS FOR LEADERS FACILITATING CHANGE

Like work in any organization, leaders must understand their system, its parts, and its people. Typically, leaders tend to work more with one part of the system and give limited consideration to its connectedness to other parts and the mutual influence they may have—and then are surprised when things don't work as they had anticipated. The major message for leaders planning for systemic work is that it is imperative to take into account the whole system plus other external factors that impinge on it. Also, as noted, attention must be directed to the interconnectedness of the parts. If the parts are not interconnected, or are "loosely coupled," then work must be initiated to enable interconnectedness and interrelationships to develop, for a loosely coupled organization will flounder. The challenge here is to work with the whole, not just some of its parts.

Similarly, acknowledging and attending to all of the system's people is required. A culture of collaboration and interdependence is helpful (see Chapter 2). This means that people at all levels of the system (executive, administrative, instructional if this is a school, sales or marketing or advertising if it is a business, support staff such as secretaries and custodian, etc.) must be involved. There are tools for planning and implementing systems change, and these tools can be found in Part Three of this book.

Systemic change, like any change, will not happen without consistent planning for implementation, taking action, and monitoring the results so that successive actions may be designed and taken. Short-term and long-range strategies will be necessary (see Chapter 9) and applied to a systemic effort. A primary strategic action by leaders must be an articulation of the vision for change that leaves some space for others in the system to add to and shape or contribute to the vision. To fail to develop a shared vision and its articulation across the system dooms the reform work to an early death.

Characteristics of Systemic Policy

Clune (1993) reported five characteristics of systemic policy: research-based goals in education practice and organization; models of new practice and knowledge; centralized/decentralized change process; regular assessment of inputs, outcomes, and process; and a coherent, sustained change-oriented political process. In the same year, the National Science Foundation noted the requirements of systemic reform: changes in financing, governance, management, content, and conduct of education (teacher preparation and enhancement, curricula and instruction, assessments), and science and math learning of all students in a diverse educational system.

Elements of Systemic Reform

Smith and O'Day (1991) articulated three major elements for systemic reform. First was unifying the vision and goals of what schools should be like; second, establishing a coherent system of instructional guidance (knowledge, skills, capacities, curriculum, materials, professional development, accountability assessment) aligned with goals; and third, restructuring the governance system (state develops outcomes and accountability, while schools determine means to achieve outcomes). An examination of Table 3.1 reveals wide disparity across the elements of attention in systemic change or reform, suggesting wide variance in what various researchers and writers deemed important as components of the system.

TABLE 3.1   Components of Educational Systems

	ANDERSON (1993)	DANEK, CALBERT, & CHUBIN (1994)	CLUNE (1993)	NATIONAL SCIENCE FOUNDATION (1993)	SMITH & O'DAY (1991)
Vision	✔				✔
Public/political support	✔		✔		
Networking/partnerships	✔				
Teaching–learning changes	✔	✔		✔	✔
Administrative roles/responsibilities	✔			✔	
Policy alignment	✔	✔			
National content standards		✔			
Ambitious student learning outcomes		✔	✔	✔	✔
Action plan/implementation		✔			
Systemic change outcomes		✔	✔		
Monitoring/evaluating/adjusting		✔	✔	✔	
Timeline for outcomes		✔			
New models of practice			✔		✔
Centralized/decentralized change process			✔		
Finance				✔	✔
Governance				✔	
Teacher preparation				✔	
Curriculum					✔
Materials					✔
Professional development					✔
Accountability/assessment					✔

WORKING SYSTEMICALLY IN SCHOOLS

In the late nineties, as frustration grew over the single shot, hit-and-run approaches to educational change and improvement, systemic change or systemic reform became more frequently considered as an alternative. Staff at one of the nation's regional education laboratories, Southwest Educational Development Laboratory (SEDL), reviewed the literature and developed a scope of transformation work employing a systems approach. The goal of this work was to transform low-performing schools into high-performing learning communities, with the work centering at the district level as well as at the school. This project's review and synthesis of the literature revealed three major parts of education systems that required attention for reform and that were incorporated into the laboratory's model: components, levels, and competencies. Stiegelbauer, Tobia, Thompson, and Sturges (2004) reported these three parts that were identified for the laboratory's work.

Components

Because all parts or components of the system are inextricably linked, support or pressure on one part exerts influence on others. This model gives attention to working across all the components that are listed here:

Standards: What students are expected to learn and be able to do

Curriculum and instruction: What is taught and how it is taught

Assessment: Testing to discover what students have learned

Policy and governance: Rules and procedures to be followed

Professional staffing: Recruiting and retaining high-quality personnel, professional development, and appraisal

Resources: Staffing, time, budget, facilities, equipment, and materials

Family and community: Support systems outside the district, including social service agencies

Quite obviously, curriculum and instruction are tied directly to standards. Assessment must be closely related to the standards; thus, assessment is aligned with curriculum and instruction. Professional development must focus on the standards and on curriculum and instruction so that the staff is prepared to effectively teach what students need to know and do. Resources must be allocated with the aforementioned components for all to function well. In working systemically—that is, paying attention to all the parts—all parts must be considered in the planning and implementation of new practices.

Levels

In addition to the components, working systemically requires all "levels" of the system be given attention. These levels are the state, district, school, and classroom.

These levels can be thought of as concentric circles, each providing expectations and demands that influence student achievement. The state creates policies and regulations that districts must implement; districts set goals to which all schools must adhere; schools provide the structures and immediate facilities in which classrooms operate; all these impinge on classrooms and the teaching and learning that occur. In reform efforts, all levels must be given attention. A third part of the system focuses on competencies to be mastered by individuals involved in the effort.

Competencies

In addition to components of the system and levels of the system that require attention, competencies for successful systemic work are needed and were identified also by Stiegelbauer and colleagues (2004):

Collecting, interpreting, and using data: This competency aids educators and others to understand where a district and its schools are; it also provides information needed to direct where the district and its schools need to go.

Creating coherence: Creating coherence is making certain that the different parts of the system reflect the beliefs and values held by the organization and that they function together to accomplish the goals of the system, including the alignment of the different components of the system.

Forging alliances: These alliances develop the communication and collaboration skills necessary for educators, family and community members, and policymakers to come together to define and accomplish the transformation work.

Building capacity: In addition to hiring personnel and providing continuous professional development, building capacity involves increasing the resources available to support the educational program and strengthening the structures to support student learning.

Promoting innovation: This competency involves investigating and trying new approaches in response to changes in the educational system or the contexts in which it operates. It does not mean randomly pursuing any new idea that is proposed, but creating an organizational culture that allows for calculated risk taking to improve student achievement. It also includes a willingness to abandon strategies that are not successful.

The Cube

Figure 3.1 graphically portrays the "cube" that contains the levels, components, and competencies of the Southwest Educational Development Laboratory's (SEDL) working systemically model. These three dimensions of the model are the focus of attention for work planned and carried out through district and school leadership teams. These teams have overlapping members. Early in the project, SEDL staff guided and directed the work in the field sites with the district and schools teams, giving their attention to the levels of the larger system and their interrelationships. The SEDL staff

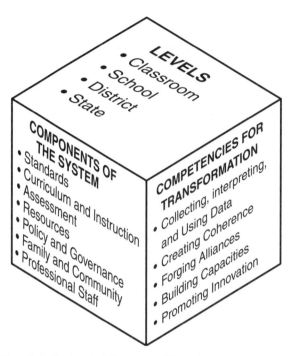

FIGURE 3.1   The "Cube" Model of Southwest Educational Development Laboratory's Systemic Change

Source: Printed with permission of Southwest Educational Development Laboratory, Austin, TX.
Copyright 2004 by Southwest Educational Development Laboratory. All rights reserved.

planned for the sites' learning of the components that must be addressed in order to improve student achievement. Particular attention was given to the alignment of standards, curriculum, instruction, and assessment, along with coordinated professional development.

The competencies received much attention from the SEDL site staff who led the district and schools in identifying root causes that could explain the student achievement data that were of concern. Building the capacity of the site educators was always the objective. This was done through well-organized staff-development sessions, as well as through follow-up coaching and assistance. Multiple phone calls and e-mails supported the efforts between the twice monthly visits by SEDL staff. When the teams were ready to provide more leadership, SEDL staff stepped back into a facilitating and supporting role.

Competencies from Other Writers

Other writers have addressed competencies needed for systemic work. Floden, Goertz, and O'Day (1995) described strategies that are needed for capacity building in systemic reform. These are enhancing teacher capacity, providing vision and leadership, and changing the organization or governance of schools; and providing guidance on curricular content and instruction, establishing evaluation or accountability mechanisms, providing resources, and facilitating access to outside sources of support. These competencies resonate with some of those mentioned earlier by Stiegelbauer and colleagues. At the state level, Timar and Kirp (1989) noted the roles, and thus the capacities or competencies, required of state-level personnel. These are to establish professional standards and expectations, provide support, and nurture organizational characteristics that foster excellence.

EFFECTS OF WORKING SYSTEMICALLY

At this time, SEDL's working systemically model should be categorized as an hypothetical model and is being tested and revised for effectiveness. As the SEDL staff has used the model to conduct field work (as described earlier) in 16 districts in the five-state region served by SEDL (Arkansas, Louisiana, New Mexico, Oklahoma, and Texas), they have fine-tuned the model and developed more specificity and a sharper focus, particularly in the competencies needed by school and district leadership to do the work. They have also seen progress in field site participants' knowledge and understanding of systemic work, as measured by the Working Systemically Survey (created and being refined by SEDL's research team), and through semi-annual interviews conducted by the research team that is following the effort.

Outcomes for Educators

The survey and interview data suggest that educators (administrators and teachers) perceive that alignment of curriculum, instruction, and assessment has improved over time. Alignment of these important components of the system is essential for systemic work. The data also indicate positive changes in alignment between instruction and assessment, curriculum and standards, and vertical alignment. The educators also perceive that leaders' capacities to promote alignment in the district and schools has increased over time. Further, the educators indicate that describing and setting expectations, monitoring, classroom involvement, and understanding data and alignment are the top roles for leaders at the school and district levels. Generally, responses to questions examining leadership roles suggested that leadership around alignment has improved somewhat from the previous year. If some positive changes have been noted in educators' capacities and actions, what about student change?

Results for Students

Although it is too early in the process to access data that would clearly identify strong trends in student results, in 13 of 16 SEDL schools examined for the current year-end report (Bond-Huie, Buttram, Deviney, Murphy, & Ramos, 2004), student results in one or more grade levels have showed decreases in the percentage of students categorized at the lowest performance categories. Out of 21 sets of test results in one of SEDL's states, 15 sets of results suggested a decrease of greater than five percentage points in the percentage of students categorized at the lowest performance levels on the state exam. Although there are positive trends in the data, there were three sets of test results that indicated an increase in the percentage of students who were categorized at the lowest performance levels as defined by the state. Obviously, investigation by the schools is necessary to determine the nature of the decline and to formulate a strategy for addressing the issues.

FACILITATORS AND BARRIERS TO WORKING SYSTEMICALLY

At the same time SEDL was working systemically in south central United States, a large-scale systemic reform effort was underway in Mexico. The Instituto Tecnologico y de Estudios Superiores de Monterrey (ITESM), more familiarly known in the United States as the Monterrey Institute of Technology, had undertaken a major effort to transform the teaching–learning paradigm across their entire higher education institution of 33 campuses spread across Mexico. The ITESM is among the first institutions of higher education to recognize the need for incorporating new learning approaches into classroom instruction throughout an entire multicampus system.

The mandated change resulted from a broad study conducted by the highest level of the university system to determine if the university was preparing its graduates for success in the twenty-first-century knowledge-based, global economy. They learned that many graduates were lacking in nine key attributes necessary for today's high-performance jobs: leadership, teamwork, problem solving, time management, self-management, adaptability, analytical thinking, global consciousness, and basic communication skills. After considering this report, and further study of the university's classroom environments and pedagogical approaches, a new vision of the teaching–learning process for the university's classrooms was developed and prepared for launching. As can be imagined, a careful attempt was made to balance academic freedom and academic performance expectations—a journey into uncharted territory.

A "top-down" mandated strategy (note that in Chapter 1, Change Principle 8 indicates that mandated change can work) was employed that involved multiple aspects of support and assistance for faculty and administrators. Several years of intensive professional development were provided to enable faculty to use a more constructivist and technology-based approach to teaching and learning. The professional development focused on multiple levels of the university's system: executive, administrative, faculty, and support personnel. It impacted resources and policy, and resulted in new ways of delivering professional development electronically. New capacities were developed throughout the staff to accommodate the implementation of the new model. So, what success was accomplished?

Facilitators of the Change

A study of one ITESM campus was undertaken to understand better how the change process was facilitated and what barriers hindered its progress (Gonzalez, Resta, & De Hoyos, 2005). The facilitators depicted in Figure 3.2 are a mix of people who provided interventions (support advisors and administrative and academic support) and conditions present in the university setting. Their brief descriptions follow:

> *Students' acceptance of change:* The ITESM students' participation and acceptance of the change that included the use of technology aided the change process.
>
> *Adoption/Adaptation of courses:* The faculty had system-level, high-quality courses available for their adoption or they could adapt existing courses for their use.

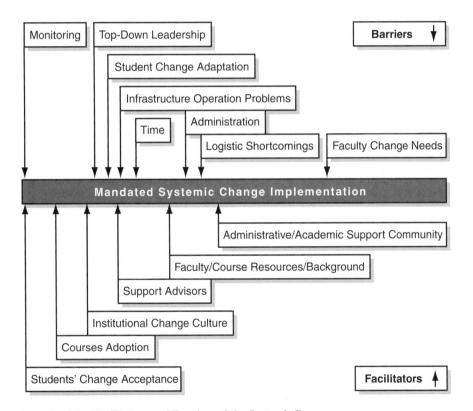

FIGURE 3.2   Facilitators and Barriers of the Systemic Process

Source: C. E. Gonzalez, P. E. Resta, and M. L. De Hoyos. Paper submitted for presentation at the annual meeting of the American Educational Research Association, 2005. Reprinted by permission of Carlos Enrique Gonzalez.

Institutional change culture: The ITESM philosophy and values-based culture promoted innovation, change, and an entrepreneurial spirit.

Ongoing support and training: Support was provided by pedagogical and technological advisors from the ITESM Learning Technology Centers.

Faculty academic background: Faculty members' individual academic discipline, years of teaching experience, and pedagogical skills supported the change process.

Professional learning community: Collegiate work in ITESM systemwide academies and local academic departments, and the appropriate organizational structure of the institution enabled the change effort to make progress.

These facilitators were identified through a five-stage process. First, administrators were asked to generate a listing of interventions that they had done that they believed were helpful to the change effort. Second, faculty were invited to identify actions that administrators had taken to facilitate the process. Third, both the administrators' and faculty's lists were submitted to factor analysis. The results were then field tested in the fourth step. These results were further analyzed in the fifth step and produced the six facilitating factors (described above) and the eight barriers, which will be described next.

The facilitators identified in Figure 3.2 were factors present across all campuses of the ITESM system. Support for implementation was provided at all levels of the system (executive, administration, and instruction). The resources and policies at all campuses were coordinated to focus systemically across the entire university on curriculum and instructional processes, and on professional development to support the change to a new teaching–learning model.

Barriers to the Change Process

Eight barriers were identified in the ITESM study:

Monitor implementation: This factor cited the lack of institutional evaluation of the implementation of the project and lack of classroom monitoring to improve.

Top-down leadership: ITESM's centralized decision-making process promotes upper-level decisions to the exclusion of a bottom-up effort.

Students' adaptation to change: There was a lack of students collaboratively developing new learning habits and adaptation to the work, and students showed apathy toward the ITESM new teaching–learning process (interestingly, students' acceptance appears to be both a facilitator and a hindrance when it is absent—easy enough to understand).

Infrastructure operational problems: This involved proper operation of technological platforms, computational servers, operational failures, and general maintenance of the infrastructure.

Time: This complaint is a typical tone—in this case, lack of time for continuous improvement of courses and interaction with students, lack of time needed to fully understand the new approach, and lack of time to become involved in the change process and for feedback during the implementation process.

Administrative alignment and support: Academic units and administrative areas had different goals and there was some lack of alignment of administrative processes with the change. Additionally, there was the issue of academic administrators' understanding of the change.

Support shortcomings: Cited were support deficiencies during the implementation process, and lack of support from technological and pedagogical advisors. (Here again is a contradiction of a factor that was a facilitator to some and a barrier to others, most likely stemming from their own personal experience with the change process.)

Faculty issues: Faculty skepticism arose about the effectiveness of the new approach, which required use of didactic methods in redesigned courses.

There are no surprises in these facilitators or barriers. All are regularly identified in change efforts. Thinking and working systemically demands attention to all parts of the system simultaneously.

Time is typically an issue of implementation, and it seems reasonable that the executive and administrative layers of ITESM could provide resources and develop policies to make time available at all campuses. In addition, policies could address administrative alignment and support. More professional development for administrators would clarify their understanding of the change so that monitoring implementation would occur more comprehensively and systemically.

The sheer scope or magnitude of conducting such a far-reaching change across 33 campuses of a very large university system challenges the intellect. What is useful here is the identification of what worked systemically to encourage implementation, and what appears to need addressing if implementation is to make additional progress across the entire system. Further, these findings represent useful ideas for the consideration and study by others who anticipate attempting such a systemic effort.

LIMITATIONS OF WORKING SYSTEMICALLY

If the definition and the expansive lists of components required for using a systemic approach to educational reform sound daunting, they are. Fullan (1993) identified two limitations of the systemic approach. First is that individuals and groups greatly underestimate the complexity of how systems operate and the daily dynamics that ensue, requiring large amounts of attention, energy, and resources. Second, it is not clear if the systemic approach or process can be extended to new situations. What is needed, Fullan suggested, is a new paradigm more in tune with the realities of systems and their dynamic complexity.

NEEDED EVALUATION, RESEARCH, AND DEVELOPMENT ON SYSTEMS WORK

Doing systemic work in organizations is in its infancy. Although systems theories have been in the literature for decades, the application of the concepts has been late developing, especially in education. Many educators use the term in their conversations, but it is not often that such individuals have a clear and operational understanding of what systemic work entails or means.

Thinking systemically is not easy. It is a challenge to accept that one's own organization is a subpart of a larger system. Lowham (1995) observed this in his study of state-initiated school reform. Each subsystem of the state—the legislature, the state education agency—has departments; each school district has schools; and each school perceives itself as a system, rather than as being a subsystem of the state system. For each change effort, determining what and where the system is a critical step.

Thus, the study and research of systemic efforts, especially in schools and districts, would be invaluable. We do not yet have a wide range of ideas about how to involve the individuals in an organization in broad and far-reaching systemic work. Do we treat these efforts as we do those that are less comprehensive? The Mexico project (ITESM) noted in this chapter suggests that many of the same interventions and tools can and should be used. More studies need to be undertaken to confirm or deny and/or to widen the recommended actions to be taken, and the effects that may be expected.

How much time is needed for successful systemic reform efforts? Can these projects be shortened, as in typical efforts, by attention to the support and assistance of the individuals involved? Just what is the array of skills and knowledge that the facilitator of systems work requires? Are there qualities or characteristics that can be suggested for the more effective facilitator?

Questions that are always asked about proposed change projects are how to launch them, develop them, and sustain them. Are systems efforts in these respects different from the existing literature on change process? A culture of cooperation and collaboration seems to be preferred for systemic efforts so that interconnectedness and interrelationships prosper; are these elements necessary, and if so, how do you initiate their development? Much remains to be known and understood about systems work—a rich opportunity for students interested in organizational change.

At this point, the reader may be haunted by the early work of Karl Weick (1976), who introduced the concept of "loose coupling" of organizations. In loose coupling, Weick explained that in viewing an organization as a system, there will be some elements that are tightly coupled, such as budgeting and spending. In other areas, there may be limited linkages, such as a nonspecific policy about how employees dress (i.e., loose coupling). Weick explained that the connections, links, or interdependence between two entities will have a degree of "coupling." Coupled individuals, groups, or events connect and respond to each other; the degree of coupling between two parts of a system depends on the activity or strength of the variables or elements that the two share. If the two have few variables in common or share weak variables, they are independent of each other.

For example, if there are no budget decision-making opportunities in the teacher's environment that are shared in the world of the principal, then the teacher and principal can be assessed as being loosely coupled with regard to the budget. On the other hand, if the principal is closely associated with teachers in instructional planning, then they are thought to be tightly coupled instructionally. Weick says, "Loose coupling simply connotes things, any things, that may be tied together either weakly or infrequently or slowly or with minimal interdependence" (1976, p. 5).

Clearly, if the parts of a system are loosely coupled, their integration and coordination are weakened. However, Weick (1976) noted that if there are rules, regulations, or prerequisites for how the subparts of the system will interact and relate to each other, then the longer the list, the tighter the coupling. One might be reminded of the introduction of site-based management in the late 1980s. Schools were given unbridled authority to act, and soon in many districts, the flotilla of schools was meandering in all directions and floundering on the shoals. For this, and other reasons, efforts have been made in many districts to "tighten the coupling" so that the district operation is better aligned with the schools and the system at large functions coherently. For systemic change to work, the components of the system must have sufficiently tight coupling so as to work with maximum interdependence. The vignette illustrates some of these points.

■ ■ ■ ■ ■ ■ ▬▬▬▬▬▬▬▬▬▬▬▬▬▬▬▬▬▬▬▬▬▬▬▬▬▬▬▬▬▬▬▬▬▬▬▬

VIGNETTE
THE HUNTER HILL SCHOOL DISTRICT

Hunter Hill, a small rural district with 1,100 K–12 students (a K–2 primary school, a grades 3–5 intermediate school, a grades 6–8 middle school, and a grades 9–12 high school) began a school improvement (SI) process 18 months ago. The four schools, with their school-improvement councils, provided the energy to respond to the superintendent's "suggestion" that they examine their data and plan for improvement. Professional development for the councils was provided by an intermediate service agency.

The councils did a substantial amount of work and seemed to be successful in guiding the schools in self-study and analysis. At the end of the fall semester, each of the schools had developed a campus action plan that emphasized their school's need for improvement—which, as it developed, was a need for attention to writing achievement of the students at all the schools.

Each of the schools selected its own writing program. As the primary school's council said, "Our colleagues in the next county found this to be a fun program for the kids." The intermediate school's principal announced that his school had studied the state's curriculum standards and selected a program that was quite congruent with the standards. The middle school principal shared that she didn't think the students were so poor in writing, and had

(continued)

decided to continue using the old textbooks for writing instruction. The high school principal, considered to be a "strange duck," was working on his superintendent's certification at a nearby university and solicited help from the university faculty. As a result, the school's faculty studied several writing programs, compared them to their students' needs and to the standards explicated by the state department for the state's students, and selected what they thought was the best all-around fit.

As the spring semester spun by, the superintendent met with the four principals as a group to check on progress with their improvement work. She inquired about the professional development in which the faculties had engaged, and what formative assessments were revealing about the students' learning in writing. Two of the principals reported that their teachers had not needed professional development as they (the principals) were sure that their teachers knew how to teach writing.

The intermediate school principal had exhausted his professional development monies and asked for additional funds to release teachers for studying their latest assessments of students and to gain additional skills in delivering the last quarter of the semester's curriculum and its appropriate instructional strategies. He further requested that the school-improvement councils and the school board look into the district's policies governing professional development for the teachers. "Teachers cannot use the new writing program without having long-term, in-depth learning of the new curriculum and its associated instructional strategies, with follow-up to help them really gain deep content and skills needed to use the new program."

While the primary and middle school principals looked puzzled, the high school principal chimed in with his concerns. "I'm wondering, even if we are giving attention to the state standards for writing at our schools (at this point, the two principals looked even more puzzled and disturbed), I wonder if our curriculum is well articulated vertically across the four schools, so that when students reach high school, they have not been subjected to gaps or overlaps in the skills needed for being successful writers. And, I worry about our assessments being aligned with the standards—and whether professional development is focusing accurately on helping the teachers develop the skills they need to teach the students so they do well on the state achievement tests and are skillful writers, as well."

At this juncture, uneasy looks were exchanged all around. The district and campus administrators collectively found themselves in an uncomfortable position. The superintendent suggested, as it was quite late in the afternoon, that they meet again in two days to further discuss their concerns and take stock of where they were in their school improvement process. She also suggested that they bring as many of their school-improvement council members as could attend on short notice.

ANALYSIS

At their meeting, the superintendent led the group in identifying and listing all the aspects of the district's system that influenced the schools' efforts to improve student writing. During their discussion and identification of the factors of the system, it became clear that everyone had failed to understand the interconnectedness and interrelationships of the various parts of the district as a system. They noted that each school had selected a different curriculum without consideration of how the curricula fit and flowed from one level of

■ ■ ■ ■ ■

V I G N E T T E   CONTINUED

school to the next. Nor had all the schools selected their programs with attention to the competencies that all students would need to accomplish, as reflected by the standards.

Resources had not been appropriately allocated for the introduction and implementation of new programs. Neither principals nor faculties knew the programs well, since professional development had not been properly considered. Giving the schools the authority and latitude to select their own programs had been a good idea, but there had been no selection criteria established to guide the district's schools in their choices of programs. One of the principals had mentioned policies and the group agreed that a districtwide committee needed to look into the policies that provided guidance to all aspects of the schools' efforts for improvement: resource allocation; time for professional development and funds to support consultants if needed; guidance for curriculum selection or development; a means to align the district's curriculum, instruction, and assessment with professional development; and a well-articulated governance structure so that issues and concerns about the district's school-improvement processes could be addressed quickly and fruitfully.

In short, the district and campus personnel had not viewed the district as a system with their schools as part of the system, but had taken free rein so that each school became its own isolated, independent entity. In other words, although tightly coupled around the state standards, district budgets, and line authority, the curriculum selection decision making was left to each school (i.e., loosely coupled).

NEXT STEPS

Since the state's achievement tests had been administered and test scores just delivered, the superintendent shared with the group their test data and led them in a review of the data, beginning with the writing scores. Interestingly, the two schools that had selected their writing programs based on the writing programs' relationship to the state writing standards had small but positive gains in student writing. They were not large enough to be totally satisfying, but they did signal the value of paying attention to the competencies deemed by the state as important for students to know and achieve.

It was clear to the school councils what was needed for making a comprehensive and concerted effort in addressing increased student achievement: more communication across all the schools and district office, and consensus as a whole system in decision making for tighter coupling and improved alignment. A number of committees were formed that would work during the summer. One group would work with the district's business manager to examine funding and to ascertain if some shifts might be made in allocations in order to provide more materials and professional development for teachers. This group had a representative from each of the district's schools. Another group whose members crossed all four of the schools would convene with the district's director of instruction and make a plan for developing curriculum that was aligned with the state standards, and to align assessments also.

A third group would meet with several school board members to explore policies that were not favorable to the execution of school change and improvement and make recommendations for additions, deletions, and changes in policies and their decision-making process. This group also included representatives from each school. The fourth group would solicit involvement of parents from each of the four schools to discuss how they

(continued)

■ ■ ■ ■ ■ ■

V I G N E T T E   CONTINUED

might be supportive of the schools in their improvement efforts, and for a district fall school year opening event that would bring district personnel, all schools, and parents, teachers, and students together.

The plan was to investigate all aspects of the district education system that affected the learning of the professionals in the schools, as well as their students. In addition, the plan was to investigate the relationships that the parts had to each other and how those relationships might be made more effective, efficient, and productive.

ONE YEAR LATER

Several of the committees addressed their work with confidence and zeal, and when they didn't know what to do, they called their regional education laboratory for advice and counsel. When committees seemed to falter or grow dispirited, the superintendent made herself an honorary member of each committee, providing attention to progress and celebrating small successes. This worked very well until the district hit a budget snag and faced a shortfall that needed immediate attention. The end-of-year state achievement tests were administered with high hopes for the results. The two schools that had gained increases the first year continued to gain the second year. The primary school principal had critical surgery soon after the Christmas season, and this school seemed not to regain its energy. The middle school suffered the loss of its band director in an automobile accident, causing an interruption in the instructional program, but revived enough to show small gains on the tests. At the close of the school year, the superintendent announced that she was accepting a position in a larger district up in the northern part of the state. All the schools and community wondered, What will happen now?

VIGNETTE CRITIQUE QUESTIONS

1. From a system's perspective, what advice would you give to the district office planners or to the community supporters of this district?
2. What systems factors contributed to the success or failure of Hunter Hill's change effort?
3. This district's parts seemed not to be able to see beyond the shadow of their own role or school setting. If you had been superintendent, what might you have done in this narrative to change this situation?

SUMMARY

Systems work, systems thinking, and *systemic change and reform* are terms that have been used for some years, but seem only fairly recently to have concrete definition. The ideas have been in the literature for decades, but this perspective has only recently been espoused for application in schools and school districts. In implementing change, it seems reasonable to consider all the parts of the system even when attempting to change only one or two. Theorists and practitioners have regularly pointed out the fallacy of not engaging in thinking about the entire system. Common sense suggests that punching on one part of the system will cause something to "pop up" in another part. Thus, in today's climate of addressing the challenge of organizational improvement, most especially school districts, attention to all parts of the system seems highly realistic. But this approach is no panacea as the citations in this text point out: There are multiple parts to any system, and this approach requires consideration of all. As with other approaches in systems thinking, monitoring the process is of high importance in order to make corrections when data deem it necessary. And, there are limitations to this approach to education and other organizational reform. Guiding and managing such efforts will require leaders who can take the "balcony view" (watching all elements of the system), who are conceptually and intellectually capable at a high level, who are quick witted and have the energy to act on short notice, and, above all, who are continually caring about the organization and its individuals. Those who would consider systems work will be advised to know as much about it as the literature makes possible.

DISCUSSION QUESTIONS

1. Why would you want a school's administrators to think about their school's change efforts systemically?

2. What difference would it make to a district's change efforts if the effort were planned and executed with systems thinking?

3. Identify and discuss the key characteristics of highly effective leaders involved in systems work.

4. List and explain strategies that should be provided for a systemic reform to be successful.

5. For systems reform, hypothesize factors that could be considered to engage the participants in developing systems thinking.

FIELDWORK ACTIVITIES

1. Do you know an organization that operates in a systemic way? If so, describe it. If not, what topics would you use to study an organization to ascertain if it operated systemically?

2. Assume that an executive or superintendent asked you to identify any of her administrators who engage in systemic thinking. What characteristics would you look for?

3. Find a district, a school, a business, or other organization that has accomplished major change through a systems approach. Query the staff to learn (a) how they started, (b) who initiated the effort, (c) what parts of the system were key, and (d) how the staff knows they were successful, or not successful.

ADDITIONAL RESOURCES

Jenlink, P. M., Reigeluth, C. M., Carr, A. A., & Nelson, L. M. (1998). Guidelines for facilitating systemic change in school districts. *Systems Research and Behavioral Science, 15,* 217–233. John Wiley & Sons.

      This how-to-do-it monograph describes the characteristics and elements of a systemic change guidance system that builds on the principles of process facilitation and systems design. It examines the integral values or beliefs related to facilitation and systemic change, the types of events and activities typically needed, the processes that form the guidance system, and how to create the guidance system.

Joseph, R., Jenlink, P. M., Reigeluth, C. M., Carr-Chelman, A. A., & Nelson, L. M. (2002). Banathy's influence on the guidance system for transforming education. *World Futures, 58,* 379–394. Taylor & Francis.

      This publication is a tribute to the work of Bela H. Banathy. The article identifies how Banathy has influenced the authors' work on systemic change in education, the crux of which is found in systems design. Systems design is a process that engages stakeholders in conversations about their visions, ideals, values, and aspirations with the goal to create their ideal educational system. The authors identify the process values and the process activities that drive Banathy's theoretical framework, and compare these to the values and activities that they have developed in their guidance system. The intention of the article, as noted in the title, is to demonstrate the extent to which Banathy's work has influenced the development of a guidance system for facilitating systemic change in public school districts.

CHAPTER 4

DIFFUSION

Communication and Change Agents

This is really a neat new approach. I really get a thrill out of trying
something new.

I think I will wait for awhile. It would be a big risk for me to try it and
have it not work out.

She says it really works well. That's good enough for me.

That person from the university extension office seems to know what he
is talking about. I understand what he is saying about why
this is a better way.

Two professors meet at an international conference and learn about a
new research method. Each returns to his/her home university and
introduces the method to their students.

If one approach to understanding change were to be selected as the grandparent of change models, the likely winner would be the *Diffusion* perspective. The groundwork for this perspective was established early in the twentieth century. This perspective now has over 100 years of accumulating research findings and widespread applications. One of the earliest contributors was French sociologist Gabriel Tarde (1903). As he reflected on change, one of his wonderments had to do with why so few innovations were actually used out of the hundreds that were conceived. Through his studies and writings he introduced many of the concepts that are still foundational to the Diffusion perspective.

A second seminal set of diffusion studies were those of Ryan and Gross (1943). They examined the rate of adoption of hybrid corn seed in two communities in rural Iowa. Before the 1930s, the source of corn seed available to farmers was the ears of corn that had been stored over the winter in a specially designed crib or shed. Researchers at Iowa State University (ISU) had been developing hybrid corn seed, specifically grown to include various plant characteristics such as disease resistance, consistent height, and a standard number of ears per stalk. In 1928, hybrid corn seed became available to farmers through the ISU Agricultural Extension Service and seed companies.

Hybrid corn seed at that time was an innovation. It also represented a new cost for farmers. Instead of using the seed available, for free, in the crib from last year's crop, farmers had to "buy" hybrid corn seed. As would be expected, some farmers made the decision to adopt hybrid corn seed quickly while others delayed for years. In the early 1940s, Ryan and Gross reviewed the history of the adoption in two communities and proposed many of the key diffusion constructs that are used to this day.

Since then, the research methods, study findings, and related constructs have been used to study a wide range of innovations and adopters. The characteristics of physicians and their rate of adoption of new pharmaceuticals have been studied. The adoptions of boiling water and steel-tipped plows by rural villagers have been studied, as has been the spread of disease such as AIDS. Diffusion constructs are regularly included in the training of sales representatives and applied to the introduction of new products and services.

Two key components of the Diffusion perspective that are reflected in the examples presented here are thinking about change as it takes place inside of *social systems* and the act of *communication.* In the Diffusion perspective, change is thought of in terms of a process whereby a "new idea" becomes distributed throughout a social system through people talking to people. For example, farmers are members of their community, which is a social system. Any single farmer talks to some farmers a lot and to others very little or not at all. Their learning about and deciding to adopt a new idea, such as hybrid corn seed, unfolds through communication.

Another important construct in the Diffusion perspective is *adoption.* Rather than change being seen as an exploration and implementation process, as described in Change Principle 1, in the Diffusion perspective the emphasis is on each individual making an *adoption decision.* Third-world villagers either boil water or they don't. Physicians either prescribe a new drug or they do not. Consumers purchase hybrid cars or SUVs. They work their way through a decision-making process and in the end adopt the new idea or continue with their traditional practice.

Today's leading scholar for the Diffusion perspective is Everett Rogers. For nearly 50 years he has been a contributing researcher, educator, and leading spokesperson for the diffusion perspective. His classic book, *Diffusion of Innovations,* which is in its fifth edition (2003), is a very informative and useful resource. Key constructs from the Diffusion perspective will be introduced in this chapter along with illustrations of how they can be used to implement change.

FOCUS QUESTIONS

1. What are the key constructs in the Diffusion perspective?
2. How do characteristics of adopters affect their decision to adopt?
3. What methods are used to understand the innovation communication process?

4. What is it about some adopters that make them so influential with those who have not yet adopted a new idea?
5. How is the innovation defined in the diffusion perspective?
6. What is the role of the change agent?

COMMUNICATION OF INNOVATIONS

In the Diffusion perspective, change is seen first and foremost as a process of communication. Initially, a new idea is introduced to a few members of a social system. Through various means of communication, word of the new idea is passed to other members. Over time, most members become aware of the innovation and may adopt it. Understanding communication processes is a core component of the diffusion perspective. Knowing who is talking with whom and what is being said about the innovation are important. Identifying the paths along which information is communicated and charting the interpersonal linkages are other important tools. Keep in mind that the medium that is used can include more than talk. Radio, print, television, and the Web are important sources for learning about an innovation.

GUIDING PRINCIPLES OF THE DIFFUSION PERSPECTIVE

1. The Diffusion perspective applies to all types of systems, including schools, businesses, and communities. A social system may be more local, such as the farmers in a geographic region or the employees in a school district. A social system may be geographically dispersed, such as the participants on a Web chatroom.
2. The amount of communication and the number of people engaged in making and receiving communications is a key to adoption rates. More communication and with more people will have a positive effect. Those with fewer connections and involvement will be slower to adopt.
3. Innovators are the first to adopt new ideas; however, they are less influential as opinion leaders. They certainly are opinion leaders, but the early adopters are most influential.
4. Perceptions of the innovation influence the rate of adoption. Innovations that are seen as having an advantage over current practice, not being complicated, being able to be sampled, and matching well with current values are more likely to be adopted.
5. Opinion leaders are a key to the rate of adoption. Their views and adoption decisions influence others. Early adopters are highest in opinion leadership.
6. Lines or channels of communication become important because those who have more access will have more information about the innovation and earlier.
7. Information about an innovation will travel fastest when there are more lines or channels of communication and where there are more people. This is true within a building as well as across a region.

Sources, Targets, and Media

An often overlooked, and certainly underappreciated, element of change is the talk that occurs between the various members of a social system. The diffusion perspective highlights the importance of these interactions. Consider each of the following quite typical interactions:

1. In a regional sales meeting the manager tells the sales representatives about a new product line that will soon be available.
2. Two teachers talk about how things are going with their students' efforts to incorporate digital photos into their reports.
3. A farmer goes to the Web to find information about the best interval to use between each planting. The farmer then shares the information with a neighbor by phone.

When reminded that change entails communication, it is easy to see how each of these actions would be especially important to the adoption of an innovation. In any change effort hundreds of these types of interactions take place.

At a minimum, change leaders and researchers need to be fully aware that there is a lot of talk taking place. Sometimes it can be useful to develop a record and count of the various communications that are taking place. A simple, but useful, coding system is presented in Table 4.1 that can be used to think about as well as systematically count the one-on-one communications. As is described in Chapter 9, this basic coding system has been used to count and categorize interventions in several year-long studies.

Sources of Communication.   Communication begins with someone initiating action. In an organization setting it can be fairly easy to find out who said something. Finding all the sources can be more difficult in social systems that are diffuse or widespread, such as a city or state. The codes introduced in Table 4.1 offer a beginning frame for thinking about and categorizing communication activity. This coding model could be adjusted and expanded to document who initiated communication actions in a single school, or any other type of organization. Obtaining information about all the sources of action across several schools, a school district, or a state would be increasingly difficult. But the same approach to coding would work. If a careful record is kept for one or two weeks, or for months, the frequency count would be informative. These data would provide direct evidence about who is initiating the most communication, as well as who may not be communicating with anyone.

Targets of Communication.   The list of codes that is developed for *sources* generally will work for *targets*. The source initiates communication with a target. The target is the recipient of the communication. Knowing the frequency with which each person is targeted provides an indication of how well informed they may be. Note that technology (e.g., e-mail and the web) is listed as a source, a target, and media.

TABLE 4.1   Codes for Use in Analyzing One-on-One Communications in a School

I. SOURCE	II. TARGET	III. MEDIA	IV. PURPOSE
IA. Principal	IIA. Principal	IIIA. Face to face	IVA. Provide
IB. Assistant Principal	IIB. Assistant Principal	IIIB. Phone	information
IC. Department Chair	IIC. Department Chair	IIIC. Cell phone	IVB. Seek
English	English	IIID. E-mail	information
Social Studies	Social Studies	Web	IVC. Non-innovation
Science	Science	IIIE. Print	related
Math	Math	IIIG. Other	
ID. Teacher	IID. Teacher		
Mary	Mary		
Alice	Alice		
Rosetta	Rosetta		
IE. Secretary	IIE. Secretary		
IF. Technology	IIF. Technology		
Web	Web		
E-mail	E-mail		
IG. Other	IIG. Other		

Media in Communication.   Another useful code addressees the form that was used to make the communication. In most change efforts face-to-face interactions will be frequent. However, other media forms are increasingly being used. E-mail and cell phones could easily be more heavily used than face-to-face in many systems.

Purpose of Communication.   The last column in the Communication Coding System in Table 4.1 addresses the *purpose* or intention of the communication. The purpose is defined in relation to the source of the communication action. What did the source intend with each communication action? The target may have a purpose, too. The target's purpose could be coded as well. One of the important cautions to keep in mind relative to the purpose is that just because there was a certain intention does not guarantee that the desired result followed. All too often what is intended in a particular communication is not what is "heard" by the target. As will be described in Chapter 11, miscommunication can have serious consequences for a change effort.

Coding Communication Actions in General.   The list of codes in Table 4.1 easily can be expanded to track communications within a particular setting, such as a school. The names of individuals could be listed, the purposes could be more detailed, and other forms of media named. The same approach can be used to code in-teractions in any type of organization or other social system. Other categories of codes could be added, such as whether the interaction is two-way or one-way, or con-current versus delayed. A simple form could be devised to code each interaction, or the key ones could be noted in a personal digital assistant (PDA). If a PDA were used, it would be easy to keep track of the date when each interaction occurred. Sometimes knowing when a certain communication took place is important information.

Lines of Communication

Many of the findings from diffusion research are obvious and interesting. Once stated, the immediate reaction can be, "Well, of course, but I had not thought about it." No matter how obvious the findings may seem, they are useful and often over-looked. In some ways, the findings from studies related to lines of communication are like this. They seem to be more obvious in hindsight than appreciated as a change process is unfolding. The basic finding is that communication about the innovation occurs along the established lines, or channels, of communication.

Interpersonal Communication.   Interpersonal sharing of information about an in-novation is core to understanding change from the Diffusion perspective. In a social system the spread of adoptions is mainly driven by communication about the inno-vation. People talk to people and that is how much of the information about the new idea or way of doing things is spread to other potential adopters. Keep in mind that in a social system the distances may be large and therefore the spread of information across the system will not be even. Face-to-face communication requires proximity, but distance is not a factor with e-mail and cell phones.

A wonderful illustration of the role of communication lines can be seen in a study by House, Steele, and Kerins (1974). In 1963, the state of Illinois established a grant program that provided state funds to school districts for gifted and talented stu-dent activities. The program was voluntary, but if school districts applied, they re-ceived funding. House plotted the statewide distribution of school districts that received the grants (see Figure 4.1). This plot graphically illustrates two key points from the diffusion perspective. First, diffusion of adoption of innovations occurs along the lines of communication. Second, adoption increases when there is close connection with others who have already adopted.

Adoption along the lines of communication is represented in this case by the U.S. highway system. In the 1960s, the network of U.S. highways was the main travel pattern within the state. Adoption of the gifted and talented grants occurred mainly along these highways. The second point is represented as well. Where there are more people, there will be more and earlier adoptions, since there is greater like-lihood of adopters exchanging information about the innovation and perhaps seeing it in use. For adoption of innovations in other settings think of the U.S. highways as a metaphor for the lines of communication. People who are "in the loop" are likely to receive more information and earlier than will those that are more isolated.

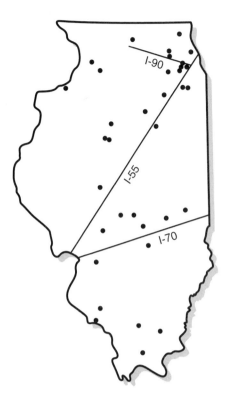

FIGURE 4.1   Spread of Gifted Programs in Illinois, 1964–1965

Source: Adapted from E. R. House, J. Steele, & C. T. Kerins, *The Gifted Classroom.* Urbana, IL: Center for Instructional Research and Curriculum Evaluation, University of Illinois, 1971.

Networks Are a Means for Communication.   Another useful tool for understanding communication about an innovation is analysis of social networks. Whether the system is a geographic region, a community, or an organization, most people will be more closely connected to some, and have little or no connection with many others. Diffusion researchers will make charts of the connections each person has with others. An example of this charting is presented in Figure 4.2. The data for this type of *sociogram* can be obtained by observing and asking about who talks to whom. Which people eat lunch together? Which departments are more cohesive? Who never attends meetings? Who seems to be most aware of what is going on across the whole system? Who plays on the softball/bowling/bridge team? Charting the interpersonal networks is very useful in understanding where information about the innovation will spread more quickly, and more slowly. People with more connections to others will be in a better position to learn more and earlier than those with fewer networks.

Implications of Communication Tools for Facilitating Change. As obvious as each of these findings from diffusion research may be, it is surprising how frequently they are ignored when change is being implemented. In some cases actions are taken that are exactly opposite of what these diffusion points suggest. Keeping track of the most active sources of communication provides clues as to whom to target to help with sharing additional information. Asking someone who does not initiate many communication actions to tell others about the innovation is not likely to result in information being spread rapidly.

Failure to attend to the lines or channels of communication is regularly observed in change efforts. Instead of thinking of a state as the social system, as was the case in Figure 4.2, think about the geography of a school campus. What are the lines of communication in this case? If an innovation is to be introduced through a pilot or demonstration, which classroom should be selected? Do not select a classroom that is far off the "highway" that prospective adopters use frequently. Instead of having the pilot done in a remote portable classroom, select a classroom that is on the direct route to the staff parking lot or on the way to the staff lounge.

Once a sociogram has been developed, use it. From the diffusion perspective, working with T36 (in Figure 4.2) makes no sense. Apparently, this teacher does not associate with any others. Therefore there will be little communication with others about T36's adoption of the innovation. The most obvious candidate to persuade to become involved early is T11. This person is interconnected with three groups. Whatever T11 says and does has the potential of being shared with 11 colleagues. If T11 likes the innovation, then a number of other prospective adopters are likely to hear about it. The corollary is also true. If T11 does not like the innovation, a number of other prospective adopters are likely to hear about it.

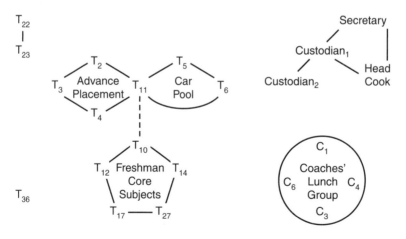

FIGURE 4.2   Social Networks in One High School

CHARACTERISTICS OF ADOPTERS

Probably the most widely studied and shared ideas from diffusion research are those related to the characteristics of adopters. An early research question for diffusion researchers is: Why do some people adopt an innovation quickly and others take longer? Even when there are obvious advantages, some people take longer to make the adoption decision. There have been literally hundreds of studies that have examined the characteristics of adopters. The Ryan and Gross (1943) studies of farmers adopting hybrid corn seed addressed the question. Many studies have been done in third-world countries as various innovations have been introduced. Out of these studies a general set of adopter categories has been agreed upon and there now are extensive descriptions of the characteristics of each. Keep in mind that each of these categories is a composite and that real people will vary from these archetypes.

Five Adopter Categories

A number of variations on the categories of adopters have been proposed. Today there is widespread use of five categories: Innovators, Early Adopters, Early Majority, Late Majority, and Laggards. Curiously, these categories and their associated characteristics tend to hold up across innovations and cultures.

Innovators. The very first people to adopt an innovation are the *innovators*. Rogers (2003) calls them "venturesome." They enjoy change for the sake of change. They are always looking for new ideas and are ready to try them. Innovators tend to be more cosmopolitan and have more extensive networks. In schools, these are the teachers who are very active in their profession regionally and perhaps nationally. Through their more extensive networks they are likely to hear about new ideas first and bring them back to the local setting. In business and agriculture, the innovators are more wealthy so that there is less risk associated with an adoption that fails. They also tend to see themselves as having control over their destiny (internality), rather than being the victim of circumstances (externality).

Early Adopters. *Early adopters* adopt new ideas quite quickly, but only after reasoned consideration. They are respected locally and tend to have been in place for extended time. Their focus is local and they are seen by their colleagues as solid, sensible decision makers. Once they adopt an innovation, then others will look more favorably on it.

Early Majority. Where the innovators and early adopters are fairly quick to adopt, the *early majority* are more deliberate. They take time and give more consideration in making the adoption decision. They are connected to others but less likely to have positions of influence, as is characteristic of early adopters. The early majority represent a large proportion of the potential adopters. Rogers (2003) estimates that 34 percent of the potential adopters will have characteristics of the early majority. This makes them an important target for those who want to see an innovation adopted by many individuals.

Late Majority.   The *late majority* are slow to adopt and tend to do so only when there is pressure from others or the need becomes very strong, If they are losing market share or can no longer afford to compete against the success of those who have already adopted, they are more likely to make the change. They approach change with doubts and caution. Rogers (2003) estimates that in the typical population the late majority represent another 34 percent. However, they tend to want to avoid risk because the cost of failure will be much higher for them.

Laggards.   This label brings with it an unfortunate negative connotation. However, as the name implies, *laggards* are very slow, and even resistant, to the adoption of new ideas. They are more conservative, more provincial or isolated, with less education and more limited resources. They are traditional in outlook and take a very long time to make an adoption decision. In other words, they are resistant to change. As one of our colleagues once observed, "They would complain if you hung them with a new rope." Laggards are a cause and a victim of their circumstances. Since, in general, they are less well educated, more conservative, and less wealthy, there is more risk in change. They also will likely have less information and understanding about the potential of the innovation and less resources to invest in making an adoption successful. At the same time, these characteristics and conditions keep them held in place.

PASSING THE WORD

As stated earlier, the primary theme in the Diffusion perspective is communication. Close attention is placed on understanding the ways and the hows of communication. Examining who communicates and how their communications are interpreted are important for change leaders to understand. These understandings can then be used to increase the rate of adoption. One important characteristic of adopters that is a key construct in the Diffusion perspective is *opinion leadership.* Another is understanding the *communication flow* between the five adopter categories.

Opinion Leaders

In any social system or organization some people will be seen as the solid citizens. They are well respected and turned to when expert advise is needed. They are the trusted colleagues and the opinion leaders. These individuals have extra influence, although they tend to be more low profile. They probably have been in the system for quite some time, are successful in their own practices, and have had some leadership roles. At the same time, they tend to not be flashy and not apt to engage in change for the sake of change. When it is important to obtain sound insight or advise about what is happening in a particular situation, the opinion leaders are the ones who are sought out.

IMPLICATIONS FOR LEADERS FACILITATING CHANGE

1. Keep in mind that communication is never done. Making on announcement in a staff meeting or sending everyone an e-mail does not mean that everyone "received" the message. It is very important to repeat messages and to use a variety of media to say the same thing. Off-site opportunities to communicate are important, too. Car pools, meetings at the district office or headquarters, and train and plane time are important opportunities to share information.

2. The metaphor of the U.S. highway system representing the lines of communication can easily be applied in organizational settings. Teachers, or other employees, travel certain routes as they come in from the parking lot, as they pick up mail, and as they go to the cafeteria. Amazingly, many change efforts do not take advantage of this phenomenon. Use it! Set up the demonstration classroom, the innovation exhibit, examples of kids' work along the lines of communication. Be visible and introduce information by deliberately inserting it into these channels.

3. The importance of opinion leadership and opinion leaders cannot be underestimated. One of the early activities in any change effort is for the change agent(s) to identify the opinion leaders. These individuals need to be courted and sold on the importance of the innovation. If they adopt the new idea, then others will follow. If they resist, others will follow their lead.

4. If the adopter category studies are accepted, then there is little reason to engage with the late majority and laggards early in a change effort. However, there are some exceptions. For example, if an individual with many of the characteristics of a laggard is a leader of a key unit, then that person must be courted. With their understanding and support, the rate of adoption will be much faster.

5. An external change agent needs to build linkages with the opinion leader(s). There is a personal side to this process, which may mean talking about hobbies, playing golf, or joining in some other "more social" activities. Most change agents are not seen as "all business."

6. Be alert to the interpersonal connections. Sociograms become a very useful tool for charting relationships. Members of one group will have similar levels of knowledge about the innovation. Knowing which individuals participate in multiple groups is important, since they can pass information across groups.

7. Keep in mind that communication is done using a variety of media. In the past, face-to-face interactions were primary. Today, e-mail is a very important medium. Cell phones might be important in some settings. Use the coding system introduced in Table 4.1 to analyze one week's interventions. Reflect on the resultant pattern in terms of ways to increase communication effectiveness.

Opinion leadership varies across the adopter categories. Innovators have some influence at home, but in many ways they are seen as the ones who are always ready to try crazy ideas. They are not always trusted to have the best advice. The early adopters are the strongest in opinion leadership. They are the ones who the other members of the system respect and turn to. If they adopt an innovation and have favorable ideas about it, others will look more favorably on making the adoption decision. Innovators may be the first to introduce a new idea, but it is the opinion leadership of the early adopters that others follow.

Communicating across Adopter Categories

A related insight from diffusion research is the general pattern of flow of communication across the adopter categories. This can be thought about in terms of where people are most likely to get their information. (This is another way to think about sources and targets.) The innovators obtain a lot of their information through their extensive external networks, whereas the laggards have very limited sources of information. In between are the other adopter categories.

Each adopter category has more communication with its adjacent adopter categories than those farther away. There also is a directionality to the flow of communication that parallels the time of adoption. For example, the early majority learns from the early adopters. As adoptions spread within the early majority cohort, the late majority is learning from them. In other words, there is a general flow of communication, as well as adoptions, from innovator, to early adopter, to early majority, to late majority, and finally to laggards.

Perceived Attributes of the Innovation

Diffusion researchers have taken a different approach to defining the innovation. Instead of defining an innovation in terms of its function, or its pieces, or its intents, they use constructs to define innovation in terms of how it is *perceived* by prospective adopters. The focus is on understanding perceptions rather than on questioning the validity of the perceptions. In many ways perception is reality. If an innovation is perceived to have certain attributes, then those perceptions must be considered as real. One of the generalizations from the Diffusion perspective is that the more positive the perceptions of the innovation, the more likely the chances are of having a favorable adoption decision. There is general acceptance in the Diffusion perspective of five perceived attributes of innovations.

Relative Advantage.   One obvious comparison for prospective adopters to make is appraising the potential of the innovation to have an advantage over current practice. There could be a perception that the innovation will have greater outcomes, profits, or consequences, when compared to what is being done currently. For example, a computer program that keeps an up-to-the-minute inventory based on today's sales could reduce warehousing costs. A particular hybrid wheat seed that is disease resistant could have higher yields. Teachers could perceive that a particular set of curriculum materials will lead to higher student test scores. Each of these examples is based on a perception of the innovation having an advantage over current practice. Relative advantage could be related to other factors besides effects. For example, the innovation may be cheaper to use in terms of money or time, or the innovation presents a potential increase in status. Perceptions that are favorable will tend to increase the rate of adoption. Inversely, the adoption rate will be slowed when there are negative perceptions of the innovation. If it is perceived not to be better, or to cost more, then there is less likelihood of it being adopted.

Compatibilty.   The degree to which the innovation is perceived to be compatible with the adopter's values, needs, and concerns influence the adoption decision. Higher compatibility increases the chances of an affirmative adoption decision, whereas perceptions of incompatibility will decrease the rate of adoption. One of the authors of this book had a Taiwanese graduate student drop his course on change "because the course was not taught by lecture." In hindsight, given the student's cultural background, it is easy to understand how he could have had the perception of incompatibility. Prospective adopters are weighing the compatibility of the innovation in terms of needs, a match with what they see as important values, and cultural norms. In some groups driving a SUV is "in," while in others it would not be seen as acceptable. These are values-based decisions.

Complexity.   The importance of this perceived attribute is obvious. Innovations that are perceived to be very complex are likely to be adopted more slowly. Innovations that are perceived to be simple to implement and use will be more readily adopted. Technology innovations are the easy example. The earliest VCRs were complicated to use, whereas the new ones require fewer commands and many now block out the advertisements, all with the push of fewer buttons. Every year the newest generation of personal computers do more things and do each in more user-friendly ways. *Complexity misperception* is a serious problem for educational innovations. Education leaders, teachers, parents, and policymakers tend to see educational innovations as simple and easy to implement. However, most are complex and subtle. These make for an interesting case of there being a favorable adoption decision followed by failure to support and sustain implementation. If the innovation is perceived as simple, then there will be less understanding of the need for extensive implementation support.

Trialability.   Innovations that are easy to try out have an increased adoption potential—in other words, trialability. Test driving a car provides useful information. It is much more difficult to try out a new assembly line process or a year-long science curriculum. To address this potential limitation, many innovation developers create samplers and trial activities. With other innovations it may be possible to test it in a limited way before making a 100 percent commitment. This happens when a farmer plants one of his fields with new seed, while planting the rest of the fields with regular seed. In schools, textbook adoption processes frequently include opportunities for some teachers to try out sample units. Being able to sample a component and experience success positively affects the adoption decision.

Observability.   Observabilty entails being able to see the innovation in use and to see the results. When observabilty is high, there is more likely to be a favorable adoption decision. Some innovations are easy to see. A drive through the Midwest in the summer presents an easy-to-see example of observabilty. Occasionally there will be a corn field that has signs in front of several rows. The signs typically are in the shape of a corn ear and will say something like "DeKalb 6746." There will be three or four of these signs, each with a different number. Each row is planted with a particular hybrid corn seed. Farmers can stop, look over each row of corn, and see for themselves what each type of seed produces. The farmer is then in a better position to decide on which seed to purchase next year. This is a classic example of observabilty. It is also a classic example of how the findings from diffusion research can be used to increase the rate of adoption of an innovation.

USING DIFFUSION CONSTRUCTS AND TOOLS TO ASSESS AND STUDY IMPLEMENTATION

The extensive history of research using diffusion constructs and tools makes it relatively easy to conceptualize new studies. Even a superficial review of the diffusion literature will yield study questions and research methods that can be applied in new situations. For example, although the adopter categories are well established in the literature, very few studies have been done with teachers or higher education faculty. The generally more difficult context of introducing change in secondary schools is especially in need of study.

Another topic area has to do with the perceived characteristics of innovations. How do these characteristics play out when the innovations are complex, such as total quality management or standards-based education? What are successful strategies for overcoming the potential for resistance due to lack of trialability and observability?

What is the role of the change agent when the innovations are complex and implementation requires new learning and extra effort? Is there sufficient difference in what is required so that once the adoption decision is made there is a need for a change agent with different expertise to facilitate implementation?

THE ROLE OF CHANGE AGENTS

A very important role in the Diffusion perspective is that of a change agent:

> A *change agent* is an individual who influences clients' innovation-decisions in a direction deemed desirable by a change agency. A change agent usually seeks to secure the adoption of new ideas, but he or she may also attempt to slow the diffusion process and prevent the adoption of certain innovations with undesirable effects. (Rogers, 2003, p. 366)

In much of the diffusion work the change agent is an external innovation expert who engages with the client system to introduce and encourage adoption of the innovation. The change agent has expert knowledge about the innovation and its use. The change agent also needs to be expert in understanding how the diffusion process works.

A good and very effective example of a change agent is the agricultural extension agent. Typically, these individuals are housed at a state university that has an agricultural research station and related academic programs. These agents also staff county extension offices. Extension agents learn from the university researchers and then travel around the state and introduce farmers to the latest findings and ideas about best practices. Pharmaceutical sales representatives serve in the same way with physicians. They are the *linking agents* who provide a personal connection between the researchers and the adopters. They are skilled at translating and applying what the researchers have been studying.

In addition to expert knowledge about the innovation and its use, change agents also need to have the interpersonal skills to interact with clients. When potential adopters perceive a commonality with a change agent, the potential of a favorable adoption decision increases. Dress, the kind of car, and even whether one smokes and/or drinks can make a difference in change agent effectiveness. Change agents may be more effective with some clients and have more difficulty in matching up with the values and interests of others. Having patience and the skill to listen are important characteristics.

Frequency of contact also becomes an important indicator of change agent effectiveness. More frequent contact should be associated with increases in adoption rates. However, it is possible to wear out one's welcome. Here again, becoming an effect change agent requires being sensitive to people and their needs, as well as being expert with the innovation.

■ ■ ■ ■ ■

V I G N E T T E

HERE WE GO AGAIN!

THE BEGINNING

When Sara Johnson returned from her meeting at the district office with other building union representatives, she couldn't wait to spread the word. She immediately talked with her close colleague who also was very active in the union. The superintendent had had some

(continued)

■ ■ ■ ■ ■

V I G N E T T E   CONTINUED

sort of meeting with a nationally prominent professor from an out-of-state research university. Now, the district was buying a new program and teachers would be receiving special training soon. Sara did not see any reason why the district should be spending money on another program when teachers needed a raise. "Besides," said Sara, "today's kids just don't study. If they spoke English and did their homework, we wouldn't even be talking about changing the curriculum."

Sara did not hear that the visiting professor was the creator of a research-based curriculum program that was designed to increase the achievement of at-risk students in urban schools. All Sara heard was that teachers were going to have to change their teaching "one more time." Her primary concern had to do with whether or not teachers would be paid for the time spent in training. Having been a teacher in the district for 27 years, she was "fed up" with having to do things without real compensation.

Bev White, the literacy coordinator, had attended the meeting and was very excited about the new program. She saw it as a real possibility for helping at-risk kids succeed. She also liked that the plan included regular visits by the professor's staff to help teachers adopt this program. Bev was immediately scheduling a meeting with the district literacy committee, which included teacher representatives from each building. Her first call was to Paul Borchardt, an outstanding literacy teacher in one of the most poverty-stricken parts of town. He listened carefully, asked a few questions, and agreed that this sounded like a good opportunity. Paul said that he would e-mail three of his fellow committee members, and would tell several colleagues in his school over lunch.

AN ANALYSIS WITH NEXT STEPS

This vignette is unfolding in a typical fashion. News about a meeting, a decision, and a new initiative are beginning to be communicated across a "user system." Different versions and different perceptions are being shared. Constructs from the Diffusion perspective can be used to diagnose the current situation and in planning next steps.

The change agent in this case is the university professor and her associates. In another way, Bev White is an "internal" change agent. Bev will have day-to-day responsibility for districtwide implementation of the change. The adopter categories can be applied, but carefully. In some ways, the categories are too simplistic and it is too easy to label someone. Still, it sounds like Sara has some of the characteristics of laggards. She and Bev have different perceptions of the innovation. Sara does not see anything wrong with current practice (relative advantage) and believes funds should be spent on teacher salaries instead of a new program (compatibility).

Paul seems to be an early adopter. Bev turns to him first, which suggests strength as an opinion leader, but he is careful although positive and ready to communicate with others. A beginning sociogram would have Sara and her fellow building representatives in one group, with Paul and the other literacy building representatives in another group.

The Diffusion perspective can help ask some questions at this point, too. Bev is connected to the district literacy committee, but what are her committee members' connections to their union building representative members? To what extent do Paul and his building union representatives network? What about Sara and the literacy building representatives in her school?

■ ■ ■ ■ ■

V I G N E T T E   CONTINUED

There also needs to be a lot of positive and timely communication to all teachers. Bev needs to get ahead of Sara's message to all teachers. There also needs to be immediate communication with the principals. The communication channels would depend on what is available. Maybe there is a listserve for teachers. Hopefully a principal meeting is taking place very soon where the superintendent can say what the agenda is. Of course, these messages will need to be repeated and sent via multiple media. For example, Bev could prepare a one-page handout that the superintendent could ask principals to share with their teachers.

The constructs of observabilty and trialabiltiy would be useful to consider. Perhaps one or two schools or classrooms could pilot the program. Other teachers could then see the program in action. Of course, the highways metaphor is an important consideration here. Paul's classroom would be logical one to choose, but we don't know if he is on the "highway" or off the beaten path.

Identifying early adopters and getting them ready to consider and adopt the new approach will be another important part of the effort. Bev should be able to assume that the teachers on the district literacy committee will be excited about the new program. Bev should ask them to start communicating back in their buildings about the importance of this opportunity and to show that they personally are supportive.

From here out, communication must continue, and as adoptions begin, it is important that the early adopters have success. They will be communicating to the early majority, and, in time, the late majority.

VIGNETTE CRITIQUE QUESTIONS

1. What about the fact that in most organizations, including schools, adoption of an innovation happens at the same time for everyone? The Diffusion perspective assumes that individuals make the adoption decision at different times. When the district decides to adopt a curriculum, all teachers are expected to adopt it. Are these two views incompatible?

2. To what extent should constructs from the Diffusion perspective be shared? Should Bev tell members of her committee that these constructs are being used? For example, sociograms could be constructed and used to plan communication activity. Who should see these? Also, in the case of sociograms, which individuals and groupings would you want to see charted?

3. In many ways, *laggard* is a pejorative term. Still, the construct seems to be real. How can it be used in positive ways? In this vignette, Sara cannot be ignored, so what should be done?

SUMMARY

The Diffusion perspective has a long and rich tradition of research and widespread application. Many of the constructs, such as the adopter categories, have become standard content in the training of sales representatives and others who have change agent roles. Diffusion constructs will be introduced to college students in business, education, nursing, communication, and other disciplines. There is a 100-year research tradition covering a wide range of settings and innovations. In addition to viewing change as a communication process, the diffusion perspective focuses on the decision to adopt. Other perspectives focus less on this decision and emphasize other aspects, such as the process of implementation. Still, the diffusion perspective offers a number of well-tested and effective tools that can be applied by those who are engaged in facilitating change and those who are studying change processes.

DISCUSSION QUESTIONS

1. Use the Diffusion constructs introduced in this chapter to analyze the quotes that were introduced at the beginning of this chapter. Which adopter categories are represented? What should a change agent do after hearing each?

2. Choose an innovation that you, or others, are currently considering or have recently adopted. Use the perceived attributes to analyze the innovation and the various communications that took place as it was being adopted.

3. Think about a change agent you have experienced. Where was this person housed: inside or outside? What was the person's level of expertise with the innovation? What were the person's interpersonal strengths?

4. Think about a social system you know well, such as a church, family, community, or business. In that setting who is an opinion leader? What characteristics are key to this person being an opinion leader? Which side of an adoption decision did he or she represent?

5. What do you think about the diffusion perspective defining adoption as a decision? In your setting is the adoption decision made by an individual? Is it a big part of the change process, or are some other aspects more significant?

6. In the Diffusion perspective, adoption of an innovation is typically seen as a decision that an individual makes. Farmers decide which corn seed to plant. Each villager decides whether or not to boil his or her water. In organization settings, the adoption of a new idea is not an individual decision. To what extent do you think the organization context reduces the usefulness of Diffusion constructs, or does it?

FIELDWORK ACTIVITIES

1. Analyzing the frequency of communication between the various members of a system can be very useful. Select a setting where you can document who talks to whom in regard to a particular new idea, innovation, or change process. Develop a version of the coding system presented in Table 4.1 and code the change-related communications that take place for a day, or several days. Summarize the frequency counts and draw some conclusions about which people are more, and less, engaged with the innovation.

2. Sociograms are fun to construct and a very useful tool for change agents. For a system where you have access, develop a sociogram of the interpersonal connections. Who sit together in meetings and at lunch? Which people are members of the same team/department? Which people seem to be isolated? Once you have drawn the sociogram, if you were a change agent, which people would you want to target first, second, and last?

3. For a system where you have more knowledge, identify a person who is an opinion leader. Interview that person about how he or she sees his or her role in the school. Also interview two or three other people about this person as an opinion leader. First, ask them who they turn to. They may identify someone else. Then explore what they see as the key characteristics of the identified opinion leader(s) that makes him or her (them) trusted sources.

CHAPTER 5

ORGANIZATION DEVELOPMENT
Problem Solving and Process Consultants

Our team is really good at solving problems. We don't jump to conclusions and always begin with examining the symptoms.

As a committee chair she listens closely to what each member says and makes sure that everyone's views are heard. She never has a hidden agenda.

We never make a decision. There is a lot of talk and the meetings go on, and on, and on. There never is closure.

I like the way he restates what someone has said and makes sure that he understands what the person meant.

This consultant comes in every month and leads training sessions. We don't deal directly with our work, but what we learn can be applied.

In our school everyone has the opportunity to present his or her view, but once a decision is made, everyone supports it.

A regular activity in all organizations is people working with others. Meetings, committees, and teams are important ways to organize tasks, assign responsibilities, and produce services and products. When these group efforts work well, a significant amount can be accomplished efficiently and effectively. There also is a feel or sense about each organization. In some groups, members feel that their ideas are heard and they are satisfied with the results. In others, many members feel isolated and unimportant. A clique may be given special treatment and there is not a shared sense of purpose.

In this chapter, the Organization Development (OD) perspective is introduced as a way of understanding the interpersonal processes in organizations. A variety of methods and tools have been developed for assessing, intervening, and growing healthy processes, especially in teamwork. Organization Development is viewed as a major approach for making long-term change in organizations as a whole.

Unfortunately, many times there is more frustration than satisfaction in group work. There can be a lot of talk with few agreements, and the same points are repeated. People talk but don't listen and agreements are difficult to reach. There is "discussion," but no "dialogue." In a discussion, each person argues his or her point of view in an attempt to persuade. In a dialogue, there is give and take along with an effort to develop mutual understanding.

FOCUS QUESTIONS

1. What is Organization Development (OD)?
2. What are key features of OD intervention strategies?
3. Do OD efforts focus only on groups?
4. What are differences between organization climate and organization culture?
5. What is the role of the consultant in OD?

Organization Development (OD) is a general model about change that focuses on individual and group skills that make for successful teamwork, and on helping the total system/organization develop and improve over the long term. The foundations of the OD perspective can be traced back to World War II and the efforts to prepare teams of military personnel to accomplish various tasks and objectives. Psychologists identified the kinds of *process skills* that more effective teams used. They also identified skills of individual members that contributed to overall team effectiveness. Following the war, attention was given to how these types of analyses and skills could be used to improve individuals and teamwork. Understanding and becoming expert in the use of OD processes can be very helpful for those engaged in implementing change, whether they are workers, leaders, or consultants. Over the years OD efforts have moved from individual and team development to addressing how to improve the health and functioning of whole systems/organizations. Today the wide array of strategies and consulting processes are applied in business and industry, with governments, in the military, and in settings all around the world.

WHAT IS OD?

Over the last 60-plus years expert consultants and trainers have developed processes to help individuals and organizations become more effective in their work. The emphases within this, the OD perspective, have varied over time, but a primary goal has continued to be to help the members of a system/organization develop expertise and the capacity to use group and individual process skills to handle whatever changes come their way. Addressing this goal now includes cross-organization processes as well. One important caveat is that in the OD perspective, the various process skills and change foci are viewed as generic. The assumption is that individuals, teams, and systems/organizations will be better able to solve their specific problems when they have developed expertise in using generalized process skills. Organization Development consultants do not introduce solutions to particular problems and needs. Instead, their focus is on helping the system/organization develop general knowledge and skill that can be used over and over as specific problems and needs arise.

OD Definitions across the Decades

Through the 1950s and 60s development of OD was parallel to development of the human potential movement. In both cases psychologists focused on the human side of change. In OD, the subjects were employees in organizations where there was an interest in improving performance; in the human potential, subjects were people who were interested in personal growth. Both movements used similar approaches. For example, rather than working with clients individually, trainers and psychologists worked with groups. Various types of group exercises were created. Each facilitated learning new skills and gathering insight into the causes of resistance to change.

GUIDING PRINCIPLES OF THE OD PERSPECTIVE

1. Developing organization members' interpersonal and group process skills are important ways to improve organizational effectiveness.
2. Organizations, groups, and individuals are important targets for developing process skills.
3. The context of OD process training is intended to be free of the organization's core technology. The assumption is that members can transfer the learning to the work setting.
4. The OD consultant comes from outside the organization.
5. The OD consultant does not introduce a specific innovation. The role is to help the organization develop more effective processes in order to be better at solving its problems.
6. Planned change is a sustained multiyear approach to improving an organization.
7. Assessment and feedback about process and skills are important activities and should be ongoing.
8. Survey feedback is an important tool for diagnosing and informing the consultant and organization members about the current state of the organization.
9. Assessing organization climate and culture can be an important step.

Training and Planning.   The earliest methods employed to improve organization effectiveness were (1) personnel training and (2) long-range organization planning (French, 1971; McGill, 1977). The personnel training method that emerged as most important was the *basic skill training group,* also known as the *T-group,* laboratory training, and sensitivity training. The training design typically had participants engaging in group work with artificial (rather than job-specific) tasks. The training process emphasized collecting data and receiving feedback about one's own behavior and the behavior of the group. The process also emphasized using the feedback to better understand oneself and others. Feedback about participants' interactions in the laboratory setting provided rich personal learning experiences that could then be applied in the workplace. The training did not directly address the workplace; rather, it was assumed that the participants could make the job-related transfer.

The emergence of systems theory (see Chapter 3) in the 1950s also became a cornerstone of OD. In systems theory the members of an organization were seen as one of many interconnected subsystems. An assumption in the OD perspective is that improving the knowledge and skill of a subsystem will lead to overall improvement in the organization. In other words, training that leads to behavioral change and improvements in the members of an organization will lead to overall improvement in the organization.

Changing OD Definitions.   As Hall and Shieh (1998) observed, one of the challenges in developing a clear definition of OD is that across the decades the definition changes. There also are variations in definition from author to author. The following sample of definitions illustrate this theme:

> Organization development is an effort (1) planned, (2) organization-wide, and (3) managed from the top, to (4) increase organization effectiveness and health through (5) planned interventions in the organization's "processes," using behavioral-science knowledge. (Beckhard, 1969, p. 9)

> Organization development (OD) [is] a philosophy of and technology for producing organization change. . . . Growing out of the human relations tradition in the forties and fifties, it is actually a pastiche of techniques developed in the behavioral sciences which focus on problems of organization learning, motivation, problem solving, communication, and interpersonal relations. (Kimberly & Nielsen, 1975, p. 191)

> OD is a planned and sustained effort at school self-study and improvement, focusing explicitly on change in both formal and informal norms, structures, and procedures, using behavioral science concepts and experiential learning. It involves the school participants themselves in the active assessment, diagnosis, and transformation of their organization. (Schmuck, 1987, pp. 1–2)

The failure of OD proponents to agree on a common definition has limited understanding and made it extremely difficult to conduct studies of its effectiveness. Although different in vocabulary and emphasis, each definition and approach reflects the importance of personal and interpersonal relationships and skill development for increasing organization health and effectiveness. For those interested in implementing change, the understandings, techniques, and strategies offered through the OD perspective can be very helpful as sources of interventions, even if the total perspective is not the framework for implementing change in a particular setting.

OD Intervention Tools and Techniques

The OD approach employs a number of methods for developing individuals, groups, and organizations. These techniques provide an operational definition for OD. When used well, these become powerful intervention tools. When they have been used poorly, resistance develops and OD as a change approach loses its credibility.

Survey Feedback.   An important theme in the OD perspective is collecting performance data and providing feedback to the participants—in other words, *survey feedback*. Floyd Mann at the University of Michigan is credited with developing this strategy (Mann & Likert, 1952). The main functions of survey feedback are to collect information about members' attitudes and opinions, to provide survey information to organization units as feedback, and to design corrective actions based on the feedback information. Various forms and formats can be used to collect the data, with questionnaires probably being the most frequently used. The regular use today of a continuum to rate each item on a questionnaire (i.e., *Likert scales*) is a direct descendent of the early survey efforts. Interviews, telephone surveys, and data about customer satisfaction or student performance are other examples of information sources. In the OD perspective, feedback of the survey data typically will be provided by an external consultant. The consultant will guide the participants in constructing an analysis and interpretation of the data. Following feedback, the consultant assists organization members in identifying steps that can be taken to improve—in other words, organization development.

Exercises.   The training situation that has been used for more than 50 years in OD for development of new skills, as well as in creating opportunities for reflection on current practice, is the *exercise*. These will range in length from half an hour to several days. Each exercise is designed to help participants, individually and as groups, learn new skills and to reflect on their learning. Standard components of each exercise include an introduction where a problem is posed. The participants will engage in a set of activities, such as building a tower using paper and masking tape, or developing a consensus set of rankings in regard to a question or topic. At some point there will be an assessment of the participants' current knowledge and skill in relation to the exercise objective. Once the group work is completed there will be a review and critique of how the *process* of the exercise unfolded and what was learned. This review and critique will focus on the process, not the product. Often there will be no "right" answer to the exercise; the focus is on the participants' skill development and reflections about how their work in this context-free situation transfers back to their work setting.

An example of a classic ranking exercise is called *Lost on the Moon*. Each group is given a handout with information (see Figure 5.1) and is asked to develop a consensus ranking of the items. The process objectives for this exercise address the group and its members in developing skills in making decisions. In this case, there is a more valid ranking, but that is secondary to learning more about group decision making. This type of exercise is based in the OD assumption that teams make better decisions than individuals.

Another exercise classic is *Five Squares*. Bavelas (1950) introduced the idea and over the years it has been adapted by many consultants and presenters, including Schmuck and Runkel (1994). Participants are organized so that each group has

FIGURE 5.1   Problem Sheet for the Exercise *Lost on the Moon*

LOST ON THE MOON: PROBLEM SHEET

You are a member of a space crew originally scheduled to rendezvous with a mother ship on the lighted surface of the moon. Mechanical difficulties, however, have forced your ship to crash-land at a spot some 200 miles from the rendezvous point. The rough landing damaged much of the equipment aboard. Since survival depends on reaching the mother ship, the most critical items available must be chosen for the 200-mile trip. Below are listed the 14 items left intact after landing. Your task is to rank them in terms of their importance to your crew in its attempt to reach the rendezvous point. Place number 1 by the most important item, number 2 by the second most important, and so on through 14, the least important.

_____ Box of matches

_____ Food concentrate

_____ Fifty feet of nylon rope

_____ Parachute silk

_____ Two .45 caliber pistols

_____ One case of dehydrated milk

_____ Two 100-pound tanks of oxygen

_____ Stellar map (of the moon's constellation)

_____ Life raft

_____ Magnetic compass

_____ Five gallons of water

_____ Signal flares

_____ First-aid kit containing injection needles

_____ Solar-powered FM receiver transmitter

Source: Adapted from J. Hall, "Decisions, Decisions, Decisions," *Psychology Today,* 5 (1971): 51–54, 86, 88. For a full description of this exercise, consult a resource such as R. A. Schmuck & P. J. Runkel, *The Handbook of Organization Development in Schools and Colleges* (Prospect Heights, IL: Waveland Press, 1994).

five members seated at a table and one or two others are designated as Observers. Each participant at a table receives an envelope with several cardboard pieces that are different in size and shape from what other participants have in their envelopes. The task of the group is to pass pieces to each other so that when the activity is completed each participant will have assembled in front of them a square. There are several important process rules that must be followed: (1) participants may not talk or gesture; (2) participants may only pass pieces to others—they cannot take pieces; and (3) the activity is concluded only when all of the assembled squares are of the same size.

The Five Squares exercise has several process objectives. Participants certainly discover the importance of talking and taking, since they are not permitted to do either in this exercise. Participants often become frustrated at not being able to talk. When several groups are doing the activity a sense of competition develops between the groups, which adds tension. Often one of the participants will pass all of his or her pieces to the other members, and then sit back with folded arms. The group experiences added difficulty in completing the task when one member does this. The process observers will be taking notes throughout the activity, which often takes more than 30 minutes.

After the activity is completed there is a debriefing about what has happened. Participants will be asked about their feelings and what the keys to success were. The experience will then be used as a metaphor to talk about how the members share and help each other back in their workplace. For example, the observers, or the OD consultant, will ask about the person who withdrew. "Does this happen at work?" "How does this affect the ability of the team/department to accomplish its tasks?"

As has been pointed out, typically, OD exercises will not directly address job-specific tasks or problems. As with the two "classics" described here, exercises are designed using unfamiliar contexts and with materials and activities that are job-neutral. The expressed intent is to remove the job-setting context so that it does not interfere with learning new skills. The explicit assumption is that once learned, the participants can make the transfer back to the work setting.

Finding and Sharing OD Exercises.   Many sources and types of OD exercises are available. One of the traditional strengths and significant norms of OD experts is their willingness to share exercises and to encourage others to add to the quality of each. Excellent beginning sources are the earlier publications of such experts as J. William Pfeiffer and John E. Jones in business, and Richard A. Schmuck and Matthew B. Miles in education. Reflecting the evolution in definition of OD, contemporary sources have a more holistic view of organization development with more reliance on case studies; see, for example, *Best Practices in Organization Development and Change: Culture, Leadership, Retention, Performance and Coaching* (Carter et al., 2001).

GROUP/TEAM AND INDIVIDUAL PROCESS SKILLS

The contributions of OD have been particularly strong in bringing about change through the identification of process skills and training for groups and individuals. Skills that were a primary focus of OD activity in its earlier days had to do with group work and team building. In most organizations, work is accomplished in departments, teams, or other group-like sets. The OD perspective brings to everyone's attention the importance of team building as a key to organization effectiveness and productivity. A number of important group skills and processes have been identified and become the focus for training. Equally important is the identification of skills that individual members of a team can use to make group work more efficient and effective.

Group Decision Making and Problem Solving

Implementing change in almost any setting entails people working in groups. With the advent of such innovations as total quality management and site-based decision making, not only is more work being done in groups, but those groups are expected to make group decisions. This can be a very frustrating and inefficient experience unless the members have developed skill in working as a group. The OD perspective offers a number of useful concepts and strategies that can greatly improve group functioning.

Decision Making.   A key premise in the OD perspective is that, on average, groups will make better decisions than individuals. This is a disturbing idea for some, especially those who are more comfortable with the traditional chain of command and organizational chart perspective, which specifies that those at the top make the decisions and those below follow orders. In the OD perspective, decision making requires groups to develop a number of processes and skills. One of the necessary decision-making skills is *brainstorming*. Rather than leaping to a decision, effective groups first work through a process of generating alternatives ideas. As with other OD skills there are sets of rules for brainstorming, which include (1) there should be no value judgments, (2) all possibilities must be accepted and placed on the list, and (3) there is an agreed-on time limit for brainstorming.

Proponents of OD place major emphasis on groups achieving consensus in decision making. Voting and decision making by the formal leader are seen as last resorts. Reaching a decision by consensus does not mean that everyone's position will be supported; however, each position is to be heard and respected. Through discussion, a decision direction emerges that has wide support within the group. As this decision takes shape, an expectation is that in the end, those whose points have received less support will still accept the decision of the group. Many of the training exercises, such as the Lost on the Moon example (Figure 5.1), provide groups with training in how to reach consensus.

Problem Solving.   Another key OD process is *problem solving.* When a problem is introduced there is a strong tendency for individuals and groups to leap immediately to offering solutions. Rather than asking questions about the facts, or brainstorming possible solutions, the tendency is to advocate for a particular solution. In OD the process of problem solving has been analyzed, a number of steps to the process have been identified, and many training exercises have been developed to help teams become better at problem solving. Figure 5.2 is a graphic of some of the steps that can be included in problem solving. Note that problem solving is represented as a cycle. Usually solving one problem leads to new problems, so the steps may need to be repeated.

A number of training exercises may be used to facilitate a group in becoming more skilled in applying each of the steps in problem solving. For example, identifying symptoms and distinguishing these from solutions is an important early step. However, many symptoms are causes of other symptoms. This analysis could lead to the discovery that what initially was assumed to be one problem is in fact a "chain" of problems. Every identified problem in the chain is not of equal importance. The key is to select one of the problems that will make the biggest difference, and to focus on "fixing" it.

Another problem-solving skill is *force-field analysis.* In this technique, two columns are presented on chart paper or with digital projection. In one column, participants list those forces that will be in support of a certain action or solution. In the other column, forces that will inhibit implementation are listed. The next part of the problem-solving process entails selecting a solution (hopefully through consensus)

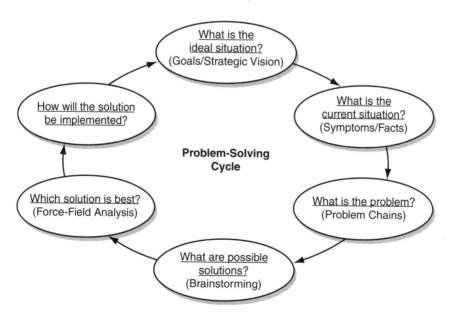

FIGURE 5.2   **Problem-Solving Cycle**

and developing a plan to take advantage of the supportive forces and tactics for off-setting the potential affects of the inhibiting forces.

Meeting Skills.   So much time in organizations is spent in meetings that one would expect that there should be ideas about better ways to run them. Skills and procedures for making meetings more efficient and effective have been identified. There are many useful resources to learn about how best to run a meeting—for example, see *101 Ways to Make Meetings Active* by Silberman (1999). Obviously, all of the exercises and skills that have been introduced here can be applied to development of meetings.

Individual Process Skills

The earlier OD perspective placed heavy emphasis on group functioning and team building. A key to the development of teams is the repertoire of process skills that team members bring to group work. Consideration of member skills is reflective of another OD value, *followership.* The designated leader of a team is expected to have certain skills. The OD perspective also places expectations on the "followers." Rather than the leader being solely responsible for leading, there are skill and role expectations for all members of the group. Team leadership is seen as a shared responsibility. The identified skills for all team members have proven useful in increasing group effectiveness. In addition, a number of tools have been developed that anyone can use for analysis of one's approach to leadership.

Individual Team Member Process Skills.   Over the years OD experts have identified a number of process skills that individual members of groups/teams can use to increase effectiveness. Training exercises have been developed to assist in learning to use these skills. There also are a wide variety of self- and group assessments that can be used to evaluate how well individuals and groups/teams are doing in using these skills. Some of these skills are described in Figure 5.3.

Today's OD experts have refined the descriptions and use of individual skills. They also have created new training materials that help individuals and teams increase their effectiveness. For example, Garmston and Wellman (2000) provide training and consultation to school districts all around the United States. Their materials provide detail about the reasoning behind each skill and offer examples of ways to say things (see Figure 5.4).

USING OD TO CHANGE WHOLE ORGANIZATIONS

As the OD field has evolved over the last 50 to 60 years one of the trends has been toward more systematic strategies for changing whole organizations. In its early days, "planned change" was a key purpose (for example, see Lippitt, Watson, & Westley, 1958). Proponents believed that organization change could be more successful when

FIGURE 5.3   Individual Skills for Increasing Group/Team Effectiveness

Encouraging: Asking another to say more, participate, elaborate, and/or lead by being warm toward and accepting of their contributions.

Clarifying: Saying an idea or point in a new way and asking, "Is this what you mean?"

Consensus testing: Asking for an indication as to where each member of the group is positioned at this time. This does not mean that it is his or her final position—it is just a check on where each person is right now.

Compromising: Offering a new position that takes into account points of disagreement and suggests a middle ground.

Gate Keeping: Inviting someone to contribute. This may be someone who has not said much or a person with relevant information.

Information seeking: Asking for information about the topic or a member's concerns.

Listening: Paying attention and carefully following a discussion.

Opinion giving: Presenting one's own position or feelings.

Paraphrasing: Restating what someone has said in order to be sure that there is shared understanding.

Perception checking: Asking a person if what you think he or she said is what the person intended to say.

Seeking opinion: Directly asking for an opinion.

Summarzing: At various points in a discussion briefly reviewing the points that have been made so far and the flow of topics.

various processes were internalized as the regular way of working. Over time, the processes for organization change became more complex and the role of the process consultant more sophisticated. Today, especially in business and industry, the range of models and strategies is quite wide. Still, core strategies continue to include addressing climate/culture, strategic planning, and process consultation. However, there have been significant increases in complexity and sophistication, as well as more rigorous research about their effectiveness.

Assessing and Developing Climate/Culture

Organization climate is an important topic for survey feedback. Over the years, many questionnaires have been developed for surveying elements of climate. For example, questionnaires can be used to measure the values and norms organization members hold about such constructs as autonomy, reward orientation, the amount of communication, and feelings about colleagues ("We trust each other") and their clients ("*Those* kids can't learn this"). The OD consultant can then work with the organization to help it become clear about its explicit and implicit assumptions. Targets can

FIGURE 5.4   Advocacy Skill Steps and Examples

ADVOCACY

Make Your Thinking and Reasoning Visible

State your assumptions. "Here's what I believe about . . ."

Describe your reasoning. "I came to this conclusion because . . ."

Describe your feelings. "I feel _____ about this."

Distinguish data from interpretation. "These are the data I have as objectively as I can state them. Now here is what I think the data mean."

Reveal your perspective. "I'm seeing this from the viewpoint of _____ or _____ or _____."

Frame the wider context that surrounds this issue. "Several groups would be affected by what I propose . . ."

Give concrete examples. "To get a clear picture, imagine that you are in school X . . ."

Test Your Assumptions and Conclusions

Encourage others to explore your model, assumptions and data. "What do you thnk about what I just said? Do you see any flaws in my reasoning? What can you add?"

Reveal where you are least clear. "Here's one area you might help me think through . . ."

Stay open. Encourage others to provide different views: "Do you see it differently?"

Search for distortions, deletions and generalizations. "In what I've presented, do you believe I might have overgeneralized, or left out data, or reported data incorrectly?"

Source: Garmston, Robert, & Wellman, Bruce. (2000). *The Adaptive School Developing and Facilitating Collaborative Groups (4th ed.).* Sacramento, CA 95762. Center for Adaptive Schools, www.adaptiveschools.com. Reprinted by permission.

be set and action plans developed for improving one or more aspects of climate as measured with the survey.

Organizational Climate Defined.   The earlier efforts to define and measure organization climate became quite confused. Many climate surveys were developed. Few had systematic research to demonstrate their psychometric qualities. Often there would be little obvious connection between the survey items and the construct being measured. For example, measuring the average size of offices might be associated with a scale called "task specialization." Quite literally, consultants would create climate surveys on the plane and apply them the next day. There was very little research to document that the various climate measures did measure elements of climate (i.e., validity) and that the measures did this consistently (i.e., reliability).

A very important conceptual and empirical analysis of the early climate measures was reported by James and Jones (1974). In the introduction to their article, they observed, "Organizational climate research occupies a popular position in current industrial and organizational psychology. However, conceptual and operational definitions, measurement techniques, and ensuing results are highly diverse, and even contradictory" (p. 1096). Actually, given the state of practice at that time, James and Jones were kind in their evaluation of the state of climate measurement. The first need was for clarity in definition of what was being measured. James and Jones proposed that there were three separate constructs being addressed under the organization climate umbrella:

1. *Situational variables* are attributes of the organization that are relatively stable over time, that require multiple measures, and that represent an objective view. These are organizational characteristics that influence the behavior of individuals and are true for the organization as a whole. Table 5.1 is how James and Jones summarized the situational components. Situational variables can be measured objectively, almost as if they were facts about a particular organization.
2. *Psychological climate* is an individual's perceptions of characteristics of the organization. Each person will have his or her view of the organization. The actual situation may be different from an individual's perceptions, but the individual's perceptions are reality for him or her.
3. *Organizational climate* is the summary of the individual perceptions of particular characteristics of the organization. At its simplest, organizational climate is the average of all the psychological climate scores.

As useful as the James and Jones (1974) definitions are, they also raise questions. For example, when there is wide variation in individuals' perceptions, what is the true picture of organizational climate? Still, the definitions continue to be useful in clarifying designs and uses of climate surveys and related feedback activities.

Climate versus Culture.   As the 1990s were unfolding, a new term, *culture,* became popular to use in survey feedback. This trend was taking place at the same time as the rise in use of qualitative research methods. Both trends were foreshadowed by the writings of Schein (1985) and others. Qualitative research methods emphasize the importance of in-depth observations in the field, developing rich narrative descriptions, and then looking for themes. These are the preferred methods for studying the culture of an organization.

A problem with climate surveys is that a standard set of items is used across organizations and an established *a priori* scoring procedure is used to determine scale/construct scores. Organization culture proponents assume that each setting will be unique in some ways and that a standardized questionnaire will miss some of the important local themes. There also is a risk that, as a consequence of a climate survey including a standard set of scales, one or another of the scale constructs could receive emphasis in a feedback session when it really is of minor relevance to a particular organization.

Assessing Organization Culture.   Assessing culture requires extensive time inside the organization. It also requires being especially observant and sensitive to how participants interpret symbols and ascribe meaning to actions and events. There is a

TABLE 5.1 Defining Organizational Climate as Situational Variables

CONTEXT	STRUCTURE	PROCESS	PHYSICAL ENVIRONMENT	SYSTEMS VALUES AND NORMS
Goals and objectives	Size	Leadership	Physical space characteristics	Conformity
Ownership and control	Centralization of	Communication	(temperature, lighting, sound, etc.)	Rationality
Charter (diversity	decision making	Control	Personnel protection	Predictablity
of mission)	Configuration	Conflict resolution	Remoteness	Impersonality
Dependence	Specialization	Change	Environment hazards	Loyalty
Age	Standardization of	Coordination	Space restrictions and confinement	Reciprocity
Function	procedures	Selection	Endurance demands	Adherence to chain of command
Level of technology	Formalization of	Socialization	Environmental stresses	Local (cosmopolitan) orientation
	procedures	Reward		Programmed (unprogrammed)
	Interdependence of	Decision making		approaches to problem solving,
	subsystems	Status and power		etc.
		Relationships		

Source: L. James, and P. Jones, "Organizational Climate: A Review of Theory and Research." *Psychological Bulletin.* 81, 12, (1974): 1096–1112. Copyright © 1974 by the American Psychological Association. Reprinted by permission.

delicate balancing task for the culture observer. He or she must enter the setting and be able to distinguish between seeing things as they are in some sort of objective view and learning how members of the organization interpret the same phenomenon. The culture observer also has to be able to understand the biases the participants bring to the setting. Many observers fall into the trap of interpreting things from their experiences, rather than hearing the meanings and interpretations constructed by the organization members. Also, organization culture is seen as a social construction. It takes shape through individual and interactive interpretation and construction of meaning.

Interviews are one of the key tools for assessing organization culture. Special interview questions need to be developed. These will be open ended and address key elements such as the role of the leader(s), the perceptions of colleagues, and the explanations for how things are accomplished. A research team in Belgium under the leadership of Roland Vandenberghe (Staessens, 1993) developed a set of questions for the team's studies of school organization culture. A sampling of their questions is presented in Figure 5.5. This research team identified three culture types: the family-school, the schools as a professional organization, and the living-apart-together school. As these names imply, leadership, goal consensus, and the values and norms were quite different in organizations with one or another of these culture types.

As with other OD tools and strategies, there are potential strengths and weaknesses inherent in choosing to apply a climate survey or to do the more in-depth fieldwork that is required to develop a picture of organization culture. Climate surveys are economical to use and the resultant information can be informative. The feedback session could include each respondent receiving feedback about his or her scores (psychological climate). The individual scores could then be compared to the average for all respondents (organizational climate). This type of process can reveal to the individual how closely his or her perceptions are in agreement with others, and provide everyone with information about the shared perceptions.

Assessing organization culture begins with extensive observation, interviews, and analysis of documents and artifacts. The resultant identification of themes will be rich and grounded in the uniqueness of the particular organization. The feedback process requires special skills and should come from a consultant who is trusted. In the feedback process the resultant themes are introduced along with examples of evidence that illustrates how the themes were identified. Some of the themes would likely overlap some organization climate survey scales, whereas others would be unique to the current organization.

Strategic Planning

Strategic planning has become a very comprehensive and extended process that is used regularly by businesses, institutions of higher education, school districts, and governments. Developing a full strategic plan can take several years. Once developed, it must be reviewed regularly and updated as progress is made or the situation changes. Typical process steps and products are presented in Figure 5.6.

FIGURE 5.5   Example Organizational Culture Interview Questions

SEEKING MEANING OF THE BEAVHIOR AND ACTIVITIES OF THE PRINCIPAL FOR TEACHERS

- Do you have many contacts with your principal? What do you talk about?
- Can you tell me what is of great importance to your principal?
- To which matters does your principal pay little or no attention?
- What does your principal expect from you as a teacher?
- What does your principal expect from you as a member of the team?
- What is the importance of your principal in your school?

DISCOVERING THE EXISTENCE OR THE FUNCTIONING OF A GOAL CONSENSUS OR SHARED VISION

- What does the staff consider as very important in this school?
- Why is this considered important?
- How can I see that this is important?
- Does everyone in the school consider this matter as important, or is this only true for a few teachers?
- How would you characterize your school during a conversation with parents?
- What exactly makes your school different from other schools?
- What are some of the stories, expressions or slogans which are used to express what is considered as very important?

DISCOVERING THE VALUES AND NORMS WHICH ARE CONSTRUCTED IN THE PROFESSIONAL CONTACTS BETWEEN TEACHERS

- How often is there a staff meeting in your school? What themes are discussed at these meetings?
- During lunch and at other times do you talk about work?
- Do you ever look in on a colleague's classroom? How often does that happen? What makes you do that? Do you discuss it afterwards?
- When you think over all the contacts with colleagues you have just described, can you say which contacts are most precious to you? Why?
- Are there things in this school that you are not able to talk about?
- Are there ever conflicts between staff members? What are they about?

Source: Adapted from Staessens, K. (1990). *De Professionele Cultuur van Basisscholen in Vernieuwing. En Empirisch Onderzoek in V.L.O.-Scholen.* [The Professional Culture of Innovating Primary Schools. An Empirical Study of R.P.S.-Schools.]. Unpublished doctoral dissertation, University of Leuven, Leuven, Belgium. For more information, see Staessens, K. (1993). Identification and description of professional culture in innovating schools. *Qualitative Studies in Education,* 6, 2, 111–128.

FIGURE 5.6   Strategic Plan Process Steps and Components

THE STRATEGIC PLANNING PROCESS ENTAILS A COMBINATION OF METHODS, INCLUDING:

- A designated leader or coordinator
- A strategic planning committee
- Retreats and workshops, including process training
- Surveys of organization members, customers, clients, consumers, and policymakers
- Sharing of plan drafts
- Top-down and bottom-up contributions
- All organization unit's activities and aspirations being nested inside the organization's plan
- Planning consultants
- Championing of the plan by the top executive leaders and governing board
- Multiyear timeline

STRATEGIC PLAN COMPONENTS

- *Action plan:* The specific objectives, tasks, activities, assignments, and timeline for the work that will be done
- *Beliefs:* A listing of core values and assumptions about the organization, its members, its clients, and how things work
- *Cost-benefit analysis:* An analysis of the direct cost (time, dollars, and other resources) to do a task, which is compared to the potential gains (tangible and intangible) and can be used to judge the potential "return on investment"
- *Goals:* General statements of the desired accomplishments for the organization over the next six months to five years
- *Indicators:* Areas of evidence that could be used to benchmark progress toward accomplishing objectives, strategies, and goals
- *Measures:* The specific pieces of evidence that will be collected and used to make judgments about progress
- *Mission statement:* An outline of the purposes and contributions of this organization that will contribute to achieving the vision
- *Opportunity cost:* An examination of the other tasks, activities, and accomplishments that will not be done, or done with less priority, in order that those identified in the plan can be done
- *Strategies:* A set of plans, resources, and activities that will be used in combination with others to accomplish each goal
- *Vision statement:* A sentence or single paragraph that describes an ideal view of the world that the organization serves (in some cases this will be an ideal view for the organization)

The strategic planning process is a very effective way to involve all members of an organization, as well as outsiders, in learning about and contributing to an organization's agenda for the future. The ideas of the many will be developed into the plan by having a strategic planning committee, which is led by a key organization executive. At intervals, drafts of the plan are circulated and feedback considered. The final plan, once accepted by the top executives and governing board, should be referred to constantly and be the basis for making major decisions. Many of the individual and group OD process skills, such as brainstorming and consensus decision making, become important to having a strategic planning process go well. Ideally, the resultant plan is a map of organization change and growth.

When a strategic planning process is introduced, the response of many is, "So what?" These people might attend the planning retreats and offer cursory feedback about the drafts, but there is no real commitment to the plan. For many, a strategic plan does not become real until the time when "real" decisions are made based on the plan. For example, if the decision on next year's department budget is heavily influenced by what the department submitted in its plan, the following year all departments will take the strategic planning process seriously. If the plan is used as a public relations document, then it will have little effect on changing the organization.

Components of strategic planning that are becoming increasingly important are the "indicators and measures." In the past, clarifying assumptions and developing a vision statement was important. There also tended to be a lot of discussion about the differences between vision and mission statements. More recently, the plan for action and the timeline have been key topics in the planning process. Now, the key focus is on what evidence has been and will be collected to indicate that there was change, and hopefully improvement. Having evidence and making decisions based in evidence is becoming the critical component of strategic planning.

■ ■ ■ ■ ■ ▬▬▬▬▬▬▬▬▬▬▬▬▬▬▬▬▬▬▬▬▬▬▬▬▬▬▬▬▬▬

VIGNETTE
THE STRATEGIC PLANNING RETREAT DAY

Paul had been looking forward to this day. Representatives from every department were meeting in a large conference room at the country club. Paul thought, "This is a good location. Plenty of coffee and everyone had to check cell phones at the door. We need to come up with some new directions today. What we have been doing will not carry us into the future." As Paul entered the room he saw the two consultants, CarolAnn and Art, talking with President Schneider. The usual chart paper and felt-tipped pens were in place and tables were arranged so that eight people could sit in a group.

The day began with introductions. President Schneider said how important this day was, but that he had to leave for another meeting. The strategic planning committee members were introduced and it was announced that each of them would chair one of the breakout goups. Jose, who is in charge of planning, led a discussion of the advance readings. Each of the articles related to some aspect of the problems and issues being faced by all of their sister organizations as well as this one.

(continued)

The agenda for the morning was to work in groups and do a SWOT Analysis. The consultants introduced the meaning of SWOT:

Strengths in the current situation and with what the organization is currently doing well

Weaknesses in the current situation and weaknesses in what the organization is currently doing

Opportunities that are out there

Threats either to the organization or in how the situation could change

The consultants emphasized the importance of keeping an open mind, and that it was a time to think differently and to introduce new ideas. They also emphasized the importance of everyone participating, "since the best ideas and decisions come out of people working together."

The consultants then reminded everyone of the rules for brainstorming:

1. Set a time limit (10 minutes).
2. Produce ideas as fast as you can.
3. Do not evaluate the ideas.
4. The priority is on producing as many ideas as possible.
5. It can be helpful to build on what someone else has said.
6. Someone needs to record all ideas.

As practice, each table had to brainstorm which animal, bird, or plant should be adopted as the organization's mascot.

Then each group began work on their SWOT analysis by spending 10 minutes brainstorming the *strengths* of the current situation. Then they were to do the same with *weaknesses* and *opportunities.* Paul saw what he thought were some good ideas being introduced, especially about opportunities. He had one frustration, though. Sally just did not understand the rules of brainstorming. She constantly kept lobbying for her single solution to everything: "We need to hire more staff. We just can't get everything done."

Following the brainstorming, each group had 10 minutes to report the results. There was a surprising amount of overlap, which the two consultants pointed out. Then each group was asked to do a force-field analysis of *threats* (the *T* in *SWOT*). As Paul heard Sally point out that staffing was a threat, he thought of several threats to add to the list but he held his breath. As a way of developing group consensus, the consultants asked the members of each group to place a red dot by the threat that they saw as most serious, and an orange dot by the second most serious threat. They also were to place a green dot by the one opportunity that they thought would really move the organization ahead. (This is a way to show visually those items where there is a developing consensus. It also is a way to reduce attention on some items that have only one or two individuals as advocates.) The consultants then asked each group to report on their top three threats and their highest-rated opportunity.

The afternoon session started with a discussion of imagination and the importance of thinking "out of the box." A very interesting video was used to illustrate how easy it

V I G N E T T E   CONTINUED

is to jump to conclusions that are based in wrong interpretations of the situation. Most of the afternoon was spent in each group preparing a presentation of the new strategic direction that they thought should be the way to go. Each group was challenged by the consultants to make their presentation interesting and to stretch the thinking of everyone. A part of their task was to develop a three- to five-year timeline with benchmarks by when tasks needed to be completed and to name roles and functions that would need to be established.

Following the group report, members of the strategic planning committee and Vice President Young asked questions and offered additional ideas that they had been considering. The day ended with the consultants explaining that over the next two days the strategic planning committee would be working with all of the notes, charts, and ideas that had been introduced during the day. One important task was to collect and compile data related to each of the four topics (strengths, weaknesses, opportunities, and threats). The strategic planning committee would then send out a draft of their report. In six weeks there would be a half-day retreat to review and further refine the plan. At some point the plan would also need to include "indicators" and "measures." The strategic plan would then go to the board and be used in making budget decisions for the next several years.

VIGNETTE CRITIQUE QUESTIONS

1. Which activities and processes described in this vignette are reflective of OD? What do you see being the process objective of each?
2. What individual and group process skills were employed in this vignette?
3. What would you predict to be the participants' reactions when President Schneider announced that he would not be there? How could the reaction be different depending on the culture of the organization?

OD PROCESS CONSULTANTS

Introducing an organization to OD and assisting members in developing skills to move through a multiyear process, such as is required for strategic planning, is the job of the OD consultant. Most OD consultants come from outside the client organization. The range of expertise of OD consultants is wide. They have to be expert in consultation and training and they must be able to diagnose problem areas and avoid inserting their own agendas. Particularly important are the interpersonal skills of the consultants. Their continued credibility is dependent on how well they can communicate with and be seen as supportive by all members of the organization. To be effective, they must be equally comfortable and eloquent in communicating with managers and workers. Since they are introducing processes and skills, rather than dealing directly with the production of the organization, they must be able to help members understand why skills and understandings of processes are important.

IMPLICATIONS FOR LEADERS FACILITATING CHANGE

1. Everyone—consultants, leaders, and followers—will be more effective as they come to understand and develop skill in using the OD process.
2. The many methods, exercises, and survey feedback techniques of OD can be applied in small-scale ways as well as in sustained whole organization planned change efforts.
3. Understanding problem solving can be very useful since so many people jump to solutions without first identifying the facts/symptoms and describing the problem.
4. Organization Development exercises and methods for analyzing and improving group decision making can be used by any team/department/unit.
5. The OD perspective addresses conflict resolution through a variety of strategies as well as the role of the consultant. The strategies can help organizations reduce conflict and/or develop positive ways of dealing with conflict.
6. Organization Development is an excellent source of interventions for facilitating change, even when OD itself is not being used as the change model.

OD Consultants at Work

Organization Development consultants bring to the organization a repertoire of process skills and understanding of organization interpersonal dynamics. They understand goal setting, communication, problem solving, decision making, conflict resolution, and the skills that groups and individuals need in order to function effectively. They also bring with them a set of "interventions." These include feedback surveys, exercises, training protocols, and skill in coaching individuals and groups at all levels of the organization.

Planned Change Steps. In its totality, OD is viewed as a way of accomplishing *planned change*. In the OD perspective a set of process steps have been identified for accomplishing change in organizations. There is a sequence to how change works, and with each step, the consultant provides relevant process training and consultation. The external OD consultant serves as coach, guide, and trainer to the organization as it addresses a need and moves through the steps entailed in changing.

From the consultants' view, planned change includes the following steps (Rothwell, Sullivan, & McLean, 1995):

1. *Entry:* In many ways, beginning a relationship involves a courtship. The prospective client is reading the actions of the consultant closely and carefully. The consultant also is engaged in an early assessment of the organization. Both are asking questions: Can I trust and work with this person? Do I have the right resources to offer? There will be several contacts before an agreement is struck, which will likely cover the first steps. Long-term commitment has to be earned.

2. *Start-up:* The first steps are careful steps. The consultant has to be a fast learner. There are bound to be mixed signals and individual perceptions that only represent part of the picture. All of the actions of the consultant are watched closely. Keys to success include identifying shared values, recognizing that the consultant has expertise, and seeing the consultant becoming sensitive to organization politics and building linkages with key opinion leaders.

3. *Assessment and feedback:* Obtaining systematic information about the current situation is important. Before deciding on a course of action, the consultant and client need to share an evidence-based understanding of where things are now. As important as gathering information is, giving feedback is even more critical. The feedback needs to be based in the assessment and presented in ways that are seen as accurate. The resultant dialogue leads to consensus about the problem and the needed change. The assessment also provides the baseline for future measurement of change.

4. *Action planning:* In order to accomplish change, actions must be taken. The process of developing the action plan should include as many of the members of the organization as possible. A change strategy needs to be selected. The plan needs to be affordable, doable, and supported by top executives.

5. *Interventions:* To accomplish the change, interventions likely will be needed at three levels: whole organization, groups, and individuals. Whole organization interventions might include strategic planning, a reorganization of production tasks, or a change in the reward system. Group and team interventions include interpersonal communication, decision making, and team skill in meeting roles and responsibilities. Addressing how individuals work in organizations could be done through self-study and reflection as well as interpersonal process skill development.

6. *Evaluation:* Collecting and using evidence is a continuing part of the OD process. Each intervention activity can be evaluated and used to refine the next steps. Evaluations should be done across time so that there are regular snapshots for viewing progress and identifying emerging areas of need. Evidence should be collected at the end to judge how successful the process has been.

7. *Adoption:* Outcome(s) have become a staple in group work and are ingrained in the organization culture. This does not mean a rigid adherence to a certain way of doing things, however. The new way continues when there are changes in key personnel and the client is no longer dependent on the presence of the OD consultant.

8. *Separation:* The consultant is no longer needed for the change to be sustained, or the consultant role is reduced to occasional appraiser of continuation of the change.

OD Consultant Issues.   As with all change perspectives there are a number of issues and potential problems with OD. One is the extent of knowledge and skill required of the OD consultant. For example, each of the OD processes and related intervention exercises is interesting. However, processing the exercise sessions is delicate and requires a high level of skill. Consultants also must be skilled at working with all levels of an organization. The consultant is likely to be contracted by a top-level executive, but he or she must also be able to work with sales representatives in regional offices as well as workers on the assembly line floor. This requires flexibility and a genuine comfort in working with diversity.

USING OD CONSTRUCTS AND TOOLS TO ASSESS AND STUDY IMPLEMENTATION

Organization Development offers a wealth of concepts, models, and measures that can be used in evaluation, implementation assessment, and research studies. The 60-year history of OD ensures that the core concepts are grounded in the reality of changing organizations. An important caveat for researchers is that most of the measures used in OD do not have available information about their psychometric qualities. Historically, OD was an applied field. Until recently there was little research and what there was had questionable quality. For example, the effectiveness studies would be conducted by the consultant (potential for bias), reliability and validity of the measures were not established (reduction in confidence of findings), there were no comparison data from a like group or organization (any changes in scores could be due to some other undocumented intervention), too many of the studies were based on participant and consultant self-report (potential for bias), and few of the studies reported direct data about increases in effectiveness or productivity in the organization's core technology.

Even with the limits of the past, the potential of OD to be used in evaluation, assessment, and research is very high. (See, for example, Volume 14 of *Research in Organizational Change and Development* by Pasmore & Woodman, 2003.) Today's research, especially in business, organization, and industrial psychology, is rigorous. Theories, models, and constructs are well defined and the study designs include systematic controls.

Study possibilities abound. For example, OD concepts related to group decision making and problem solving are ripe for use in education. Most public schools are required to develop school improvement plans each year. This is intended to be a schoolwide and community-involving effort. Many schools have difficulty with the process. Intervention studies using OD methods and techniques could be conducted to see if the school improvement process improves and the quality of the plans is enhanced. In higher education, there are parallel dynamics as they engage with strategic planning.

Studies of organization climate and culture could use concept definitions identified in the various measures that OD consultants have developed. For the quantitatively inclined, factor analytic studies similar to those of James and Jones (1974) could be conducted to test for the existence of constructs and to develop research verified measures. Of course, those with a qualitative bent should become immersed in an organization for the purpose of describing elements of culture that support or inhibit planned change efforts.

Since OD consultants come from outside, they have to earn their continuing involvement. Their contract can be terminated at any time. They must work well with the executives. They also should continually remind themselves that their primary client is the organization, not just the top executive(s). They must do all of this while maintaining confidentialities with everyone. Consultants will have knowledge of impending strategic decisions and various employee personal problems. They must be responsible to the people, the organization, and the planned change effort.

SUMMARY

Organization Development (OD) represents a different perspective for understanding and implementing change. The focus on process, the role of the external process consultant, and the planned change steps represent a systematic approach to change. The OD perspective does not focus directly on the core technology of the organization. There is an avoidance of expertise or offering of assistance in whatever the organization's product or service may be. Instead, the OD perspective focuses on the personal and interpersonal dimensions of people in organization settings. A core assumption of OD is that the members of the organization will be better able to solve their technology problems as they become more skilled in the "technology" of OD.

DISCUSSION QUESTIONS

1. Have you ever participated in an OD planned change effort? What was it like? What processes were used?

2. Have you ever participated in an OD training exercise? What skills were being developed? Did you find that you were able to bring the skill training back to your work setting? Why or why not?

3. Planned change efforts using strategies such as strategic planning and school improvement are designed to involve everyone in reviewing the current situation and setting an agenda for the future. As a leader, how would you see using OD concepts and methods?

4. Participants in OD are often slow to see any connection between the time spent in doing exercises and doing their job. What do you think about the OD reasoning of not using the work context in process skill development? What would be gained/lost from embedding the training in the work context?

5. The OD consultant represents himself or herself as not bringing a solution to any particular problem and not representing a certain direction for the organization. By comparison, the change agent in the diffusion perspective openly represents and advocates for adoption of a specific innovation. In many ways OD and the consultant are innovations that must be adopted. To what extent do you think that OD and the consultant are innovations? What is the innovation(s)?

FIELDWORK ACTIVITIES

1. Observe several meetings of a group. This could be a committee, a department, a team, or a complete staff. Use the skill list presented in Figure 5.3 to observe the group's process. Which skills do individual members of the group apply? How are decisions made? Does the leader make them, or is it by consensus or voting? Are there other skills that if used would help the group in accomplishing its tasks?

2. Seek out an OD reference that includes training exercises. Select one that you could process for a group. Work closely with your instructor on all that is entailed in serving as the process consultant with the selected exercise. Develop a feedback form to evaluate your role in leading the exercise and your skill as the consultant. Select a group of colleagues or fellow students and try facilitating a session. At the end, be sure to critique the exercise and your role as the process consultant.

3. Examine a strategic plan, school improvement plan, or similar product from a whole organization planned change effort. Interview several of the participants. Ask them to reflect on the process, as well as the product. Who led the work? Was there a process consultant? If so, what role did that person play? Develop an analysis of the OD processes that were in place. Were any introduced by the leader or consultant? In hindsight were there other skills that if employed might have been of help?

ADDITIONAL READINGS

Carter, L., Giber, D., & Goldsmith, M. (Eds.). (2001). *Best Practices in Organization Development and Change, Culture, Leadership, Retention, Performance and Coaching.* San Francisco: Jossey-Bass/Pfeiffer.

> Case studies along with assessment instruments and evaluation tools are described as they are being used with a variety of companies. The cases are organized around five topic areas: (1) organization development and change, (2) leadership development, (3) recruitment and retention, (4) performance management, and (5) coaching and mentoring.

Clegg, S. R., Hardy, C., & Nord, W. R. (1996). *Handbook of Organization Studies.* Thousand Oaks, CA: Sage.

> Although not an OD book, this volume is an excellent resource for those who are interested in the recent models, research, and thinking about organizations. The chapters in this handbook document the increased rigor in thinking, theory building, and research that is true of OD and the extensive field of organization studies. The handbook chapters are organized within three parts: (1) frameworks for analysis, (2) current issues in organization studies, and (3) reflections on research, theory, and practice.

French, W. L., & Bell, C. H. (1998). *Organization Development: Behavioral Science Interventions for Organization Improvement* (6th ed.). Upper Saddle River, NJ: Prentice-Hall.

> For a traditional view of OD, how it works and keys to its success, this is the book. The authors are long-time scholars and practitioners in the field of OD. The history, current practices, and examples of efforts to make long-range change in organization culture and social processes are described. In many ways this book reflects the dynamic and evolving nature of OD, from its earlier human potential days to today's context of globalization and contemporary innovations such as total quality management.

March, J. G. (Ed.). (1965). *Handbook of Organizations.* Chicago: Rand McNally.

This is a one-stop resource for reading about the historical foundations chapters cover a wide range of topics, including those closely related to OD. The chapters are organized within the categories of foundations, methodologies, theoretical-substantive areas, specific institutions, and applications.

Silberman, M. (1990). *101 Ways to Make Meetings Active.* San Francisco: Jossey-Bass/Pfeiffer.

This book offers 101 tips and activities that can be used to make meetings more effective. There are suggestions for preparing for and beginning meetings, as well as for stimulating discussion, facilitating creative problem solving, and managing controversy and conflict. A number of the activities and suggestions address building consensus and commitment.

PART III

TOOLS AND TECHNIQUES FOR UNDERSTANDING THE PEOPLE PART OF CHANGE

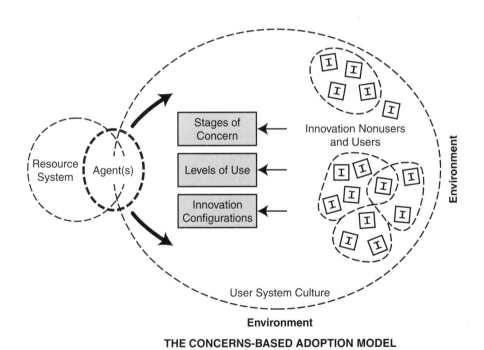

THE CONCERNS-BASED ADOPTION MODEL

Change is most definitely a part of life and work for all people. Regardless of the workplace setting or social situation, change is experienced personally and individually. Researchers have studied how people individually and collectively experience change processes. Out of this research a number of useful constructs and tools have been developed. Chapters 6, 7, and 8 present three well-established ways of thinking about and understanding change at the individual level.

Clarifying what "it" is is the subject of Chapter 6. In most change efforts, different people have surprisingly different images of what full implementation looks like. This results in different **Innovation Configurations (IC)** being implemented by different users. An important step for change success is to develop consensus about what full implementation should look like. One way to do this is to develop an *Innovation Configuration map (ICM),* which is similar to a rubric for assessing innovation implementation.

There is a personal side to change. The people who are involved in a change effort have personal reactions and feelings about the innovation and about their involvement in the change process. This is stating the obvious, but understanding and using the obvious as a means for anticipating and providing appropriate responses is the goal of Chapter 7. The research-based construct of **Stages of Concern (SoC)** about the innovation is introduced and used to illustrate ways of addressing the personal side of change.

Chapter 8 introduces a third way to understand individuals and their approach to change, **Levels of Use (LoU).** The chapter focuses on the *behaviors* of each person as he or she gradually learns about and becomes a competent user of an innovation. The research-based construct, Levels of Use, becomes very useful to charting implementation progress across time. It is useful in planning for training and other supports as the change process unfolds, and in conducting outcome evaluation studies.

Two caveats are important to note here. First, although each of these chapters has described a way of understanding, assessing, and facilitating change for individuals, this does not mean that individuals cannot be grouped and clustered and addressed as a whole. Each chapter will include examples of how to facilitate change for groups and whole organizations. However, the interventions are based on first understanding the dynamics of change as experienced by individuals.

The second caveat has to do with the amount of information that is necessary before a new idea can be used well. As is the case with many new ideas (innovations), the level of information provided in each chapter is likely to be just enough to make a prospective adopter/user "dangerous." Most people need further study and possibly some training in order to use any new idea, program, or practice effectively. Before adopting any of the constructs and tools, investing in additional learning will be an important and responsible subsequent step.

■ ■ ■ ■ ■ ▬▬▬▬▬▬▬▬▬▬▬▬▬▬▬▬▬▬▬▬▬▬

CHAPTER 6

CLARIFYING THE CHANGE

Innovation Configurations

Why can't they [instructors] just read the lesson as written and do what it says? When you go out in the field, some of the things that are going on you will not believe!

—Curriculum developer

The district mathematics liaison stopped by yesterday and said I was doing a good job! To tell you the truth, I still don't know what I am supposed to be doing, so I just make it up as I go along.

—Middle school teacher

Well, the teacher's guide is so clear and the training gave me the opportunity to practice, so I understand what is expected. I am able to do all of the activities in each lesson just as they are described in the guide and how I saw them in the video examples.

—Social studies teacher

My hospital volunteer group is trying hard to explain to new members what our roles are as nurses aides—what can we do to describe it?

—County hospital volunteer

A frequent problem for teachers and others who are expected to implement new practices is that they are not clear about what they are being asked to do. Even when training and materials are provided, there is a big leap from preparing to do something to actually doing it. In the end, what teachers do in the classroom may bear little resemblance to what the creator(s) of the change had in mind originally. All of the teachers may call it the same thing, but in practice what they do may look very different. In this chapter we will examine the *innovation,* or the change itself: How to describe it and how to measure it in classroom use are central themes. A key purpose of this chapter is to identify a concept and tool that can be used to construct a common understanding of the change by everyone involved.

FOCUS QUESTIONS

1. Should all teachers in a school be doing the same thing in their classrooms relative to reading, science, mathematics, and the other subject areas?
2. How do you specify an intended change?
3. What key issues result from a lack of clarity about how to use an innovation?
4. How can a clear vision of a change serve as a road map to successful implementation?
5. How can you determine which classroom practices really make a difference in student learning?
6. What is an Innovation Configuration map? Who should be involved in developing one?
7. How many "components" and "variations" will be needed to make a really good Innovation Configuration map for a company's managerial responsibilities?
8. What are some of the uses of an Innovation Configuration map?

THE CHANGE: WHAT IT IS AND IS NOT

A major reason that widespread change often occurs only modestly across a school is that the implementers, change facilitators, and policymakers do not fully understand what the change is or what it will look like when it is implemented in the envisioned way. When there is such confusion, principals and other facilitators may give conflicting signals, and teachers will create their own versions of the change as they try to understand and use the materials and/or processes that have been advocated. Evaluators then have serious difficulties in appraising whether the new way is better than the old. This is particularly problematic when what is being done under the name of the innovation is different in various classrooms. This phenomenon led those of us working with the Concerns Based Adoption Model (CBAM) to add a third diagnostic dimension to the paradigm—*Innovation Configurations (IC)*—which is the topic of this chapter.

Before beginning the description of Innovation Configurations, a definitional issue must be addressed. For any change or innovation there will be one or more architects, or creators, who may be national expert(s) or local developer(s). Frequently the creators of the innovation are curriculum experts from outside the school or district, such as a national project or publishing house. Others are a local team or committee of teachers who have experimented in their classrooms and developed an approach that they wish to share with others. Still other changes are driven by local school boards, state legislatures, and federal policies; some are even initiated by court decisions. In the CBAM approach to change, we have used the term *developer* to represent any and all of these sources.

INNOVATION ADAPTATION

The concept of Innovation Configurations addresses both the idealized images of a change developer as well as the various operational forms of the change that can be observed in classrooms. The focus in the IC diagnostic dimension is on developing and applying word-picture descriptions of what the use of an innovation can look like.

Previously, a typical means of determining whether a new program or process was being used in classrooms was to count how many classrooms contained the program materials. Alternatively, *use* of the new way would be assumed because the teachers had participated in a workshop or the principal would report that teachers were "doing it."

The uncertainty of whether there was high-quality use of a new program or process was discovered early in the original CBAM verification studies. The implementation of two innovations was being studied: teacher teaming in elementary schools and college professors' use of instructional modules. In each case, when the so-called users were asked to describe what they were doing, a surprising range of practices was outlined, but in all cases the interviewees would claim to be using the same innovation. For example, when teachers in Texas, Nebraska, and Massachusetts were asked to describe their teams, they provided very different pictures of the innovation of teaming:

> *Team Texas* consisted of three teachers and two aides who served approximately 110 students. They "teamed" all day and were housed in a pod that was equivalent to three classrooms in size. The students were taught by all of the teachers, and each teacher took the lead in planning for one subject area.

> *Team Nebraska* consisted of three teachers, each of whom had a homeroom class. For half the day, students would move from classroom to classroom as they were grouped and regrouped for lessons. Teachers kept their own students for the afternoon. Teachers specialized in teaching all students particular subjects.

> *Team Massachusetts* consisted of two teachers, each of whom had a regular classroom with 25 to 30 students. The teachers exchanged lesson plans once a month, but each kept and taught his or her own students all day.

As these examples illustrate, how the change is thought about in theory may bear little resemblance to the activities that are done in classrooms under the name of that innovation. In each of the schools just described, the teachers were quick to say,

"Oh, yes, we are teaming," but what they were doing under the name of teaming was very different.

An early conclusion in our studies was that users of innovations tend to adapt and, in many cases, mutate innovations! In other words, the innovation in action can take on many different operational forms or configurations. Once the phenomenon of Innovation Configurations is recognized and accepted as a natural part of the change process, a number of implications emerge. For example, the outcomes from the use of different configurations of an innovation will likely vary. Users of some configurations will be associated with higher outcomes than those using other configurations. Also, to further their implementation, training and coaching users will need to target different aspects of the innovation, depending on which configuration is in use. There is a philosophical issue here too. To what extent is there a need to advocate for close adherence to the developer's intended model (i.e., a "fidelity" approach)? When, or should, all users be doing the same thing? In other words, how necessary and appropriate is a fidelity model of change? The concept of IC and its related measurement procedure help address these questions.

The purpose here is not to make judgments about how good or bad it may be to adapt an innovation. Instead, the goal is to point out (1) that in most change efforts, innovation adaptation will occur; (2) that there is a way to chart these adaptations; and (3) that these adaptations have direct and indirect implications for facilitating and assessing change processes. In the concluding section of this chapter we will return to issues related to fidelity and some of their implications, but first, Innovation Configurations as a concept and its mapping procedure need to be described.

INNOVATION CONFIGURATIONS AS A CONCEPT

Anyone who has been involved in change recognizes the phenomenon of Innovation Configurations. The tendency to adapt, modify, and/or mutate aspects of innovations is a natural part of the change process; it is neither malicious nor even explicitly planned. It happens for a number of interrelated reasons, beginning with uncertainty about what is supposed to be done. Most people, especially teachers, want to do the "right" thing. Therefore, when teachers are asked to use an innovation, they will try. The problems begin when the details of how to do it are not made clear.

In nearly all cases the innovation as operationalized by different users will vary along a continuum from being very close to what the developer had in mind to a distant zone where what is being done is nearly unrecognizable. Creating different configurations of an innovation is not unique to education. For example, consider cars as the innovation. As Figure 6.1 illustrates, and as any parking lot confirms, a car can be and has been significantly adapted from the initial conception of a two-door sedan. A whole range of "configurations" can be observed, ranging from changes in color, to the addition of mag wheels, to rebuilding as a race car, to some forms that some might claim are cars that the rest of us would say, "No, those are not cars!"

FIGURE 6.1   A Continuum of Innovation Configurations for a Car

This same continuum of configurations exists for educational innovations, only determining what is and is not the innovation is more difficult than with the car example. All too frequently the developers of an educational innovation have not thought clearly about what the use of their change will really entail. They have thought more about what is needed to support its implementation, such as training and materials. In addition, because teachers, like the rest of us, are always short on time, they will tend to reduce the amount of change and effort they have to invest whenever they can. If there is limited training and support for the change, it is likely that it will not be fully implemented. Although the teachers may genuinely believe that they are using the innovation, an expert observing their classroom may conclude, "Hmm, is that the way it should be done?"

The different configurations of educational innovations are easy to picture. Take, for example, the innovation of integrated use of technology. What is envisioned here is classroom use by students and teachers of various forms of technology for information retrieval, processing, and communication. Some of the relatively simple configurations that could be observed are as follows: (1) classrooms with only a few computers with no Web access, which are used mainly for drill and practice; (2) classrooms with computers that are linked within the school and include CD-ROM databases but no Web access; (3) classrooms with computers with Web access, projection devices, and video, where students work individually and in groups to research, plan, develop, and communicate presentations about their learning; and (4) schools in which all computers are in a lab or media center and used on an assigned schedule for groups of students.

Once it is recognized and accepted that there will be different configurations of an innovation, an important next issue is how to describe those configurations. Answering this question entails development of an Innovation Configuration map (IC map).

GUIDING PRINCIPLES OF IC MAPPING

1. Always type the word *draft* on each page of your IC map.
2. Always type your name and the date of the current draft on each page. This will reduce confusion over whether someone is referring to the most recent version of the IC map.
3. Watch out for IC map components that simply taper off as they move from the *b* or *c* to the final variation. If this is happening to one dimension, make sure you have a second dimension that increases from *a* to the final variation. After all, if the ideal dimension is decreasing, some other practice is taking its place.
4. Remember that the *d* and *e* variations are not "bad" or simply pejorative descriptions; they should be descriptions of alternatives that represent other ways of doing things.
5. A completed IC map should serve as a record of how an innovation is being used; its purpose is not to explain how the information about practice is to be collected, which may be done by interview, observation, or user self-assessment. Some caution is needed in terms of reliability and validity, especially for certain types of IC map components. For example, there will be much lower validity for a teaching process component that is self-assessed than one that is recorded by a trained observer.
6. An IC map is only good for the innovation for which it was designed. With a different innovation, the map-building process will have to be done again.
7. Strive to have very descriptive word pictures for each variation. Address the presence or absence of each dimension in each variation.
8. Be careful about having too few and too many dimensions in a component. Very rarely should a component consist of only one dimension or more than four.
9. Remember that the consensus-building process and debate among the mappers is key. The talk about "what you mean" and "what I mean" is critical to developing a useful and valid IC map.
10. Do not insert fidelity lines until after the IC map has been through several generations of drafts and there are clear reasons to do so.

MAPPING INNOVATION CONFIGURATIONS

The scenarios just described are very familiar to teachers, principals, and other leaders. The situation in which teachers are not sure about what they are to do occurs in part because innovation developers have a hard time imagining the extent to which their innovation can be adapted. Another reason for the uncertainty is that change facilitators and teachers do not have clear images and descriptions about what the use of the innovation can look like. To address these needs, we have developed a process and tool that can be used to visualize and assess the different configurations that are likely to be found for any particular innovation. We call the process *Innovation Configuration mapping* and the resultant tool an *Innovation Configuration map.*

Innovation Configuration Maps

The concept of a map was deliberately chosen for this work because, just as a road map shows different ways for getting from one place to another, so does an Innovation Configuration map. A highway map will picture interstate highways, U.S. highways, and county roads. These are alternate routes, all of which make it possible to complete the trip. The IC map does the same thing for change facilitators and users of innovations by identifying the major components of an innovation and then describing the observable variations of each component. The IC map is composed of "word picture" descriptions of the different operational forms of an innovation or change.

IC Map Components.   Consider the very simple IC map component presented in Figure 6.2, which describes the units that a teacher presents. In the *a* variation, all units and most activities are taught. The quantity of units and activities that are taught decreases in the other variations, with the *e* variation describing the classroom where none of the units or activities is taught. Even without naming a specific program, it is possible to use this component with its different variation descriptions to visualize different degrees of coverage of units and activities. It is part of the "map," just as is a highway map.

The purpose of the IC map is to present carefully developed descriptions of different ways of doing the innovation. An IC map will have a number of components (typically 8 to 15), and each component will have a number of variations (typically 2 to 6). The number of components will vary depending on the complexity of the innovation and the amount of detail needed. There is a dynamic trade-off between the number of components and the level of detail represented. Normally, in an IC map with fewer components, each component will have more information, which at some point makes the descriptions too dense and difficult to visualize. On the other hand, in an IC Map with many components, each one may be too finely ground to be useful. In the end, the team that develops an IC map has to decide what is best for its situation.

FIGURE 6.2   A Simple IC Map Component (from the Science Program)

COMPONENT 1: UNITS TAUGHT

(A)	(B)	(C)	(D)	(E)
All units and most activities are taught	Most units and activities are taught	Some units are taught	A few selected activities are taught	No units or activities are taught

The major goal in writing each component description and each variation description is to be as visual as possible. The better the word pictures, the easier it will be for teachers, principals, and others to see what successful use of the innovation entails.

Developing Clear Word-Picture Descriptions.   The IC map component presented in Figure 6.2 was deliberately chosen because of its simplicity. A more typical IC map would have much richer component descriptions, as shown in Figure 6.3. These components were selected from the Instructor Profile for Fast Trac II (Novak, 1992), a 10-week course for business entrepreneurs. In this project, which was done by the Center for Entrepreneurial Leadership of the Kauffman Foundation, there was interest in developing an IC map that depicted the role of the course instructor that could be used as part of the quality control check as the course was disseminated nationally. The resultant IC map was used also to select content for instructor training, since instructors were to be skilled in doing each of the map's components. The map was also used by the instructors in planning and self-reflection, and by trained assessors in determining instructor certification by viewing videotapes of their classes.

One of the interesting aspects of the Fast Trac IC map was that the innovation was the role of the course instructor. An IC map could also have been developed around the role of workshop participants or around what they, as entrepreneurs, applied from the course to their businesses. Deciding which innovation will be the focus for IC mapping is a critical first step.

Note, in Figure 6.3, how the component and variation descriptions in Component 2 have been stated. The basic component is the same, but more information is presented for the component than in Figure 6.2. However, as IC mapping expert Paul Borchardt would say, this is still a "boring" component, since it basically just evolves from "all" (*a*) to "a little" (*d*). A component of this type could be made much richer by adding a second dimension, or practice, that increased in occurrence from *a* to *d*. For example, the dimension of excessive time being spent on one or two modules could gradually increase across the variation descriptions.

A much higher quality example of an IC map component and its variations is Component 11 in Figure 6.3. Note how the word-picture descriptions of each variations are richer, and how four different dimensions—variety, type, relevance, and length—are addressed in each variation. An IC map notation technique is to present a key word for each dimension within brackets following the component label.

Indicating Ranges of Quality and Fidelity.   Figures 6.2 and 6.3 illustrate a number of additional features of IC map components as well, including the implicit value in the sequencing of the variations. As one moves from the *e* variation toward the *a* variation, the behaviors and practices described increasingly approach the more ideal practices as viewed by the innovation developer or some consensus group, usually those who developed the IC map. Laying the component variations along such a continuum from more to less desirable can be very helpful. Note that this IC mapping technique can be used only to implicitly signify when some variations are valued

FIGURE 6.3 Two IC Map Components for the Instructor's Role in the Fast Trac II Course for Business Entrepreneurs

FAST TRAC II COURSE INNOVATION CONFIGURATION MAP

Site _____ Session _____ Instructor _____ Observer _____ Date _____

A. FULL COURSE OVERVIEW

2) Balanced Coverage of the Six Core Modules —Entrepreneurial Mind Set —Management & Organization —Finance [6 covered, equal emphasis]
—Legal Entities —Marketing —Negotiations

(a)	(b)	(c)	(d)	(e)	(f)
All six modules are developed and with equal emphasis.	All six modules are developed but with one or more given less emphasis.	One or more modules is not systematically addressed.	One or two modules become the course.		

LECTURE SEGMENT

11) Use of Examples by the Instructor during the Lecture   [Variety, type, relevance, and length]

(a)	(b)	(c)	(d)	(e)	(f)
Examples are used throughout. Examples are interesting, varied, to the point, and congruent with the issue or topic at hand. Examples include retail/service/manufacturing and participants' expertise with examples from their businesses.	Examples presented are to the point and congruent. There is limited variety in terms of retail/service/manufacturing and participants' businesses.	Examples and stories are not always relevant to the issue or topic at hand and tend to be drawn out, or a few businesses are overused as examples. Examples may not be clearly explained.	So many examples and war stories are shared that complete coverage of the points is hindered.	So many examples and war stories particular to the instructor's personal experience are shared that there is little variety and complete coverage of the point is hindered.	There are few examples and/or all of the examples are based in one or two businesses.

Source: Reprinted by permission from the Kauffman Center for Entrepreneurial Leadership at the Ewing Marion Kauffman Foundation.

118

more highly than others. The authors of this text are not arguing for or against such a fidelity perspective, but merely showing how it can be noted on the IC map.

Another IC mapping technique that can be helpful with a fidelity perspective is use of what we call *fidelity lines,* which are represented by the vertical dashed and solid lines between certain of the variations of the components in Figure 6.3. A solid line signifies that all of the variations to the right have been judged to be "unacceptable" ways of doing that component; all of those to the left of a dashed line are considered "ideal" practices, while those between the solid and dashed lines are viewed as "acceptable." Determining the placement of these lines in this case was done by the Fast Trac course developers. Whether to have lines and where to place them are important decisions for IC mapping groups. No matter who is to make the decision about the inclusion of fidelity lines, *no lines should be added until after the IC map has been through several versions and has been used in data collection.* The insertion of fidelity lines should not be arbitrary or capricious. There should be a very good rationale and, hopefully, empirical data to support their placement.

Student Roles in IC Maps.   One of the first decisions in IC mapping is to determine which role(s) will be the focus of the map. For example, as mentioned earlier, the Fast Trac map shown in Figure 6.3 could have focused on the participants or the regional dissemination administrators instead of the instructors. Normally, IC maps will deal not just with the role of the teachers and their use of the materials but with the role of the students too. For example, Figure 6.4 describes one aspect of student performance in a constructivist approach to teaching mathematics (Alquist & Hendrickson, 1999), which is based on the National Council of Mathematics Standards. Figure 6.5 is a student component from the IC map for standards-based education of the Douglas County School District in Colorado. The rich and observable descriptions of each variation in these examples were the result of intense and sustained effort.

Other Roles in IC Maps.   The National Staff Development Council (NSDC) created IC maps of five role groups of educators (Roy & Hord, 2003) to describe expectations for their activities when conducting staff development that exemplified the 12 NSDC standards for staff development (National Staff Development Council, 2001). Figure 6.6, the Cross Walk, is the result of organizing all the desired outcomes (in these maps, *desired outcomes* is the term used for *components;* there are no variations in the Cross Walk) of all five role groups of educators.

The desired outcomes of teachers are presented as the first column in the Cross Walk. Then the desired outcomes of the other role groups are placed horizontally to the teachers in order to show which desired outcomes relate to each other. This depiction suggests how the four role groups (principal, central office staff members, superintendent, and school board) support and enable the achievement of the desired outcomes for teachers.

The idea is to read horizontally, beginning with the teacher, paying no attention to the numerals of any of the outcomes (unless you wish to refer back to the ICs presented in the book of maps). Notice that in some rows of desired outcomes, all

FIGURE 6.4 Student IC Map Components

INNOVATION CONFIGURATION MAP FOR THE TEACHING AND LEARNING OF MATHEMATICS
DoDDS-Hessen District Superintendent's Office, Rhein Main, Germany

DRAFT	DRAFT	DRAFT

B. Engagement with Task/Investigation

3) Student Engaged in Mathematical Tasks throughout the Lesson [engagement, time]

a	b	c	d
Most students are engaged in mathematical tasks, most of the time.	Most students are engaged in mathematical tasks, part of the time.	Some students are engaged in mathematical tasks. Many are off task most of the time.	Few students are engaged any of the time.

4) Students' Understanding of Problem-Solving Strategies [knowing your goal, where you are now, knowing the steps to get to the goal, reflection]

a	b	c	d	e
Students view the open-ended problem as a whole and analyze its parts. They create, select, and test a range of strategies. Students reflect upon the reasonableness of the strategies and the solution.	Students grasp the open-ended problem as a whole and analyze its parts. Students pick an established/traditional strategy to try to solve the problem, which is applied without considering alternatives. Students reflect upon the reasonableness of the solution but not the strategy.	Students approach the open-ended problem as a whole but do not have a clear understanding of the parts. The primary focus is on getting an answer. The students' reflection is on whether the answer is right rather than the reasonableness of the strategy.	Students approach open-ended problems as unconnected/unrelated parts and do not see the problem as a whole. Students may manipulate materials and numbers, but are not clear about the reason/purpose. If observable, reflection is about procedures.	Students calculate and compute using rote and routine procedures. Students are not clear about the final goal or the relationship of the tasks to that goal. There is little or no reflection about what is being learned.

Property of Hessen DSO, Unit 7565 Box 29, APO AE 09050—Contact the authors of the IC Map for the latest version.

DRAFT

Source: From "Mapping the Configurations of Mathematics Teaching" by A. Alquist and M. Hendrickson, 1999, *Journal of Classroom Interaction, 34*(1), 18–26. Reprinted by permission.

FIGURE 6.5 Student IC Map Component for Standards-Based Education (Douglas County School District, Castle Rock, Colorado)

DOUGLAS COUNTY SCHOOL DISTRICT—LEARNING SERVICES STANDARDS-BASED EDUCATION—CONFIGURATION MAP

Component #5—Student Ownership and Understanding of Learning; (understanding of standards or checkpoints, understanding of progress in relation to standards or checkpoints, understanding of what is needed to improve performance in order to achieve standards or checkpoints)

(I)	(II)	(III)	(IV)	(V)
Students' focus is on the **current activity.**	Students' focus is on **the requirements of the class and grade** they receive.	Students can use the **"language" of standards.** They **can state the standards and checkpoints** that they are expected to learn, but are **unclear about where they are** in meeting the standards or checkpoints or **what they need to do to** achieve them.	Students **understand** what they are **expected to know and be able to do** and can **articulate in specific terms** what it means to reach the standards or check-points. They can **describe where they are** in regard to the standards or checkpoints but are **unclear what they need to do** to achieve them.	Students **understand** what they are **expected to know and be able to do** and can **articulate in specific terms** what it means to reach the standards or check-points. They can **describe where they are** in regard to the standard and know what they **need to improve** to achieve it.

Examples:

"We are reading *The Diary of Anne Frank*, and I will be writing some kind of report when we are finished."	"We are studying how to use primary source materials. I need to get at least a B on the final report."	"I know that we are studying how to select and evaluate primary source materials as related to the Holocaust. I'm not sure exactly what I'll need to know about primary sources, or if I am any good at using them."	"I know that we are studying primary source materials as related to the Holocaust, and that's why we are reading *The Diary of Anne Frank*. I know that we will be evaluating and interpreting sources for their usefulness in understanding the Holocaust. I can find sources, but I am not sure how to evaluate their relevance and quality. I am not sure what I'll need to do to become proficient in evaluating these sources."	"I know that we are studying primary source materials as they relate to the Holocaust and that's why we are reading *The Diary of Anne Frank*. I know that we will be evaluating and interpreting sources for their usefulness in understanding the Holocaust. I am pretty good at locating primary sources, but I have trouble knowing whether they are really quality sources. My teacher has shown some interesting ways to judge the quality of a source, but I need some more practice with them."
				April, 1999

Douglas County School District Re-1

Source: Douglas County School District Re-1, Castle Rock, Colorado. Reprinted by permission.

FIGURE 6.6 Cross Walk of Five Role Groups for National Staff Development Council's Standards for Staff Development

STANDARD: LEARNING COMMUNITIES

TEACHER	PRINCIPAL	CENTRAL OFFICE STAFF MEMBERS	SUPERINTENDENT	SCHOOL BOARD
	1.4: Creates and maintains a learning community to support teacher and student learning.			1.2: Takes collective responsibility for the learning of all students.
	1.3: Understands and implements an incentive system that ensures collaborative work.		1.1: Understands and implements a recognition and incentive system that rewards collaboration that achieves district goals.	1.1: Supports a recognition and incentive system that rewards collaboration that accomplishes districtwide goals for student learning.
1.1: Meets regularly with colleagues during the school day to plan instruction.	1.1: Prepares teachers for skillful collaboration.	1.1: Prepare administrators and teachers to be skillful members of learning teams.	1.3: Ensures district administrators are prepared to be skillful leaders and members of learning teams.	

1.2: Aligns collaborative work with school improvement goals.	1.2: Creates an organizational structure that supports collegial learning.	1.2: Maintain and support learning teams.	1.2: Creates policies and structures that support the implementation of learning communities within the district.	1.3: Functions as a learning community.
1.3: Participates in learning teams some of whose membership extends beyond the school.	1.5: Participates with other administrators in one or more learning communities.	1.3: Participate with others as a member of a learning team.	1.4: Participates in learning communities that focus on continuous improvement.	1.4: Supports individual, team, school, and system-wide learning at the local, regional, state, and national levels.
		1.4: Support learning team use of technology		

Source: Reprinted from *Moving NSDC's Staff Development Standards into Practice: Innovation Configurations,* by Shirley Hord and Pat Roy (NSDC, 2003) with permission of the National Staff Development Council, www.nsdc.org, 2004. All rights reserved.

squares are not filled. This effort with the Cross Walk is to illustrate the systemic approach to professional development and the role that all educators play.

More Complex and Richer IC Map Components.   When there is the need and time, IC map components can be made even more complex and richer. In one such project the innovation itself was very subtle and complex, and developing each component had to be done in ways that built in the nuances of the philosophy of the developer as well as clear descriptions of how this approach would be seen in classroom practices. The innovation, the ESSENTIAL Curriculum, is an educational program that provides children and young people with the knowledge and skills that will directly assist them in their development as capable and ethical people (Dunn & Borchardt, 1998). Although there are lessons and activities in the program, its philosophy of how people should treat each other is expected to be expressed in the classroom throughout the day. Because of this, the IC map included components that described practices during a lesson as well as others that addressed practices to be used throughout the day.

To help teachers, change facilitators, and evaluators assess implementation of the ESSENTIAL process, the IC map components became much more complex. One of those components is presented is Figure 6.7. There are a number of readily apparent differences between this IC map component and the earlier examples. First, the range of variations is greater, and there is a common dimensionality built into each one that deals with how holistically the teacher is integrating use of the program's principles. The *f* variation, for example, describes the case when nothing that is related to that component is observed. The *g* variation addresses behaviors and actions that are actually *antithetical* to the intent of the program, information that can be very helpful. Another important addition to this component is the open-ended list of examples under each variation description. Although they will not represent all that is in a particular variation, nor will they necessarily be exclusive to that variation, they do describe the kinds of behaviors that are indicative of it.

The Process of Developing an IC Map.   Developing an IC map is a challenging endeavor. It also is energizing for those who really are interested in having implementation of an innovation succeed. There are moments of discovery about the intent of a particular innovation and how it should be used. There is also the initial struggle to figure out what the components are and then to develop useful word-picture descriptions for each variation. Additional rewards come when the first draft of the IC map is shared with interested teachers, principals, and other change facilitators. Often, this is the first time they will have seen written descriptions of what they can do when using the innovation.

Often, the first reaction of people who examine an IC map is to do a self-assessment of where they would place themselves on each component. A second reaction is to consider some of the other variation descriptions and whether they should try them. The IC mappers receive very helpful feedback from these dialogues, which can be used in further refining the map.

FIGURE 6.7 A Dense and Complex IC Map Component with Indicators

THE ESSENTIAL CURRICULUM IC MAP

II. All Day in the Classroom

D. Teacher

6) The Principles and Concepts are applied throughout the day by the teacher [teacher application, all]

Consistent reliance on and integration of program (Complete Integration) (a)	Deliberate and concious application of principles and concepts (Deliberate Application) (b)	Emphasizes selected principles and concepts (Selected Emphasis) (c)	Program delivery as designed (Motions) (d)	Presentation of parts and pieces at random (Parts & Pieces) (e)	Non-use (Nothing) (f)	Opposition to principles and (Antithesis) (g)
Principles and concepts are integrated without conscious effort into activities of the day. ■ Teacher and students acknowledge mistakes in words including "oops, I goofed." ■ Teachers teach students through steps of correcting errors seamlessly. ■ Students have "Driver's Licenses" and "Drive" to other parts of the building using self-control. The license can be suspended for lack of self-control.	All principles and concepts are developed and consciously applied throughout the day. ■ When opportunities arise, teacher and students draw connections to and apply specific principles and concepts. ■ When faced with opportunities, teacher and students talk out loud about the relevant Principle or Concepts.	Selected principles and concepts are emphasized and applied appropriately throughout the day. ■ Teacher leads students in applying principles of "self control," but does not refer to other concepts. ■ Teacher recognizes opportunities around "making mistakes," but misses opportunities related to other Principles and Concepts.	Lessons are taught, but no extrapolations to situations outside the Essential lesson context. ■ When obvious opportunities to refer to principles and concepts arise, teacher does not make connection. ■ Teacher handles fight on playground without reference to any Essential principle.	Some activities are purposefully selected to teach the concept. ■ Tap and Trade game is played without Principles being taught. ■ Social studies curriculum happens to lend itself to the selection of Essential lessons.		Principles and concepts applied in classroom are antithetical to Essential. ■ Indiscriminate use of praise (unearned). ■ Self esteem activities teaches principles and concepts counter to Essential's Principles and Concepts. ■ "In this classroom we will not make mistakes." ■ "I can give my students self esteem." ■ Mistakes are punished without any processing.

Source: From *The Essential Curriculum,* The Teel Institute, Kansas City, Missouri. Reprinted by permission.

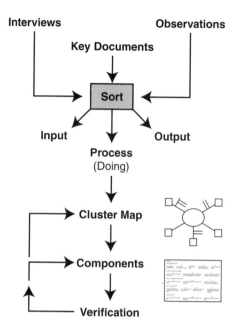

Note: This is a dynamic, interactive, consensus-building process.

FIGURE 6.8   The IC Mapping Process

Developing an IC map is definitely an interactive process. An individual working alone is very unlikely to construct a map that is as useful as one that evolves from a team effort. Typically, three to seven key people work together for five or six days to devise a complete first draft of an IC map. One of the major outcomes of this interactive process is that the IC mappers develop a consensus about what the innovation should look like when it is in use. Up to that time, they likely will not have been using the same terms and detailed images of use. This regularly observed lack of explicit agreement in understanding adds greatly to teachers' confusion about what they are supposed to be doing.

The general process that is followed in developing an IC map is presented in Figure 6.8. The beginning steps entail reviewing all of the available printed material and then interviewing the innovation developer and/or experts. Following this, a range of classrooms where the innovation and similar practices are in use should be observed. It is important to observe a variety of classrooms, because an IC map needs to have word-picture descriptions that cover all possible variations. Three key questions that should be asked throughout this process are:

1. What does the innovation look like when it is in use?
2. What would I see in classrooms where it is used well (and not as well)?
3. What will teachers *and* students be doing when the innovation is in use?

A key part of IC mapping is the orientation that is taken. The focus is on developing pictures of the operational forms of the innovation, not statements of its philosophy or a listing of its implementation requirements. Innovation creators have a tendency to focus on implementation requirements. They may say something like, "You have to use these materials and spend at least 30 minutes doing so every day." However, this is the wrong answer for those building the IC map, who instead need to know *how* those materials are being used and *what* happens in the classroom when they are.

The initial document review, interviews, and observations should lead to the development of a *cluster map,* which is a schematic map of the array of possible components, their clustering, and some of the possible variations for certain components. The first goal is to develop a holistic organizing scheme of possible components and clusters of components that represent what the innovation is like when it is used.

Following this is the task of agreeing on which components are key and should be developed. Then comes the intense work of negotiating the wording of components and component variations. Once there is a draft, it needs to be tested in what we call the first "dose of reality." Without exception, when IC mappers try out their first full draft, they discover a number of points that need clarification. They also are likely to discover that other components need to be mapped.

Developing an IC map is a highly interactive and iterative process. Our experience has been that innovation developers cannot develop high-quality IC maps by themselves. Also, it is always best to have three or more people drafting an IC map. An earlier technical document on IC mapping (Heck et al., 1981) may be of some help. The Guiding Principles of IC mapping presented on page 115 also provide additional technical information and tips to consider in reviewing map drafts.

IMPLICATIONS FOR LEADERS FACILITATING CHANGE

The concept and way of working of professional learning communities (Chapter 2) is in substantial need of information and understanding about facilitating the creation of these structures in schools.

Although some information is available about this challenge, much more would be desirable. To produce such data, change facilitators would create IC maps of PLC (or other reform structures or practices), use the maps to guide and support development of the PLC, and assess both staff and student outcomes as the staff reaches various points on the map.

In this way, interventions that support participants could be related to how far they have moved on the map in terms of the variations of the components. Interventions could be catalogued as they relate to the development of each of the five dimensions of PLC (components) in the map.

The IC map is an invaluable tool to use in the creation of new practices. Tracking interventions on the IC map will provide clear examples of how to use Innovation Configuration as a diagnostic tool for supplying interventions that facilitate a significant reform practice (i.e., PLC). Building and using an IC map helps to develop consensus about what "it" looks like when implemented.

INNOVATION CONFIGURATIONS: APPLICATIONS AND IMPLICATIONS

There are many applications and implications of the Innovation Configuration concept and IC maps. We have selected a few to introduce here to stimulate further thought about this important aspect of the change process. The points included address some facets of facilitating change processes, conducting research, and drafting IC maps.

Using IC Maps to Facilitate Change

Once an IC map is developed, it should not be kept a secret. Share it with all of the potential and current users of the innovation and with all change facilitators. This was done, for example, for the nine innovation bundles in the Kentucky Education Reform Act. Under the leadership of Roger Pankratz and the Kentucky Institute of Education Research, nine cross-state constituent teams of 6 to 10 members each, met for a week to develop the first drafts of the IC maps. Each team was assigned to one bundle. Copies of their IC maps were then sent to all 1,230 schools in the state. This was the first time that teachers and principals had word-picture descriptions of what they could be doing under the labels of each of the reform initiatives.

An IC map is also a diagnostic tool for planning training and development. For example, a large number of teachers could be observed and an IC map completed for each, with the information then summarized by component. The summary would be a tally of how many teachers were at each of the variations for each component. Then it would be possible to identify those components where implementation was going well (i.e., many teachers using *a* and *b* variations) and any components where implementation was lagging (i.e., many teachers using *d* and *e* variations). This information could be used to plan a training workshop to address less well implemented components.

IC maps can be a useful coaching tool as well. Principals and other change facilitators could observe classrooms to provide help to teachers, but often they are not given guidelines and specifics about what to look for. The IC map provides a set of descriptions that can be used to focus their observations. There might also be a preobservation discussion where the teacher and the facilitator agree that certain IC map components will be targeted during the observation. Since many of the components focus on what the students are doing, teachers are less likely to perceive the use of an IC map during an observation as an evaluation threat. In all cases, if the focus is kept on the innovation instead of the teacher, personal concerns will be lower.

Using IC Maps in Research, Evaluation, and Implementation Assessments

A serious problem in most research and evaluation studies has been the failure to document implementation before making judgments about the effects of various treatments, programs, and innovations. Typically, implementation is assumed to have occurred if teachers were trained or the materials were purchased. An IC map provides one clear and direct way to record the actual extent and quality of what has been implemented.

NEEDED EVALUATION, RESEARCH, AND DEVELOPMENT

The innovation configuration map has been widely embraced across the English-speaking cultures/nations as an excellent tool to define and support implementation of new practice. Its "sister" tool, Stages of Concern (SoC) (Chapter 5), in the diagnostic set of CBAM concepts and measures has been likewise embraced; however, SoC has been translated and has traveled across international boundaries.

It seems plausible to translate the procedures and a sample of IC maps into other languages (Spanish, for example) for use by colleagues in non-English-speaking countries. This would require the appropriate translation, of course, but also a testing of the process and sample ICs in the native tongue and setting. (see research to support the original IC work in Heck et al., 1981). Such a research and development project would permit wider use of this tool.

In a number of research studies, IC maps have been developed and data collected to assess implementation. For example, Bridge (1995) conducted a number of studies of the implementation of the Integrated Primary program in Kentucky. The *a* variations were formulated using the state's reform initiative and the standards of the National Association for the Education of Young Children. Bridge found that children had higher achievement in primary-grade classrooms where there were higher levels (i.e., more *a* and *b* variations) of implementation of the developmentally appropriate practices. Koon (1995) had similar findings in a study of the extent of implementation of YESS! Mini-Society (Kourilsky, 1983), an innovation designed to introduce concepts of business and entrepreneurship to students.

THE FIDELITY ENIGMA

The work of both Bridge and Koon had a fidelity orientation, or an established vision of which practices were more preferable. In both studies, the IC maps were developed accordingly, and higher student outcomes were associated with higher fidelity implementations. An issue that needs discussion is whether it is appropriate to ask for or insist on high-fidelity use of an innovation. From one point of view, teachers are being told what to do, which reduces their teaching freedom. On the other hand, if student gains are higher when the innovation is used in specified ways, should not teachers be expected to use the verified practices? Although we do not have a simple or universally applicable answer to this critical question, we believe that it needs to be openly asked, discussed, and addressed in each change effort. The following vignette illustrates how an IC map could serve as a guide for teacher reflections.

■ ■ ■ ■ ■

VIGNETTE

USING AN IC MAP COMPONENT FOR REFLECTION AND PEER OBSERVATION

Two teachers are discussing their understanding of standards-based education (SBE) and what they think their students understand about it.

> **JOSÉ:** I think that I am finally understanding what SBE is about. It really has been a big change for me. I have been used to providing information and teaching with the discovery approach. The idea that I should make sure up front that the students understand the desired outcome has been a big change for me.
>
> **MARY JO:** I know what you mean. I have always wanted my students to learn, but I too thought that they should have to figure it out from scratch.
>
> **JOSÉ:** I still don't think my students get it. They can give me a general idea about the standards and the specific benchmarks we are working on, but they don't seem to be very clear about it. I wish I could somehow get them to understand what their responsibilities are.
>
> **MARY JO:** I know what you mean. Do you remember that implementation rubric handout that Elliott [the district SBE coordinator] gave us last August? There was a student component. Maybe we should look at that.
>
> **JOSÉ:** I know what you mean. I just happen to have a copy in my file. I am going to look it over and see if it gives me any ideas.
>
> **MARY JO:** Why don't you pull a copy and then tomorrow, when you have your break, come observe my physical science class and see what you think? Don't use the whole thing, just the component that focuses on student learning.

This story points out two important applications of an IC map. First, it can be used by teachers for self-reflection. Teachers can read each component, assess where they are, and then think about what they wish to continue doing and what they might want to change. An IC map can also be used for peer observation, as teachers observe each other's classrooms using an IC map as the rubric. They can focus the observation through preobservation discussion, and then debrief one another afterward.

Note that only one component of the IC map was used as the focus for the planned peer observation in this case. This is a very efficient and useful way to go about it. The selected component was one that dealt with student behaviors, which was a very good choice. When teachers focus on what they would like students to accomplish, there can be a very direct connection back to what the teachers need to do to help students succeed in the desired ways.

VIGNETTE CRITIQUE QUESTIONS

1. Think about using an IC map for teacher self-improvement. Under what conditions would you want to use the whole IC map? When would it be best to use one or two components?
2. Would you ever want to share the IC map with students? Why or why not?
3. Would you ever consider sharing an IC map with parents? Why or why not?

SUMMARY

In this chapter we have introduced the idea that an innovation can be made operational in many different forms or configurations. We have advocated developing Innovation Configuration maps and openly sharing the drafts with all parties. Along the way we have pointed out some of the conceptual, operational, and philosophical implications of this process. Key points to remember from this chapter are summarized as Guiding Principles.

One of the important benefits of developing an IC map is the consensus building that it encourages. Without such agreement, the various leaders and change facilitators all too frequently deliver different messages to the nonusers and users, which adds to the confusion and frustration about the change. It sometimes also leads to early adopters of the innovation establishing practices (i.e., configurations) that are later determined to be inappropriate or even not in keeping with the original design. Change processes will be more efficient and effective when there is careful consideration of the possible components, variations, and clusters from the outset. This is not to say that images and values of the innovation cannot change with time. In fact, this is one of the reasons why it is important to type "draft" on each page of the IC map. Still, it is better to begin with the best possible estimate of a shared vision rather than starting with conflicting conceptions.

In conclusion, efforts to implement changes in schools—new processes, practices, organizational structures, and the like—have long been highly ambiguous. We believe that the typically elusive visions of what the use of an innovation entails has been a primary reason for the lack of widespread successful change. When a variety of configurations are implemented, there is little likelihood that significant gains in student learning will be detected across all classrooms. As has been described in this chapter and illustrated in the vignette, the Innovation Configuration map is a multipurpose tool that change leaders and implementers can use to improve this situation. Evaluators and researchers have also found it to be valuable in promoting specificity and unstacking innovation bundles. As one constituent enthusiastically reported, "The IC map is the best thing since sliced bread!"

DISCUSSION QUESTIONS

1. Describe an experience that you have had where the innovation as used was different from what the developer had intended. Why did this occur?

2. What key steps would you take to introduce the idea of developing an IC map to a school/district staff?

3. How could a teacher use an IC map?

4. How could a principal use an IC map?

5. How could a corporation or private sector manager use an IC map?

6. What do you see as an important implication of Innovation Configurations for evaluation and research studies?

FIELDWORK ACTIVITIES

1. Develop two or three configuration components, with their variations, for an innovation that you know. Try to draft your IC map by observing or interviewing someone who is using the innovation. What did you learn about the innovation and its implementation from this experience?

2. Critique an IC map that someone else has developed. Can you visualize the ideal use of the innovation from studying the map? Which variation descriptions present clear word pictures? What are the dimensions within each component? Does each component contain an appropriate number of variations? Which would you suggest be changed or clarified?

3. After studying all of the available materials related to a particular innovation, sketch a cluster map of possible components and some of the variations. Then interview or observe someone who is using the innovation. How does your cluster map need to be changed?

4. Make a presentation to your CEO and/or board of directors about the desirability of creating IC maps to support use of your new golf ball promotional strategies by the sales teams. In addition to the teams, what other individuals should have an IC to guide their work in this promotion? Explain why.

ADDITIONAL RESOURCES

For accessing training in the use of and creation of Innovation Configuration maps, contact the authors, or Southwest Educational Development Laboratory, 211 East Seventh Street, Austin, Texas 78701, 1-800-476-6861.

CHAPTER 7

UNDERSTANDING FEELINGS AND PERCEPTIONS ABOUT CHANGE

Stages of Concern

You see. She wasn't interested in what we think. They have already decided what is going to happen.

—A teacher's comment following an exploratory school staff meeting with the superintendent

I don't have time to go see what someone else is doing; I have more than I can get done right here.

—Reaction to a curriculum consultant's suggestions to observe what someone else is doing

My kids have been doing terrific things with manipulative materials in mathematics. Now José and I are talking about bringing our two classes together to do some cooperative groups.

—One teacher's thoughts in the third year of use of a new approach to teaching mathematics

The quotes above are all too familiar to those of us who have spent time in schools working with teachers and other workers as they have been engaged in change. Many feelings and perceptions are expressed, and many more are only whispered or left unspoken. No matter how promising and wonderful the innovation, no matter how strong the support, implementers will still have moments of self-doubt about whether they can succeed with this new way, and whether they even want to. There are also moments of euphoria when the change works well, as well as times it seems it will never succeed.

We all know what it is like during that first year of doing something new and different. We tire more easily. We need more time to prepare. And we can't predict everything that will happen. We never feel like we are really on top of things.

Yet, after several years, the new becomes familiar and readily doable. Our thoughts shift from the struggles of figuring out what to do to the satisfactions of seeing what happens with students, and of talking with others about the benefits of the change and about how to fine-tune it to work even better.

Across all of these experiences, there is an affective dimension, for we are not just doing but continually thinking and feeling about how the change is working, how well we are doing, and what effects it is having. This personal side of change is experienced by everyone—executives, parents, students, sales representatives, secretaries, and governors—whenever we are involved in implementing change.

FOCUS QUESTIONS

1. How do you handle those personal feelings and perceptions that come out as part of the change process? Should any of them be ignored?
2. Do all of the implementers in a building or region have the same types of concerns, or are they different for everyone?
3. When you are talking to someone, how can you discover what his or her concerns are?
4. Is there a predictable pattern to the feelings and perceptions that people have as the change process unfolds?
5. Do the Stages of Concern always move forward, or can they be arrested or move backward?
6. How fast can implementers move through the stages of concern?

THE PERSONAL SIDE OF CHANGE

Feelings and perceptions about the innovation and the change process can be sorted and classified in to what we call *concerns*. In fact, there is extensive research about how our feelings and perceptions evolve as the change process unfolds, which we have named the *Stages of Concern*. These stages give us a way of thinking about people's feelings and perceptions about change. Additionally, through research and experiences a set of techniques have been established for assessing concerns.

Understanding the Stages of Concern and using the assessment techniques can result in significantly more effective one-on-one coaching sessions, more relevant workshops, and strategic plans that take into account the personal side of the change process. In this way, the process can be both facilitated and increasingly personalized. A description of the Stages of Concern (SoC), the assessment techniques, and their applications is the central topic of this chapter. In subsequent chapters examples of how the SoC construct can be used with other diagnostics to asses and/or facilitate the change process are described.

STAGES OF CONCERN ABOUT AN INNOVATION

The idea of calling one's feelings and perceptions *concerns* was originally proposed by Frances Fuller (1969), a counseling psychologist at The University of Texas at Austin who took an interest in student teachers as a result of teaching their required educational psychology course. When she started teaching the course, she worked diligently to make it a good one, but the evaluations at the end of the semester showed that 97 out of the 100 students rated the course "irrelevant" and "a waste of time."

Fuller was an exceptional educator. As Howard Jones, a colleague of ours from the University of Houston likes to tell, she did not react as you might expect to the students' evaluation of her course. Instead of being completely discouraged, she asked, "What did I do that turned those 3 students on?" This was a breakthrough question. When she looked at the 3 students who had rated the course positively, she found that they, unlike the other 97, had had some sort of previous experience with children. They had either taught a church class or were parents already. Thus, they had a different background with which to understand and appreciate the introductory course on educational psychology. Fuller hypothesized that their *concerns* were different as a result of their experiences.

Fuller's Unrelated, Self, Task, and Impact Concerns

Fuller proceeded to conduct a series of in-depth studies of the concerns of student teachers. She then proposed a model outlining how, with increasing experience in a teacher education program, the student teacher's concerns moved through four levels: unrelated, self, task, and impact.

Unrelated concerns are found most frequently among student teachers who have not had any direct contact with school-age children or clinical experiences in school settings. Their concerns do not center on teaching or teaching-related issues. Instead, they more typically focus on college life (e.g., "I hope I can get a ticket to the concert") and college studies removed from professional education courses (e.g., "I hope I pass that geography course"). These students do have concerns, but they are not teaching-related concerns.

Self concerns tend to be most prevalent when student teachers begin their student teaching or other, more intense clinical work. Now they have concerns about teaching, but there is an egocentric frame of reference in terms of what the experience will be like for "me" and whether "I" can succeed. Beginning student teachers with self concerns will be asking questions such as: "Where do I park my car when I get to the school?"; "Can I go in the teachers' lounge?"; and "I hope that I can get along with my cooperating teacher so that I get a good grade." These expressions indicate concerns about teaching, but with a focus on themselves rather than on the act of teaching or the needs of children.

Task concerns show up quite soon after the start of student teaching, as the actual work of teaching becomes central. Typical expressions include: "Oh! I am so tired, I had to stay up until midnight grading papers"; "When three groups are going at once, my head is spinning; I don't know where to turn next!"; and "These materials break too easily—there are pieces everywhere, and they just play with them!"

Impact concerns are the ultimate goal for student teachers, teachers, and professors. At this level the concerns focus on what is happening with students and what the teacher can do to be more effective in improving student outcomes. Improving teaching and student learning are what the talk and thought are about: "My kids are doing great; they understood what I was trying to do!"; "I am thinking of adding some new interest centers. They might attract those children who don't seem to get it this other way"; and "There is a workshop next Saturday on involving kids with special needs in cooperative groups. I am going to take it."

In her studies, Fuller found that over two-thirds of the concerns of preservice teachers were in the self and task areas, whereas two-thirds of the concerns of experienced teachers were in the task and impact areas. She also observed that at any given time teachers may have concerns at several levels, but that they tend to concentrate in one particular area.

Connecting Concerns to Teacher Education

Fuller (1970; Fuller & Bown, 1975) proposed a different model for the content and flow of a teacher education program, which she named *personalized teacher education.* In such a program, the courses and field experiences are linked with the developing concerns of the students. She believed that becoming a teacher entailed *personalogical development,* or the development of one's own style and philosophy, and that the best way to achieve this end was to address the student's concerns when she or he had them. In the design of a teacher education program, this means offering the courses and field experiences in a sequence that parallels the developing concerns of the students, rather than a sequence that parallels the professors' concerns.

Thus, when teacher education students have self concerns, this is the time for early field experiences, low-ratio teaching activities, and educational psychology courses on children of the same age as those being observed. For students with task concerns, the timing is ripe for the "how-to" components of methods courses. The history and philosophy aspects of teacher education are seen by the students as being much more relevant when offered to parallel the development of their impact concerns, which typically occurs near the end of their program. This personalized approach does not mean that all content that is important from the professors' point of view is left out. Instead, the information is provided when it is most relevant to the students' developing interests and perceived needs. In terms of cognitive psychology it means that the students have accumulated sufficient prior knowledge, or have schema constructed so that they are able to draw connections between what they currently understand and what they need to be learning next.

GUIDING PRINCIPLES OF CONCERNS THEORY

1. We all have personal concerns (Stage 2) when first confronted with change. Rather than condemning someone who has a high level of personal concerns, you first need to be empathetic and work to determine why these concerns are so intense. Then efforts can be made to resolve them.
2. When you find teachers with impact concerns, be sure to take time to encourage them. Although these are the types of concerns that we wish educators had all the time, they are unfortunately less frequent than we would like. Spend more time with teachers who have impact concerns. They will find your interest supportive, and you will feel better by being around such positive teachers.
3. Stage 5 Collaboration concerns are very rare in any organization, including schools. When a number of employees have such concerns, it strongly indicates that the leader has been doing something special. In terms of interventions, do all that you can to nurture and support collaboration concerns. A school where both Stage 5 concerns and Stage 4 Consequence concerns are intense truly exhibits an interest in students and collegiality about teaching.
4. The Stages of Concern can be applied to both individuals and to groups. In fact, this chapter deliberately does not identify which are being discussed. The concepts and thinking are the same for both. However, because group SoCQ profiles are by definition an average, they can mask individual differences.

CONCERNS AND THE CHANGE PROCESS

As you may have already seen, our research on the concepts and issues related to change has clearly documented that the concerns phenomena that Fuller identified are not limited to college students going through teacher education programs nor to teachers. In fact, everyone involved in change exhibits the same dynamics seen in the education students confronted with the "innovation" of student teaching.

The same *unrelated, self, task,* and *impact* pattern of concerns is found in people involved with all types of innovations and change processes. In addition, choosing the types of "interventions" that are to be done to facilitate the change process is based on the same personalization model. What facilitators of the change process do needs to be reflective of the concerns of those engaged with the innovation and those considering its use. In fact, if the example is simply changed from teaching to a school innovation, the same types of expressions of concerns are typically heard:

Unrelated: I am not really interested in _____ [this innovation]. My mind is on . . . .

Self: I don't know if I can do this. Also, I am concerned about what my boss thinks.

Task: Using this material is taking all of my time. You can't imagine all the pieces and steps that are entailed in just doing one step!

Impact: Yesterday, I was talking with Mary. Both of us have found that with the new approach, all of the students (clients) are engaged in and picking up on the concepts much more quickly.

As these quotes illustrate and the findings from our research and that of our colleagues document (Van den Berg & Vandenberghe, 1981; Persichitte & Bauer, 1996; Shieh, 1996), the same types of concerns exist when people are engaged with any change. Further, the personalized idea about what the leaders need to say and do is the same. Interventions to facilitate change need to be aligned with the concerns of those who are engaged with the change. For example, when teachers are in the first year of implementing an innovation such as standards-based education, and they have many task concerns, the most valued and effective facilitator is a teacher or consultant who is highly experienced with the details and mechanics of using the innovation and can offer specific "how-to" tips. Teachers with intense task concerns don't want to hear about the philosophy; they want help in making the innovation work more smoothly. The more abstract and subtle aspects of innovation use are of greater interest to teachers with impact concerns.

Identifying the Stages of Concern

Through our research, we have identified and confirmed a set of seven specific categories of concerns about the innovation that we call *Stages of Concern,* or *SoC* (pronounced "ess-oh-see;" not "sock"!), as presented as in Figure 7.1. We also developed a more comprehensive definition of the term *concern:*

> The composite representation of the feelings, preoccupation, thought, and consideration given to a particular issue or task is called *concern.* Depending on our personal make-up, knowledge, and experiences, each person perceives and mentally contends with a given issue differently; thus there are different kinds of concerns. The issue may be interpreted as an outside threat to one's well being, or it may be seen as rewarding. There may be an overwhelming feeling of confusion and lack of information about what "it" is. There may be ruminations about the effects. The demand to consider the issue may be self-imposed in the form of a goal or objective that we wish to reach, or the pressure that results in increased attention to the issue may be external. In response to the demand, our minds explore ways, means, potential barriers, possible actions, risks, and rewards in relation to the demand. All in all, the mental activity composed of questioning, analyzing, and re-analyzing, considering alternative actions and reactions, and anticipating consequences is *concern.*

FIGURE 7.1 Stages of Concern: Typical Expressions of Concern about the Innovation

		Stages of Concern	Expressions of Concern
	6	**Refocusing**	I have some ideas about something that would work even better.
IMPACT	5	**Collaboration**	I am concerned about relating what I am doing with what my co-workers are doing.
	4	**Consequence**	How is my use affecting clients?
TASK	3	**Management**	I seem to be spending all of my time getting materials ready.
SELF	2	**Personal**	How will using it affect me?
	1	**Informational**	I would like to know more about it.
UNRELATED	0	**Awareness**	I am not concerned about it.

To be concerned means to be in a mentally aroused state about something. The intensity of the arousal will depend on the person's past experiences and associations with the subject of the arousal, as well as [on] how close to the person and how immediate the issue is perceived as being. Close personal involvement is likely to mean more intense (i.e., more highly aroused) concern which will be reflected in greatly increased mental activity, thought, worry, analysis, and anticipation. Through all of this, it is the person's perceptions that stimulate concerns, not necessarily the reality of the situation. (Hall, George, & Rutherford, 1979, p. 5)

With further study and application in schools, colleges, and, to a lesser extent, business, we and our colleagues developed paragraph definitions for each of the Stages of Concern, which are presented in Figure 7.2. Note that the original ideas of unrelated, self, task, and impact have been preserved, but, based on the research findings, the self and impact areas have been clarified by distinguishing stages within each. Self concerns are now divided into two stages—informational and personal—and impact concerns into three—consequence, collaboration, and refocusing.

If you think about it, these stages make intuitive sense, and you certainly hear people express these kinds of concerns. For example, at the beginning of the change process teachers (and others) say:

Well, at this point I don't know much about it, other than we have been told that we will be adopting it (Stage 1 Informational). I don't know what the principal thinks about our doing this (Stage 2 Personal), or if he even knows about it (Stage 1 Informational). I just hope that I don't have to stop doing what I have been doing and start all over again (Stage 2 Personal). I hope that we learn more at the next faculty meeting (Stage 1 Informational).

FIGURE 7.2   Stages of Concern about the Innovation: Paragraph Definitions

Impact	**6 Refocusing:** The focus is on the exploration of more universal benefits from the innovation, including the possibility of major changes or replacement with a more powerful alternative. Individual has definite ideas about alternatives to the proposed or existing form of the innovation.
	5 Collaboration: The focus is on coordination and cooperation with others regarding use of the innovation.
	4 Consequence: Attention focuses on impact of the innovation on clients in his or her immediate sphere of influence. The focus is on relevance of the innovation for clients, evaluation of outcome including performance and competencies, and changes needed to increase client outcomes.
Task	**3 Management:** Attention is focused on the processes and tasks of using the innovation and the best use of information and resources. Issues related to efficiency, organizing, managing, scheduling, and time demands are utmost.
Self	**2 Personal:** Individual is uncertain about the demands of the innovation, his/her inadequacy to meet those demands, and his/her role with the innovation. This includes analysis of his/her role in relation to the reward structure of the organization, decision-making, and consideration of potential conflicts with existing structures or personal commitment. Financial or status implications of the program for self and colleagues may also be reflected.
	1 Informational: A general awareness of the innovation and interest in learning more detail about it is indicated. The person seems to be unworried about himself/herself in relation to the innovation. She/he is interested in substantive aspects of the innovation in a selfless manner, such as general characteristics, effects, and requirements for use.
Unrelated	**0 Awareness:** Little concern about or involvement with the innovation is indicated.

Source: From *Measuring Stages of Concern about the Innovation: A Manual for Use of the SoC Questionnaire* (Report No. 3032) by G. E. Hall, A. A. George, and W. L. Rutherford, 1979, Austin: The University of Texas at Austin, Research and Development Center for Teacher Education (ERIC Document Reproduction Service No. ED. 147 342).

All of these concerns are in the *self* area, but they represent two component parts. The person knows a little, but would like to know more (Stage 1 Informational), and is also concerned about where he or she stands in terms of the principal's knowledge and position and what he or she will have to give up when the innovation arrives (Stage 2 Personal).

Impact concerns are even more complex. Stage 4 Consequence deals with increasing effectiveness and impact in one's own use of the innovation; Stage 5 Collaboration focuses on concern about working with one or more colleagues; and Stage 6 (Refocusing) indicates that the person has ideas about a more effective alternative. Remember, however, that the overarching theme of Stages 4, 5, and 6 is always concern about improving the *impact* of the innovation on clients/students.

IMPLICATIONS FOR LEADERS FACILITATING CHANGE

1. Assume that all change processes will begin with most everyone having more intense Self (Stage 1 Informational and Stage 2 Personal) concerns. From the very beginning, interventions should address these concerns.
2. Early and frequent offering of information is the key to reducing the potential for aroused Stage 2 Personal concerns. Once aroused, Personal concerns must be addressed in ways that facilitate their resolution; this often means dealing with issues that are not directly related to the innovation.
3. The first cycle (year(s)) of implementation is when Task (Stage 3 Management) concerns will be intense. Strategies, such as providing an on-site implementation facilitator, technical manuals, and websites with how-to-do-it tips, should be established that directly anticipate and address Task concerns.
4. An important condition for the arousal of Impact (especially Stage 4 Consequence, Stage 5 Collaboration) is first facilitating the resolution of Self and Task concerns.
5. Concerns-based interventions can be targeted toward all implementers, especially during the early phases of the change process. As implementation progresses, key organization units, such as individual schools and departments, will increasingly need to be the targeted units for interventions. Each unit is likely to change at its own pace and interventions will need to be customized to address each unit's unique concerns profile.
6. The SoC Questionnaire can be overused, which results in resistance to filling it out "again." Being skilled at using the one-legged interview and interpreting open-ended concerns statements are much more useful for those engaged in the daily activity of facilitating change processes.

WHY ARE THEY CALLED "STAGES" OF CONCERN?

The research studies clearly document that there is a quasi-developmental path to the concerns as a change process unfolds. However, the flow of concerns is not always guaranteed, nor does it always move in one direction. *If* the innovation is appropriate, if the leaders are initiating, and if the change process is carefully facilitated, then implementers will move from early self concerns to task concerns (during the first years of use), and ultimately to impact concerns (after three to five years).

Unfortunately, all of these "ifs" are not always present. More often than not, the support needed for the change process over time is not forthcoming, or the leaders fail to facilitate effectively, or, in the case of schools, the district, state, and federal governments annually add more innovations to the point that none is being fully implemented. In these situations, concerns do not progress from self to task to impact. Instead, progress is arrested, with Stage 3 Management concerns continuing to be intense. If these conditions do not change, in time many teachers return to self concerns.

In the first conception of the Concerns Based Adoption Model, the term *Stages of Concern* was deliberately chosen to reflect the idealized, developmental approach to change that we value (see Hall, Wallace, & Dossett, 1973). Unfortunately, in most instances, as we pointed out in Chapter 1, change is not viewed and treated as a process but as an event. When this event-mentality is applied, the stages model breaks down, and people are forced into sustained self and/or task concerns.

CAN THERE BE CONCERNS AT MORE THAN ONE STAGE?

When presenting the Stages of Concern, we are frequently asked if it is possible to have concerns at more than one stage at the same time. Of course it is possible. In fact, most of the time a person will have intense concerns at more than one stage. For example, although a teacher may have intense task (Stage 3 Management) concerns, concerns about students are still influencing his or her instructional decision making. In general teachers will have a conglomeration of concerns representing several of the stages, with some more strongly felt than others, and some absent all together.

Graphically, we represent this conglomeration or array of concerns of varying intensities by using a *concerns profile*. By representing the Stages of Concern on the horizontal axis and the relative intensity of concerns on the vertical, a general picture of a person's concerns can be displayed. The peaks indicate stages that are more intense, and the valleys show those that are less intense.

Different, commonly observed scenarios can be envisaged using concerns profiles. For example, we have already described the first-year user of an innovation with intense Stage 3 Management concerns. That person's concerns profile would have a peak on Stage 3, whereas the other stages would be lower. If the person were also a first- or second-year teacher, he or she might have more intense Stage 2 Personal concerns about surviving the evaluation process and receiving tenure. In this case the concerns profile would likely have two peaks, one for Stage 3 Management concerns and a second peak for Stage 2 Personal.

Another teacher might be very experienced and truly a master teacher. His or her concerns profile could be most intense on Stage 3 Management concerns too, relative to first-year use of the innovation. But her or his second-highest stage could be Stage 4 Consequence, indicating more concern about how use of the innovation is affecting his or her students.

Many combinations of concerns can be imagined and have been observed. In each case, once the profile of concerns has been identified, the important work can begin. As interesting as it is to see and attempt to analyze a concerns profile, the crucial step is in using it to make *concerns-based interventions* that will be able to resolve the concern and move the person toward more advanced use of the innovation.

ARE THERE TYPICAL CONCERN PROFILES?

Stages of Concern profiles are a very informative way to illustrate movement and nonmovement during a change process. When concerns profiles are collected at different points in time, each is a snapshot of that moment. The time series of profiles becomes a motion picture of how concerns evolved and hopefully developed.

As the name *stages* implies, and as the numbering of the stages suggests, there is a hypothesized pattern in the concerns profiles when the change process unfolds successfully. This progression takes the form of a "wave motion" of intensity that begins with self concerns being more intense prior to first use of the innovation. Then, as implementation begins, task concerns become more intense, and there is a gradual reduction in self concerns. With time (three to five years), impact concerns can increase in intensity as the self and task concerns decrease. A graphic representation of this wave motion pattern is presented in Figure 7.3.

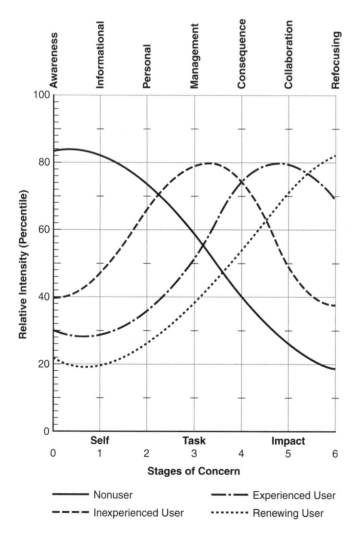

FIGURE 7.3   **Ideal Wave Motion Development of Stages of Concern**

As we have pointed out, this idealized evolution does not always occur. Attempting to change humans in an organizational context is a very complex, dynamic, and, in many ways, subtle enterprise. However, by looking for the patterns, being knowledgeable about what has been learned about change, and being grounded in the uniqueness and intricacies of the situation, it is indeed possible to plan and facilitate a change process that will unfold in the manner shown in Figure 7.3. But since there is a high likelihood that there will be convoluted turns and unexpected happenings along the way, change facilitators must continuously engage in monitoring and adjusting.

TECHNIQUES FOR ASSESSING
STAGES OF CONCERN

The monitoring of the change process should include regular and ongoing assessment of the Stages of Concern of all participants, including the change facilitators. There are three ways to assess concerns:

1. One-legged interview
2. Open-ended concerns statement
3. Stages of Concern Questionnaire

Each of these techniques has its strengths and appropriate uses, as well as its inherent weaknesses.

USING STAGES OF CONCERN CONSTRUCTS AND TOOLS TO ASSESS AND STUDY IMPLEMENTATION

Assessing Stages of Concern has become an established way to monitor how well a change process is going. One of the advantages of assessing SoC is that both the researcher and change facilitators can understand and use the information. This is a decided advantage for the evaluator/researcher. Instead of having to explain and interpret the findings, change facilitators can understand and use the SoC findings in their daily efforts. They press the evaluator/researcher for the data.

For research and evaluation studies, the SoC Questionnaire is the best measure. It has sound psychometrics and does not take long to complete. It often is helpful to add an open-ended concerns statement following the 35 items. The narratives provide context that can help in understanding why certain stages are more, and less, intense. Be sure to obtain and use the technical manual (Hall, George, & Rutherford, 1979). *Do not change the wording of the 35 SoCQ items.* Changes in wording will upset reliability and validity. Also, for the teacher version of the SoCQ, the scores for Stage 0 Awareness generally run very high. Therefore, do not identify Stage 0 as the most intense; instead, set aside interpretation of Stage 0, especially for group data.

Many studies have been done where concerns have been assessed before and after a particular intervention, such as a workshop or a year-long implementation effort. No matter what the quality of the change facilitation, there will likely be changes in SoC. What is missing from most of these studies, and much needed, is analysis of why particular interventions contribute to the arousal and resolution of particular concerns. Most studies have addressed early concerns: Self and Task. Few have addressed the arousal of Impact concerns. This topic, developing understanding of the dynamics of concerns arousal and resolution, is a priority focus for our research and theory building.

The SoCQ can provide informative longitudinal data. Systematically collecting SoCQ data two or three times each year provides a time series set of snapshots. Each new SoC profile can be compared with the previous one(s) and with the general "wave motion" (Figure 7.3). These pictures provide one clear way of documenting how well the change process is going.

Don't forget that analysis of subgroup and individual SoC profiles can be very informative. All too often researchers and evaluators address only the high and low stages, and profile, for the whole group. Stopping at this point results in much rich information being missed. There is a tendency to perceive that with a large group it would take too much time and be too difficult to examine subgroupings. In fact, this is not the case. At a minimum, respondents can be organized into subgroups such as individual schools or departments and their high/low stages compared.

Individual SoC profiles can be analyzed, even for a very large group. For example, in one study one of the authors examined 800 individual SoC profiles related to teacher use of a laptop computer. The individual profiles fell into seven subgroups with less than a dozen left over. In the implementation assessment report the whole group and each of the seven subgroups were described, along with recommendations for the next steps in facilitating the whole group and each subgroup. Of course, this researcher is expert in interpreting SoC profiles.

The One-Legged Interview

Many of the CBAM research studies have carefully documented the numerous interventions that school principals, school improvement teams, lead teachers, staff developers, and others have used to facilitate an innovation (Hall, Hord, & Griffin, 1980; Vandenberghe, 1988; Entrekin, 1991; Schiller, 1991; Stassens, 1993; Shieh, 1996). One of the major findings has been that schools that are more successful in change have statistically significantly more of the very small, almost unnoticed interventions that we call *incidents*. Most of these take the form of a brief conversation between a change facilitator and an implementer about use of the innovation, which we call *one-legged interviews (OLIs)*.

In the busy work of schools, there is little time for extended conversation; everything happens on the run. The clock is ticking, the bells are ringing, and the students are moving. When the adults do meet, their available time is short. Maybe there are a couple of minutes for a quick chat as they pass in the hall, go to the office to pick up their mail, or gather in the lounge during the lunch period.

CBAM research shows that these brief moments are *critical opportunities,* whose frequency will determine the final degree of implementation success. Because the time available is so brief, you must make it count.

One interesting insight into the concept of the one-legged interview came when a principal suggested that we should call them "flamingo interviews." This seemed like a good idea until, when telling a Floridian about the suggestion, she pointed out that, yes, a flamingo does stand on one leg, but it also puts it head under its wing! This would not be a very effective way to assess concerns.

The important beginning of a one-legged interview is to encourage the client (e.g., a teacher) to describe what he or she is doing and how the client feels about what he or she is doing, or thinking of doing, with the innovation. The facilitator should not assume that he or she understands the situation, but instead should ask and listen. The trained facilitator can quickly hear and, if necessary, probe lightly to clarify the concerns

Following this quick diagnosis, the second part of the OLI is for the facilitator to do something to address in some way the indicated concerns. This is an important time to keep the "wave motion" in mind. The focus of the intervention needs to be on helping to resolve current concerns as well as anticipating the potential arousal of others.

There are advantages and disadvantages to using the one-legged interview to assess concerns. Advantages include that it can take place whenever you are in conversation, whether it is face to face or by telephone. Also, it is unobtrusive, with none of the obvious probing involved in paper-and-pencil methods. Another strength is that the facilitator shows interest in what the teacher is doing, which in and of itself is supportive. This is a very useful technique for sales representatives as they assess customer needs.

The major disadvantage is accuracy. Different facilitators can hear the same words and offer very different interpretations. So be very careful about leaping to conclusions based on a diagnosis derived from a one-legged interview. Things must be checked out and, as with all concerns-based diagnoses, treated as tentative until more is known.

The Open-Ended Statement

The first systematic measure of concerns that Fuller used was to ask teacher education students to write a description of their concerns, which was then content analyzed. This open-ended statement has continued to be helpful. Collecting the information is straightforward. Respondents are given a blank piece of paper that has the following written at the top:

> *When you think about [the innovation] what concerns do you have? Please be frank, and answer in complete sentences.*

These papers are then collected and content analyzed as described in a manual by Newlove and Hall (1976). The first step is to read the statement to determine if the overall theme is unrelated, self, task, or impact concerns. The statement is then reread, and a Stage of Concern is assigned to each sentence in order to make a holistic assessment. Note that the individual sentence scores are not totaled and averaged. There is no such thing as a "3.5 concern" or a "5.7 average concern." Instead, the entire statement is judged.

This technique has a number of strengths. An obvious one is that the concerns are in the respondents' own words. Also, this technique can be used at any time. For example, if a staff meeting or workshop is coming up, ask the participants to submit an open-ended concerns statement two weeks in advance. This information can then be used to plan the meeting or workshop so that it responds to the expressed concerns. Participants can thus have input in a nonthreatening way.

As with the one-legged interview, there are disadvantages with the open-ended format. One is that different respondents will provide different amounts of information. One person may write three paragraphs, while another may write only one sentence. Some people will only provide a list of topics instead of complete sentences, which means that there is no concerns statement to be scored. And some people will turn in a blank page, which is very hard to interpret. The other major problem with open-ended concerns statements is reliability. Even thoroughly trained judges have difficulty in agreeing on how to rate them. But for most staff-development and meeting situations, where an estimate of concerns is useful, the open-ended statement is an excellent tool.

The Stages of Concern Questionnaire

The most rigorous technique for measuring concerns is the Stages of Concern Questionnaire (SoCQ), which is a 35-item questionnaire that has strong reliability estimates (test/retest reliablities range from .65 to .86) and internal consistency (alpha-coefficients range from .64 to .83). The SoCQ was constructed to apply to all educational innovations. The questionnaire items stay the same, with the only change being the insertion of the name of the specific innovation on the cover page.

It is possible to use the SoCQ to construct concerns profiles. Because the questionnaire has been designed so that there is a raw score for each stage, a graphic representation of the data can be made using a percentile table for conversions. Study and practice, as well as training, will develop one's skill in interpreting these profiles.

Copies of the SoC Questionnaire and the SoC Quick Scoring Device are included as Appendixes to this book. A technical manual (Hall et al., 1979), which includes additional scoring and interpretation information, as well as guidelines for appropriate applications, should also be studied closely by those who wish to use the SoCQ. No one should consider using the SoCQ without study and direct access to this important reference. There is also a specially designed questionnaire for assessing the concerns of change facilitators and a technical manual for its use (Hall et al.,

1991). Although the original SoCQ was developed several decades ago, it continues to be seen as a reliable and valid measure.

The advantages of the SoCQ technique for assessing concerns include strong reliability and validity, and the capability of using it to develop concerns profiles. The SoCQ is particularly useful for formal implementation assessment efforts. One disadvantage is that respondents often do not want to fill out this questionnaire, or any other. This most formal way of assessing Stages of Concern should thus be used sparingly. Normally in our school studies we will use the SoCQ twice a year (e.g., early October and late April). Sometimes we have gone to a third assessment in January. We always include space for an open-ended statement on the last page to give the respondents another opportunity to point out something they may think is being missed.

Characteristic Stages of Concern Profiles

Many of the commonly observed SoC profiles are easy to interpret by studying the technical manuals and developing an understanding of concerns theory. Some profiles are in fact "classic"; we have seen them many times, and their meaning is well understood. A couple of these are presented here to illustrate our thinking about diagnosis and implications for concerns-based intervening.

Remember that one of the keys to interpreting concerns profiles is to look for the peaks and valleys. It does not matter if the overall profile is at the eightieth percentile or the twentieth; it is the overall shape that must be considered first. It is the high and low points on that profile that serve as the beginning frame of reference.

The second step is to study closely the full definitions of each stage presented in Figure 7.2. A peak on a profile indicates that the type of concerns that are described for that stage are intense, whereas a valley shows that there is little or no concern for that stage. When there is a peak at more than one stage, the profile must be interpreted by combining the definitions for those stages. In most cases this level of interpretation will serve well.

However, to illustrate that there is always more to be learned about concerns theory and assessment, a couple of the more interesting variations in concerns profiles are described next. For each profile we offer a brief interpretation and ideas about the types of interventions that would make sense.

One, the "Big W" Concerns Profile (so named for its configuration of peaks and valleys), has been observed all too frequently (see Figure 7.4). In this profile Stage 3 Management concerns are very intense, while Stages 1 Informational, 2 Personal, 4 Consequence, and 5 Collaboration are of much lower intensity. This profile would not be so significant if it were not for the "tailing up" on Stage 6 Refocusing. This combination of peaks and valleys indicates that there are strongly held ideas about what ought to be done differently with this innovation (Stage 6) that are related to the very high (and unresolved) management concerns. Teachers with this profile can be quite adamant about their situation and how things should be changed.

More than a one-legged interview will be needed to address the underlying cause of such high management concerns. We know from a number of studies that this

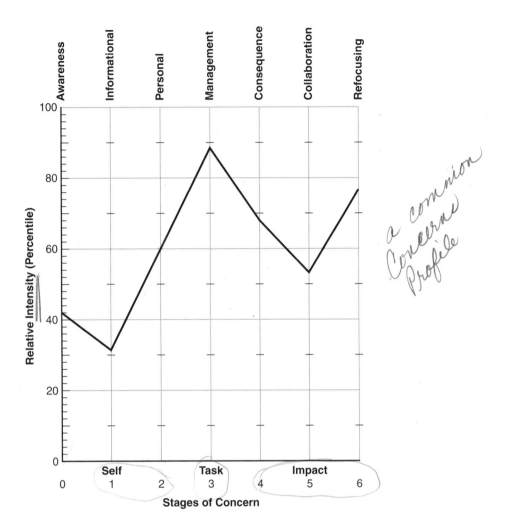

a common Concerns Profile

. **FIGURE 7.4   The "Big W" Concerns Profile**

concerns profile is frequently found in schools where the principal has displayed the responder change facilitator style (see Chapter 10). Part of the strategic action may thus be to strengthen the principal's support of the teachers' use of the innovation.

High Stage 4 Consequence and Stage 5 Collaboration in a concerns profile (see Figure 7.5) represent the ideal goal of a concerns-based implementation effort. After all, the essence of good schooling is teachers with high impact concerns about the effects of the use of the innovation in their classroom (Stage 4 Consequence) and about linking with other teachers in using the innovation (Stage 5 Collaboration). The research of Judith Warren Little (Little & McLaughlin, 1993) on teacher collegiality confirms the importance of this dynamic for teachers and their students. Unfortu-

an "ideal" profile

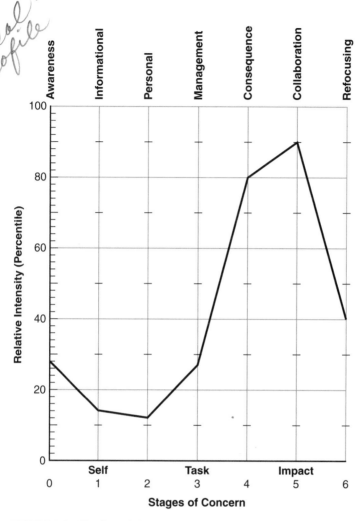

FIGURE 7.5   The Goal of Concerns-Based Implementation Expressed in an Impact Concerns Profile

nately, finding individual teachers and school staffs that reflect this concerns profile is very rare. To develop to this point means that change truly has been treated as a process, that the innovation has been given sufficient time to be implemented, that there has been a principal with an Initiator Change Facilitator Style, and that the innovation, or more likely an innovation bundle, was significant and matched the school's vision well.

Intervening on this profile should include a celebration. Clearly the teachers and the principal have been hard at work and doing some special things. They should be congratulated, supported, and cherished. Also, this is a fragile system state. A change in a key player (e.g., the superintendent or the principal) or the arrival of some new mandate from the school board, state, or federal government can sidetrack and undercut the energy and momentum that have been built. Therefore, a second set of interventions would be to protect and encourage the continuation of the impact concerns, with a special emphasis on facilitating the development of collaborative work for impact concern reasons.

When a large number of SoC profiles are available they can be sorted into subgroups according to common characteristics. For example, Matthews, Marshall, and Milne (2000) had in excess of 700 SoC profiles from teachers engaged in their first year of use of laptop computers. Nearly all of the SoC profiles could be placed in one of six subgroupings.

IMPLICATIONS OF RESISTANCE IN STAGES OF CONCERN PROFILES

We haven't yet talked about resistance, which is a natural part of change. In the CBAM work, most of what is called *resistance* will show up in the Stages of Concern diagnostic dimension, especially self concerns. Here again, we advocate listening before intervening. Often, what change facilitators see as resistance are aspects of Stage 2 Personal concerns. There is an uncertainty about what will be expected and self-doubts about one's ability to succeed with the new way. There may also be some grieving over the loss of things that were currently being done successfully. Another aspect of this, which is all too frequently overlooked, is the failure to have addressed, early on, Stage 1 Informational concerns. When people don't know what is happening, it is perfectly normal for Stage 2 Personal concerns to become more intense. The less information that is provided, the higher the Stage 2 Personal concerns will be.

At the beginning of a change process, when self concerns are more intense, be sure to use many channels to communicate what is coming. Communication needs to start during the spring, before implementation is to begin. Also, don't simply make a one-time announcement and expect everyone to get the message. People with Stage 1 Informational concerns need to receive small bits of information, repeated across time. They do not want all of the details at once. And don't forget their Stage 2 Personal concerns; they want to hear enthusiasm and promises of continuing commitment to and support for the change.

Of course, there can be real resisters. The reasons for their position are varied. Some may simply not understand the proposed innovation. Others may have a different agenda or a real philosophical disagreement with the innovation. Sadly, there may be one or two who have serious problems elsewhere in their lives, which none of us are equipped to handle. In a concerns profile, especially high personal concerns (Stage 2) in what would otherwise be a nonuser profile (remember Figure 7.4), and a slight "tailing up" of Stage 6, are the indications of what typically is called a "hostile" nonuser.

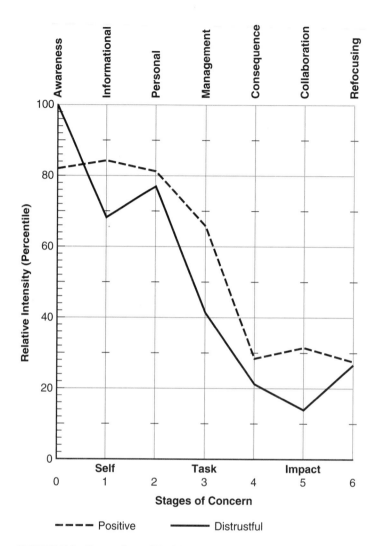

FIGURE 7.6   Comparison of Positive and Distrustful Nonuser SoC Profiles

Let's look more closely at these dynamics. Figure 7.6 presents both the typical positive nonuser profile and the typical hostile nonuser profile. Consider some of the standard comments of the hostile nonuser:

"Where is the research to show that this is better?"

"We've always done it this way. All you have done is put a new name on it."

"Ah. This is just old wine in new bottles. You know how education is. It's just a pendulum swinging back and forth from fad to fad."

The tendency of change facilitators is to react to such attitudes by saying something like, "Oh, no. This really *is* different." However, from a concerns profile perspective, this is the wrong intervention. What the facilitator is hearing is the "tailing up" on Stage 6 Refocusing—that is, strongly held ideas about how things ought to be different. But which concerns are the highest? Stage 2 Personal, and right behind these are Stage 1 Informational. This indicates that the so-called resister actually does not have enough information about the innovation and thus is personally uncomfortable about it. So telling this person that this innovation really is different is *interpreted* (see Chapter 11) as follows: "You are telling me that I don't know what I am talking about and that further threatens me." The result is less ability to listen, still higher personal concerns, and probably stronger "tailing up" on Stage 6 Refocusing.

A better intervention approach (although there is no quick cure once this profile is established) would be to express empathy and understanding for the person's concerns. Don't attempt to explain a lot in the first contact. Try to have a series of one-legged conferences to get a sense of what is producing this concerns profile, and then gradually provide pieces of information about the change, the change process, and how they will be supported. There is no simple remedy for this, or for many other concerns profiles. However, what needs to be done to facilitate change in most cases is relatively straightforward: provide information, resources, and support that are aligned with the person's concerns. Read the vignette presented here to see how Stages of Concern can be used in a districtwide change process.

■ ■ ■ ■ ■ ▬▬

V I G N E T T E
A DISTRICTWIDE USE OF STAGES OF CONCERN

In one large suburban school district, the science department coordinators and staff developers engaged in a collaborative project with CBAM researchers to do a concerns-based implementation of their revised science curriculum. Ultimately, this project was very successful in terms of teacher success in implementing the curriculum and was recognized with a special award from the American Educational Research Association based on the practitioner-researcher partnership.

THE IMPLEMENTATION GAME PLAN

From the beginning, an accepted assumption was that change is a process, not an event. Further, the Stages of Concern were used as the guiding dimension when planning training workshops, newsletter content, and other interventions. The SoCQ was administered twice a year (in early October and late April) for three years, and science facilitators were trained in doing one-legged interviews.

Due to the large size of the district (80 elementary schools plus many secondary schools), it did not seem reasonable to expect that all schools could be supported in implementation at the same time. So the district was divided into thirds, and there was a phased

(continued)

■ ■ ■ ■ ■

implementation for one-third of the schools at a time, beginning at six-month intervals. (There were many year-round schools in this district, so the traditional nine-month school year did not apply throughout.)

ADDRESSING TASK CONCERNS

The school board had budgeted for three all-day in-service sessions. Rather than holding all of these at the beginning, they were distributed over the first year and a half of use of the curriculum. This made great sense from a concerns-based perspective, since Stage 3 Management concerns last for at least a year. Also, task concerns are most clear and intense when teachers are engaged in teaching specific lessons. By stretching the time between the in-service days, it was possible to offer each near the time when teachers would have questions about specific lessons they were about to teach.

A cadre of lead teachers was identified and trained to design and conduct the in-service workshops. These teachers had field-tested the materials and were experienced science teachers. They were trained in the Stages of Concern, in how to interpret SoCQ and open-ended data, and in doing one-legged interviews.

The lead teachers established an overall design for workshop days as well as a special version for each grade level. Then teachers from across the district were brought together by grade for the workshops. A newsletter was used to guide teachers in pacing themselves from lesson to lesson and to alert them about upcoming logistical steps. A special class of interventions was the "comfort and caring" sessions, which were hosted by an experienced science teacher after school. Here again, face-to-face opportunities were provided to address the "how-to" questions (Stage 3 Management) as they arose.

SELF CONCERNS AND THE PRINCIPAL

The important role of the school principal was anticipated as well. All too frequently the principal is bypassed, and only teachers are trained. Most principals, however, like to know what the teachers are being asked to do. In addition, the change-facilitator role that the principal assumes makes a major difference in how successful teachers will be with implementation (see Chapter 10). Remember, one of the early concerns is Stage 2 Personal, when a common question has to do with principal support. Having principals know what is expected and anticipated can help them be more supportive.

Thus, early in the district project it was decided that principals should be given information first, before their teachers, although they did not receive as much information nor the same information. A half-day session was held with the principals, who were shown the materials, the teacher's guide, and sample lessons. All of this addressed their self concerns. They were also told about some of the questions and problems that their teachers would likely have. They were introduced to the lead teachers and to the special telephone hot line and the other implementation support resources that were designed to help them and their teachers implement the revised science curriculum.

EARLY SELF CONCERNS OF TEACHERS

According to concerns theory, teachers are likely to have some kinds of self concerns in the school year prior to implementation of the innovation. (Remember the "wave motion"

■ ■ ■ ■ ■

VIGNETTE CONTINUED

shown in Figure 7.3?) To address these early nonuser Stage 1 Informational and Stage 2 Personal concerns, a one-and-a-half hour afterschool meeting was held in the spring before implementation was to begin. As the staffs from two neighboring schools met at one of the schools, one of the science department coordinators and a lead teacher hosted an introductory session about the new curriculum, what would be expected, the timeline, and the availability of supplies.

These briefing sessions were conducted in an upbeat tone. The expectation was made clear: "Use of this curriculum is board policy." The timeline for in-service sessions and the resources that would be available to help teachers were described briefly. Remember, at this point teachers do not want all of the details. They instead need positive reinforcement and a general picture of what will be happening. At this time, Stage 1 Informational concerns are being addressed and Stage 2 Personal concerns are being anticipated. If the dispersing of information is paced well, and if the support is in place, the intensity of Stage 2 Personal concerns should not increase disproportionately.

At the end of the introductory sessions, teachers were offered the opportunity to take the teacher's guide with them: "I know that some of you will want to do some preplanning this summer. In case you do, here is a copy of the teacher's guide. You don't have to look at it before the first workshop, but it is here if you would like it."

IMPACT CONCERNS?

It was expected that more intense impact concerns would be felt by some teachers, such as those who had field-tested the innovation and those who were experienced science teachers. Although they still had to learn about the curriculum, they were ready to consider some of the more advanced and subtle aspects of innovation use. Interventions for them had to be different in some ways.

To address the varying levels of teachers' concerns, the workshops were designed with alternate routes for parts of the day. One route, which allowed teachers to stay in a small-group setting and to work with an experienced teacher on specifics of lesson preparation, materials, and activities, was chosen by teachers with more self and task concerns. The second route, which gave teachers the choice to work independently or in pairs through a series of self-paced modules, films, and exercises, was selected by teachers with higher impact concerns.

Another strategy that focused on impact concerns was to wait three years before training all teachers in some of the more subtle aspects of the innovation. It was decided at the outset that the first goal was to have all teachers teaching science, instead of having just some teaching science very well. Given the limits on resources and the large size of the district, it would not have been possible to achieve both outcomes at once. It was also not possible from a concerns perspective. As a result, a new round of workshops was started in the third year to prepare all teachers to use cooperative groups in science teaching. Although this had been planned from the beginning, it was not emphasized until after the task concerns about materials, lessons, and scheduling had been resolved.

In summary, the first three years of the implementation were designed to have all teachers teaching science by addressing their self and task concerns. During the next three years, other innovations (e.g., cooperative learning), in what was now an innovation bundle, were introduced and supported. With this phasing approach an entire district came to have quality science teaching in most of its elementary classrooms.

(continued)

■ ■ ■ ■ ■

VIGNETTE CRITIQUE QUESTIONS

1. What characteristics of the interventions used in this district made them especially relevant to each identified Stage of Concern?
2. What would need to happen in a school that continued to have task concerns?
3. Typically, it takes three years for a school staff to resolve their task concerns. What could be done in the third year of implementation to facilitate the arousal of impact concerns?

SUMMARY

In this chapter we have introduced and briefly illustrated the Stages of Concern diagnostic dimension. It is clear that Stages of Concern can be experienced, observed, and documented in most change processes. We also know that it is a cross-cultural phenomenon. For example, Shieh (1996) observed the same categories of concerns in teachers in Taiwan that we have seen in the United States, and earlier Van den Berg and Vandenberghe (1981) documented SoC in Belgium and the Netherlands. The various technical manuals and research reports should be studied before launching a major Stages of Concern initiative. Talking with experts and participating in training sessions are important steps too. At all times keep the guiding principles in mind as a guide to thinking about using SoC as a diagnostic approach to making facilitating interventions.

DISCUSSION QUESTIONS

1. Think about someone you have talked with recently about implementing an innovation. What were his or her concerns? What did you say or do in response?

2. What was something that someone did for you when your concerns were really high? At what stage were they?

3. What could be done to help teachers with intense Stage 4 Consequence concerns? What would not be appropriate?

4. What happens to your concerns when your supervisor has high Stage 2 Personal concerns? How do your interactions change?

5. Think about one of the great teachers you have had. Generally, what were his or her most intense Stages of Concern?

6. In your experience, which workshops have you considered to be the best and the worst? How did each match with your concerns at the time?

FIELDWORK ACTIVITIES

1. Attend a workshop and observe the concerns of the participants. How well did the content and process of the workshop match those concerns?

2. Collect and analyze open-ended concerns data from people who are attending a staff meeting or workshop. Analyze the statements. (Obtain a copy of Newlove and Hall's [1976] manual to help with this.) Develop a recommendation about what should be done and how to address the participants' concerns.

3. Conduct a one-legged interview with a person, and then ask someone else who understands Stages of Concern to do the same, with the same individual. See how well you both assess the person's concerns.

4. Collect Stages of Concern Questionnaire data about a particular innovation for a school or other population. Do this before and after a workshop, or at two points during the semester. Analyze the interventions that were done, and how they relate to changes and nonchanges in the concerns profiles. Be sure to refer to the technical manual for the SoCQ (Hall et al., 1979).

CHAPTER 8

EXPLORING THE USE OF INNOVATIONS

Levels of Use

I am happy to report that I have worked the bugs out of how to use math manipulatives with third-graders, and I have a system that works!

Can you help me order the equipment for the sophomore's earth science units? I'm getting things ready to start in September.

My marketing director told me to find out how our sales staff is working with the new product; we may need to give them more training if they are not pitching the new product in a well-organized and consistent way.

I telephoned a colleague at another school to inquire about the problem-based social studies program his school is using and whether it stimulates the kids in critical thinking.

Another teacher and I have worked together with this approach. The changes that we have made this year are really helping students to succeed.

Through our research studies we have learned that use of a new program is not automatic, nor is it a matter of some persons using it and others not. Using new programs or processes is not a simple case of, "Yes, he's using it," or "No, she is not." In any given change effort, implementers will be operating in very different ways with new practices, thus, the real question is, "How is she or he using it?"

Before we began to address this question, use of new curriculum, instructional methods, or organizational structures was assessed in terms of whether the materials and/or equipment required were present in the classroom. Little attention was given to whether the materials ever left the storage closet.

The implicit assumption was that initial training plus materials equaled use. Instead, our observations and studies document a number of different behavioral patterns for nonusers and users. To understand this phenomenon of the change process, the diagnostic dimension of Levels of Use (LoU) was born.

Stages of Concern. Levels of Use. The terms have a deceptively similar ring. However, we are about to make a significant conceptual switch, for whereas Stages of Concern (SoC) addresses the *affective* side of change—people's reactions, feelings, perceptions, and attitudes—Levels of Use has to do with *behaviors* and portrays *how* people are acting with respect to a specified change.

This chapter explores the behaviors of people as they seek to learn about new practices for their classrooms and schools or perhaps ignore such matters entirely. It also examines individuals' behaviors as they adopt and implement new ideas and innovations. Eight Levels of Use will be explained, and examples and applications will be given. Levels of Use is a second diagnostic dimension of the CBAM, and the behaviors of so-called users and nonusers are the basis for describing where people are in the change process and for diagnosing their progress in implementing a change project.

Further, the LoU framework makes it possible to understand and predict what is likely to occur with people in change. Facilitators who understand and apply the LoU concept and its measures are able to provide appropriate interventions that will be relevant and helpful to those involved, or expected to be involved, in change. LoU is a very important concept for evaluators, too. A critical step in determining whether a new approach is making a difference is to determine first if the innovation is being used. Otherwise, as Charters and Jones (1973) observed, there is a risk of evaluating "nonevents."

FOCUS QUESTIONS

1. What is the concept of Levels of Use?
2. What advantage does Levels of Use provide in evaluation of change efforts?
3. How can an individual's Levels of Use be assessed?
4. How can a person be further described by categories at each Level of Use?
5. What does a person look like at each Level of Use?
6. How can Levels of Use be applied to facilitating change efforts?

THE LEVELS OF USE CONCEPT

Eight classifications, or levels, of how people act or behave with a change have been identified and verified through our research. Since Levels of Use deals with behaviors, it was possible to develop operational definitions of each level (see

FIGURE 8.1   Levels of Use of the Innovation

Users	**VI**	**Renewal:** State in which the user re-evaluates the quality of use of the innovation, seeks major modifications of or alternatives to present innovation to achieve increased impact on clients, examines new developments in the field, and explores new goals for self and the system.
	V	**Integration:** State in which the user is combining own efforts to use the innovation with related activities of colleagues to achieve a collective impact on clients within their common sphere of influence.
	IVB	**Refinement:** State in which the user varies the use of the innovation to increase the impact on clients within immediate sphere of influence. Variations are based on knowledge of both short- and long-term consequences for clients.
	IVA	**Routine:** Use of the innovation is stabilized. Few if any changes are being made in ongoing use. Little preparation or thought is being given to improving innovation use or its consequences.
	III	**Mechanical Use:** State in which the user focuses most effort on the short-term, day-to-day use of the innovation with little time for reflection. Changes in use are made more to meet user needs than client needs. The user is primarily engaged in a stepwise attempt to master the tasks required to use the innovation, often resulting in disjointed and superficial use.
Nonusers	**II**	**Preparation:** State in which the user is preparing for first use of the innovation.
	I	**Orientation:** State in which the user has recently acquired or is acquiring information about the innovation and/or has recently explored or is exploring its value orientation and its demands upon user and user system.
	0	**Nonuse:** State in which the user has little or no knowledge of the innovation, no involvement with the innovation, and is doing nothing toward becoming involved.

Source: From *Measuring Levels of Use of the Innovation: A Manual for Trainers, Interviewers, and Raters* (pp. 171–195) by S. F. Loucks, B. W. Newlove, and G. E. Hall, 1975: Austin: The University of Texas at Austin, Research and Development Center for Teacher Education.

Figure 8.1). These definitions enable a change facilitator or evaluator to place an individual at one of the levels (Hall et al., 1975). However, the individual assessments can be aggregated for a school- or systemwide view of the extent of use of a particular change.

The first distinction to be made is whether the individual is a user or a nonuser. Three nonuse and five use levels have been identified. Each is described briefly in the following paragraphs, and suggestions about appropriate interventions are offered.

GUIDING PRINCIPLES OF LEVELS OF USE

1. With any innovation, each person exhibits some kind of behaviors and thus can be identified as being at a certain Level of Use.
2. The decision points that operationalize the levels and the information related to categories contribute to the overall description of an individual's Level of Use.
3. It is not appropriate to assume that a first-time user will be at Level III Mechanical Use. Nor should it be assumed that a person who has used the innovation several times will not be at LoU III.
4. An interview is the only means by which to successfully and efficiently collect LoU information. A written format cannot sufficiently account for an individual's varying responses at each LoU. The only alternative to the LoU interview would be extended ethnographic fieldwork using the LoU chart as the observation and interview guide, which is what was done in the original LoU interview validity study (Hall & Loucks, 1977).
5. Informally gathered information about an individual's LoU can be used for facilitating implementation of change; more rigorously collected LoU data can be used for conducting research studies of change and for evaluating the extent of implementation.
6. The Levels of Use are presented in a logical sequence, but this is not always followed by everyone. Typically, people move sequentially from LoU 0 to LoU IVA, and then may move up, down, or stay at LoU IVA.

Nonusers

Rather than classifying all nonusers in the same way, three very different types have been identified. It is important to understand the behavioral distinctions between them, since the support and assistance that is appropriate for each will vary accordingly. And although the behaviors of each are quite different, all three describe nonusers of the change from an evaluation perspective.

Level of Use 0 Nonuse.   When a person knows very little or nothing at all about an innovation or change, and exhibits no behavior related to it, that person is said to be at Level of Use 0 Nonuse. Further, the LoU 0 person will not display any knowledge of or interest in the innovation, and will take no action to learn about it. If such a person receives a brochure in the mail, it is not read. If there is an orientation presentation about the innovation, he or she does not attend, or, if required to attend, grades papers or engages in some other form of off-task activity. Again, there is no action related to the change.

If it is not important for such an individual to become involved with the particular change, a facilitator may ignore this person. However, if the person is expected to be involved, the facilitator's challenge is to design and deliver interventions that stimulate interest and support movement to learn about the change. Level of Use 0 Nonuse people are potentially an excellent source of data for the evaluator who is looking for a comparison or control group. However, much to the chagrin of change facilitators and evaluators, significant proportions of LoU 0 people are found in the *treatment* schools.

Level of Use I Orientation.   When a person takes action to learn about an innovation, or exhibits interest in knowing more about it, he or she is characterized as being at LoU I Orientation. Typical LoU I behaviors include attending an overview session about the innovation, examining print materials displayed by a vendor, asking questions of colleagues, or writing to a vendor for descriptive materials about various approaches that might work. The behaviors of the individual are related to learning more about the innovation, but no decision has been made to use it.

The facilitator will find it easy to respond to such a person, since he or she is actively looking for information. Thus, relevant interventions include providing information in the most provocative and interesting manner possible, so that adoption and use will be encouraged.

Level of Use II Preparation.   An individual who has decided to use the new program or process and names a time to begin is at LoU II Preparation. At this level, use has not started, but the intention and a specific start-up time have been indicated. The person typically is preparing materials and himself or herself for initial use.

It could be that the decision to begin use has been made for the individual—for instance, by a state or district policy that mandates action, or by the principal in concert with faculty peers who are pressing for use. In any case, while how the decision is made is of interest, it does not figure into Levels of Use, which focuses on behaviors. Obviously, the facilitator's role is to be as supportive as possible, providing assistance so that when use does begin, it can proceed as efficiently and smoothly as possible.

The three classifications of nonusers have been verified through studies of change efforts in K–12 schools, universities, medical schools, and business settings. Because the three levels represent three different behaviorial profiles, they provide understanding and guidance to change facilitators in supporting each individual in his or her actions to learn about, consider, and prepare for first use of an innovation. Strategic planners should keep in mind that in order for an entire organization or macrosystem to change, the individual members will need time and appropriate interventions to move beyond these nonuse levels.

Users

Implementation may be said to start in earnest when users and their clients (i.e., company staff, teachers and students) begin interacting with it in the company, classroom, or other setting. Five Levels of Use of users have been identified and described. A key in making these distinctions is the type of adaptations that are being made by the user in use of the innovation or in the innovation itself. How this plays out will be discernible as each of the five levels is described here. Keep in mind that although these descriptions are presented in a sequence that is logical, each person will not necessarily follow the sequence. Each LoU is independent of the other; LoU is not a straight-line hierarchy.

Level of Use III Mechanical.   At this level the user is actively engaged with the innovation in the workplace. This LoU is characterized by experimentation by the user as he or she endeavors to make the change work for him or her. Adaptations are made in managing time, materials, and other logistics. There is a short-term day-to-day focus on planning and a general inefficiency in how the innovation is used. If it is a classroom innovation, the implementer is making adaptations in its use or in the innovation itself in order to master use of the new practice.

The facilitator's task is to help implementing teachers with the frequently harrowing experiences of finding and organizing materials and scheduling time to plan for use, while they manage classrooms and students and experience the use of the new practices. The lack of knowledge about what will happen next affects such users' efforts to make innovation use more efficient for them.

Successful facilitators of LoU III users are those who are willing to do all sorts of seemingly low-level, nitty-gritty tasks to help the implementer achieve short-term success in use. They offer many "how-to" tips and may publish a newsletter and establish a telephone hot line to answer mechanical-use questions as they arise.

Successful facilitators have been known to organize materials in the closet, co-plan with the teacher, run and fetch what is needed, bring in substitute materials when glitches occur, and co-teach or demonstrate teaching in the LoU III teacher's classroom. As noted in the discussion of adaptations, LoU III implementers typically make a series of changes in their use of the innovation to find a system that works for them. A knowledgeable and experienced facilitator can be a highly significant source of help—and thus can receive immediate expressions of gratitude.

Level of Use IVA Routine.   If the user has been given sufficient time and adequate help, LoU IVA Routine may be reached. At this level, the implementer has mastered the innovation and its use, and has established a regular way of working with it. At this level, users do not plan to make any adaptations or changes; instead use is stabilized. These users may be heard to comment, "Why should I change? My way is working fine." Thus, the LoU IVA person is making no adaptations.

The facilitator may conclude that this user needs no help, since use is established. In this case, congratulations and some celebratory symbol from the facilitator could be wise. On the other hand, a discussion with the user, or an observation to determine how this person's use aligns with the ideal variation on an IC map (see Chapter 6), could be very informative and ultimately lead to a new set of actions, perhaps a move toward LoU IVB.

Level of Use IVB Refinement. Some users begin to observe and wonder how well their use of the innovation is working for the benefit of their clients (in the case of classrooms, this would be students). Based on their reflection and assessment, they make adaptations in the innovation or in their use of it to increase benefits for their clients. These actions signify LoU IVB Refinement. The key here is making adaptations for the clients' benefit (not for the benefit of the user, as in LoU III). Note again how the factor of adaptations helps to understand and distinguish the Levels of Use.

The facilitator is typically welcomed warmly by the LoU IVB person, who is looking for new ways to make the program as successful as possible for students. Since the LoU IVB user is wondering how well the program is working, a key action of the facilitator is to suggest or to help the teacher to find assessment or evaluation tools or rubrics to check on student work. Conversation about adaptations or adjustments in the program to accommodate the assessment findings would be helpful to the LoU IVB user. Providing journal articles and examples of what other users have done will also be useful to this person.

Level of Use V Integration. The LoU V Integration person, like the LoU IVB individual, makes adaptations for the benefit of clients, but the LoU V action is done in concert with one or more users. The collaboration is between users, not between a user and a resource person such as a counselor, librarian, or principal. The two or more users collegially plan and carry out adaptations in their use of the innovation that will benefit their students.

LoU V is a significant phase for the evolution of a change process and for the professional culture of the school. Change facilitators should do all that they can to nurture and facilitate its development and continuation. The facilitator's task is to make it possible for people who wish to work together to do so. Thus, seeking accommodations in the schedule to include concurrent planning periods and other logistical arrangements will be greatly appreciated by these users.

It should be noted that some users wish to work together to better manage the new program and its demands, and to increase the users' efficiency and decrease the workloads that new programs frequently demand. This can be a wise means of providing additional help and support to peers. However, this reason for working together is part of LoU III Mechanical Use, not LoU V, which entails collaborating to make adaptations in use for *client* benefits, not *user* benefits.

Level of Use VI Renewal. At Level of Use VI Renewal, the user is exploring or implementing some means to modify the innovation in major ways or to replace it altogether. The modification may constitute one very significant addition or adjustment, or multiple small adaptations that add up to significant change. In either case, the adaptation is intended to benefit clients. Again, making the adjustments is central, and it is the size or number of adaptations that places a person at this level. Curiously, persons at Level of Use VI comprise a small part (2.5 percent) of the CBAM database.

Facilitators for persons at this level may applaud them and stay out of their way. However, these users may be called on or may offer to provide additional materials or resources that will translate their adaptations into reality. For example, the LoU VI individual might be invited to provide professional development activities for and with others to share a possible new direction. Or the user may be asked to join a design team that is planning an entirely new replacement program or a revision of the current program. On the other hand, if the program is meant (through the decision of someone in authority) to be used without changes in its design, the facilitator may find himself or herself in the position of having to tactfully explain that the proposed adaptations are not in line with the expectations of the school, district, or state.

In summary, the operational definitions for each LoU are behavior based and action oriented. Levels of Use does not focus on attitudes or feelings; Stages of Concern does that. Because these actions can be observed, facilitators find the LoU construct and definitions useful for observing and analyzing what users are doing, for better understanding their needs, and for further facilitating implementation. Assessing LoU is critical in evaluation and research studies. Otherwise, there is no certainty that the so-called treatment group only contains users and that there really are no users in the control group.

ASSESSING AN INDIVIDUAL'S LEVEL OF USE

Whereas information about a person's Stages of Concern may be obtained in several ways (see Chapter 7), LoU may be assessed only through long-term observation or use of a specially designed focused interview protocol (Loucks, Newlove, & Hall, 1975). Various researchers and others have attempted to develop a paper-and-pencil measure to determine LoU, although we have consistently stated that it will not work. Measuring behaviors through self-report (as is done in assessing feelings through the Stages of Concern Questionnaire) is like trying to decipher semaphore signals by listening to a radio. In a word, using a questionnaire to rate one's behaviors and to make the distinctions across the levels is not possible.

There are two configurations of LoU interviews: (1) the LoU branching interview and (2) the LoU focused interview. In both, the person's placement at a LoU is determined by decision points, which are the distinguishing actions or behaviors. In the earlier descriptions, the factor of adaptations was used as an abbreviated way to introduce each decision point. Figure 8.2 offers a fuller explication of each LoU and the decision points that are used to define them.

The LoU Branching Interview

In the one-legged interview, the facilitator visits with the user in a brief and casual way to gain a broad view of an individual's Level of Use in order to offer appropriate assistance. In a word, the outcomes of this conversation are for facilitation pur-

FIGURE 8.2   Levels of Use of the Innovation with Decision Points

Decision Point F: Begins exploring alternatives to or major modifications of the innovation presently in use.

Level VI, Renewal: State in which the user re-evaluates the quality of use of the innovation, seeks major modifications of or alternatives to present innovation to achieve increased impact on clients, examines new developments in the field, and explores new goals for self and the organization.

Decision Point E: Initiates changes in use of the innovation for benefit of clients based on input from and in coordination with colleagues.

Level V, Integration: State in which the user is combining own efforts to use the innovation with related activities of colleagues to achieve a collective impact on clients within their common sphere of influence.

Decision Point D-2: Changes use of the innovation to increase client outcomes based on formal or informal evaluation.

Level IVB, Refinement: State in which the user varies use of the innovation to increase the impact on clients within his or her immediate sphere of influence. Variations in use are based on knowledge of both short- and long-term consequences for clients.

Decision Point D-1: Establishes a routine pattern of use.

Level IVA, Routine: Use of the innovation is stabilized. Few if any changes in use are made. Little preparation or thought is given to improving innovation use or its consequences.

Decision Point C: Makes user-oriented changes.

Level III, Mechanical Use: State in which the user focuses most efforts on the short-term, day-to-day use of the innovation, with little time for reflection. Changes in use are made more to meet user needs than the needs of clients. The user is primarily engaged in an attempt to master tasks required to use the innovation. These attempts often result in disjointed and superficial use.

*(Left margin: **Users**)*

Decision Point B: Makes a decision to use the innovation by establishing a time to begin

Level II, Preparation: State in which the user is preparing for first use of the innovation

Decision Point A: Takes action to learn more detailed information about the innovation

Level I, Orientation: State in which the individual has acquired or is acquiring information about the innovation and/or has explored its value orientation and what it will require

Level 0, Nonuse: State in which the individual has little or no knowledge of the innovation and no involvement with it, and is doing nothing to become involved

*(Left margin: **Nonusers**)*

Source: From *Measuring Levels of Use of the Innovation: A Manual for Trainers, Interviewers, and Raters* (pp. 173–195) by S. F. Loucks, B. W. Newlove, and G. E. Hall, 1975: Austin: The University of Texas at Austin, Research and Development Center for Teacher Education.

poses—to make a quick assessment of a person's LoU and to do something that will facilitate further use of the innovation.

The branching interview is constructed so that the facilitator, through a series of questions, gains information about the user's innovation-related behaviors (see Figure 8.3). To gain this quickly assessed estimate of the overall LoU of the individual, the initial question is, "Are you using the innovation?" The response separates nonusers from users, and depending on the response, the "no" or "yes" branch is followed. Then the facilitator needs to ascertain which of the three types of nonusers or five types of users the individual may be. The key in the interview is to stimulate the person to descibe and provide examples of behaviors that he or she is taking in relation to the innovation. The interviewer then refers to the decision points and LoU definitions to determine the person's LoU, which provides the guidance in structuring help and assistance.

The LoU Focused Interview

For research, implementation, assessment, and evaluation studies, more rigorous and detailed data are needed. For these purposes, the prospective LoU interviewer undergoes a three-day training and certification program to prepare for using a more formalized interview protocol, to gain data on levels and categories, and to reliably rate interviews. The result of this process is a matrix constructed by the interviewer to portray a more descriptive account of the individual's behaviors (for training manual on this process, see Loucks et al., 1975). The key to this process is employing questions that are based on a set of seven categories or dimensions that compose each LoU: knowledge, acquiring information, sharing, assessing, planning, status reporting, and performing (see Figure 8.4).

Knowledge.   This is the individual's practical and theoretical understanding of the change—its characteristics or elements, how to use it, its potential effects, and the advantages and disadvantages of its use. Unlike the other categories, which relate to the implementor's behavior, this cognitive dimension is not expressed as a behavior. Rather, the knowledge category reflects the degree of complexity and sophistication of one's understanding of the innovation and its use. The higher the LoU, the more complex the knowledge schema.

Acquiring Information.   This category focuses on actions taken to seek information about the innovation through such behaviors as questioning colleagues and others, reviewing printed materials supplied by a vendor, visiting sites where the innovation is in place, or writing to request descriptive material.

Sharing.   Sharing reflects what individuals tell others about their innovation use (or nonuse), including related ideas, problems, and plans. Through this report of what is

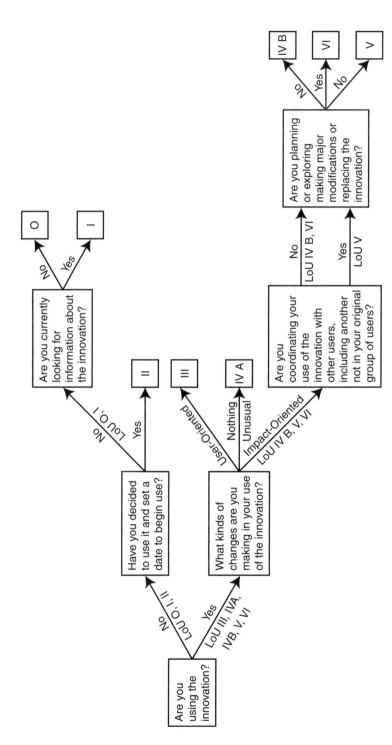

FIGURE 8.3 Format for the LoU Branching Interview

Source: From *Measuring Levels of Use of the Innovation: A Manual for Trainers, Interviewers, and Raters* (p. 22) by S. F. Loucks, B. W. Newlove, and G. E. Hall, 1975: Austin: The University of Texas at Austin, Research and Development Center for Teacher Education.

FIGURE 8.4   Levels of Use Categories

Knowledge: That which the user knows about characteristics of the innovation, how to use it, and consequences of its use. This is cognitive knowledge related to using the innovation, not feelings or attitudes.

Acquiring Information: Solicits information about the innovation in a variety of ways, including questioning resource persons, correspondence with resource agencies, reviewing printed materials, and making visits.

Sharing: Discusses the innovation with others. Shares plans, ideas, resources, outcomes, and problems related to its use.

Assessing: Examines the potential or actual use of the innovation or some aspects of it. This can be a mental assessment or can involve actual collection and analysis of data.

Planning: Designs and outlines short- and/or long-range steps to be taken during the process of innovation adoption (i.e., aligns resources, schedules activities, meets with others to organize and/or coordinate use of the innovation).

Status Reporting: Describes personal stand at the present time in relation to use of the innovation.

Performing: Carries out the actions and activities entailed in operationalizing the innovation.

---

shared with others, the LoU interviewer gleans information relative to what the individual is doing with the innovation.

Assessing.   Mentally exploring actual or potential innovation use to determine its strengths and weaknesses is the focus of assessing. Informally or formally collecting and analyzing data about what is being done and its effects are examples of assessing. However, assessing may also be only mental reflection about use of the innovation.

Planning.   Thinking ahead to design and outline short- and long-term actions to take, relative to use of the innovation, constitutes planning. The individual is looking beyond today's use to next steps.

Status Reporting.   This category entails the individual's reporting his or her own views of overall use of the innovation. The information about the individual, derived from the interviewer's questions in this category, provides a general description of the person's LoU.

Performing.   The performing category represents actual use of the innovation and what it looks like in the workplace (frequently classrooms or in business when implementing new processes). In the LoU interview, specific examples of use will be rated in the performing category.

One of the interesting aspects of the LoU categories is that all, with the exception of performing, represent actions relative to innovation use that occur outside the actual moments of its delivery in the classroom. As is obvious, much activity related to using innovations occurs beyond the classroom, or use site, and significant time and activity are invested in such behavior.

How the levels and categories relate (for further explanation, see Hall & Hord, 1987) is depicted in the LoU Chart in Appendix 3. For each LoU, the category behavior that occurs is different. Description of these behaviors is found at the intersection of the horizontal row that describes a particular LoU with the vertical column that addresses each category. The trained LoU interviewer is skilled at asking questions that allow the user to describe what he or she is *doing* in relation to each category. The trained LoU interviewer can also rate the bits of information obtained in an interview in order to determine the overall LoU.

IMPLICATIONS FOR LEADERS FACILITATING CHANGE

In this section there is significant discussion and multiple suggestions of interventions that may be employed at each Level of Use to support and enhance the effective implementation of new programs, practices, or processes. These ideas, however, should not be used in a cookbook fashion. It is very important for the change facilitator to be skilled in facilitation of change using Levels of Use.

■ The facilitator should have deep content knowledge of the innovation, understanding its essential components and characteristics, as well as its philosophical (and historical, perhaps) basis, the assumptions that accompany it, and the purposes or goals for which it may be used (see Chapter 6). The facilitator's superficial knowledge base can provide only superficial support to the implementation of the innovation users.

■ In addition to knowing the innovation, the facilitator must have a deep understanding of the concept of Levels of Use, and the operational definitions of each of the levels. This requires careful and thorough training in the concept and its measures. Being able to accurately recognize and identify users' (and nonusers') behaviors associated with the levels is obviously important. To do this, training followed by practice and feedback to refine such identification skills is needed.

■ The effective facilitator not only knows well the innovation and the Levels of Use tool but also uses appropriate interactions with individuals in the interview process in order to obtain useful information—and to supply or suggest relevant interventions to enable the individual to move to higher levels of use. These skills and qualities have direct implications for the preparation and competence of facilitators to use LoU in change efforts.

APPLYING LEVELS OF USE

There are two major ways in which Levels of Use can be employed. One is in planning for and facilitating the change process; the other is in conducting evaluation and research studies. The first can be considered formative use; the latter involves the summative domain.

Facilitation of Change

Like Stages of Concern, Levels of Use provides an understanding of implementers' relationship to the innovation. However, unlike SoC, which represents affect about innovations, LoU focuses on the implementers' behaviors. Thus, the LoU concept and its measures contribute in a second way to describing change at the individual and group levels. These descriptions enable the change facilitator to understand where each person is and to determine appropriate support for furthering the change process. For facilitating purposes, the first need is for an overall estimate of the LoU of the individual, which can be obtained with a one-legged conference or an informal branching interview.

Frequently, it is desirable to obtain an estimate for a group of persons, for instance, all the kindergarten and first-grade teachers, or an academic department in a high school. This is done by interviewing each individual and aggregating the data. This assessment is followed by provision of interventions for the group. Similarly, data could be collected from all or a sampling of individuals to assess the Levels of Use in a school or system. This may well be the case for planning. If district and even state data are desired, representative sampling could be done across the unit.

We strongly believe that each person's Level of Use and success with a change is in large measure influenced by the facilitation he or she receives. If no support and facilitating interventions are offered, many will never fully implement the innovation, and others will remain nonusers. Further, those who are at LoU III Mechanical Use need interventions that will help them move beyond this level, or they may adapt the innovation to make it easier for them to manage, or they may stop using the new practice altogether. There are, however, effective actions that change facilitators can take to assist individuals in moving up the use levels.

From a strategic perspective, assuming that all potential implementers across a system should ultimately be users, the facilitator's first challenge is to intervene in ways that support individuals in moving from LoU 0 Nonuse to LoU I Orientation. Although, hopefully, intended users would have been involved to some degree in deciding to adopt or to develop the innovation, this is frequently not the case. The facilitator, therefore, may need to begin by making people aware of the impending innovation and all expectations regarding the individual's role with it. The first objective is to stimulate people to actively seek information (Decision Point A), thus moving them to LoU I Orientation. Keep in mind, however, that each person must move through Decision Point A in order to be characterized as being at LoU I Orientation.

At LoU I Orientation and II Preparation, information is needed from the facilitator about the purposes and requirements of the change, and the timelines for implementation. This information should be general so as not to be overwhelming, yet specific enough to allow people to move to the next level. At these nonuse levels, individuals also need information about required materials and equipment—their purchase and preparation—and about how to get started. The advice should be practical, with only a moderate amount of attention to theory.

As use is inititated, most if not all first-time users of an innovation will be at LoU III Mechanical Use. Typical behaviors reflect concerted effort to find and organize materials. Effort is invested in searching for time to plan for and put new ideas into practice. These users try multiple ways of handling various parts of the innovation. There are innovation-related surprises as well as a short-term focus to planning (e.g., for the next day). During this period, then, the user typically needs help in finding, ordering, and organizing materials.

Help in finding the time for managing these logistics and for experimenting with the innovation is imperative. Facilitators who can help LoU III users do this will be greatly appreciated. "How-to" workshops to develop management skills and to provide guidance in structuring tasks are essential. Making it possible for users with common problems to meet with an experienced user to ask technical questions is another effective intervention that can be a high priority for LoU III users at this time.

If people have appropriate facilitative assistance and time, they typically move to LoU IVA Routine. They have established a way to use the innovation that they believe works for them and their students or other clients. By definition, the LoU IVA user does not experiment with the program further, makes no adaptations in the program or in her or his way of delivering it, and states that she or he plans to continue the current use. This is an especially important time to check on the user's Innovation Configuration (see Chapter 6).

If the LoU IVA user meets the expectations set forth in the goals of the change effort, one intervention here is to celebrate. Give praise and other recognition to reinforce the person's efforts. If, on the other hand, a user is using a less-than-desirable configuration of the innovation and has become stable (LoU IVA Routine) in this pattern, the facilitator needs to encourage further refinements in use. Interventions to help the user continue to change may be in order at the same time that encouragement is being provided.

LoU IVB Refinement users are typically a pleasure for facilitators. These people are searching for new materials, activities, or other refinements that will benefit the students. Importantly, they are also mentally assessing how well the innovation and their use of it are working for their students. Thus, these users welcome suggestions for assessing effectiveness and new ideas for improving varied aspects of the program or practice. Putting them in contact with others to access new information is a key intervention. Bringing others to visit them to see their ideas at work is confirming and rewarding. In addition, LoU IVB users may be potential facilitators.

If individuals are interacting with other users to coordinate their use and are making efforts to work together for their clients' benefits, they are diagnosed as LoU V Integration. Through collaboration, they are making adaptations in their use for client gains. In classroom innovations, they may be regrouping their collective students to take advantage of their interests, or reorganizing activities and/or materials to accommodate differing ability levels. The facilitator supports the LoU V users by making it possible for them to more easily coordinate their efforts (e.g., by restructuring schedules, space, etc.). Time for planning together will be of utmost importance. If the integration involves several people, training for them in shared decision-making could be relevant.

Normally, not a lot of a facilitator's time is directed to LoU VI Renewal users. In typical change processes, very few people reach this level, and those who do have typically done so by virtue of their own creative abilities and energy. Further, these users are interested in significantly modifying the innovation, which may or may not mesh with the planned goals of the change effort. These users can be a very positive force in change because they have ideas, and because their ideas are focused on improved outcomes for their clients. They could, however, be headed in a completely different direction from the one the innovation's designer intended. Their work should thus be either supported and applauded, or channeled in more productive ways that are consistent with organizational goals.

Motivation for Movement in LoU

One aspect of LoU that has been the source of interesting speculation but little research is the causes for change in LoU. Does change come about simply as a result of increasing experience with the innovation, or is it related to affective aspects of the person? What causes people to move to higher Levels of Use? Are there particular keys to understanding why people move to lower LoUs and from use to nonuse? Do certain kinds of interventions make a significant difference in movement? Although each of these questions is intriguing, there has been little research to aid in developing answers. One reason for this is the multivariate nature of the questions, which means that they would be best answered with a longitudinal design, a project few researchers are willing to undertake.

The simplest way to think about the motivational aspect of movement in LoU would be to assume a one-to-one correspondence with movement in Stages of Concern. There is an obvious correspondence between LoU and SoC. For example, task concerns correspond to the LoU III Mechanical Use, Stage 5 Collaboration concerns correspond to LoU V Integration. But we know that this picture is too simplistic. Using large databases from cross-sectional studies, we have been able to predict one diagnostic dimension from knowing the other only at the extremes. In other words, if a person is a nonuser, it can be predicted statistically that he or she is likely to have more intense self concerns. If the person is at the higher LoUs, it can be predicted that she or he is likely to have aroused impact concerns. However, no prediction of SoC is possible when a person is at LoU IVA Routine, which means that any SoC profile seems possible in this case.

Our preferred hypothesis about the relationship between movement in LoU and motivation is as follows. At the lower Levels of Use, the actions cause the arousal of concerns. For example, when a person attends an orientation workshop, the Stage 1 Informational and Stage 2 Personal concerns increase in intensity; use is driving concerns. At the higher levels, concerns would seem to drive LoU. A teacher who has concerns about certain students not doing well in mathematics will take action to learn about alternative approaches (LoU IVB Acquiring Information). A teacher who is developing concerns about working with a colleague, so that they can serve more students (Stage 5 Collaboration), is likely going to start talking with the colleague about what they might be able to do (LoU V Integration). All of this is speculative, but does have a great deal of attractiveness. The simple linear relationship, although initially logical in an intuitive way, is too simplistic. Human emotions and behaviors are much more complex, especially when it comes to their dynamics during times of change.

Evaluation of Change

In using LoU for evaluation of implementation, the three-day formal training and certification in the rigorous LoU focused interview, data collection, and data coding are required (see Loucks et al., 1975). Such training permits the evaluator or researcher to ascertain with reliability each individual's Level of Use in each of the categories and the overall LoU. Having such a precise measure of LoU makes various interpretations possible: How effective was the implementation plan? How effectively has facilitation been conducted? How far has the change process moved? Has institutionalization been achieved?

For instance, if users are at LoU III Mechanical Use, student/client outcomes are not likely to be higher than would be found in a control group of nonusers. (Remember all those evaluation reports with no significant differences?) On the other hand, if teachers are at LoU IVB and are making changes in the innovation or in their use of it to increase student outcomes, this information is helpful in interpreting how effective the innovation may be. Whether for facilitating the change process or evaluating implementation, Levels of Use is a valuable tool.

SIDELIGHTS ABOUT LoU

Two final little items: You might have noticed that Stages of Concern uses Arabic numerals for its naming system, while Levels of Use employs Roman numerals. This is simply an effort to further differentiate the two concepts and their classifications. We are also careful to say *Stages* of Concern and *Levels* of Use, and not vice versa.

NEEDED EVALUATION, RESEARCH, AND DEVELOPMENT ON LEVELS OF USE

Levels of Use as a concept and way to describe individuals involved in change has been thoroughly researched. The concept is valid and translates across numerous nationalities and cultures. The process for measuring LoU using the focused interview has been tested for reliability and validity. Levels of Use can be used with confidence and the resultant data trusted.

Further, descriptions of how individuals are acting or behaving in change efforts are usually understood easily by those who are not students of the change process because behaviors can be observed and identified.

What would be useful are studies that examine different formats and structures for reporting LoU to different audiences: the company manager, the school district research and evaluation division, the school board, principals, lead teachers, and so on. Exploring the efficacy of various types and styles of reports to particular audiences and inquiring of their effectiveness would be very useful:

Should reports to researchers and evaluators rely only on quantitative data?

Should stories or narratives (qualitative data) be reserved for parents and school board?

What is an appropriate mix of methods and language that best conveys information to any target audience?

Needed also are more studies of the uses of LoU in the business or private sector. How and when would the LoU tool be best used to support formative and summative assessment of implementation, and evaluation of change efforts? Who in the private or corporate sector is best positioned to use LoU (another inquiry that could produce useful information for facilitating change)?

Another study useful to consider is the cost and benefits of conducting LoU work. Are there ways to minimize costs and maximize benefits? Gaining an understanding of these issues in both the private and public sectors would inform change facilitation practice.

You might have wondered why Level of Use IV is the only one divided into two sections, LoU IVA and LoU IVB. The answer is one of history and pragmatics. When the initial LoU verification study was launched, there were only seven levels, 0 through VI. However, as the research team went about its explorations, the need for an additional classification became very apparent. To add this level, without having to renumber the entire database, LoU IV was split into two levels: IVA Routine and IVB Refinement.

In the vignette that follows, we will use an individual teacher, rather than a school, as an example of LoU in a change process. And, rather than supplying analysis at the end of the vignette, we will analyze this individual as we learn her story.

■ ■ ■ ■ ■

VIGNETTE

TIME SERIES SNAPSHOTS OF HYPOTHETICAL USER

Students of CBAM have suggested that it is easier to understand Levels of Use if the example of a "real live person" is provided for each level. Therefore, we introduce Louise, a hypothetical language arts classroom teacher in a high school. We will trace Louise through all the Levels of Use, describing her at each one, including the decision points. But please remain aware that in reality, people do not move hierarchically from one level to the next. Sometimes an individual may skip a level, move back to a lower level, or reach a level and move no further. At other times a user may drop the innovation entirely (this is not rare, particularly at LoU III) if she or he receives no help and becomes increasingly unable to make sense of the change or to use it efficiently.

Louise, who has been in the school for four years, is considered a good teacher by the students and is respected by her peers. Her principal told her that he had heard that the state board of education was recommending that schools think about including a service project in the curriculum, and he asked Louise what she thought. Louise expressed a lack of information and interest, as she was not sure what it was all about (LoU 0 Knowledge). Further, she had just purchased a new home and had a new lawn planted, and was busily occupied with preparations for the school year that would begin shortly. She gave no attention to service learning (LoU 0 Performing), and asked the principal no questions (LoU 0 Acquiring Information).

[Overall, Louise is at LoU 0 Nonuse with regard to service learning.]

At the end of September, the gentle autumn rains had come to Louise's lawn, and to her classroom came a student from another high school in the city, who asked Louise if the class would be doing a service learning project. Louise said, "No, I don't think we'll do that this year." However, the topic came again on Saturday, when Louise was playing tennis with some colleagues, one of whom mentioned going to an orientation session on service learning and asked Louise what she thought. She described her student's question and borrowed materials from her tennis partner's workshop to review (LoU I Acquiring Information and Performing).

[Because Louise has taken action to learn more about service learning (Decision Point A), she has moved to Level I Orientation.]

The principal supported Louise's expression of interest and encouraged her to learn more. Louise found the materials to be highly interesting (LoU I Assessing). She talked with her language arts department chair and called her language arts coordinator to find out what was available in the school and district relative to service learning (LoU I Acquiring Information). The principal suggested that Louise visit the American history teacher in the school who had begun implementing service learning.

Subsequently, she attended a second district in-service session on service learning and became quite excited about the ideas (LoU I Acquiring Information and Assessing).

V I G N E T T E   CONTINUED

She shared what she was doing with her second-period junior-level language arts class, whose members asked questions and expressed interest (LoU I Sharing). Louise decided that she would attend a series of three workshops. Her principal said that the school's budget would support teachers who wanted to attend the workshops that focused on the philosophy of service learning and on how to use it with high school students. As a result, Louise said that she would begin to "do" service learning with the second-period class immediately after Thanksgiving.

[Because Louise has decided to use service learning and sets a specific time to begin (Decision Point B), she is at LoU II Preparation.]

Louise attended the workshops on service learning and considered them to be quite good. She thought that the philosophy and values of service learning were well articulated and that they provided a meaningful basis for selecting the materials and choosing activities for students (LoU II Assessing). She began to collect materials and to make lesson plans for her class that would engage in service learning (LoU II Performing). Further, Louise and the other workshop participants were networking and sharing tips on how to get started, even though some people were from rural areas some distance away from the city (LoU II Sharing and Acquiring Information).

On schedule, Louise initiated service learning with her second-period class after the Thanksgiving break. Since the holiday season of giving and sharing with others was in the air, Louise had thought this might be a good time to launch service learning.

It was a good time, but it was also a maddening time. Louise had prepared all the suggested materials to teach the first activities, but was unsure about how (or with whom) to make contacts for doing service projects in the community (LoU III Knowledge). The students were excited by the plans and clamored to be quite independent in all phases of the service projects, while Louise was trying to keep up with finding and providing materials, activities, and ideas (LoU III Planning and Performing). She made a number of unproductive phone calls to community members to enlist their support and placement of projects. She commented, "Everything seems to take more time than I had anticipated" (LoU III Status Reporting). A crisis almost occurred one day when she had not prepared sufficiently for the class and a school board member stopped by.

Parents telephoned, and some came to the class, to find out what was going on, which was a mixed blessing for Louise in the midst of all that she was trying so hard to do. The parent inquiries were both useful and distracting. It took significant time to explain service learning and their children's role in it to each one, although after hearing about the projects, many parents offered their support, time, and resources. She tried to train one of the parents to make assignments for the students, but this required more of her time than was helpful, so she dropped this idea (LoU III Performing). The principal checked in regularly, providing support and some suggestions and ordering materials that were needed. Somehow Louise made it to the holiday break.

[Because Louise is using the innovation and making user-oriented changes (Decision Point C), she is at LoU III Mechanical Use.]

During the December–January break Louise reflected on her work with service learning and how disappointing her use had been (LoU III Assessing). She decided that she definitely would not expand it to other classes until she had ironed out the wrinkles, and that in the spring semester the second-period class would do only two projects and that there

(continued)

would be a great deal of planning (LoU III Planning). Louise would invite the students to reflect on their experience, and together they would correct their errors and discuss frustrations. She would guide them to an area of language arts curriculum that would fit well with the projects, thus integrating service learning so that it and language arts were more meaningful. More importantly, this would save her valuable classroom time (LoU III Planning). She talked this over with the langage arts coordinator, who supported her assessment and plans (LoU III Sharing).

At the end of the school year, Louise breathed a sigh of relief. She and the second-period juniors had accomplished the two projects, the second coming off more smoothly than the first (LoU III Assessing). Louise had asked the workshop leader and the history teacher to come into her classroom several times to give her pointers and ideas (LoU III Acquiring Information). This had helped a great deal. Having someone in the building who was more experienced with service learning had been especially meaningful. Louise and the students assessed the triumphs and traumas of the two spring projects, and all felt that they had made significant strides in how to do service learning successfully (LoU III Assessing). Further, the principal congratulated the students and Louise publicly on their efforts.

In the fall, Louise continued to do service learning with that year's second-period junior class, using the improved methods that she and her students had developed during their spring projects. She made no adaptations in the projects nor in her way of working with students for the fall semester (LoU IVA Performing).

[Because Louise has determined a satisfactory way to do service learning and has repeated her approach in the fall (Decision Point D-1), she is at LoU IVA Routine.]

In the following spring semester, Louise and her class did two service projects and each went well. But for the second one, after talking with her principal and carefully training and planning with the students, she gave them the opportunity to make their own contacts to initiate their projects. She felt this additional responsibility would improve the students' understanding of the community and of how to go about making arrangements in the "real world" (LoU IVB Assessing). It did indeed make the students feel very empowered and capable. This move was also applauded by the parents, who saw it as an opportunity for their children to develop poise and confidence while giving service to others.

[Because Louise has adapted her use of the innovation to increase client outcomes (Decision Point D-2), she is at LoU IVB Refinement.]

In May, the principal dropped a hint to the local newspaper's editor, a friend in the Rotary Club, who picked up on the story of Louise's students and sent a reporter to interview the class. Louise suggested that the reporter also interview the history teacher (Thomas) and his class about their service learning experiences. The discussion between the two teachers and the reporter after the interviews focused on the local railroad museum and its need for exhibits, publicity, and docents to guide tours for lower-grade children.

Later that night, Louise had an idea—in the fall, why couldn't she and Thomas organize the senior students from their classes into task forces that would explore the museum's needs and determine how to address them (LoU V Planning). The senior students, who would have experienced service learning and who could offer the content and capacity of their history and language arts courses, would be allowed to develop plans and procedures for the various parts of the project, although they would be monitored carefully by their teachers.

At the beginning of the fall semester, Louise and Thomas and their classes began to meet together during second period in the media center, where there was space to accommodate them. Louise worked in-depth with various groups of students while Thomas floated to facilitate and support the others. The two teachers did extensive planning for this team-taught, blocked cohort of students. They would frequently exchange assignments so that each played various roles with the students, keeping their work fresh and their ideas stimulating to the students (LoU V Performing). They occasionally invited the principal to actively participate in their project.

[Because Louise has initiated student-oriented change in the innovation in coordination with Thomas (Decision Point E), she is at LoU V Integration.]

Louise was quite pleased with her work with Thomas (LoU V Assessing). The history students had led the research among community "old-timers" to gain information about the early days of the railroad. The language arts students supplied leadership in designing publicity about the museum. All students developed scripts about the various exhibits and trained each other to deliver the information to younger children. They made schedules for the children's visits and assigned themselves as docents to guide the tours. Louise and Thomas were very excited about working in tandem with their students (LoU V Performance).

Then, during the Thanksgiving holiday, Thomas moved to another state, which forced Louise to consider a new dimension to service learning. Stimulated by the gift of some computers and related equipment from her uncle, during the winter holiday she began to explore how her students might use e-mail to connect with students of the other teachers in her workshop network (LoU VI Assessing).

The language arts coordinator and principal conferred with Louise about the new idea. They decided that the students from various schools who would communicate by e-mail would select a common service topic for investigation in their respective communities, and then use the technology to share information, report needs, brainstorm solutions, develop plans, critique each others' ideas, and share results of their projects.

[Because Louise has explored major modifications in how to plan for and execute service learning (Decision Point F), she is at Level VI Renewal.]

This is not the end of Louise's story, but it is quite enough for now.

VIGNETTE CRITIQUE QUESTIONS

1. Consider the time line of Louise's journey through Levels of Use. What reaction, if any, do you have to the pace of her movement?
2. What, if anything, should Louise's principal and/or curriculum supervisor do with her now?
3. Does Levels of Use give you a means for understanding the process of using new programs? Explain your response.

SUMMARY

In this chapter, Levels of Use, a second diagnostic dimension of the CBAM, was introduced and described. The decision points, which differentiate the levels that include the nonusers and users of innovations, were presented as a means for precisely identifying individuals at the various levels. An additional means for illuminating the eight levels is the use of seven categories, which were also described.

As outlined in this chapter, two procedures—one that is informal, which is used for facilitation purposes, and one that is more rigorous, which is used for research and evaluation purposes—may be used to assess individuals for their Level of Use. How Levels of Use may be employed to facilitate the change process was discussed, as were abundant examples of interventions that can be applied to assist individuals and groups in their movement to higher Levels of Use.

A vignette of a teacher's LoU as she learned about and used service learning was shared, along with rich descriptions of her use as she proceeded through her hypothesized journey. Similar to the work that a rater of LoU interviews would do, codings of the level and category were given to pieces of information and data that were revealed in the case story. While this case is purely an invention, it reflects real life and provides an intimate portrait of a user of an innovation at various Levels of Use.

We also made reference to the importance of documentiong Levels of Use in research and evaluation studies. In doing such studies, it is crucial to assess LoU in the control/comparison group as well as in the treatment group. We almost guarantee that both groups will contain a mix of users and nonusers.

DISCUSSION QUESTIONS

1. Using LoU, describe a sequence for training workers on the production line as they are introduced to and gradually become skilled at using a new machine, procedure, or process.

2. Describe an experience you have had with a change wherein you can identify the different LoUs.

3. How does the factor of change discriminate each of the five levels of users?

4. Use examples to illustrate and discuss how the categories expand the descriptions of an individual's LoU.

5. What are the two major LoU applications to a change effort; how are they similar and different?

6. Think of an innovation, such as technology or problem-based learning. How could LoU be used as a diagnostic tool to plan for its implementation?

7. How might teachers' Levels of Use of a new math program be used to explain student outcome scores three years after introducing the program?

FIELDWORK ACTIVITIES

1. Interview three people (e.g., teachers) about an innovation. Use the LoU branching interview technique to estimate each individual's LoU, and then design an appropriate intervention for each. If you can't find three teachers, use classmates. Remember that they don't have to be users for you to assess their LoU.

2. Plan how Levels of Use could be employed at the school district or state level to assess implementation of a systemwide school improvement project.

3. Identify a change effort that is early in its initiation at your campus or in your workplace. Explain how you would use Levels of Use to develop and guide a three-year implementation plan.

4. Consider the Innovation Configuration (IC) of your new product or practice (in operation) (see Chapter 6); describe how you would use the IC in tandem with an LoU interview to learn the status of implementation of your organization's latest process.

ADDITIONAL RESOURCES

For accessing training in either the LoU branching technique, or LoU focused interview, contact the authors.

PART IV

THE IMPERATIVE FOR LEADERSHIP IN CHANGE

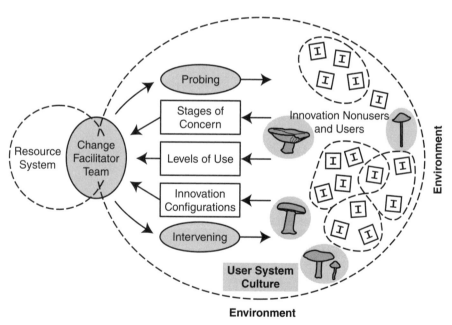

THE CONCERNS-BASED ADOPTION MODEL

A continuing theme in business, government, and education is discussion, examination, and cries for effective leaders and leadership. Although it is not acknowledged as frequently, today's leaders must be able to lead change processes. The success of all organizations requires that they make changes and that they accommodate changes in their environment. Each of the earlier chapters in this book presented a key perspective, theories, models, constructs, and tools that leaders can use to facilitate change. In Chapters 4 and 5 a consultative role was defined. In the diffusion perspective, it is the *change agent;* in the OD perspective, it is the *OD/process consultant.* Up until this point the formal leaders of organizations have not been addressed directly. In the next three chapters the actions, approaches, and consequences of the leaders are examined.

In Chapter 9 the actions that leaders take, their **interventions,** are described. Researchers have developed schemes for describing, classifying, and counting interventions. The resultant categories are useful for planning and reflecting on the various actions that leaders and others take as they are engaged in implementing change. Analysis of interventions have been informative in understanding how to better facilitate change processes.

In Chapter 10 the **Change Facilitator Style** of leaders is the topic. The research on interventions has led to the identification of three different styles of leaders. These styles are correlated with the varying degrees of success in implementing innovations. An important point to keep in mind as this chapter is studied is that in most settings there will be more than one person with formal responsibility for leading a change initiative. The way these individuals work together as a Change Facilitator Team will be heavily influenced by the Change Facilitator Style of the leader.

Chapter 11 introduces a very different category of interventions: **mushrooms.** Up to this point the explicit assumption has been that change leadership and change facilitating interventions are made by leaders, followers, and consultants. Intervention mushrooms represent a very different source of interventions. Just as the name implies, mushroom interventions grow in the dark and can be nutritious to the change process. Intervention mushrooms also can be toxic and cause serious drag on a change process.

Note that the accompanying figure on page 182 now has added icons of various mushrooms, and in the intersection of the User System and Resource System, the **Change Facilitator Team** is named. Two other elements having been added: **Probing** and **Intervening**. These represent the importance of leaders being systematic in having a systemic aproach to facilitating change. This completes the graphical representation of the **Concerns Based Adoption Model (CBAM),** which is the framework that the authors have used for their extensive careers in research, consultation, training, and professional development.

CHAPTER 9

DESCRIBING WHAT CHANGE FACILITATORS DO

Interventions

I am so pleased. Our school improvement team just finished writing a grant for $50,000 that will supply resource materials and equipment for our new science program.

What can I do? My teachers have been to the fall series of three workshops and they still don't understand how to operate the Students-Plus Tutoring process. It appears that one-to-one help is now needed.

Interdisciplinary curriculum development and teacher teaming have required a significant amount of time and resources across these first three years for their support, but they are well launched in our school, and we are preparing to report to the board about our efforts.

You know—the staff in my design division don't seem to really get it. What can I do to help them "see" my vision for our new product that will surely make a great deal of money for our company?

For decades there has been a lack of understanding of and attention to the process of leading change efforts. There exists generally, in the public and professional minds, an assumption that change just happens. We are reminded of two theories articulated by Chin and Benne (1969):

1. The rational empirical approach to change postulated that a good program or process provided to good people would find its way into their practice. (The clue here is *good* program and *good* people.)

2. The power coercive approach maintained that a good program or policy delivered to good people through the offices of a power or authoritarian figure would certainly ensure change in practice. (The key here is *power* and its influence.)

Even today these two approaches tend to be employed by would-be change agents who assume that change will just happen if an attractive or needed innovation is presented (or mandated). What is typically overlooked by such would-be reformers is that most change implementors have full-time (or more!) jobs, and don't have the opportunity to carefully and methodically design a self-changing approach. There are particular difficulties if the innovation is one vastly unfamiliar to the persons who will implement it.

What we know from our own research and review of the literature on successful school change is that facilitators are needed in a major way to support implementors. The main purpose of this book is to help would-be change facilitators to understand this and to develop the insights and skills needed to address successful change. And these facilitators are very active, as has been abundantly discussed in previous chapters. Through the reviews of school change success stories, we have with certainty identified many of the actions required of facilitators. These change facilitation actions are the topic of this chapter.

FOCUS QUESTIONS

1. What do we mean by interventions?
2. Who delivers interventions?
3. Are interventions really necessary?
4. To support successful change efforts, what six basic kinds of interventions are needed?
5. What additional kinds of interventions may be considered by facilitators?
6. What are the sizes of interventions that researchers and practitioners use for studying and planning change?
7. How can an individual intervention be analyzed and studied?

INTERVENTION DEFINITION

We have used and will continue to use the term *intervention* with great regularity in this book. We know, as stated, how significant the work of facilitators is in the process of supporting change efforts. Facilitators provide the interventions that can increase the potential for the success of change or allow it to fail. Thus, we think it is important to understand this term as we use it in this chapter. Our explanation and definition follow; please bear with us.

GUIDING PRINCIPLES OF INTERVENTIONS

1. Successful implementation of new policies, programs, processes, practices, and even new personnel does not just happen. Assuming that the announcement of such changes is sufficient is tantamount to little or no implementation, or very superficial implementation at best. Interventions both small and large make the difference.

2. While principals have been identified as change facilitators or significant suppliers of interventions, others also make many of these actions. Whoever will assume the role and responsibilities—whether they are teachers, parents, central office personnel, community members, or others—can serve in these capacities.

3. Many types of interventions must be provided to ensure the success of change efforts. Facilitators must acquaint themselves with and use their knowledge of interventions in planning, monitoring, and assisting their organization's efforts to change and improve.

4. Because change is accomplished at the individual level, facilitators will need to use diagnostic tools for shaping the interventions supplied to individuals, as well as to remember to provide groups with the array of interventions necessary to ensure each implementer's success with change.

5. Interventions may also be targeted for whole system change, remembering to employ them across all the persons in the system.

6. Since *learning* new information, skills, and behaviors is at the heart of any change project, facilitators would do well to keep this basic premise in mind as they consider, design, and deliver the interventions necessary for change process success.

If a central office curriculum coordinator brings microscopes to a teacher who is implementing a new life-science curriculum, this is an intervention to support the teacher's use of the change. If a university professor coaches three principals in developing instructional leadership, this is an intervention in behalf of the principals' new roles. If a principal conducts staff development for all the faculty in cooperative learning techniques, the principal has provided an intervention to the staff. If the division chief sends notes or gives a party of appreciation for the company's staff in recognition of their efforts, that is an intervention. If two teachers talk about what they think of the innovation, that, too, is an intervention.

In the context of the change process, any *action* or *event* that influences the individuals involved or expected to be involved in the process is an intervention (Hall & Hord, 1987, p. 143). Notice the use of the terms *action* and *event*. An action is deemed to be planned and focused deliberately on an individual, group, or all users or prospective users of a new program or practice (see Figure 9.1). Such an action could be sending an article about the use of math manipulatives to all primary teach-

FIGURE 9.1   Definition of an Intervention

An Intervention is an

Action	or	Event

that is typically

Planned	or	Unplanned

and that influences individuals (either positively or negatively)
in the process of change.

ers who teach mathematics. Discussion in a staff meeting about how implementation is going is another intervention.

An event, on the other hand, is something that occurs outside the deliberations and plans of the change process. Has this ever happened to your effort? Because we have observed that events do indeed influence the process of change, we have included them in our intervention definition. Events that we have observed in our work include:

A blizzard that prevented all truckers from delivering necessary equipment for a district's new astronomy program

A fire in the intermediate service center's print shop that caused a three-week delay of materials for the high school's drug prevention pilot effort

A learning styles consultant's accident on a mountain trail that resulted in rescheduling campus-based facilitators' preparations and planning for the project

Whether the intervention is an action or event, its related influence may be either positive or negative. In the preceding examples of actions, the influence was intended to be positive, but the examples of events all suggest negative influence. This does not mean that all actions are positive, nor that all events are negative. A refusal to approve funding for a "how-to" workshop (action) can be negative, whereas a flat tire that forces teachers to carpool (event) and thereby take the opportunity to share success stories could be positive.

We have seen and recorded wide-ranging interventions—from quite simple and short-term actions to multiyear strategic plans. An example of a short-term intervention would be a school improvement team member stopping by to say hello to another teacher and then asking her if she has any needs regarding the new computer technology. Another, more complex example is a change facilitator observing an implementer and providing feedback on his use of a new instructional strategy. An intervention's simplicity or complexity may be analyzed, and this, as well as the various levels of interventions that constitute a typology of interventions that facilitators can consider in their work, are addressed later in this chapter.

INTERVENTION DELIVERY

Who are the deliverers of interventions? The research and stories of successful school change are almost unanimous in identifying the principal as the primary catalyst and facilitator of site-based change. And, yet, as we will discover in this chapter, the principal is not alone in this endeavor. It is easy to assume that principals and superintendents, because of their positions, are change facilitators. While this is desirable, it is not always true. Even if it is the case, almost inevitably, because of the multiple roles of principals and superintendents, others share in the change facilitation (see Table 9.1).

Thus, based on our observations, we suggest that innovation-related interventions and change facilitation support and assistance may be delivered by any person who assumes the role and responsibilities of the change facilitator (whether implicitly or explicitly).

One implication is that many change process participants do not realize that they take actions that influence an individual, a group, or perhaps the entire change process. Another implication is that many people can be involved in the delivery of planned interventions. One significant result is that the burden of support and assistance to the users and nonusers is shared. This is important in view of the limited time that people in schools typically have to invest in facilitating change. Sharing the responsibilities of the facilitating role means also that the role is not necessarily positional, but may be operationally defined by what the facilitator does, which is the focus of the discussion that follows.

SIX FUNCTIONS OF INTERVENTIONS

The Southwest Educational Development Laboratory (SEDL), headquartered in Austin, Texas, is one of the federally funded regional labs committed to educational change and improvement. At the SEDL, considerable time and attention were given in 1990–95 to the matter of implementing planned change in the schools and districts of its region. The SEDL staff had previously spent much time and effort assisting these schools and districts in planning for their school improvement efforts. Although planning activities for change seemed generally to receive useful attention by school

TABLE 9.1 Sources of Interventions

CAMPUS	DISTRICT	COMMUNITY	STATE
Principals	Superintendent	Parents	Policymakers
Key teachers	Curriculum coordinators	Business representatives	State board/ superintendent
Counselors	Instructional supervisors	Legislators	
Students			

practitioners, the issue of implementing the change seemed to fall between the cracks (a point that was made in Change Principle 2 of Chapter 1).

The SEDL staff believed that focusing on implementation was critical for the success of school change and thus improvement. In an effort to ascertain if practical materials and activities were available for schools to develop important implementation knowledge and skills, the SEDL staff conducted a national exploration. Suspicions about the lack of such materials proved correct; little was found for practitioner use. As a result, the SEDL staff undertook a broad review of the leadership and change facilitation literature to identify relevant research-based concepts and information that could support the development of effective facilitative leaders for school improvement projects. To help these busy practitioners get to the center of change facilitation work, this wide-ranging review of the literature focused on the actions and behaviors of leaders who were facilitating change (Hord, 1992)—in other words, on interventions. What could be more important, the staff asked, than assisting potential facilitators in understanding the demands of the role and the interventions required?

The literature review resulted in identifying these interventions, which were organized into six types or functions (see Figure 9.2). A major source of this informa-

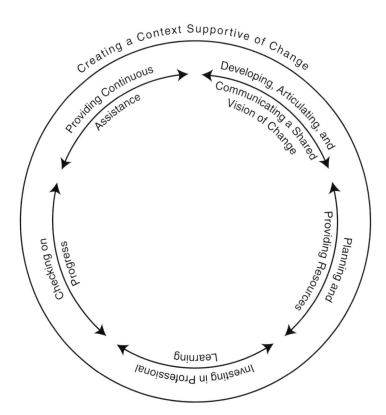

FIGURE 9.2   Six Functions of Interventions

tion came from the CBAM research, specifically the Principal/Teacher Interaction Study reported by Hord and Huling-Austin (1986) and the conceptualization of Game Plan Components in an intervention taxonomy done by Hall and Hord (1984). These six functions were deemed necessary for making change happen, and they constituted the job description of the change facilitator. They also provided the framework for a training and development institute that was designed to enable busy educators to assist local schools and districts, as well as to prepare state departments of education staff and others to realize successful change in their respective organizations (Boyd et al., 1993). These six functions, as described next, are designed for students early in their study of the change process. Additional functions and concepts of interventions follow thereafter.

Function I: Developing, Articulating, and Communicating a Shared Vision of the Intended Change

A first step in moving toward a changed and improved future is the development of a shared dream or vision of what will be—that is, a vision of the future that increases student outcomes. The goal of increased student outcomes results from specific changes or innovations that are selected for adoption and implementation. Many change efforts fail because the participants do not share mental images or pictures of what classroom and/or school practice will look like when an identified change is implemented to a high quality. Picturing the change in operation provides the target for beginning the change journey. A part of this process can be creating an Innovation Configuration (IC) map of the change—a useful way of defining what the change/innovation will look like when it is actually and actively in operation in its intended setting (see Chapter 6).

The elements of the shared vision of change must be as clearly defined as possible, and facilitators must continuously communicate this vision to enable implementors to move toward high-quality implementation. When there is a shared vision, facilitators can be consistent in supporting individuals and groups.

Specific facilitator interventions for developing a shared change vision could include but are not limited to engaging the school staff and community in identifying its beliefs and values regarding the purposes of the school; determining areas of the school program in need of change and improvement; selecting solutions to address the areas in need; and collectively developing clear mental images of the solution (i.e., the vision of change) when it is in operation in the school or classrooms.

The shared vision can be communicated in multiple settings: in the media, such as the public press and school and district newsletters; at school board and other community meetings; at the local coffee shop; and even on the golf course. The idea is to continually remind all constituents, in various ways, of the vision and where the school is in relationship to realizing it. Related is the understanding that attention to the vision needs to be provided throughout the process of change in order to capture and capitalize on (or diminish) evolving changes in the vision.

For further material on vision and on the six functions of basic interventions, see the Additional Readings at the end of this chapter.

Function II: Planning and Providing Resources

When an initial vision for change has been established (the vision can certainly evolve and change as the school staff experiences, learns, and gains more expertise), planning for its realization is both possible and necessary. All logistical factors and resource allocations, along with policy implications, must be considered. Although it seems obvious, the planning and provision of resources represent an important means by which implementors are enabled to initiate implementation and sustain the change process. We have observed change efforts that lacked necessary resources, which forestalled the expected beginning of the change process and doomed the entire effort.

Planning is not a one-time event. Like a holiday trip, destinations sometimes change, and frequently, unexpected additions may be made for increased effectiveness and/or satisfaction. Thus, while a plan is essential for understanding where the change journey is moving, it should never be considered to be cast in concrete. Likewise, the resource requirements for a change are altered across time as implementors become more expert in the use of an innovation and as the configuration of use may make differing demands on materials. Not to be forgotten is the regular depletion of program materials and equipment and the need for updating supplies to teachers and students.

One of the most important, and most typically lacking, resources for change is time: time for planning, time for staff development, time for sharing, and so on. Also important, of course, is time for facilitators to do *their* work. School administrators and facilitators would do well to find or create quality time to devote to the change effort. And, scheduling time for teachers to meet together to discuss successes and problems during implementation has proved to be valuable to change efforts.

Other specific actions of facilitators related to this function include developing policies related to the change or innovation; establishing rules and guidelines by which the implementation will be executed; staffing new roles and/or realigning existing ones; scheduling meetings and other regular and nonregular events; seeking and acquiring materials and equipment; providing space; and accessing funds needed for the new program or practice.

Function III: Investing in Professional Learning

Change means developing new understandings and doing things in new ways. If faculty are going to use new curricular programs or instructional practices, they must learn how to do that. Thus, *learning* is the basis of and the corollary to change. Formal training and other forms of staff and personal development, then, are essential to prepare implementers for the change. Such learning opportunities for the implementers should be ongoing as they develop more expertise in using the identified change. All too frequently, training workshops are scheduled only at the beginning of a change process. Stages of Concern (SoC) can be used to design and shape the development and learning sessions in the preimplementation period of preparation as well as during implementation, when implementors are changing from novices to mature users of the new practices (as discussed in Chapter 7). Note also that different levels of understanding and different learning are characteristic of peoples' knowledge at each Levels of Use (LoU; see Chapter 8).

Leaders of the change effort will need to consider the following interventions, and others, in the learning and development category: scheduling training and development sessions across time as the implementers move from novice toward expert; identifying and contracting with trainers and other consultants (internal and external); providing information about the change; teaching the skills required of the innovation; developing positive attitudes about use of the new program; holding workshops; modeling and demonstrating innovation use; and clarifying misconceptions about the program or practice. At this point the training is characterized as formal; that is, it is provided as large-group instruction. Professional learning interventions at the individual or small-group level are found in Function V.

It is important that training and development are innovation related and focused on the vision of the change. When this occurs, implementors gain the information and learn the skills necessary for the new way of behaving in the classroom and school. Too often, professional development has been vague and off-target. With a focus on the staff's concerns about their new program and practices, and on the vision of what the change will look like in operation, investing in professional learning will pay large dividends.

Function IV: Checking on Progress

Because change does not happen overnight, the process must be continuously assessed and monitored. Even though a clear articulation of the change has been expressed and material and human resources have been provided, the change journey is not without its bumps and detours. A significant set of facilitator interventions focuses on keeping a hand on the pulse of change. One-legged or informal interviews are an excellent way to check with individual implementors to identify needs, clarify questions, and solve problems. Not only does this enable the facilitator to assess progress but it also signifies to the implementors that their efforts are valuable and worthy of notice and support.

Decision makers and regulatory agencies have always known that what is measured or monitored is likely to be given attention. A change effort will be given more attention if facilitators assess its implementation.

More often than not, the change effort is lost when the leadership team, or whatever the facilitating team is called, fails to routinely check the progress of each implementer. Important checking actions include gathering data about the implementers' needs; collecting information about the knowledge and skills of the implementers; collecting feedback at the end of workshops and providing feedback on the feedback; systematically measuring, analyzing, and interpreting SoC, LoU, and IC; and talking informally with users about their progress. It is important that data collected about implementation are analyzed, carefully interpreted, and used to guide subsequent interventions.

Function V: Providing Continuous Assistance

Assisting is directly coupled to assessing, as discussed earlier. When needs or problems are identified, a response is required to support implementation. Assistance may take the form of supplying additional materials, providing formal or informal learning activities, teaming with the implementer to demonstrate refinement of practice, and coaching. It makes sense to assess progress in order to identify needs and then to provide assistance to respond to the needs. This coupling of *assessing* and *assisting* is labeled *coaching, consulting,* or *follow-up,* and typically occurs with individuals or very small groups of implementors.

These are crucial behaviors by facilitators. Other assisting actions of facilitators include stopping by to greet implementers and simply asking, "How's it going?"; responding to individual's questions and confusions; encouraging individuals in their use of the innovation; assisting single and small-group implementers in problem solving; providing follow-up and technical assistance; conducting quick conversations about the implementors' use and reinforcing what they are doing; and celebrating successes both small and large, publicly and privately.

Function VI: Creating a Context Supportive of Change

Increased attention is currently being paid to the context, climate, and/or culture of the school and how this factor influences the workplace of the professionals involved and subsequently their responses to change. For example, Boyd (1992b), in a review of the literature on context that supports or inhibits change, defined two components of context. One is the *physical,* or nonorganic, aspects of an organization—its building facilities, schedules, policies, and the like. The second component is the *people* element—the beliefs and values held by the members and the norms that guide their behavior, relationships, attitudes, and so on. While the context is identified by its two parts, the parts are interactive and influence each other. For example, a small faculty in a small facility (but one with an available meeting space) will find it much easier to come together to interact and build trust than a much larger faculty spread over multiple buildings. A supportive context decreases the isolation of the staff; provides for the continuing increase of its capabilities; nurtures positive relationships among all the staff, students, and parents/community members; and urges the unceasing quest for increased effectiveness so that students benefit. (For further discussion of the characteristics of a supportive context for change, see Chapter 2.)

In such a context the participants value change as a means for improving their effectiveness and seek changes in order to improve their practice. Boyd (1992a) reports that school leaders can take actions, such as the following, to create this context:

IMPLICATIONS FOR LEADERS FACILITATING CHANGE

The six functions of interventions provide a practical framework to facilitators for supporting and guiding change. These are the "sacred six" kinds of actions demanded for the success of change projects.

An interesting way of generating actions or specific interventions for these functions is in employing the Innovation Configuration map as a guide. Function I is the articulation of a shared vision of the intended change when it is implemented in a high-quality way. The IC map is the written product that represents the creation of a shared vision of the change. When this IC map is completed, it can be used for designing the Function II interventions, Planning and Providing Resources. The map indicates the desired outcomes—what actions are taking place in the innovation's setting—and is the point of reference for making an action plan to reach those desired outcomes. It can also be referenced to determine fiscal and human resources needed to reach the desired outcomes, or the vision of the change.

Referring to the IC map provides clarity for identifying professional development for staff (Function III) needed to reach the actions delineated on the map. Professional developers use the map to plan training and development for participants. But, that is not the end of the change process, though many seem to believe if initial training is provided, the process is complete—not true.

The map is used for Function IV, Checking on Progress. The facilitator uses the map as an instrument to ascertain where each individual is in the change effort, so that Function V, Providing Continuous Assistance, may be planned appropriately to support individuals in moving closer to the ideal variation of each component on the map.

An IC map may not address directly Function VI, Creating a Context Supportive of Change. But a map of such a context for change could be produced to guide the facilitator in designing interventions to enable the creation of a more supportive context in the organization.

1. *Shaping the physical features of the context* by manipulating schedules and structures (such as faculty meetings) so that people can come together and share improvement ideas, by allocating resources to support the improvement effort, and by developing policies for enhancing staff capacity.
2. *Modeling* the behaviors and norms desired of the staff by interacting and cooperating in a significant way with all staff, by working with focus and commitment, and by being highly visible in the daily routines that they hope the staff will emulate.
3. *Teaching and coaching* by reading, studying, and subsequently sharing materials that will nurture and develop the staff's expertise, by attending professional development activities with the staff, and by attending conferences and sharing their substance with the staff.

4. *Addressing conflict* by facing it rather than avoiding it, and thus using conflict as a vehicle to resolve disputes and build unity.
5. *Selecting, rewarding, and censuring staff* by recognizing their work publicly and privately, by inviting the staff to share their efforts and experiences related to improvement goals, and by insisting that staff commit to school goals through the selection and termination processes.

In summary, the six types of basic interventions or functions, identified from the SEDL's Leadership for Change Institute (Boyd et al., 1993), have been widely used as a framework for developing the knowledge and skills that facilitators need to plan for change, monitor its progress, and evaluate its outcomes in terms of degree of classroom implementation.

ADDITIONAL KINDS OF INTERVENTIONS

Four of the six basic intervention types discussed—planning and providing resources (developing supportive organizational arrangements), investing in professional learning (training), checking on progress (monitoring and evaluation), and providing continuous assistance (providing consultation and reinforcement)—accounted for the majority of interventions identified in earlier CBAM studies; the original CBAM names are shown in parentheses (Hall & Hord, 1984, 1987; Hord & Huling-Austin, 1986; Hord et al., 1987). Two of the six categories of interventions—developing a shared vision of the change and creating a context for change—were identified by Hord (1992).

The CBAM studies revealed two additional Game Plan Components that are less frequently executed but quite important in change efforts: communicating externally and disseminating information. We examine the importance of these interventions next.

Communicating Externally

An important but often neglected set of interventions are those actions taken to keep individuals and groups external to the implementation site informed about what is happening. In order to gain their support or approval, they need to be informed by the on-site participants. One of the quotes at the beginning of this chapter reports that the change effort on interdisciplinary curriculum is going well and that a report on progress will be made to the board. It is easy to understand the politically and economically astute reasons for communicating externally to such an influential group, but too often too little is done too late.

Activities related to this category of interventions include describing the change and its purpose to those outside the school, publishing a monthly newsletter, making presentations at various district and community meetings, keeping the external members of the site council and the PTO informed about progress and setbacks, informing all possible constituents about progress, and developing a campaign to gain the support of the public and other relevant groups.

Disseminating Information

Efforts to share information about the new program or practice and to let others know of its value and positive impact, with the intention of persuading them to adopt the program, are dissemination interventions. In broadcasting the virtues of the innovation, broader support and influence may be gained as well, but in this category the primary intent is to inform prospective adopters from other sites.

In order to accomplish the purpose of this category, the facilitators engage in various activities, including mailing descriptive information to persons external to the school, making presentations at regional and national meetings, encouraging others to adopt the innovation by reporting its benefits, making large-group presentations about the innovation to potential adopters, providing free sample materials, and training expert colleagues to represent the innovation.

Note that it is not necessary to do disseminating interventions in order to have change success at the home site. As a matter of fact, spending too much time on disseminating, especially early in implementation, can draw needed energy and resources away from the project. Early dissemination also runs the risk of appearing premature, since everything may not have been worked out at the home site. Four or five years into a change process can be an excellent time to begin disseminating actions for at this point they can serve to reward and expand the perspectives of successful implementors while increasing visibility for all.

In the early work, these CBAM intervention classifications were labeled "Game Plan Components" and were part of a system that provided for further detailed and enriched planning and analysis of a change endeavor. The additional concept of sizes or levels of interventions, identified in the intervention taxonomy, was developed for research purposes. However, many experienced change facilitators have also found them to be instructive and useful.

SIZES OF INTERVENTIONS

Game Plan Components constitute one size of interventions, but we have also identified other sizes of interventions which are distinguished by their relative duration and the degree to which they affect few or many people. In classifying by these two factors, policy-level interventions are identified as the most comprehensive of the interventions. Strategies, tactics, and incidents are additional interventions that can be distinguished by size (see Figure 9.3).

Policies

Since they affect the whole organization and exist typically for an extended amount of time (years), the policies of an organization must be taken into account when planning for change or when studying a planned change project. Policy interventions

FIGURE 9.3   The Relative Size of Interventions

Policies: Decisions that affect the whole organization for an extended period

Game Plan Components: Major functional groupings of interventions

Strategies: Interventions that operationalize the Game Plan Components into actions

Tactics: Sets of small actions that comprise the strategies

Incidents: Brief in-time actions that focus on one or a few users or nonusers, and that may or may not add up to tactics

could include contract specifications that restrict staff development to the school day. Or there may be a policy that prohibits staff development during the school day, thus requiring its scheduling for after the formal school hours, with stipends being paid to the teachers who participate. Such overarching interventions can have significant and far-reaching influence on a change process. Facilitators ignore them at their risk.

Game Plan Components

Earlier in this chapter, these interventions were referred to as "functions." This size intervention, which represents a major planning device for a change effort, is a clustering of behaviors into meaningful and functional groupings that provide a framework for the facilitator.

Strategies

These interventions make the Game Plan Components more explicit and translate them into describable actions. Strategies are long-term, and are designed to accomplish specific change process objectives and operationalize the Game Plan Components through their impact on a large number of the implementors. For example, under the Game Plan Component of monitoring and evaluation (checking progress), the strategy of one principal who was closely guiding and supporting change in his school was to collect, every Friday, samples of students' work related to the innovation. This strategy led to another strategy that became a part of the providing consultation and reinforcement (providing assistance) component, as the principal led the staff in reviewing the students' work every other week. This strategy informed the teachers about additional possibilities for students related to the innovation and reinforced and/or encouraged various teachers in their use of the innovation.

Tactics

This intervention is defined as a set of small, interrelated actions. A day-long workshop would be a tactic that is part of the strategy of designing and providing training sessions across the first year of implementation. The strategy is, in turn, part of the Game Plan Component of training.

Other examples of tactics are visiting each implementor in his or her classroom over a three-day period to solicit concerns about training sessions for the new computers and scheduling a consultant to be in the school for a week to provide technical assistance to any teacher who indicates interest.

Incidents

We have learned with certainty how significant the small and more individualized interventions known as incidents are. They are short in duration, focus typically on one or just a few implementors, and occur in informal ways. This is not to say that they are unplanned, for they are so powerful that they should be on the mind of every facilitator. It is in these little day-to-day, moment-to-moment actions (which frequently take the form of the one-legged interview described in Chapter 7) that the change effort is most frequently won or, unfortunately, lost. We and our colleagues have observed that in schools where there are significantly more incident interventions, teachers have greater implementation success due to this personalized help and support. There are many opportunities for enacting incident interventions, such as the following:

- When meeting a user or nonuser in the hallway, the facilitator can offer comments to support his or her hard work with the innovation or to increase his or her interest in learning about it
- At the staff mail box, the facilitator can share requested information with the teacher who is early into use of a new mathematics program
- Crossing the parking lot to go home, the facilitator can inquire about the innovation equipment that was sent to a teacher the day before
- In the cafeteria line, the facilitator can provide a brochure about professional development sessions

The effective facilitator uses the small interactions to provide help and assistance.

If the facilitator or policymaker thinks only of workshops as the key interventions for a change effort, the implementers will be short-changed. In our studies of interventions, we have found a wide range of incident interventions in the Game Plan Components that provide resources, assess progress, and provide assistance. It is in these one-to-one interventions that individuals and small groups have their idiosyncratic—and vastly important—concerns attended to. It should be noted also that incidents form the building blocks that become tactics and ultimately strategies.

In a bit more detail, incidents may be further described as one of five types: isolated, simple, chain, repeated, and complex.

Isolated Incident.   This singular action is distanced in time, space, and purpose from any others. It is given little time and generally is addressed to a single individual. An example is requesting a teacher to respond to a request from a parent for information on language manipulatives.

Simple Incident. Although this single-action intervention is typically short and aimed at one or only a few individuals, it is linked in its purpose to other interventions. When a facilitator stops by to see the two second-grade teachers to check on their concerns about their new science curriculum, this is an example of a simple incident. Peer faculty could also provide this same intervention to their colleagues on a one-to-one basis. An innovation-related announcement about an upcoming workshop made in a staff meeting would also be a simple incident intervention.

Chain Incident. As suggested by its name, this is a series of short incidents provided to multiple targeted individuals by the same person and for the same purpose. A facilitator dropping by to remind each teacher of the afternoon's workshop in the cafeteria is an example.

Repeated Incident. Unlike the chain incident which delivers the same action to multiple audiences, the repeated incident delivers the same action to the same target multiple times. The central office's Director of School Improvement reminding the assistant principal three times to complete the implementation report for the superintendent is such a repeated incident.

Complex Incident. This incident involves a set of related incident actions that occur within a short period. An example in the definition section of this chapter was the feedback conference with a teacher held following an observation. This complex intervention could also include the development of a growth plan for supporting the

---

NEEDED EVALUATION, RESEARCH, AND DEVELOPMENT

Not much research on intervention has been conducted, although we have learned about the actions of the interventions, their size, type, and elements.

What would add productively to our knowledge base would be studies of who most effectively provides which interventions—more specifically, studies to determine priority intervention roles for internal and external facilitators. Are some interventions more effectively provided by internal or external facilitators, and under what conditions? Such studies could contribute to the knowledge base of facilitators and provide the information for developing guidebooks for both internal and external facilitators.

Studies of the distribution of interventions as a change process unfolds would be useful. Some interventions, such as training sessions, are expensive. When is the best time for such expensive interventions? A related question has to do with the strategy of using turnkey trainers. Is this an effective strategy in terms of the time it takes for these trainers to become competent (LoU IVA Routine Use) and confident users (low Self and Task concerns) of best practices (as exemplified in an IC map)?

teacher and a number of related topics, such as scheduling a follow-up focused observation.

The sum of all these intervention sizes or levels is a comprehensive set of actions undertaken to provide nonusers and users with what they need to successfully implement any given change. But an even more specific exploration, known as the Anatomy of Interventions (Hall & Hord, 1987), may be done by researchers and facilitators to analyze a change effort.

THE ANATOMY OF INTERVENTIONS

The interventions just described address the different sizes of interventions. The internal parts of an intervention can also be analyzed in terms of codes related to each part: source, target, function, medium, flow, and location (see Figure 9.4). Such an analysis and coding of interventions across time make it possible to ascertain who is providing intervention actions to whom, for what purpose, how, and when. Thus, redundancies and gaps may be identified and corrections taken so that all persons involved receive the supportive interventions that are needed.

Source

The source of an intervention is the person who is initiating the action. Typically, this will be a facilitator who has determined the need for the intervention and designed it to respond to that need. However, the source could be any campus or district person who makes a change process–related action. Teachers, as well as persons more external to the implementation site, do initiate actions. However, in our studies, it is clear that principals and others on a leadership or school improvement team are the most frequent sources of interventions.

Target

The person who will receive the action is the target. The target may be a single individual with particular concerns or many persons (such as participants in a workshop). If hundreds of persons are targeted, the intervention will obviously be less

---

FIGURE 9.4   Internal Elements of Incident Interventions

Source: Person(s) providing the action

Target: Person(s) receiving the action

Function: Purpose of the action

Medium: Means by which the intervention is delivered (telephone, face to face, etc.)

Flow: Directionality of the intervention action (one-way, interactive, etc.)

Location: Where the action took place

---

personalized. The diagnostic dimensions—Stages of Concern, Levels of Use, Innovation Configurations—provide data useful in designing interventions that will be relevant and effective for the target.

Function

Function is the purpose of the action. Interestingly, an intervention can have multiple functions. In analyzing interventions, it is frequently difficult to identify a single purpose to any one action. On the other hand, it's quite useful for functions to be multipurposeful. For instance, it is easy to imagine that when a facilitator (particularly a principal) drops by a classroom to ask the teacher how the new instructional strategy is working, the teacher can feel supported and also somewhat pressured to be using and improving use of the strategy. The visit signals that the principal considers the new practice important (pressure) and is also interested in supplying help (support). The same intervention also provides the principal with information about how the innovation is going.

Source, target, and function can provide the facilitator with important information about who is being attended to in a change effort, by whom, and for what purpose. Redundancies (which do not occur very often) and gaps in the provision of intervention actions may be revealed by analyzing these subparts of interventions. For research purposes, the three subparts noted above—along with medium, flow, and location—may be coded using a set of carefully defined codes and coding rules. (See Hall and Hord [1987] for additional information.)

This chapter has provided increasingly finer "cuts" at analyzing interventions. The following vignette returns to the basic six functions of interventions.

■ ■ ■ ■ ■ ▬▬▬▬▬▬▬▬▬▬▬▬▬▬▬▬▬▬▬▬▬▬▬▬▬▬▬▬▬▬

V I G N E T T E

IMPLEMENTING A NEW CAR

Perhaps a simple story of the integration of a new product into everyday life will be helpful in illustrating what so frequently happens when something new is introduced to individuals.

In 1989, Mrs. H challenged her husband's practice of securing two heavy but speedy, gas-demanding Oldsmobiles for the family by researching and purchasing a new four-door Honda Civic hatchback. This car, silver in color, had a standard transmission, heat, air conditioning, and windshield wipers, and that was it—no radio, no frills. Fortunately for Mrs. H, this car proved abundantly successful, until after 13 years and nearly no visits to the mechanic except for the recommended periodic checkups, the Honda service technician proclaimed that, at 195,000 miles, "Silver Belle" was "terminal."

Not surprised, although she had planned to run this car to 350,000 miles (a record in effect at this dealership), Mrs. H presented herself at the Honda showroom. Now note the parallels between this personal experience of change—buying a new car—and the steps in the six basic interventions recommended for any change process:

(continued)

V I G N E T T E   CONTINUED

CREATE A CONTEXT SUPPORTIVE OF CHANGE

The Honda showroom was filled with shiny autos, festive balloons, and coffee and cookies for the potential customers. A charming and not unattractive young salesman, Jeff, offered to help Mrs. H review the auto possibilities.

DEVELOP A SHARED VISION

Jeff was quite insightful in playing to Mrs. H's concerns for information and her growing interest in a "fine, new car." He was descriptive and persuasive in developing the mental images in the prospective buyer's mind of sailing along the highways in a handsome and upscale new car.

PLAN AND PROVIDE RESOURCES

When Mrs. H decided to make a purchase, Jeff planned the process, developed a contract, and queried Mrs. H about her resources to pay for the car. Although her personal concerns erupted over the prospects of writing such a large check, Jeff assured her that she was doing the right thing, thus decreasing these concerns. Further, he asked her to give him 30 minutes when she picked up the car the next day.

INVEST IN LEARNING

When Mrs. H arrived the next day, Jeff sat behind the wheel, with Mrs. H leaning in the car window, as he recited his litany: this button does this, that one does that, the lever on the left is, this knob controls that, and so on. At the conclusion, he handed Mrs. H the keys, told her to have fun, and thanked her for her business.

   At this point, Mrs. H's management concerns escalated and she left the dealership parking lot with some trepidation (albeit excitement also), but successfully executed the traffic, hills, and curves to her home.

CHECK ON PROGRESS

To this day, nearly two years later, Mrs. H does not know how to play a CD in the car (although she keeps a supply of them ready just in case). When does she think about using the CD player? When she is sailing down the freeway, which is not a good time to refer to the user's manual. Finally realizing that this was an unacceptable situation, she brought the manual into the kitchen so that she could study it.

PROVIDE CONTINUOUS ASSISTANCE

"You goose," Mrs. H said to herself, "this is not the appropriate place to study the car manual; you should be in the car." She was also still not clear about how to tune the radio. Further, certain buttons and thingamajigs on the dashboard were befuddling.

   The lesson of this not-untrue fable is that the training in use of the car that the change facilitator/salesperson provided was perfunctory, with no hands-on experience, no practice, and no feedback. Further, he did no checking into Mrs. H's use of the car. The lack of personalized training, with the absence of checking progress, followed by no follow-up, has left Mrs. H as a very low-quality user of her car.

■ ■ ■ ■ ■

V I G N E T T E   CONTINUED

Mrs. H and her car provide an excellent example of what happens far too often to teachers in classrooms. They become interested in new programs after learning how they work in similar places and developing a vision of how they can contribute effectively to their work so that students benefit. Many times adequate resources are provided, although this is not always the case. Staff development in the new program/practice is provided at the beginning in very ineffective ways (as it was for Mrs. H). Almost without exception, poor training is followed by an absence of the continuous help and assistance that can assure that high quality (rather than perfunctory) use results in classrooms and contributes to students' growth, learning, and success.

VIGNETTE CRITIQUE QUESTIONS

1. Have you had an experience similar to Mrs. H's with a new product (such as a new computer, microwave oven, or cell phone), when you did not receive proper support? Reflect on your experience and consider what might have been done to make your implementation of the new product more successful.
2. It would appear that sales personnel, school administrators, and others who are interested in changing their public's products or practices assume a great deal about their clients' capacity with those innovations. How could you help Jeff, the car salesperson, or a school or district administrator understand the real needs of clients for supportive and appropriate interventions?
3. Why would we use a story about purchasing a car in a chapter on interventions? How does it relate to what happens all too frequently when new programs and practices are introduced in schools and classrooms?

SUMMARY

The concepts, strategies, and tools described in this chapter were created and designed with change facilitators in mind (whether they be school principals, district supervisors, key teachers on the campus, or others in the private sector). Typically, interventions are made without prior thought. Our intent in this chapter was to focus on the concept of interventions and to introduce a number of ways that they can be considered, classified, and assessed.

It is absolutely clear that in those change processes where there are statistically significant more innovation-related incident interventions, teachers have greater implementation success. It is also clear that in schools where there is coherence in incident interventions that accumulate to form tactics and ultimately strategies, change is more successful. And, if interventions focus on LoU V Integration, there is a more collaborative culture and greater sharing of a vision. Strategies will be needed to promote collaboration if that element of culture is desired in the staff's workplace.

Interventions take time and thought. Without them, members of the organization work in isolation and innocence in terms of use of the innovation. As we admonish in our workshops, "Change facilitators, *do* something."

DISCUSSION QUESTIONS

1. What preparation relative to interventions should be provided to a person who will serve as a change facilitator? Would your prescription be different if the facilitator was based at the school, district, or state level?

2. What length of time should be allotted for implementing a new curriculum such as a constructivist-based mathematics program? What strategies should be included? Provide a rationale for your response.

3. *Little Things Mean a Lot*—how might this song title apply to the various types of interventions?

4. How might a campus-based practitioner, a state policymaker, or a researcher employ the information on interventions in this chapter?

5. Which of this chapter's intervention concepts are most applicable to the corporate world, or private sector?

FIELDWORK ACTIVITIES

1. Obtain the implementation plans for two schools' or other organizations' change efforts. Which basic kinds of interventions are included and which are absent in each case? On this basis, compare, predict, and explain the results likely to be gained in each organization.

2. Develop a plan for making a presentation to the school board using the six basic types of interventions as a framework to explain the attention and resources needed to further a change process.

3. Develop a plan of interventions to be supplied to a school whose staff will be implementing problem-based learning or some other complex innovation. Be as thorough and comprehensive as possible, identifying key strategies within each Game Plan Component and examples of relevant incidents.

ADDITIONAL RESOURCES

Professional development focused on developing the knowledge base and skills of facilitators related to the six intervention functions is available as a three-day institute. For information about *Leadership for Changing Schools,* contact Southwest Educational Development Laboratory, 1-800-476-6861.

A leader's guide, videotapes, audiotapes, and copy for handouts and transparencies from the *Leadership for Changing Schools* institute is available as a "stand-alone" set of materials and activities. For information, contact, Southwest Educational Development Laboratory 1-800-476-6861.

ADDITIONAL READINGS

Developing, Articulating, and Communicating a Shared Vision

Barth, R. S. (1990). *Improving schools from within.* San Francisco: Jossey Bass.

Blumberg, A., & Greenfield, W. (1980). *The effective principal: Perspectives on school leadership.* Boston: Allyn and Bacon.

Cuban, L. (1985). Conflict and leadership in the superintendency. *Phi Delta Kappan, 67*(1), 28–30.

Fullan, M. G. (1992). Visions that blind. *Educational Leadership, 49*(5), 19–20.

Hord, S. M., & Estes, N. (1993). Superintendent selection and success. In D. S. G. Carter, T. E. Glass, & S. M. Hord (Eds.), *Selecting, preparing, and developing the school district superintendent* (pp. 71–84). Washington, DC: Falmer Press.

Planning and Providing Resources

Brandt, R. (1987). On leadership and student achievement: A conversation with Richard Andrews. *Educational Leadership, 45*(1), 9–16.

Louis, K. S., & Miles, M. B. (1990). *Improving the urban high school: What works and why.* New York: Teachers College Press.

Peterson, K. D., Murphy, J., & Hallinger, P. (1987). Superintendents' perceptions of the control and coordination of the technical core in effective school districts. *Educational Administration Quarterly, 23*(1), 79–95.

Investing in Professional Learning

Fullan, M. G. (1985). Change processes and strategies at the local level. *The Elementary School Journal, 85*(3), 391–422.

Hord, S. M., & Boyd, V. (1995). Staff development fuels a culture of continuous improvement. *Journal of Staff Development, 16*(1), 10–15.

Joyce, B., & Showers, B. (1980). Improving inservice training: The messages of research. *Educational Leadership, 37*(5), 379–385.

Murphy, J., Hallinger, P., & Peterson, K. D. (1985). Supervising and evaluating principals: Lessons from effective districts. *Educational Leadership, 43*(2), 78–82.

Checking on Progress

Fullan, M. G., with Stiegelbauer, S. M. (1991). *The new meaning of educational change.* New York: Teachers College Press.

Murphy, J., & Hallinger, P. (1986). The superintendent as instructional leader: Findings from effective school districts. *The Journal of Educational Administration, 24*(2), 213–231

Rutherford, W. L (1985). School principals as effective leaders. *Phi Delta Kappan, 69*(1), 31–34.

Providing Continuous Assistance

Bush, R. N. (1984). Effective staff development: Making our schools more effective. *Proceedings of Three State Conferences* (pp. 223–238). San Francisco: Far West Laboratory for Educational Research and Development.

Coleman, P., & LaRocque, L. (1990). *Struggling to be good enough: Administrative practices and school district ethos.* London: Falmer Press.

Creating a Context Supportive of Change

Boyer, E. L. (1995). *The basic school: A community for learning.* Princeton, NJ: Carnegie Foundation for the Advancement of Teaching.

Deal, T. E., & Kennedy, A. A. (1982). *Corporate cultures.* Reading, MA: Addison-Wesley.

Deal, T. E., & Peterson, K. D. (1990). *The principal's role in shaping school culture.* Washington, DC: U.S. Department of Education.

Garmston, R., & Wellman, B. (1995). Adaptive schools in a quantum universe. *Educational Leadership, 52*(7), 6–12.

Hord, S. M. (1997). *Professional learning communities: Communities of continuous inquiry and improvement.* Austin, TX: Southwest Educational Development Laboratory.

Little, J. W. (1982). Norms of collegiality and experimentation: Workplace conditions of school success. *American Educational Research Journal, 19*(3), 325–340.

Senge, P. (1990). *The fifth discipline: The art and practice of the learning organization.* New York: Currency Doubleday.

CHAPTER 10

DEFINING CHANGE FACILITATOR STYLE

Different Approaches Produce Different Results

His attitude is so positive that it is often mistaken for expertise! You can't help but like him.

As she uses a finger to draw several loops that converge in the air, a staff person observes, "The principal draws in things I didn't even know were out there. She always is thinking about how all the pieces can fit together."

Everything is so well organized and gets done on time. He always focuses first on resources. He is like a cook who follows the recipe.

Leaders and leadership are popular topics for discussion and research. There are debates about whether a certain person is a good leader and what the characteristics of effective leadership are. There are literally thousands of research studies that examine characteristics and behaviors of leaders in a never-ending quest to answer the age-old question of how leaders can make a difference. In this chapter we consider leadership in a special context—*implementing change.* We will examine recent studies that have focused on leadership during change processes and describe how different approaches relate to implementation success. By the end of this chapter, you will have a set of rubrics to assess yourself and leaders you have known. You also will have some clues about how to work with and influence different types of leaders.

FOCUS QUESTIONS

1. What are the important variations in how different leaders facilitate change?
2. How is the concept of style different from behavior?
3. What are the key differences between the Initiator, Manager, and Responder Change Facilitator Styles?
4. Which Change Facilitator Style will be most closely correlated with higher levels of implementation success?
5. Which type of change facilitator do you like to have as a supervisor?
6. Which Change Facilitator Style do you prefer to use when you are in a leadership role?

Each of us has our favorite stories about leaders who were great to work for, the ones who respected our skills and potential, who let us take on extra responsibilities, and who helped us to grow professionally and personally. We also have stories about the leaders who did not trust us, who maintained control over the smallest details, and who would not give genuine consideration to our ideas. And then there are those leaders who were very friendly, who always had time to chat, and who verbally encouraged us to try anything, but in hindsight we can see that they never made a definite decision and that each attempt at change seemed to fall apart during implementation.

These types of experiences with leaders are typical rather than atypical. There are varied approaches to leadership, and different people lead in different ways. Further, there are patterns and similarities among those leaders who do make a difference and among those who do not make a difference. Depending on how the leader leads, the followers and the organization will have very different change process experiences, and the ultimate results of the change will differ as well.

We have identified different approaches to leadership that we call *Change Facilitator Styles,* which are defined by the use of different interventions and of different perspectives about how to approach change processes. Depending on their styles, they send different signals to their staffs and spend their time doing different things. The effects of these different Change Facilitator Styles can be observed in the amount and degree of success that the followers have in implementing and using the change.

In this chapter the concept of Change Facilitator Style and its implications for leaders will be introduced. Although the focus of our research has been on the formal heads of organizations, namely school principals, keep in mind that leadership in change efforts is not something that is done only by the designated administrator(s) at the top. *Everyone who is engaged in change has a responsibility to assist in facilitating the process.* In addition, everyone will have a particular Change Facilitator Style. In other words, although most of the research presented in this chapter was done with school principals, the findings have implications for anyone who is facilitating change.

Two sets of implications of this work on Change Facilitator Style need to be kept in mind: First, regardless of your position in an organization, you have a potential role to play in helping to facilitate the change process, and in doing this you will have your own Change Facilitator Style. (What will it be?) Second, the formally designated leaders of the change process will have their Change Facilitator Styles. (How can you best work with each?) Everyone, whether principal or teacher, plant manager or assembly-line worker, has a potential role in facilitating the change process. Whether they knowingly assume this role and how they go about it is the main topic to be addressed in this chapter. You also will be introduced to some ways to analyze Change Facilitator Styles and to think about implications for working with others in change leadership.

THE HISTORY OF RESEARCH ON LEADERS AND LEADERSHIP

Which way did they go?
How many of them were there?
I must find them!
I am their leader!

This oft-cited refrain summarizes much about leadership in general and especially as it relates to leadership in change. It is used here to introduce you to a number of important questions: What do you believe are the important characteristics of good leaders? What kind of leader do you like to work with? And how do you lead?

The metaphor of a dog-sled team can be used to introduce some of the important differences in the way that leaders lead. Some leaders are like the lead dog. They like to be at the front, checking out the view ahead and breaking trail for those behind them. Others like to lead from within the team. They often say that they are not comfortable with the visibility that comes with being at the front, while those who like the front position point out that the view is always the same for those behind. Still other leaders stay at the back of the sled, like the drivers, riding the rails of the sled, pushing the sled, and barking out commands to those on the team who are not pulling hard enough. Some leaders seem to be more like the spectators and race officials. They watch from the side while the team, sled, and driver travel by. They are ready to evaluate, and occasionally cheer, the performance of the team and driver, but do not enter the race themselves. So again, which kind of leader do you like to be with? How do you lead? And which type do you think makes the biggest difference?

The Legacy of Research on Leadership

Leaders and leadership have been the subject of study and theorizing for most of the twentieth century. In fact, so much has been written about these subjects that there are major anthologies that just summarize the history of study and examination of leaders and leadership (see, for example, Bass, 1990). Earlier studies of leaders examined particular traits, such as height. Different models of leadership have been proposed, such as the important work by Fiedler (1978) suggesting that the style of effective leaders is contingency dependent. In other words, a different style of leader is needed for different situations. Others have studied specific behaviors of leaders in the hopes of identifying a critical set of needed skills and competencies (see, for example, Leithwood & Montgomery, 1982). Many have proposed models of leadership that suggest that how a leader leads needs to be considered across two dimensions: a task dimension and a people, or relationship, dimension (see, for example, Blake & Mouton, 1964). According to some, the "best" leaders are those who exhibit high levels of both task and relationship behaviors. Others advocate shifting the balance of task and relationship behaviors depending on the "maturity" of the followers (see, for example, Hersey & Blanchard, 1988).

This long and extensive legacy of research, theory, and model building about leaders and leadership has focused primarily on business and industry contexts. Very little has been done with education organizations, and even less with leaders and leadership during change processes. One notable exception would be the 60-year history of activity and action research related to *Organizational Development (OD)* (see Chapter 5), which has an extensive legacy of writing about models and practices with implications for schools (see, for example, Schmuck & Runkle, 1994; Miles, 1971). Unfortunately, the research findings indicate that the OD approach has not lasted in school settings (Fullan, Miles, & Taylor, 1980), although there has been a recent revival of interest in applying it in supervision processes (Hall & Shieh, 1998).

Studies of Leaders during the Change Process

Nearly all of the research and models about leaders and leadership had their beginnings in studies of individuals in leadership positions or in theorizing about what people in leadership positions should be like. By contrast, our research on leaders and leadership in change had a very different beginning. Rather than starting with an agenda to look at change leaders, we stumbled onto the need to look at leaders because of some research findings about teacher success and lack of success in implementing change.

As a research team, we were analyzing a very extensive set of data about teachers' Stages of Concern (SoC), Levels of Use (LoU), and Innovation Configurations (IC). We had just completed a two-year study of teachers' implementation of a very innovative science curriculum in a large (80 schools) suburban school district. All of the teachers had participated in carefully designed workshops that were presented by lead teachers. SoC, LoU, and IC map data had been collected twice a year, and the district office change facilitators had devoted themselves to coaching teachers. So we expected that at the end of two years all of the teachers would be at the same point in terms of implementation. Wrong!

In the SoC, LoU, and IC map data we found very distinct variations that appeared to represent school by school differences! We were able to sort the schools into three groups according to how the implementation data differed. To use the SoC data as an illustration, in Group A were schools that exhibited a gradual lowering of self and task concerns and an arousal of Stage 4 Consequence concerns. In Group B were schools that revealed generally flat concerns profiles that were low on all stages. In Group C were schools whose teachers had the "Big W" concerns profile. In other words, they had high Stage 1 Informational concerns, high Stage 3 Management concerns, and a serious "tailing up" on Stage 6 Refocusing concerns. These teachers were not pleased with having unresolved task concerns and had some very strong ideas about what should be done to make things better.

We were puzzled about how to explain these data. All the teachers had received the same district workshops and the same curriculum materials. The schools were generally alike in terms of student socioeconomic status and the like, and they all had had two years to implement the new curriculum. So we decided to present the three stacks of school data to our district change facilitator colleagues and ask how they would explain the clustering of the schools. With very little hesitation they said: "It's the principals! In the schools in Group A, the principals are very active and supportive of teachers using the new curriculum. In Group B the principals are well organized, but they don't push their teachers to go beyond the minimum. In Group C schools, the principals don't help their teachers. They talk a good game, but they don't follow through."

The outcome of these discussions with our school-based colleagues was a set of studies to document and analyze the intervention behaviors of school principals to see, if indeed, what they did as school leaders could be correlated with the extent of teacher implementation success. From these and the earlier studies of teachers engaged in change processes, the concept of Change Facilitator Style emerged. These studies did not originate with some a priori model of leadership or theories about what good leaders do. As with other CBAM studies, the work on Change Facilitator Style came out of what happens to real people living and working to implement change.

THE CONCEPT OF CHANGE FACILITATOR STYLE

Interestingly, as obvious as it is, many school district leaders, staff developers, and researchers miss the fact that *all principals are not the same*. Principals view their role and priorities differently, and they operationally define their roles differently in terms of what they actually do each day. One implication of this fact was that in studying principals as change facilitators, we needed to sample schools so that we had representatives of different ways in which principals lead change efforts. Our emerging concept of Change Facilitator Style provided the means for doing this. We could select study schools using the descriptions of principal leadership that had been discovered in comparing schools in Groups A, B, and C.

Note that so far we have been talking about "style." For the rest of this chapter, it will be very important to understand that there is a big difference between the concept of style and the idea of leader behaviors. Style represents the overall tone and pattern of a leader's approach. Behaviors are a leader's individual, moment-to-moment actions, such as talking to a teacher in the corridor, chairing a staff meeting,

---

GUIDING PRINCIPLES OF CHANGE FACILITATOR STYLES

1. Change Facilitator Style is the overall pattern that is derived from accumulated observations of individual leader behaviors. CF Style provides the context for understanding and interpreting the moment-to-moment actions of a change leader.
2. Initiators focus on doing what will be best in the long term for students and the school, rather than primarily on making people happy in the short term.
3. Schools with Manager leaders attain implementation success. However, there is little effort to move beyond the acceptable minimums.
4. Responders ask about concerns but are less active in attempting to resolve them and in facilitating change. They just tend to keep checking on how people are feeling about issues in general.
5. Influencing leaders with different CF Styles requires customized approaches. Responders are most interested in staff feelings, Managers focus most on administrative and organizational efficiency, while Initiators want to hear the facts and reasons about how student success will be affected.
6. Change Facilitator Styles do not change quickly. Individual behavior will change from setting to setting, and each action will be interpreted in terms of the overall style. But a change in one's style, if it occurs at all, appears to be caused only by a major change in circumstances or the passage of time.

---

writing a memo, and talking on the telephone. The overall accumulated pattern and tone of these behaviors form a person's style. Interestingly, more effective leaders understand that each of their individual behaviors is important in and of itself as well as a sign of their overall style.

Three Change Facilitator Styles

Our studies of principals revealed that there are three distinct Change Facilitator (CF) Styles: the Initiator, the Manager, and the Responder. We know that these three do not represent all possible styles, but, they do represent three contrasting approaches that are regularly seen in change processes. In this section, each of these CF styles is described. To make the descriptions come alive, we have included some of our favorite examples and anecdotes from the studies. Formal definitions of each Change Facilitator Style are presented in Figure 10.1.

While reading these descriptions keep in mind several questions:

1. How well do these descriptions match with leaders you have experienced?
2. Which CF Style do you think is most highly correlated with greater teacher success in implementing changes?
3. Which CF Style do you use?

FIGURE 10.1   Descriptions of Three Change Facilitator Styles

Initiators have clear, decisive long-range policies and goals that include but transcend implementation of the current innovation. They tend to have very strong beliefs about what good schools and teaching should be like and work intensely to attain this vision. Decisions are made in relation to their goals for the school and in terms of what they believe to be best for students, which is based on current knowledge of classroom practice. Initiators have strong expectations for students, teachers, and themselves. They convey and monitor these expectations through frequent contacts with teachers and voicing clear explications of how the school is to operate and how teachers are to teach. When they feel it is in the best interest of their school, particularly the students, initiators will seek changes in district programs or policies, or they will reinterpret them to suit the school's needs. Initiators will be adamant but not unkind; they solicit input from staff and then make decisions in terms of the goals of the school, even if some are ruffled by their directness and high expectations.

Managers focus on resources and organization of activities. They both demonstrate responsive behaviors toward situations and people, and initiate actions in support of the change effort. The variations in their behavior seem to be linked to their rapport with teachers and central office staff and to their understanding and acceptance of a particular change effort. Managers work hard to provide resources and basic support to facilitate teachers' use of an innovation. They keep teachers informed about decisions and are sensitive to teacher needs. They will defend their teachers from what are perceived as excessive demands. When they learn that the central office wants something to happen in their school, they become very involved with their teachers in making it happen, yet they do not typically initiate attempts to move beyond the basics of what is imposed.

Responders place heavy emphasis on allowing teachers and others the opportunity to take the lead. They believe their primary role is to maintain a smoothly running school by focusing on traditional administrative tasks, by keeping teachers content, and by treating students well. They view teachers as strong professionals who are able to carry out their instructional role with little guidance. Responders emphasize the personal side of their relationships with teachers and others. Before they make decisions, they often give everyone an opportunity to have input so as to consider their feelings or to allow others to make the decision. A related characteristic is their tendency to make decisions in terms of immediate circumstances rather than longer range instructional or school goals. This seems to arise in part from their desire to please others and in part from their more limited vision of how their school and staff should change in the future.

Initiator Change Facilitators.   Initiators have clear and strongly held visions about what their school should be like. They are motivators who are continually articulating what the school can become. When issues come up, they listen to all sides and quickly make decisions based on what they think will be best for students and what will move the school closer to their vision. Initiators set high expectations for teachers. They expect them to be engaged in teaching, supporting students, and contributing to the effort to continually improve the whole school. For example, one elementary school had a goal of children writing every week. To encourage teachers and students in this effort, the Initiator principal asked teachers to give him samples of all students' writing each week. He then displayed the samples around the school halls and common areas.

Initiators push teachers, students, parents, and personnel in the district office to support the things that will help students learn, teachers teach, and the school move forward. Sometimes they push too hard, which makes some feel pressured and uncomfortable. They also are knowledgeable about how the system operates and on occasion will work with the philosophy that it is easier to seek forgiveness than prior approval.

Initiators consciously question and analyze what *they* and others do. They reflect on what others have told them, on what issues may be emerging, and on how well tasks are being accomplished. They listen to teachers and students. They not only make decisions but consciously work to make sure that all decisions and actions move people and the school in the desired direction. They are focused on assessment, instruction, and curriculum. Initiators also have a great deal of passion. They care deeply about their students, teachers, and the school. Their pushing, monitoring, and bending of the rules are done to support everyone in doing his or her best. They also have what we are calling *strategic sense,* which means that they do not lose sight of the big picture while they are doing the day-to-day activities. They anticipate what might happen and envision alternative responses that they may need to employ.

Manager Change Facilitators.   Managers approach the leadership of change efforts with a different set of behaviors and emphases. They are skilled at making their school run like a well-oiled machine. They focus first on resources, schedules, and logistics. The bells ring on time, everyone knows how to get supplies, schedules are planned well in advance, and the various forms are filled out correctly and processed promptly. As proposals for change are made by teachers or those outside the school, Managers do not rush in. When asked by an external facilitator or a teacher to try something different, their first response will likely be, "Well, that is an interesting idea, but my teachers are real busy right now." Managers buy time, which they use to study and learn more about the change and to consider whether they should have the school engage with it.

An important consequence of this delaying is that teachers and the school are protected to some extent. This dampening of the initiation of change also buys time for the principal and teachers to learn about the proposed change and to prepare for an efficient implementation. As a result, when changes are implemented, they tend to proceed smoothly and to acceptable levels.

Manager principals also try to do many things themselves rather than delegating to others. They arrive at school very early in the morning, stay late in the evening, and return on the weekends to do more of the tasks. They work to meet the needs of the staff and to get the jobs done. In many ways, they demand more of themselves than they do of others. They often decide, "It is easier for me to do it right the first time than to have someone else do it and then have to fix it."

IMPLICATIONS FOR LEADERS FACILITATING CHANGE

Being successful and effective in working with different Change Facilitator Style leaders can be a challenge. It also can be interesting and very rewarding. Each CF Style—Initiatior, Manager, and Responder—brings with it certain advantages and disadvantages. Supervisors, coaches of leaders, and their followers will find that success in working with each leader requires different strategies.

SELECTING A PILOT/DEMONSTRATION SITE

Suppose there was a need to establish a demonstration site for an innovative program, or some other new approach such as a magnet school or a new manufacturing technology. Which CF Style would be best, and why? The Initiator would seem to be the logical choice. However, there will need to be a sales presentation. If the Initiator sees how the new initiative will benefit his or her organization and its clients (teachers or customers), then there will be full support for implementing the pilot. However, if the Initiator is not convinced that there are benefits for clients and the organization, then it will be a hard sell, and quite likely little active support for the initiative. The Initiator will ask, "How will *we* and *our* clients benefit?" The Manager will state, "*I* will need more resources to do this." One Manager who one of the authors has worked with will usually go further by stating an ultimatum based in the need for more resources: "If *I* don't get more resources, then *my* unit will have to stop what it is doing." The Responder will say, "Go ahead, *you* do it." The italics have been inserted here to point out the differences in frame of reference for each CF Style.

SUPERVISION AND COACHING DIFFERENT CF STYLES

Supervisors who wish to differentiate their working with each of the leaders "below" them in the organization can use the CF Styles as a guide. The same can be done by coaches of leaders. Responders will generally understand less and get less done, so closer supervision and more frequent contact will be necessary. In our experiences, Responders often do not understand the deeper reasons and nuances. They tend to focus more on the surface and count on their friendly, non-threatening style to carry the day. At the same time, they have the potential to be busy behind the scenes, spreading gossip and rumors with peers.

Managers focus heavily on the perceived need for more resources, no matter what the issue or opportunity. Some are fun to coach, especially those who are interested in becoming more effective as leaders. Their efficiency and organization skills can be very important to implementation success and organization effectiveness.

Initiators are the ones who focus first on the needs of clients/students and are continually looking for programs and strategies that can make a positive difference. One of the consequences for their supervisors and coaches is that Initiators don't wait for you to come to them. They come to you! They will push for what they want for their unit. They also make their peers uncomfortable, since they will push and compete with them. As a result, one of the bur-

(continued)

IMPLICATIONS FOR LEADERS FACILITATING CHANGE CONTINUED

dens for their supervisor is having to spend time in resolving conflicts and perceptions of favoritism. Problems also can develop when Initiators "forget" about a rule or procedure and just go ahead and do what they think will be best for their unit.

LEADERSHIP TEAM DIFFERENCES

The kind of dynamics inside leadership teams will vary CF Style of the leader. In CBAM research a special role has been identified for what we call the *Second Change Facilitator,* or *consigliere.* This person has a key role in change process success.

In the Initiator-led team, the Second CF does as many interventions as does the leader. They truly work as a horizontal team with both going out and working with the staff in complementary ways. Contrary to what might be predicted, it is the Initiator-led team that is most collegial and collaborative. There is a shared agenda. Each member of the team will give the same answer to questions and will have the same priorities in working with others.

In the Manager CF Style team, the Second Change Facilitator makes fewer interventions, such as one-legged-interviews, and the Manager makes more. In fact, when compared to Initiators and Responders, the Managers make significantly more interventions. However, the total number of interventions across all members of the Change Facilitator Team will be highest with the Initiator-led team. In addition, the relationship between the Manager leader and the consigliere is different from what has been observed with Initiators. It is much more of a supervisor–subordinate dynamic.

The Responder CF Team is different again. There are significantly fewer interventions in support of the change process and the Second CF/consigliere does not have clear and ongoing support to facilitate implementation. The Responder also is significantly less active.

Each of these CF Teams requires different approaches to supervision and coaching. The Initiator team will keep on going. The Manager team will get the job done and tend to stop. And the Responder-led teams will tend not to get organized or to be able to focus on facilitating implementation.

Responder Change Facilitators.   Responders approach leadership with a primary focus on what is happening now. They do not have many ideas about what the school should be like in the future or where education is going. Instead their attention is on others' present concerns and perceptions. Therefore, when they do one-legged interviews with teachers and others, their purpose is to discover concerns and perceptions about current topics and issues. Responders also spend time on the phone checking with other principals about their perceptions of what the assistant superintendent was talking about in the last principals' meeting "when she said . . . ." They engage in the same sort of discussions with community members and students. The pattern to their talk is chatting, social, and listening to concerns.

Responders are most willing for others to take the lead. For example, if a teacher wants to try a different curriculum approach, the Responder principal will say, "Go ahead. You know we always like to be innovative in this school." If someone from the district office or a nearby university wants to start a new project in the school, the Responder will welcome that person as part of the overall goal of trying to keep everyone happy. As a result, many disparate projects and activities can be going on in different parts of the school.

In contrast to Initiators, Responders delay making decisions. They want to have first heard from everyone about their concerns and perceptions. When they do have to make a decision they tend to do it at or shortly after the deadline. And, the decision will be most heavily influenced by the last person who talked to them. Thus, it is possible for a teacher or someone else to influence a decision right up to the last moment.

Another part of the Responder CF pattern is the tendency to minimize the size and significance of proposed changes. They often feel that a change proposal is not as innovative as it advocates claim. "So what's the big deal?" a Responder may say, "We have been doing most of this already; you just have a different name for it." Also, Responders tend to hire strong and independent teachers believing, "They know more about teaching than I do. It is my job to work with the community and do the other things so that they can teach."

DISCUSSION AND IMPLICATIONS OF CHANGE FACILITATOR STYLE

Now that the different Change Facilitator Styles have been introduced, it is important to think about some of the implications, issues, and questions. If the style descriptors offer nothing else, they can help you think about yourself and what you think are important characteristics of leaders during change processes. The different CF Styles described here do not represent all principals, nor do all principals fit perfectly into one of these styles. However, they do appear to represent the more commonly found approaches to change leadership.

A Continuum of Change Facilitator Styles

One way to think about the relationship of one CF Style to the others is to place them on a 100-point number line (see Figure 10.2). The stereotypic Responder is positioned at point 30, the stereotypic Manager at point 60, and the Initiator at point 90. Then, by using the paragraph definitions (Figure 10.1), it is possible to envision what persons who are combinations of the three styles would be like. For example, one principal might behave somewhat like a Responder but overall tend to be more of a Manager. That person could be placed around point 50 on the number line. A leader who is developing a clearer vision about the school and is sometimes thinking of more long-term goals might be somewhere between the manager and initiator CF Styles, around point 75.

FIGURE 10.2   A Continuum of Change Facilitator Styles

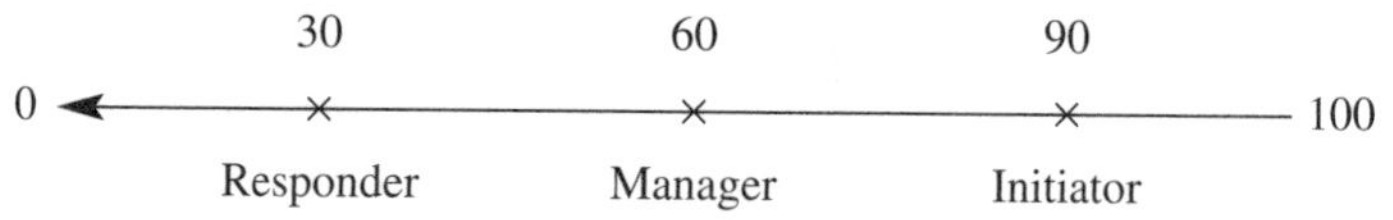

Other CF Styles can be imagined by envisioning what people would be like at the extreme ends of the continuum. For example, a leader that scores above 100 would be a despot that does not listen and just decrees, while a person at the 0 end would display an extremely laissez-faire approach, neither taking a position nor helping with the change. Off the chart, far to the left would be the covert saboteur who works behind the scenes to scuttle the change effort.

Additional Research and Support for Change Facilitator Styles

One could question whether these different CF Styles actually exist. How can we be assured that they are not just figments of the authors' imaginations? Addressing this question is one of the important purposes of research. This is also one reason we took the time in the introduction to this chapter to explain the background studies that led to the hypothesis that there are different Change Facilitator Styles. In this section, some of the related and more recent research studies are introduced.

The first research study on Change Facilitator Styles was the Principal/Teacher Interaction (PTI) Study (Hord & Huling-Austin, 1986). In this study full-time ethonographers systematically documented the interventions of nine elementary school principals for an entire school year. Implementation was assessed by measuring teachers' Stages of Concern, Levels of Use, and Innovation Configurations. Statistically significant differences were found in the quantity and quality of the principals' interventions and that they could be clustered according to the three hypothesized Change Facilitator Styles (Hall et al., 1984; Hall & Hord, 1987).

Studies by a number of other researchers in the United States have independently confirmed that principal intervention behaviors can be clustered according to these three styles (see, for example, Trohoski, 1984; Entrekin, 1991). In addition, studies have been done in Belgium (Vandenberghe, 1988) and in Australia (Schiller, 1991) with similar results. In a major test of the cross-cultural generalizability of the three Change Facilitator Styles, Shieh (1996) documented the intervention behaviors of six elementary school principals in Taiwan and observed the same differences in style and surprisingly similar anecdotal examples of perspectives and approaches to change leadership. Thus, although they certainly do not represent all possibilities, these three Change Facilitator Styles do have a basis in systematic studies in a number of settings and do offer a way to think more holistically about change leadership.

Research Relating Change Facilitator Style to Implementation Success

The relationship between principal Change Facilitator Style and teacher success in implementation has been studied also. For the PTI study, the CBAM diagnostic dimensions of SoC, LoU, and IC provided very useful benchmarks, or mileposts, for assessing the degree of implementation. Teachers who moved to higher Levels of Use of more sophisticated configurations, with reduction of Self and Task concerns and arousal of Impact concerns, would be considered as having had more implementation success. Their degree of implementation success could be compared with the intervention behaviors of their principals and the principals' Change Facilitator Style. In most of the studies cited above, this comparison was made. In the original PTI Study a correlation of .74 was found between Change Facilitator Style and teacher implementation success. In the other studies (for example, Schiller, 1991, 2002, 2003; Vandenberghe, 1988; and Shieh, 1996), similar patterns have been observed.

The general finding was that teachers with Initiator principals have the highest levels of implementation success. Teachers with Manager principals are successful too, but not to the same extent as teachers in Initiator schools. Teachers with Responder principals are rated a distant third in terms of implementation success. One way to summarize these findings is to suggest that the Initiator principals "make it happen." They have the vision, passion, and push to help things move in the desired direction. They make decisions quickly and there is consistency. Manager principals "help it happen." They see that things are well organized. They protect their teachers, but when implementation becomes an objective, it is accomplished efficiently. However, unlike the Initiators, they do not have the excitement and energy to keep doing more.

The conditions in schools led by Responder principals are quite different. These leaders "let it happen." Yes, they do listen to perceptions and concerns, but they seldom resolve issues with certainty. They continue to be open to new input and as a result do not bring closure, or else will hear another piece of information and change their minds. They are statistically significantly less active in terms of the number of change-related interventions they make. The result for teachers is less implementation success and a tendency to have "Big W" SoC profiles (see Figure 7.4). Shieh (1996) observed that in the first months of implementation teachers in Responder schools tend to use more of the less desirable variations of the innovation, whereas teachers in Initiator schools tend to use more of the desirable variations.

Metaphors for Change Facilitator Styles

Metaphors can be a useful way to summarize a great deal of information and ideas. A metaphor that should help in thinking about the totality of each CF Style is that of a game.

The Initiator is a chess player. Just as chess has many pieces, each with its own rules for being moved, the Initiator sees the individual differences in the school's people and activities. And just as good chess players use strategies and anticipate many moves ahead, Initiators not only engage in doing the day-to-day activities of change leadership but are also constantly thinking about what needs to be done next. Most importantly, Initiators have several strategies in mind in anticipation of possible scenarios that could unfold.

Manager leaders play a board game too, but it is a simpler one—checkers. There are different pieces and rules of movement, but the view of the organization is less complicated. With checkers there are tactics rather than strategies, prediction is simpler, and winning is less complex. Still, in checkers, as in the Initiator style, there is a sustained purpose to the actions.

The game metaphor for Responders is that of flipping coins. Each flip of the coin is an act that is independent of the one that came before and the one that will follow. To a surprising degree, this is the case for the intervention behaviors of Responders. Each action tends to be taken independently. Much less consideration is given to stringing together such actions as individual one-legged interviews, faculty meetings, announcements, and notes to teachers. For example, a teacher may be told at the beginning of the school year that they are responsible for maintaining the materials closet, but the Responder principal never checks to see if the teacher is doing the task. Interventions do not accumulate to make tactics and strategies or to develop coherent themes that teachers can see.

UNDERLYING DIMENSIONS OF CHANGE FACILITATOR STYLE

In more recent research we have been examining some of the underlying dimensions of Change Facilitator Style. For this work we have developed the Change Facilitator Style Questionnaire (CFSQ) that asks teachers how they view the intervention actions of their principal (Hall & George, 1988, 1999; Vandenberghe, 1988). Through this work we have identified six underlying dimensions of change Facilitator Style, each of which can be rated separately. Different combinations of these dimensions then describe different Change Facilitator Styles. The six dimensions of CF Style are defined in Appendix 4. Three examples of principal profiles, identified by the CFSQ, are presented in Figure 10.3; each represents the norm group for one of the styles. Profile interpretation is guided by the six scale definitions that are presented in Appendix 4.

Teachers see Initiator principals as being high on Social/Informal, Formal/Meaningful, Administrative Efficiency, and Vision and Planning dimensions. This profile fits with what would be expected from the earlier descriptions of Initiators, with the possible exception of being high on the Social/Informal scale. This research finding brought home an important point: Initiators have many one-legged interviews that not only are related to use of the change/innovation (Formal/Meaningful) but also deal with personal and general topics of discussion (Social/Informal). In other words, Initiators talk with teachers about how the change process is going and find time for social chat too.

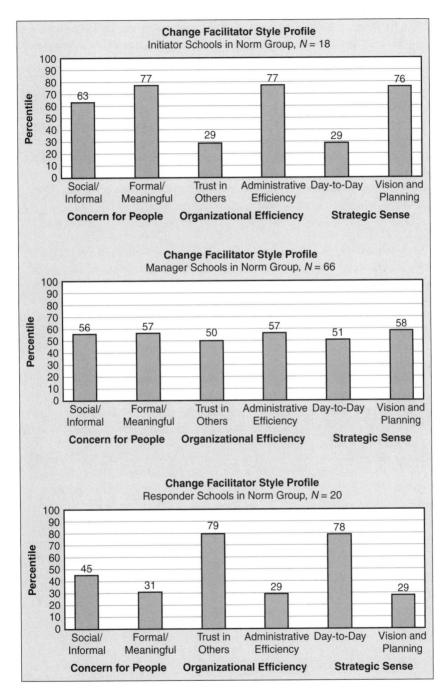

FIGURE 10.3   Stereotypical Change Facilitator Style Profiles for Stereotypical Initiator, Manager, and Responder Styles

The CFSQ profile for Manager principals is relatively flat and at the midlevel of each scale. Teachers see Manager principals as doing about the same amount of intervening relative to each of the six CFSQ scales.

Teachers view Responder principals as being high on the dimensions of Trust in Others and Day-to-Day. These findings are consistent with the Change Facilitator Style descriptions presented earlier in this chapter. Responders tend not to focus on making the school run efficiently nor on engaging in long-term Vision and Planning. What is particularly interesting about this profile is the low score on Social/Informal. Based on our description of the Responder style, one would expect that a Responder would be rated highly on informal, nontask-related talk and chat, but this is not how they are seen by their teachers.

Changing Change Facilitator Style

How easy do you think it is to change one's CF Style? Take the case of a very talented Initiator elementary school principal (see Figure 10.4.) At the time of our study, she had been the principal at this school for nearly 10 years. She and her school have received a number of significant state and national awards. This school had developed well and was continually doing new and exciting things for children. As would be expected in a school led by an Initiator, in the past the teachers had rated this principal very high on Vision and Planning. They had seen her as having some focus on the Day-to-Day and Administrative Efficiency dimensions, which Initiators consider to be the foundation on which they are able to lead change processes. She had had a high score on Formal/Meaningful, which we would expect as well, since Initiator change facilitators spend a lot of time in one-on-one interactions that are directly related to teacher use of the change. The Social/Informal scale of this principal's CFSQ

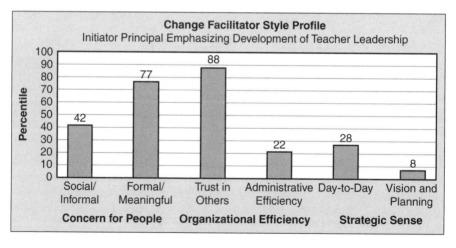

FIGURE 10.4   Change Facilitator Style for an Initiator Principal Emphasizing Development of Teacher Leadership

profile was what would be predicted too, since Initiators spend time informally and personally with their staffs. That was her CFSQ profile in the past. The accompanying CF profile (Figure 10.4) shows that leaders can change their style. However, the CF Style change described here did not occur until the principal had been in the school a number of years.

The important as well as interesting points in this profile, which are not characteristics of all Initiators, are the very high score on Trust in Others and the low Vision and Planning score. When the principal was asked about these changes, she pointed out that she had been at the school long enough so that she was not doing as much leading by herself. Instead she now was trying to develop and empower her teachers to do the leading for various projects and tasks. She has teachers doing more presentations around the state, and she is pushing her teachers to lead more within the school. As a result of this shift in her style, her teachers now rate her much higher on the Trust in Others scale and low on Vision and Planning.

It is not easy to change one's style. It is easier to consciously work on adjusting one's behaviors so that they fit each situation. In other words, change facilitators are not likely to change their style, but they most certainly should do different things depending on the current SoC, LoU, and IC of their clients.

CHANGE FACILITATOR STYLE AS A SIGNIFICANT FACTOR IN CHANGE

Change Facilitator Style is an important factor in determining change process success. Another major theme in this book has been how the actions of change facilitators accumulate to form the larger patterns of interventions that we call tactics and strategies (see Chapter 9).

Of course, the three CF Styles of Initiator, Manager, and Responder do not represent all the possibilities but rather certain basic types that differ in a number of important ways. The concepts and distinctions of Change Facilitator Style can have various applications, some of which have been suggested above; others are summarized next.

Change Facilitator Style as a Heuristic

The concept of Change Facilitator Style can serve as a heuristic, or a device that helps us think about what we should do in leading change processes. Using the CFS concepts, we can ask ourselves questions such as:

1. What kind of Change Facilitator Style do I want to have?
2. In the successful change processes of which I have been a part, what was the Change Facilitator Style of the leader?
3. When I interview for a new position, what characteristics will I look for in my new supervisor?

Working with Different Change Facilitator Styles

Change Facilitator Styles also offer clues about why and how to be more influential with different leaders. Each leader by definition will be emphasizing particular aspects of the change process and elements of use of the innovation. They consider different factors when making decisions, and the amount of time that they need to make decisions varies considerably. Teachers and others who have determined the leader's style will have more influence. They also will be more accurate in predicting what the leader will decide. For example, when teachers would like their principal to make a decision in a particular direction, what they say to influence the decision making and when and how they say it, will need to be adjusted to fit the principal's CF Style.

Whatever the issue to be resolved, Initiators will want to have reasons and evidence that explain how the decision will affect student success and advance the school. They will expect teachers to have well-developed ideas and clear descriptions, supported by facts. Timing is important, since Initiators tend to think far ahead. They like to be able to anticipate what will work as well as what might go wrong. Providing them with information early in the process is key. Once they have heard what is being suggested, they may need to consult with others, but will make a decision fairly quickly.

In contrast, Responders will be less interested in hearing specifics and more likely to encourage "going ahead" without careful thought or fully understanding all that may follow. In their effort to be encouraging, they frequently will agree to two or more initiatives that overlap and may actually compete. In other words, do not count on continuity of support and follow-through. One piece of good news is that Responders will allow and even encourage an array of change initiatives. Don't forget, however, that if what is being asked involves a major decision or may create controversy, Responders are very slow to agree. They will want plenty of time for talk, which may seem like a way to avoid making a decision. A good approach when dealing with a Responder is to begin with casual social chat and then raise the general topic. An important side strategy would be to regularly and continually monitor other related decisions that the Responder is making.

When making a request or a suggestion to Manager leaders, remember that they will want to hear about the time, logistic, and cost implications. The structuring of work and scheduling are important considerations for them. Be prepared to know what resources will be needed and have suggestions about how your ideas can be managed. Managers can decide quite quickly if what is being asked is in line with initiatives that are already up and running. However, an entirely new proposal is likely to run into the dampening effect, which results from a combination of Managers' desire to protect and maintain stability, and their need to first study and ponder.

The Relationship of Change Facilitator Style to Other Factors

The possible relationships between CF Style and other characteristics of leaders have not been studied, although many hypotheses can be offered. For example, there appear to be connections between CF Style and aspects of personality. Some forms of intelligence and creativity may be at play as well. However, there have been no empirical studies of these issues, nor of the Stages of Concern of leaders with different Change Facilitator Styles. One hypothesis would be that Initiators move more rapidly from Self to Task to Impact concerns during a change process. Another would be that Responders rarely have high Impact concerns. In testing any of these hypotheses, it must be remembered that change in Stages of Concern will, at least in part, be related to the context. What happens to people's concerns, even for leaders, is to some degree dependent on what is going on with others above and below them in the same organizational context.

Changes in Change Facilitator Style

For the most part, Change Facilitator Styles do not change quickly. From all that we know, a person's CF Style is quite stable. It does not change from day to day or from innovation to innovation. Of course, there will be changes in behaviors, the intervention actions that are taken moment to moment and day to day. The priority that a leader gives to different innovations can vary, as can the leader's actions, but the person's overall Change Facilitator Style will remain constant.

USING CHANGE FACILITATOR STYLE CONSTRUCTS AND TOOLS TO ASSESS AND STUDY IMPLEMENTATION

At this point the existence of the three Change Facilitator Styles in school principals has been established through research studies in the Australia, Belgium, Taiwan, and the United States. There even has been a study of change facilitator style of officers in the U.S. Navy (Jehue, 2000). Still, additional studies are needed to test how well the CF constructs hold up in different context. Examining relevance and implications of CF Style in higher education and business leaders could be especially informative.

Another promising area for study is examination of the relationship between the CF Style of the leader and the functioning of the leadership team. What is the balancing of tasks and functions between the leader and the other members of the leadership team? In larger change initiatives and in larger organizations there will likely be a third, and perhaps a fourth, change Facilitator. How do these roles function and interrelate? How do they change with different CF style leaders?

The bottom-line question of relationship of leadership to change success needs much more study. Given time constraints, it is most likely that short-term and smaller change initiatives will be the subjects of study. In many places leaders turn over too quickly to do longer-term studies. However, longitudinal studies are needed that document what happens when leaders do stay in place and when the changes being implemented are large and/or strategic.

This assertion of only limited short-term change in style being likely contradicts the position of a number of current leadership experts. For example, various workshops are offered to help leaders analyze and change their "style." The clear implication is that workshop participants will learn, in these two- or three-day sessions, how to change their overall approach to leadership. In other words, they will learn how to change their style. Our research and experience suggest that only in times of major changes in context can leaders quickly change their overall style. Even then, we see more cases where the leader has been unable to adapt his or her style to sudden changes, than we have of successful short-term change to match the new realities. One quick way to test our position on the limited capability of leaders to change their style is to look at political leaders to see whether their styles change. Think about recent American presidents, each of whom was associated with an overall style, which the press made stereotypical in many ways. Can you think of times when these presidents broke away from their preferred/dominant style? How long did it last?

The Relationship of Change Facilitator Style to Organizational Variables

Change Facilitator Style can be related to organizational climate and organizational culture. It seems reasonable to expect that there would be relationships between the Change Facilitator Style of the principal and the climate and culture of the school. How teachers feel about their school and their perceptions of what counts should be a reflection of the style of the leader. In a few of the early studies, estimates of organizational climate were found to be related to the principals' Change Facilitator Style. The general trend was that organizational climate was more positive in schools with Manager and Initiator principals than with Responder principals. Studies of Belgian schools (Staessens, 1993) have clearly documented that the organizational culture is much more positive and professional in schools with principals whose style more closely resembled the Initiator. Again, the organizational culture in schools with Responder principals seems to be much less healthy and professional. This topic is explored further in Chapter 12.

■ ■ ■ ■ ■ ▬▬▬▬▬▬▬▬▬▬▬▬▬▬▬▬▬▬▬▬▬▬▬▬▬▬▬▬▬

V I G N E T T E
PRINCIPAL SUCCESSION

One of the interesting applications of the work in Change Facilitator Style is its use in envisioning different scenarios when there is a change of principals. This analysis could be done from one or more perspectives. For example, if you have accepted the position of principal, you should be interested in finding out about the Change Facilitator Style of your predecessor. You could also be interested in this analysis if you are a teacher in a school that is going through a turnover in principals, or if you are on the interview committee or in the district office with an assignment to advise on the selection of a new principal for a partic-

V I G N E T T E CONTINUED

ular school. In any of these cases, having an understanding of CF Style concepts would be helpful. They can be used to understand the kind of leader the school needs next and to anticipate what the problems will be in the transition. Let's imagine what some of the transitions could be like. To do this we will use a combination of real cases and hypothetical examples.

Frequently, an Initiator principal is hired to replace a Responder. Consider the setting that the newly assigned Initiator will enter. To begin, Responder-led schools are characterized by the "Big W" concerns profile (see Figure 7.4). Teachers are not happy about their continually high Stage 3 Management concerns which is reflected in the "tailing up" on Stage 6. They have some very strong ideas about how things ought to be. Remember too that a Responder principal does not make clear and final decisions. We also know that in a Responder school a small clique of teachers will have more control over what happens and a large number of teachers will have little say in what occurs. In addition, each teacher tends to be strong and independent, because the Responders attitude is, "I hire strong teachers who know more about teaching than I do." The result is that the teachers rarely agree on anything, ranging from which texts to use to where to place the coffee pot.

Administrators in the district office are delighted that a well-known Initiator principal has agreed to take over this school and "turn it around." This principal is known for having a strong focus on student success, and she insists that all the teachers work toward the betterment of the school: "My expectation is that they should lead, follow, or get the hell out of the way."

Given your understanding of Change Facilitator Style, what do you predict will happen in this situation? Will the transition go smoothly? What kinds of issues will be problematic? Will students be more or less successful? And what will the district office administrators do as the scenario unfolds?

In our case files are a number of examples of a transition from Responder to Initiator Style. One of the opening steps for Initiators is to study closely the achievement data of students and the records of the teachers. The Initiator arrives with a set of key themes, such as "treat students as you want to be treated," that she emphasizes repeatedly.

In our case study of the previous Responder principal, there was an unequal distribution of resources, with certain teachers getting more and some getting little. The newly arrived Initiator principal expects that resources will be distributed evenly and that there will be no favoritism. She also presses for teachers to use certain teaching practices and curriculum materials. All of the new principal's actions are intended to move things in the direction of her vision.

The reactions of teachers are aligned with how their influence has been affected and the degree of change that is expected of them. The clique of teachers that had more influence with the Responder principal are unhappy with the changes. In fact, some of them are complaining to the district administrators, and some even go directly to the school board. When asked, teachers who were not part of the influential clique but who are now being treated fairly express appreciation for the new principal, but they do not express their satisfaction to the district administrators or school board.

Typically, the administrators in the district office start to worry when they hear that things are not going well at the school. In this case, as with a number of similar transitions that we have observed, the district administrators maintained a hands-off stance, leaving the

(continued)

■ ■ ■ ■ ■ ■

Initiator principal to sink or swim, on her own. One district administrator observed, "Well, I don't know if Teresa is going to make it." Ironically this was the same administrator that placed Teresa in this situation. Rather than moving to address the concerns of the complaining teachers or to overtly encourage and support the new principal, the district administrators merely listened to the one-sided reports from the school. Fortunately, this vignette can have a happy ending. Two years later Teresa was acclaimed for having turned the school around.

Obviously there is more to this case that could be told. The purpose here was to briefly introduce the strategy of using Change Facilitator Style concepts to examine transitions in school principals. In thinking about sucessions, it is important to consider the CF Style of the departing as well as the incoming leaders. It is also necessary to understand what the school has been like and what the new principal will expect it to become. Remember too that teachers, parents, district office administrators, and students may perceive and consider aspects of the principals' CF Style differently.

VIGNETTE CRITIQUE QUESTIONS

1. What do you see as being the critical characteristics of the Responder and the Initiator in this vignette? Was there a clear change in leadership style? How did the leaders differ in what they considered to be important? What should the district administrators have done?

2. What is the Change Facilitator Style of your current principal/leader? Describe some of the things that you have learned to do to work effectively with this person. How do you think your role/work would change if your principal/leader had a different CF Style?

SUMMARY

In this chapter, the focus has been on characteristics of those who lead change processes. Three Change Facilitator Styles have been proposed and confirmed through studies that documented the moment-to-moment and day-to-day intervention behaviors of principals. Findings from research have been used to illustrate and explain these different approaches to change leadership. One important point that was made early in this chapter was that *everyone* who is part of a change process has the opportunity, and some responsibility, to help lead. Also, attention must be given to distinguishing between facilitators' individual actions or behaviors and their overall style. As will be discussed in Chapter 11, the very same action by leaders with different Change Facilitator Styles will be perceived and interpreted very differently by their followers. In other words, often what counts is not what you do but how others interpret what you do.

The style of change leadership makes a major difference in the implementation success of the followers. There are many implications of being able to distinguish the different Change Facilitator Styles, including their use by the followers, who need to work with leaders with different styles, as is illustrated in the vignette, and by the leaders themselves, who may want to analyze and reflect on their approach to change facilitation. In conclusion, it is crucial to remember that, since principals and other leaders, like students and teachers, are different, we should not treat them as if they were all the same.

DISCUSSION QUESTIONS

1. The research findings described in this chapter describe a strong correlation between teacher success in implementation of educational innovations and the Change Facilitator Style of the principal. Why do you think the correlation is so strong? What is it about the different CF Styles that makes for more, and less, implementation success?

2. In small groups, use specific behavior examples to discuss and analyze the Change Facilitator Style of a leader such as a principal, district superintendent, college president, dean, or department chair. You also could use a state or national leader, such as a governor or U.S. president. Use examples of specific behaviors and actions as well as the more general description of overall style to place this person at a specific point on the continuum presented in Figure 10.2.

3. Develop a brief description of your own Change Facilitator Style and be ready to discuss it. Describe your behaviors during one change effort. In hindsight, what style were you using? What do you now know that you could have done differently?

4. Develop a chart or summary figure that identifies and describes actions and approaches that you should and should not take to positively influence (i.e., to get along with) supervisors each of whom uses one of the three Change Facilitator Styles.

5. One of the heuristic applications of Change Facilitator Styles is to apply them to various succession scenarios. For example, what happens when a Responder follows an Initiator, or when a Responder follows a Responder? A number of succession patterns are possible. Pick one and predict what would happen in the organization with the professional staff, support staff, and change initiatives. Would change occur more quickly, more slowly, or at the same pace? Would the same change initiatives continue? How long would it take for effects of the new leader's style to be detected?

FIELDWORK ACTIVITIES

1. Ask two people to describe how they work to facilitate change. One of the people you interview should have a formal administrative position and be a designated leader. The other person should be one of the so-called followers. When interviewing the follower, keep in mind that at first the person is likely to say that he or she has no lead-

ership role. But delve further by asking how he or she participates in planning meetings or helps other people who are engaged with the change process. Use the CF style constructs to explain how change processes have worked in their setting.

2. Ask someone who has worked for a number of administrators to describe what it was like to interact with leaders with different CF styles. Develop a report on the person's feelings and perceptions when he or she was engaged in change. You also should ask about the times when change was more and less successful.

3. One of the themes in this chapter has been that a critical factor in change process success is the Change Facilitator Style of the leader. If you were to interview prospective leaders of a change effort, what kinds of questions would you ask? Develop a list of the questions and explain how you would expect the answers to differ depending on the person's Change Facilitator Style. You could also use this activity when you are being interviewed for a new position. After all, the leadership style of your prospective supervisor will make a difference in how successful you can be.

CHAPTER 11

CONSTRUCTING UNDERSTANDING OF CHANGE
Intervention Mushrooms

District A: Following the second round of restructuring and downsizing of the district central office, the superintendent announces that it's all done and that everyone should get to work and do what is best for the district. The typical employee response is, "Why should I believe you now?"

District B: Teacher from School R: "I was so surprised last week, when my principal stopped me in the hallway to ask about what I was doing with the new computers. He never asks me anything about what I am doing in the classroom. I wonder what he was after?" Teacher from School I: "I don't see anything unusual about that. My principal is always stopping by and asking me about what I am doing. Sometimes he makes really interesting suggestions." Teacher from School M: "My principal stops by sometimes, but she only wants to see if I have enough supplies."

District C: First teacher: "Wasn't that neat—what the superintendent said in her talk with our school faculty? She really cares about us and what we teach our students." Second teacher: "Yes, it is the same points that she made at the districtwide meeting in the beginning of year. Best teaching practices and student success are important priorities for her." Third teacher: "Yes, it is so great to be in this school district."

The critical point that will be made repeatedly in this chapter is that it is not what you do that counts, but how other people perceive and interpret what you do. As the preceding quotes illustrate, participants in a change process develop a wide range of impressions and interpretations about what the change effort is about and what different change facilitators intend. Just because the leaders of a change effort are well intentioned does not mean that the participants will see them that way. Each participant individually, and each group of participants collectively, will construct their own understandings about what was intended and what it all means. Regardless of what was intended, participant interpretations will have an affect on implementing change.

FOCUS QUESTIONS

1. How is the interpretivist perspective different from the more traditional behaviorist perspective?
2. What is an Intervention Mushroom? Are mushrooms nutritious or poisonous?
3. What kinds of perceptions and interpretations of change will an individual develop at different Stages of Concern?
4. How will an individual's perception and interpretation of an intervention vary depending on the Change Facilitator Style of the intervenor?
5. What kinds of mushrooms develop through group construction of understanding of change processes and events?
6. How is group construction of understanding affected by different Change Facilitator Styles and Stages of Concern?

Fortunately, the constructs and principles about change that have been introduced in the preceding chapters can be used to better understand the different interpretations that people may develop about a change effort. The earlier constructs, such as Stages of Concern and Change Facilitator Style, can be used also to predict the types of interpretations that are likely to be constructed. Additionally, these same constructs can be used to more effectively plan interventions and facilitate the change process using the new understandings that will be developed in this chapter. In other words, all of the concepts introduced in the preceding chapters remain very relevant, and can be applied in new and interesting ways when considering how participants construct their own interpretations. The key in this chapter will be to make a shift in thinking about and using the constructs introduced earlier. Here the various ideas will be used to explain and predict the interpretations and meanings people construct about the change process as they experience it. After reviewing the manuscript for this chapter, Carolee Hayes, formerly the Director of Staff Development for the Douglas County School District in Colorado, observed:

> This chapter represents a major shift in the book. Up to this point, the authors have taken a fairly left-brained approach to making sense of change. In this chapter, the reader will sense a shift to considering the uncontrollable, unpredictable factors in change and is drawn into a process of integrating the controllable, predictable factors with those that are controlled only by individual and shared interpretations.

INTRODUCING MUSHROOMS: A UNIQUE FORM OF INTERVENTION

In previous chapters a great deal of attention was given to discussing the different forms, sizes, and functions of interventions. In all of those descriptions and analyses, there was an assumption that change facilitators *initiated* the interventions. In this chapter, we will describe a different form of change process intervention, for which change facilitators are not the source and, in fact, over which they have little control. This new category of interventions is called *mushrooms* (see Figure 11.1).

The metaphor of mushrooms is particularly salient for describing this special class of interventions. Just as mushroom plants can be nutritious or poisonous, so can Intervention Mushrooms. Some help advance the change process, while others erode it. Just as mushroom plants come in many colors and shapes, mushroom interventions in a change process take different forms. There may be none, one, or a great variety. Just as mushroom plants grow in the dark and are fed manure, mushroom interventions grow in the shadows of a change process and are fed by the actions of the change facilitators and other participants. Just as it takes an expert to identify and pick the good mushroom plants, some change facilitators are much more skilled than others at detecting and sorting mushroom interventions; taking advantage of the positive mushrooms and discouraging the growth of poisonous ones.

Two Ways of Knowing: Objectivist and Interpretivist

Before explaining the construct of intervention mushrooms further, it will be useful to review briefly two research traditions that have been very influential during the last three decades. Each of these traditions has made significant contributions to our understanding of the change process. As is true in most fields, there has been a history

FIGURE 11.1   **Intervention Mushrooms Come in a Variety of Shapes and Sizes**

GUIDING PRINCIPLES OF MUSHROOM INTERVENTIONS

1. Mushrooms grow out of individual interpretations of actions and events as a change process unfolds.
2. A mushroom may be constructed by an individual or by a group.
3. A critical aspect of understanding a mushroom is to be able to see the overall pattern of actions that have contributed to growth of its constructed theme.
4. Mushrooms may be nutritious or poisonous to a change process.
5. In most cases, intervening in response to individual actions will not kill a poisonous mushroom but instead will contribute to its further growth.
6. Contrary to what one might predict, both positive and negative mushrooms can be constructed by people at each Stage of Concern.
7. An important change facilitator skill is to keep one's antennae tuned for actions that could be the beginning of negative and positive mushrooms.
8. To sustain or kill a mushroom, interventions must be aimed at its constructed theme, not one of the individual actions.
9. Think about what you and others do to contribute to the growth of mushrooms, especially the poisonous ones. Keep in mind how others may interpret your actions.

---

of disagreement and competition between proponents of each of these traditions. Interestingly, each can be complementary of the other. In this chapter, these two research traditions will be used in combination to better explain and illustrate the concept and dynamics of mushrooms.

The Objectivist Perspective of Change. From the 1950s to late in the 1980s, the dominant way of thinking about learning was labeled *behaviorism*. The focus in this approach was on observable behaviors. For example, classroom teachers were expected to describe student learning in terms of what the students could *do,* not what they "understood." Curriculum developers and teachers were trained and required to write behavioral objectives. The design of the research was influenced by the behaviorist perspective as well. Researchers focused on describing and counting the observable behaviors of teachers, such as the quantity of questions asked and the frequency of giving management directions. All were admonished to never ever use the word *understand* because one cannot see "understanding." Instead, they were to deal only with what could be observed.

Since the primary emphasis in behaviorist research and practice was on being absolutely objective about what one did, the term *objectivist* was applied to this approach. The goal was to remove the biases and perspectives of the observers (e.g., teachers and researchers) by describing events in terms of cold, hard facts, or in other words, objective descriptions of observed behaviors. This perspective dominated research on organizations throughout the twentieth century.

The Interpretivist Perspective of Change.   As Kuhn (1970) so eloquently proposed, there comes a time in the study of any field of science when the regular way of thinking and working (i.e., the established paradigm) is challenged by a new model (i.e., a competing paradigm). When the established paradigm fails to predict some aspects of a phenomenon, a new, competing paradigm is proposed. Such a revolution in organization and in education research and theory has been represented by the recent movement toward *constructivism,* which emphasizes how the learner develops, or "constructs," his or her own "understanding," or "interpretation," of reality. *Interpretivists* strive to analyze how understanding is developed by studying the way people interpret and give meaning to events (e.g., by examining the quotes like those at the beginning of this chapter). Rather than simply dealing with observable behaviors the interpretivist paradigm stresses unearthing and describing the interpretations and meaning that people attach to an action, event, or concept.

INTERVENTION MUSHROOMS ARE CONSTRUCTED

So what does this discussion of paradigms, behaviorism, and interpretivism mean for understanding the change process? Combining elements of the objectivist and interpretivist paradigms is very useful for explaining a very important but little understood component of change process dynamics—intervention mushrooms. To be sure, change processes are affected by the behaviors (aka interventions) of the change facilitators. But there is another class of interventions that grow out of the participant's interpretations of what the actions of the change facilitators and others mean.

There are observable behaviors associated with mushrooms. For example, a teacher complains about having to go to a workshop. Both the teacher's complaint and the workshop are observable and describable change process–related actions, or interventions. Holding the workshop is a change facilitator–initiated intervention. But what about the teacher's complaint? It fits the definition of an intervention in that it is an action or event that can influence the change process. However, it has the potential to be come more. Depending on how the complaint was stated and what the teacher does next, the complaint could be forgotten or start to grow into a mushroom. If nothing more is heard, then the teacher's complaint disappears as an isolated incident. However, as is illustrated in Figure 11.2, if the teacher complains repeatedly and with increasing animation, a mushroom intervention is born.

We contend that most mushrooms can be anticipated. For example, to determine if the workshop complaint will grow into a mushroom, we first need to understand more about the interpretation that the teacher has given to the announcement that there will be a workshop. A number of plausible interpretations can be imagined. For example, does the teacher see the workshop as useless in terms of content because she already knows the subject? Or is there a scheduling conflict because the teacher is committed to making an exploratory visit to a site where the innovation is in use? Or is she concerned that her lack of knowledge might be exposed and that she could be embarrassed? Depending on the reason for the teacher's complaint, not

FIGURE 11.2   Initial Growth of an Intervention Mushroom

Action 1:	In a hallway conversation with Teacher B, Teacher X complains about having to attend a workshop.
Action 2:	In the lunchroom, Teacher X complains to a friendly colleague (Teacher W), who does not want to attend the workshop either.
Action 3:	In the parking lot, Teachers X and W again complain and plan to talk to their department chair.
Action 4:	The next day during planning period, Teacher X catches the department chair and complains about having to attend the workshop.
Action 5:	The department chair talks with the principal about the complaint.
	Theme: (Some) Teachers are complaining about having to attend the workshop.

wanting to attend the workshop could have very different implications for that teacher, other teachers, and the success of the change process. This is where the interpretivist perspective is key to understanding the change process. Carolee Hayes has summarized nicely:

> The metaphor of mushrooms provides an image of fungi creeping into a system without any nurturing or intention on the part of the leadership. That is a powerful image, one which all leaders have experienced when best efforts become interpreted as something otherwise. It reminds us that being right or well intentioned is only one perception of a situation.

Four Aspects of Intervention Mushrooms

There are four features of Intervention Mushrooms that can assist in understanding their origination and growth. The interpretivist and objectivist perspectives that were just discussed can be used to understand these features. First, the interpretivist component of mushrooms addresses the *interpretations* that an individual or a group constructs about the meaning and intention of a change facilitator's interventions, the innovation, and the change process in general. Second, the objectivist component of mushrooms addresses the *behaviors,* or the statements and actions, that emanate from the constructed interpretations.

Two other important features of mushrooms are *potential effects* and *individual* or *group construction.* As with mushroom plants, intervention mushrooms can be either nutritious or poisonous for a change process. Some mushrooms, such as growing enthusiasm of teachers that the change is working, are positive and help move the process ahead. However, poisonous mushrooms, such as a growing number of teacher complaints about the quality of the materials, can negatively affect the change process. The fourth feature emphasizes the point that Intervention Mushrooms can be constructed by single individuals or by a group. Each person involved in a change process will, at least to some extent, have developed his or her own interpretations of events and intentions. Some interpretations will be discussed with others, and through these discussions a shared interpretation will be developed.

A brief example of mushroom construction will further illustrate these features. When the seed for a potential mushroom is planted, the individual develops his or her own interpretation of what a particular action or event means. Something as simple as the superintendent's statement at a school board meeting that a curriculum director from the district office will be reporting on a new initiative at the next meeting could trigger the growth of a mushroom or no reaction at all. A principal who had heard the superintendent's comment could develop an "educated guess," based on extrapolations from past experience, that a big change is coming. The principal's interpretation is his or her own (i.e., an individual construction) until he or she says to another principal, "Guess what I heard at the board meeting last night?" Then group construction begins. There is a high probability that this mushroom will grow quickly with the theme being: The superintendent has another big change coming.

THE LIFE CYCLE OF INTERVENTION MUSHROOMS

Mushrooms are constructed out of the interpretations that each person makes of the unfolding actions and events in a change process. People look for ways to make sense of and to explain what is happening to them and around them. Efforts to make sense and explain increase during a time of change. Each participant develops his or her own interpretation and understanding based on past experiences as well as on the themes and patterns that are characteristic of his or her organization. For example, if the principal always runs a staff meeting in a certain way, the staff comes to expect that this is the regular pattern. But if one day the principal changes the way the meeting is run, it may be seen as a sign of something. At first, what the "something" is will be uncertain. If the principal explains why the change occurred, this additional intervention will alter the teachers' growing interpretations. If no explanation is offered as the meeting unfolds, each staff member will begin to develop his or her own explanation, or hypothesis, about what the change means.

The Birth of a Mushroom

Regardless of whether the principal explains the reason for the change or each staff member develops his or her own explanation, some staff may exchange interpretations following the meeting. Then there will be gradual development of a shared interpretation of what the change means. This group development of a shared understanding is often called *social construction.*

The shared interpretation becomes the *constructed theme* of the mushroom. In the example here, which is mapped in Table 11.1, one teacher thinks that the principal just forgot to do the usual routine. Another teacher thinks that the principal is

TABLE 11.1 Mapping a Mushroom Intervention

SEQUENCE OF EVENTS	ACTIONS	PARTICIPANT INTERPRETATIONS	CHANGE FACILITATOR'S ISOLATED RESPONSES	ACCUMULATED EFFECT(S)
0	Principal changes meeting process.	Some notice, some don't, some are surprised.	Principal explains the change	None observed
1	Teachers talk with each other about the change.	Some see it as no big deal; some think it means something.	—	Some energy going into examination of what the change means
2	More teacher dialogue occurs.	"The principal is looking."	—	More energy going into constructing shared interpretation
3	Superintendent makes an unannounced visit.	"The principal is being checked out."	—	Increasing talk and distraction
4	Principal says to the secretary, "I am ready for a change."	"The principal *is* looking/ leaving!"	—	More support for the mushroom and less work activity
5	Principal closes the door to take phone call.	"The principal has a call about the new position."	—	More support for the mushroom and less attention to teaching and learning

Constructed Theme

"The principal is leaving."

Change Facilitator's Responses to the Total Mushroom

None

Accumulated Effect(s)

Time and energy being drawn away from teaching and leaning

238

using some new techniques that she picked up at a principals' conference last week. Two others believe that the change means that the principal is looking for a new job and is practicing a different leadership style. No one knows for sure what the principal is doing, but all have an individual interpretation to share and advocate. Arising out of the discussions is a *first consensus* that the principal is looking for another job: "She has been here for five years; it's time." A mushroom is born.

The Growth of a Mushroom

In the following two days, one teacher overhears the principal say to the assistant principal that she really is ready for a change. The teacher did not hear all of the conversation, but is certain about what she did hear. Another teacher, who had been at the administration building to pick up a book, heard that there is an opening for a principal "downtown." Both of these individual events are shared and interpreted by all as further confirmation of "the-principal-is-looking" mushroom. The mushroom is growing and beginning to take on a life of its own.

The Maturity of a Mushroom

Over the next several weeks, other actions and events occur that, if the mushroom did not exist, either would not have been noticed or would have been interpreted differently. However, with a rapidly growing mushroom, many otherwise innocuous actions are interpreted as support for the mushroom theme and contribute to its continued and quick expansion. For example, the superintendent's unannounced visit to the school and closed-door meeting with the principal further feeds "the-principal-is-looking" mushroom. Teachers begin comparing the frequency of principal visits to the lounge with memories of her past behavior; "She is not in the lounge as much now." Something as simple as the principal closing the door to take a phone call adds further support to the mushroom. Events and actions, many of which may in fact have nothing in common, are thus interpreted as being part of an overall pattern and theme. As can be seen in this very simple example, it is quite easy for a mushroom to get started and for its growth not only to be assisted, but also to race ahead without any of the change facilitators being aware that it is happening.

KEYS TO THE CONSTRUCTION OF INTERVENTION MUSHROOMS

There are several ways to analyze mushrooms. Some of the techniques can be used to anticipate the growth of new ones, while other approaches can help to explain those that already exist. Most of the constructs introduced in earlier chapters are very powerful tools for understanding the different ways that mushrooms can start as well as the dynamics of their growth. Here, the constructs of Levels of Use, Stages of Concern, and Change Facilitator Styles will be used to illustrate how mushrooms are constructed, and why they turn out to be nutritious or poisonous.

Levels of Use as a Rubric for Developing Understanding of Mushrooms

Levels of Use (LoU) was introduced in Chapter 8 as a way to describe and understand a person's gradual development of skills and expertise in using a change/innovation. In that chapter, Levels of Use was described in purely objectivist terminology. Very strong emphasis was placed on the fact that Levels of Use is a behavioral diagnostic dimension. Further, LoU was defined in operational terms, and the Levels of Use chart (see Appendix 3) is composed of behavioral descriptions and indicators that are characteristic of each level. The method of assessing LoU is a special focused interview procedure that is based purely on soliciting and coding examples of the interviewee's innovation-related behaviors. Obviously development of the Levels of Use concept and its measurement relied heavily on the objectivist research tradition.

Levels of Use from a Constructivist Perspective.   Levels of Use can also be viewed and described in a constructivist tradition. Notice in particular the Knowledge Category in the operational definitions of Levels of Use in Appendix 3. If cognitive theory were applied to the LoU descriptions, the Knowledge column of this table would be seen as presenting snapshots of gradually increasing sophistication and complexity of "understanding" about how to use the innovation. Each Knowledge level represents a major step in the transition from nonuser to novice to expert. At the lowest levels, the schemas are very simplistic and incomplete. As one moves to higher Levels of Use they become more complex and multifaceted. In other words, although the early development and studies of LoU were based in the behaviorist paradigm, LoU can be explained in terms of the constructivist paradigm as well.

LoU-Based Mushrooms.   LoU can be a very useful tool for predicting and understanding mushrooms. First of all, the types of mushrooms that an individual constructs will be different depending on the person's level of understanding (i.e., his or her knowledge rating). As obvious as this may seem, we frequently fail to recognize that there could be a number of potential mushrooms growing in relation to a person's level of knowledge and understanding about what the innovation is and how it can be used. For example, a person at LoU I Orientation may have such limited knowledge that even when the innovation is described in minute detail, he or she cannot make the link back to how the change would work in his or her situation. As a result, the person might reject the innovation because it is perceived as being too complex, confusing, and unrelated to the immediate problem/need.

This episode could be the beginning step in the growth of a poisonous mushroom. The mushroom could disappear if the next facilitator intervention helps the person develop a clearer connection between his or her current understanding of the innovation and his or her needs. However, if the subsequent interventions are also detailed and intricate, they could reinforce the developing perception that this innovation is too complex and not relevant (See Perceived Attributes of an Innovation in Chapter 4.) Then an individual mushroom of resistance to the innovation could begin growing.

The same intervention of providing minute detail about the innovation could easily lead to growth of a positive mushroom for a person who is at LoU IVB Refinement. He or she already has a full understanding of how the innovation works in the classroom and how it can be fine-tuned for special needs. If this person were to meet and plan with another LoU IVB individual, they both develop an interest in taking something new back to their classrooms. If these decisions were to happen several times and with several other teachers, a positive mushroom related to collegiality and collaboration could begin growing. In this case, there would be clear indication of movement toward LoU V Integration.

Stages of Concern as a Source of Mushrooms

Stages of Concerns (SoC) are a powerful catalyst for the development of mushrooms. The perceptions and feelings that one has in relation to a change process are constantly in flux, and there is a high sensitivity to everything related to the instability of change. Therefore it is important not only to be assessing SoC for use in planning interventions, but also to use SoC assessments to recognize developing mushrooms and to anticipate the potential for others to grow. Here again, the mushrooms that are constructed can be either nutritious or poisonous, and can be limited to one individual or shared by a group.

Personal Concerns: A Significant Source of Negative Mushrooms.   Stage 2 Personal concerns represent a particularly sensitive time for individuals and groups. When personal concerns are high, the antennae are up and looking for anything and everything that might represent a threat to the person, real or imagined. By definition the person with high personal concerns is interpreting actions and events chiefly in terms of what they mean for him or her. They are not as concerned about what the change might mean for students or others; the concerns are centered on implications for themselves. Note that the real intentions of the change facilitator are not at issue here, but rather how someone with high Stage 2 Personal concerns perceives and *interprets* actions and events.

Persons with high Stage 2 concerns can easily interpret whatever occurs as an attempt to undercut or attack them. If this happens only once, there is no mushroom. However, if over a few days or weeks there are several events that are seen by the person as suspicious, a poisonous individual mushroom of insecurity and resentment will start to germinate: "The principal doesn't care what *I* think. He has his mind made up already." "I can't do this. I am just going to close my door and hope that nobody will see that I am not doing it." "You know the superintendent is all politics. She doesn't care at all about kids."

When two or more individuals who are growing such "insecurity mushrooms" talk to each other, the social construction process works overtime. "You are right. The superintendent doesn't care at all what we think, or how hard we have to work." "Why, the last time we did this, do you remember how she went on and on about this being such a good thing? It turned out to be an absolute disaster." At this point the individual insecurity mushrooms have combined into one that is shared and is ready for rapid growth through continued group construction. If a Stages of Concern profile were made, it would show high Stage 2 Personal concerns as well as a "tailing up" on Stage 6 Refocusing concerns. With this sort of concerns profile, the "here-we-go-again,-I-don't-buy-this-one-either" mushroom can grow faster and taller than Jack's beanstalk.

Intervening on Insecurity Mushrooms.   There are many wrong ways for leaders to respond to insecurity mushrooms. One very risky approach would be to say such things as, "This really is different," or "Trust me. It will work well." "Trust-Me" interventions usually accelerate the rate of growth of already rapidly expanding poisonous mushroom: "Sure. I should trust her. She doesn't have to do it. What does she know?" Another intervention that must only be used if carefully thought out is to put something in writing. Persons who have high personal concerns and are cultivating a shared insecurity mushroom will be able to come up with interpretations of a written document that were never intended, or even imagined, by the author. No matter how well a document is written, it can be perceived by those with high Stage 2 Personal concerns as further proof of the theme of the negative mushroom. "See, I told you so. She has no interest in what we think. She already has made the decision."

One potentially effective intervention would be to talk individually with people with high Stage 2 concerns and present a positive, straightforward stance of interest in and support for them, with reassurances that the change process will work out well. It is especially important for the leaders of the change process to constantly and continually act positively with such individuals. They also need to carefully monitor their own statements and actions for any that could be interpreted as negative or in some way doubting the chances of success. Those with supertuned personal concerns antennae will pick up on any hints of doubt or uncertainty within the leaders.

Impact Concerns: A Significant Source of Positive Mushrooms.   Frequently overlooked in change processes are those people with various forms of impact concerns, who have some combination of high concerns at Stages 4 Consequence, 5 Collaboration, and 6 Refocusing. All are concerned about the impact of the change on clients, especially students. Impact-concerned people are positive and enthusiastic, and talk to each other about the strengths and successes they are experiencing in using the innovation. These are the people who naturally grow positive mushrooms within themselves and through dialogue with others.

The research and concepts related to organizational culture, such as those that were introduced in Chapter 7, are important to keep in mind in relation to the growth of positive mushrooms, which are more easily recognized in such a culture. Positive norms are positive mushrooms. By talking to each other about teaching and student learning, teachers are growing a positive mushroom related to teacher collegiality and a shared focus on students. Interestingly, positive mushrooms such as this are quickly claimed by the change facilitators: "I know that we are collegial in this school. I have been doing a number of things to help this happen." From a practical point of view, who gets credit for positive mushrooms is of little consequence. However, researchers as well as change facilitators need to understand when and how positive mushrooms develop, since by definition, mushrooms are not knowingly created by change facilitators. All mushrooms begin their growth "in the dark"; it is the more finely attuned change facilitator who detects the beginning of a positive mushroom and actively intervenes to nurture its further growth.

Intervening on Positive Mushrooms.   A frequently observed problem is that change facilitators spend little or no time attending to positive mushrooms. In fact, they often fail to see their constructed themes. They may react to individual statements of enthusiasm, but are slow to see the whole theme. More deliberate effort needs to be given to recognizing and supporting the Impact-concerned people and the positive mushrooms that they generate. Facilitators tend to be compulsive about addressing the persons with Self and Task concerns while failing to realize that people with Impact concerns are a key source of supportive interventions.

Frequently, all that is needed is to take the time to offer a compliment or a word of encouragement. Visiting a classroom and observing the innovation in use can be very supportive of the further growth of positive mushrooms generated by Impact concerns. Another effective approach is to point out the existence of the positive mushroom. Once it has been identified, claim it as a strategy that all can nourish.

Change Facilitator Style and Mushrooms

Another frame to use in examining the growth of mushrooms is the Change Facilitator Style (CF). In the literature there has been a long-running debate about the relationship of leader behaviors to style and whether a leader can easily change his or her style. Our studies and those of our colleagues, as summarized in Chapter 10, lead us to conclude that leaders cannot easily or automatically change their overall style. Ideally, they will adapt or adjust their behaviors from situation to situation, but they do not readily change their overall style. Therefore, one source of continuity and predictability is the CF Style of the leader. Whether he or she is an Initiator, Manager, Responder, or something else, that style represents a pattern within which individual actions can be understood.

One of the generalized activities that participants in a change process engage is constructing a shared description of the styles of the various leaders. The individual actions of the leader are interpreted within constructed context of his or her overall style. As one veteran teacher said to a first-year teacher after the principal had growled at her: "Oh, don't worry about that. That is the way he always is. He doesn't mean anything by it." The principal had made a comment that by itself could be interpreted as demeaning of the new teacher. However, when it was interpreted by the veteran in the context of that principal's style, the meaning was mollified. *Once again, it isn't only what you do, it is how others interpret what you do.*

Different Change Facilitator Styles Have Different Meanings. An interesting example of the importance of understanding style is how the same action can have very different meanings depending on who does it. In other words, the same action done by leaders with different Change Facilitator styles will have very different meanings for their followers.

Consider a simple change facilitator action, a one-legged interview in the hallway, as the principal stops and says to a teacher, "How's it going with your use of the new computers?" This is a simple incident intervention that could be coded, using the objectivist paradigm outlined in Chapters 5 and 9, by source (the principal), target (a teacher), location (the hallway), and so forth. If a number of these types of interventions were recorded, a quantitative analysis could be done and different principals could be compared in terms of the frequencies of occurrence of different types of interventions and the difference that these made on teacher success in implementation. This is exactly what was done in the original Principal/Teacher Interaction Study and the subsequent studies that confirmed the three different Change Facilitator Styles. This work was described in depth in Chapters 9 and 10.

An analysis of the same one-legged-interview using the interpretivist paradigm would be different. Instead of coding and counting the parts of the action, the analysis would focus on the interpretation of the action that a teacher constructs. In other words, what does the intervention mean to the teacher who receives it? Our hypothesis is that it will depend on the Change Facilitator Style of the principal.

An Initiator principal meets a teacher in the hallway and asks, "How's it going with your use of the new computers?" What goes through the mind of the teacher? First, the teacher will place this individual action in the context of the CF Style of the principal. Given that this is an Initiator principal, the teacher will know that the principal is expecting several things of the teacher, including: (1) the teacher's use of the computers, (2) descriptive information about what is happening with students, and (3) the identification of any need or problem. Further, the teacher knows that if something needs to be done to support the teacher, the principal will see that it is done. Based on this interpretation, the teacher goes ahead and describes some "neat" things that are happening with students, which leads to a short dialogue and ends with a commitment by the principal to stop by to see the sixth-period class in action.

If a Manager principal met a teacher in the hallway and asked, "How's it going with your use of the new computers?" the teacher's interpretive processing would be different. The teacher would understand that this principal is interested in knowing whether (1) there are any logistical or mechanical problems, (2) the schedule is working; and (3) there are enough supplies. Of course the principal is interested also in how the students are doing, in a general sense. So the teacher responds that having some additional chairs or printer cartridges would help. The dialogue continues with discussion of the need for additional rules about student uses of computers outside of class.

Interpretation of the same opening statement from a Responder principal would differ from that of either the Initiator or Manager principals. If a Responder principal stopped the teacher and asked, "How's it going with your use of the new computers?"

IMPLICATIONS FOR LEADERS FACILITATING CHANGE

Change efforts can be won, and lost, based on the array of intervention mushrooms that are in place at the beginning and that grow as the implementation process unfolds. Too many poisonous mushrooms can kill a change process before it even begins. A very difficult challenge for external change facilitators is to detect and map the array of mushrooms at the beginning.

For example, if Self concerns are very high, there is a high probability that there are poisonous mushrooms already growing. If there are Impact concerns, then open and fair consideration should be given to the new initiative. If Task concerns have been high for a long time, there is a strong possibility that the new initiative will be seen as "too much work."

One of the biggest challenges for leaders, internal change facilitators, and especially external change facilitators is to understand enough about a setting so that the birth of mushrooms can be anticipated. This is a rare skill. However, it can be very useful to be able to make an educated guess about the potential for mushroom growth. One of the problems for the change leaders is that members of the organization will not always tell them what they are thinking and sharing with each other, especially if it is negative.

In one situation, one of the authors was in a major administrative position and none of his direct reports would tell him what they were talking about with each other. Based on little tidbits that were dropped and given some policy and leader changes that were taking place higher up in the organization, it seemed likely that at least one poisonous mushroom was growing. For example, it was discovered that there were frequent off-campus lunch meetings that were never referenced in open meetings. Without going into all of the details, with time it became clear that the prediction was correct; a toxic mushroom was being constructed. The problem in these situations is that if there is no way of knowing a mushroom is growing, it is very difficult to address its themes. Change facilitators must develop and continually refine their skills at mushroom detection. Unfortunately, in many settings detection is based on having been there before and/or making educated guesses using the constructs and reasoning that has been outlined in this chapter.

the teacher's first reaction would be to mask surprise and to try to recover from the shock of being asked at all, since the normal style of the Responder principal is to chat in general about school topics or about some current issue in the community or in professional sports, not about what was going on in the classroom. The typical response of the teacher would be to offer some generalities such as, "Things are going well," and see what the principal says next.

The point here, as throughout this chapter, is not to present intricate depictions of principals' and teachers' actions and interpretations. Instead, the purpose is to use brief anecdotes to illustrate the mushroom concept and to ask you to shift the way that you think about an important aspect of the change process. Rather than thinking solely in terms of what the change facilitators do, consideration needs to be given to the interpretations that the participants ascribe to the actions. Again, it is not only what you do, but the meaning that others assign to what you do that counts. Further, there are both individual and group-constructed interpretations, as well as interpretations of isolated events and of perceived patterns drawn across a number of events and experiences, all of which can result in nutritious and/or poisonous mushrooms.

Mushroom Detection by Change Facilitator Style.   Mushrooms may not be created knowingly, but once they occur, they can be maintained knowingly. As we stated at the beginning of this chapter, mushrooms tend to grow in the dark. Still, their presence may be detected at any point in their growth, and intervention can occur. The positive mushrooms need to be nurtured and the poisonous killed. Interestingly, Initiator leaders seem to detect positive mushrooms almost as soon as they are born. The Initiators then support and nourish their further growth. For example, they will offer encouragement to individuals. They will link the Impact-concerned people with some of those with Task and Self concerns. They will provide extra resources or offer a special award to keep a positive mushroom growing. They may make a special point to acknowledge a positive mushroom in a faculty meeting, and attempt to recruit others to do things that contribute to its development. On the other hand, Initiators are telepathic about sensing the emergence of poisonous mushrooms and quick to take actions to kill them, neutralize their toxicity, or turn them into nutritious mushrooms.

By contrast, Responder leaders do not see mushrooms. Also, there seem to be very few positive mushrooms growing in their schools, while negative mushrooms are thriving. Responders tend not to see the overall mushroom pattern and theme, which means that when they do react, they tend to respond to some of the individual actions of the mushroom instead of its constructed theme. The result is a lot of flitting around from complaint to complaint as a number of actions are taken that may contribute to the growth of existing negative mushrooms and even foster the development of new ones.

DEALING WITH A GROWING MUSHROOM

Don't forget that mushrooms can be nutritious as well as poisonous to a change process. For example, teachers excitedly and continuously chatting with other teachers about the helpful things that parents are doing in classrooms is a positive mushroom that should be nurtured. Taking advantage of positive mushrooms should be a straightforward process, assuming that the different individual actions are seen in the context of the larger pattern of the mushroom. Unfortunately, in our research studies we have regularly observed leaders and change facilitators who did not see these patterns. Instead, many react to the individual actions as if each were occurring in isola-

USING INTERVENTION MUSHROOM CONSTRUCTS AND TOOLS TO ASSESS AND STUDY IMPLEMENTATION

Our understanding of Intervention Mushrooms is much more limited than for the constructs that were introduced in the preceding chapters. In order to understand more, there is a need for better methods of charting identified mushrooms. In addition, before they can be charted, they must be identified. Better procedures for identification would be of help in research and in training change leaders in detection. Since mushrooms are individual and social constructions, it is likely that more of the studies will use qualitative methods.

A working hypothesis, based on clinical experience with change processes, is that Initiators are quite good at detecting mushrooms. Assuming this is the case, how do they do it? What are their clues? They also are better at reducing, killing, or turning toxic mushrooms. How do they do this? Spending intensive time in an organization, identifying and mapping Intervention Mushrooms and observing how the leaders respond is needed. In several cases, we have observed Initiators anticipate the birth of mushrooms. What do they look for and what frames of analysis are they employing?

It appears that there are more poisonous mushrooms in organizations led by Responders. If so, why is this the case? What could be done to reduce the potential for the occurrence of poisonous mushrooms? What drives their construction, especially when they hurt individuals and the organization as a whole?

The growth of positive mushrooms certainly is desirable. What are the conditions that contribute to this happening? What are the characteristics of the leaders and the followers? What types of actions support and sustain positive/nutritious mushrooms?

Another set of questions has to do with the relationship between the construct of Intervention Mushrooms and characteristics of organizational culture. We suggested in this chapter that the themes of mushrooms seem to be similar to cultural norms. Theoretical knowledge and fieldwork could contribute to our having a better understanding of both constructs and the extent of their overlap. One interesting subquestion has to do with how dynamic each may be. Culture researchers seem to see norms as stable, while the themes of mushrooms may continue to grow, or in some cases be addressed and disappear. How are enduring mushrooms and their themes the same as or different from norms?

As will be pointed out in Chapter 12, leader succession is an important area for study. Depending on the CF Style of the past leader, how will the new leader be received? The array of intervention mushrooms that are in place at the time of leader succession most certainly needs to be understood by the new leader. They also are likely to be related to how long the new leader's honeymoon can last.

tion. They do not see that there is a theme of accumulating actions that *together* are affecting the change process.

It is critical for change facilitators to become skilled in mushroom detection. They must continually be looking for positive themes arising out of individual actions and strive to support their further growth. On the other side, they must be constantly tuned to the potential for negative mushrooms, growing in the dark, at the edges of the change process. When a negative mushroom is detected, effort needs to be directed toward destroying its constructed theme, rather than responding to each individual action independently. The mushroom needs to be recognized and dealt with in its totality. Targeting individual actions in isolation will only lead to more rapid growth of poisonous mushrooms. Unfortunately, many leaders do not see the overall pattern of individual actions that aggregate to make a mushroom. In these situations, the change process does not advance as well, and there is an increased likelihood that teachers will develop "tailing up" on Stage 6 Refocusing concerns, which leads to negative mushrooms being created.

EVERGREEN MUSHROOMS

Some mushrooms simply will not go away. No matter what is tried, they just keep coming back. We call them "evergreen" mushrooms. One example of an evergreen mushroom that we have experienced several times is the "two-against-one" mushroom that grows in offices staffed by three secretaries. Due to the intensity of the work and the extensive time in the same work environment, on occasion two of the secretaries become upset with the third. The two start having whispered conversations and leave the third out. After a while, work tasks are dropped or a key piece of information is not communicated. In an attempt to stop the growth of the mushroom, the leader talks to each secretary individually and asks what can be done to resolve the issue. This seems to take care of the problem. The three return to working as a team.

However, within months, two of the secretaries will be at odds with the third. It may be a different two, but the same scenario starts to unfold. This time all three are taken out to lunch, and the problem is talked through. Perhaps some tasks are restructured or schedules are changed. However, no matter what interventions we have tried, in time this evergreen mushroom returns.

There are many other evergreen mushrooms that could be discussed, such as the annual panic to create the revised strategic improvement plans, the trauma surrounding yearly evaluations, and the disbelief over administering standardized achievement tests to all students in the fall. These examples won't be mapped out here, but the key point is to remember that part of the wisdom of leading and facilitating change is in recognizing when something is not likely to go away. There are some parts of the change process, such as evergreen mushrooms, that need to be understood and then worked around.

■ ■ ■ ■ ■ ▬▬▬▬▬▬▬▬▬▬▬▬▬▬▬▬▬▬▬▬▬▬▬▬▬▬▬▬▬

VIGNETTE

GROWING A NUTRITIOUS MUSHROOM

Poisonous mushrooms are easy to find. We all have experienced them, and in many cases have helped to grow them. Nutritious mushrooms are less well understood and rarely celebrated. There is something about the compulsive nature of educators that makes them overlook or discount the positive aspects of their work. Therefore, we decided to present a short story about one nutritious mushroom.

This nutritious mushroom, which we shall call "enthusiasm for teaching and learning science," grew in one elementary school as a new science curriculum was being implemented. This innovation contained the usual elements: manipulative materials, living organisms, cooperative groups, no textbook, and field trips. All teachers had been given released days to participate in a series of all-day training workshops. The workshops had been designed to be concerns-based by regularly assessing Stages of Concern and adjusting each day's sessions accordingly.

Across the district, teachers in most schools were implementing the new approach and had the predictable array of Stage 3 Management concerns, such as, "The daphnia are dying" and "The crickets escaped!" In a few schools there were negative mushrooms about all the work, the mess, and the uncontrollable students.

In one school, however, we found no negative mushrooms. In reviewing the data, it was clear that the principal in this school was an initiator. He was very supportive of the new approach to teaching science. He advocated for the new curriculum and did the little things that signaled he was willing to help. For example, when he overheard a teacher in the lounge expressing concerns about not having enough microscopes for a particular lesson, without saying anything he found the microscopes and placed them on the teacher's desk. He made sure teachers attended the training workshops. He visited classrooms when science was being taught.

Teachers were discovering that their students liked the new approach and were asking to have science classes everyday. Parents began commenting about their children's enthusiasm for science. The district office science coordinators too were pleased with how implementation was progressing in this school. We researchers were intrigued that the SoCQ profiles were low on Stage 1 Informational, Stage 2 Personal, and Stage 3 Management concerns. Further, there was an arousal of Stage 4 Consequence concerns. All of these actions and indicators document the spontaneous birth and growth of a nutritious mushroom. Everyone was talking positively about what was occurring around use of the new approach.

When we pointed out this nutritious mushroom to the principal, he said that it had been part of his plan along. As the researchers, however, we had a different hypothesis: As positive actions began to occur, the principal reinforced and nurtured their expression and sharing. He also was making every effort to reduce the occurrence of actions that could lead to the growth of any poisonous mushrooms, such as providing the needed materials. In summary, either way in which the construction of this nutritious mushroom is diagrammed, the clear consequence was dynamic and positive schoolwide implementation success.

(continued)

■ ■ ■ ■ ■ ■ ▬▬▬▬▬▬▬▬▬▬▬▬▬▬▬▬▬▬▬▬▬▬▬▬▬▬▬▬▬▬▬▬▬▬▬

V I G N E T T E   CONTINUED

VIGNETTE CRITIQUE QUESTIONS

1. What do you see as the key actions that contributed to the construction of this nutritious mushroom? Were all of the actions needed?
2. What type of action would lead to the death of this mushroom? How long would it take to kill it?
3. In this case, the principal claimed that the nutritious mushroom had been part of his plan from the very beginning. Do you think this was true?
4. What was the principal's role in the continued growth of this nutritious mushroom? How did the teachers contribute? Did the students also have a role?

SUMMARY

The success of any change effort is dependent not only on what the change facilitators do but also on how the participants individually and collectively interpret and understand these actions and events. All participants in a change process are looking for ways to explain and simplify what is happening. The individual and social construction of mushrooms serves as a very useful strategy for doing this. Whether the resultant mushrooms are poisonous or nutritious depends on the Change Facilitator Styles of the leaders and the Stages of Concern of all participants. Success in facilitating change also depends heavily on one's ability to detect mushrooms early in their genesis. More successful change facilitators are skilled at early detection. They are quick to see the overall pattern and themes of both positive and negative mushrooms, and then take actions that are aimed at their totality, rather than just some of the individual actions.

In the ideal setting, the most effective change facilitators are both objectivist and interpretivist. They observe behaviors, and they assess how things are going. They use these diagnostic data to anticipate likely interpretations that could be made, and they listen for individual and social construction of meaning. They check for understanding and map the overall pattern of each mushroom. By keeping the big picture in mind, they are better able to respond to individual actions and events as they unfold. With this approach, mushrooms grow for a shorter period in the dark, and more of them can be put to positive use as the change process continues to unfold. As a check on your understanding, review the Guiding Principles for reminders of how to recognize and attempt to influence the growth of mushroom interventions.

DISCUSSION QUESTIONS

1. Describe and analyze a nutritious mushroom that you have seen in your organization. What name would you give it? What was done to sustain it?

2. Describe and analyze a poisonous mushroom that you have seen in your organization. What name would you give it? What was done to kill it? What was done to sustain it?

3. What are some critical means of detecting mushrooms? What skills will help change facilitators detect nutritious and poisonous mushrooms?

4. What are important ideas to keep in mind when intervening on positive and negative mushrooms?

5. For each Stage of Concern, predict likely positive and negative mushrooms for a staff that has high concerns at that stage.

6. Describe experiences you have had or observed about the construction of mushrooms with leaders using different Change Facilitator Styles. Did they react to individual incidents or to the totality of mushrooms?

FIELDWORK ACTIVITIES

1. Interview a change facilitator about the degree to which he or she is sensitive to and watches for overall patterns in a change process. See if this person can describe examples of positive and negative mushrooms he or she has experienced. What did he or she do to support or discourage the growth of particular mushrooms? As was done in Table 11.1, develop a map for one of these mushrooms to share in class. Estimate the person's Change Facilitator Style and consider whether that style is related to his or her perception and handling of mushrooms.

2. Follow the national news for several weeks; you are bound to find mushrooms growing. For example, a politician may make one small comment that the media magnifies, such as President Clinton's "I didn't inhale" statement. The media may have taken the idea out of context, or it may have been an innocent statement that begins to grow. When the politician attempts to respond in order to kill the mushroom, the response only leads to its further growth. Identify the theme and map the growth of such a mushroom. Give it a name. Then consider what you would recommend that person do if you were an advisor?

PART V

COMBINING VIEWS AND TOOLS

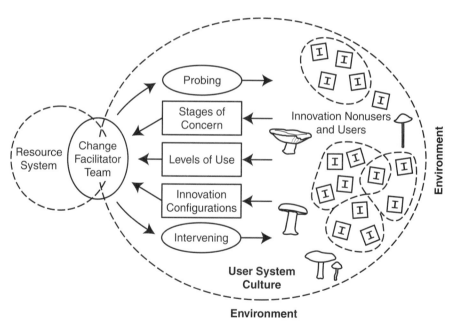

THE CONCERNS-BASED ADOPTION MODEL

In Chapter 12 several examples of how the perspectives, constructs, tools, and techniques introduced in Chapters 1 through 11 can be applied are described. Some of the examples come from research and evaluation studies, while others are drawn from the "real world" of implementing change. Another perspective that has implications for implementing change, postmodernism and critical theory, is introduced. Related issues and dilemmas are presented also. The intents of this chapter are four:

1. Illustrate how some of the ideas and tools introduced in the earlier chapters can be used to facilitate change.
2. Report on some of the research and evaluation studies that have been conducted in which change process constructs and measures have been used.
3. Stimulate further thought and reflection about how the change process works, how to better facilitate change, and the raising of questions that could be the subject of future research.
4. Stimulate consideration of ethics. When do efforts to facilitate change become manipulation?

In addition, the reader needs to keep in mind that there is more—more to be read and more to be learned about how better to facilitate the implementation of change at the individual, organization, and social system levels.

■ ■ ■ ■ ■

CHAPTER 12

IMPLEMENTING CHANGE
Applications, Implications, and Reflections

In this, the final chapter, we offer several short illustrations of how various combinations of the perspectives, constructs, and methods described in Chapters 1 through 11 have been used to think about, facilitate, evaluate and study change. Each of the perspectives represents a unique view of the change process and emphasizes certain factors. Each of the constructs introduced has a solid depth of research that supports its validity and utility. None represent all that can be considered. Each offers instructive ideas and methods for thinking about, facilitating, and studying change processes. The goal is to show how combining constructs and methods across perspectives can be helpful and informative.

This also is the chapter where a very different perspective, postmodernism, is introduced. Although more difficult to grasp, there are several potentially significant implications of this perspective when, and if, it is applied to implementing change. The final topic is the question of ethics. Those engaged as change agents, process consultants, change facilitators, and change leaders need to ask themselves regularly, "Am I being responsible and appropriate in what I am doing and what I am asking others to do?" The chapter begins with additional discussion about the target(s) of interventions.

FOCUS QUESTIONS

1. What are the key units of change and how do these relate to units of intervention?
2. How can constructs and measures introduced in Chapters 1 through 11 be used to assess the extent of implementation and relationships to outcomes?
3. Should development of a PLC-type organization culture be the first priority, or should the focus be on implementing certain innovations?

4. What about new and different perspectives, such as postmodernism and critical theory—do these views have any implications for implementing change?
5. In reflecting on all that has been introduced, are there any ethical issues or questions about responsibility when involved with implementing change?

DIFFERENT UNITS OF INTERVENTION

An important question to answer early in a change effort is: What is the unit of change? Is it an entire system or organization, certain departments, or particular individuals? The answer to this question tells a lot about what should be the target(s) of interventions. Regardless of the answer, without exception some individuals will be expected to implement change. Systems and organizations may adopt change, but individuals implement change. This statement was made earlier in this book. It is useful here to consider further where interventions can be targeted so that individuals and the organization can be supported to change and improve. There are four levels for targeting interventions: the individual, teams, an entire organization, and large systems (see Figure 12.1).

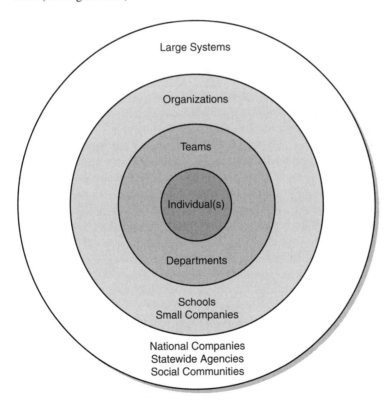

FIGURE 12.1   Units of Change, Targets of Interventions

The System as the Unit of Change

Oftentimes, large systems such as the farmers in Iowa (Chapter 4), a national company, the statewide delivery of a service, or a school district are targeted for change. For example, a corporation may determine that the introduction of a new product line requires the attention of the entire nationwide company. A school district may direct the attention of all schools, and all departments of the central office, to a new data collection, analysis, and management system in which all parts of the system will be impacted. Or, as Hartford Public Schools has done, administrator evaluation and the role of central office departments are realigned to show how they support each school's implementation of its improvement plan. These are systemwide changes, but their implementation may not be done in systemic ways.

There often is an assumption in large-scale change initiatives that all parts of the system must do the same thing. For example, the federal education mandates around No Child Left Behind (NCLB) treat all states, school districts, and schools equally in terms of expectations and consequences for lack of performance. In this "one size fits all" approach, all subparts or subsystems of the system are given the same directives, rules and regulations, and consequences. There is a belief that the "mandate" intervention is all that is needed for change to occur. Although the whole system is being targeted, the approach is not very systemic.

A full systems approach would build in adaptations for various subsystems. For example, adjustments would be made for Connecticut and California, which have been focusing their testing around growth. Other adjustments could be based on the distribution of English language learners, teacher professional development, and state-required testing. When the entire system is the target and no differentiated support is provided for subsystems, there is the strong likelihood that not much change will actually occur.

An entire system can change, if, as in the example of the ITESM, Monterey (Mexico) Institute of Technology effort, a clear goal is stated and held to, there are wide ranging and multiple years of professional development, and administrators provide support and assistance (see Chapter 3 on systems change). There has to be systemic thinking and adaptations along the way based on the interactions and needs of each subsystem (i.e., campus). Without guiding and supporting interventions customized for each subsystem, it is nearly impossible to achieve systemwide change. A small percentage of individuals who may already have the capacity to enact the identified change will proceed, whereas most others became late adopters at best.

One of the key strategies for having successful change across a large system is to differentiate professional development and support for the leaders of the various subsystems. Leader training and development should be different from that provided to the front-line implementers. The leaders must be skilled in guiding and providing support and assistance to the implementers, rather than being implementers of the change themselves. In a systemic approach there also will be differentiations in interventions based in considerations of each leader's Change Facilitator Style.

An Organization as the Unit of Change

An organization as the unit of change could be a particular business site, such as the local fast-food restaurant, or a specified school within a district. Each of these units does not operate independently of the system of which it is a part, but each unit has a local context that should be considered in efforts to improve its services and products. In each case, there is a unit leader with a particular Change Facilitator Style (Chapter 10) who is responsible for rallying the "troops" and convincing them that the change is important and beneficial. This person must be cognizant of the executive level of leadership at the top of the system and its directives, as well as pay attention to the needs and wishes of the staff in their unit. Explanation of the change and professional development to create the capacity to perform the change are key interventions at this level (Stages of Concern must be addressed). The entire organization should receive the same message that focuses on what the change is and how it will work. But the individual departments or teams will be led by their team leaders who should customize their interventions to better fit each division or team. In these cases, the leader of the organization must attend to change for the unit, but also accommodate the unit being a part of a larger system that sets certain parameters.

Teams or Divisions as the Unit of Change

In the smaller intervention units of a teams and departments it is possible for the leader to craft interventions in ways that address individual concerns and still meet the needs of the larger organization. For example, the marketing division will need support and assistance that differs from the sales division. At this level, the interventions can be tailored in more personalized ways and still address attaining the desired outcomes. It should be feasible for the leader to meet with the members and solicit their ideas for support and assistance in implementing the change. Quite obviously, at this smaller unit, it is easier to become more personalized in the design of the interventions that each person will receive.

The Individual as the Unit of Change

The Concerns Based Adoption Model (CBAM), which has been a major focus of this book, was created to serve change facilitators and to focus attention on the needs of the individual so that change facilitation is personalized. There are some who have assessed this model and its diagnostic and prescriptive dimensions as a "truly humane" approach to change, since it addresses the individual. After all, persons differ measurably from each other, in terms of their understanding, accepting, and implementing change. Some will change readily, others will come to understanding and accepting later, and some will never reach acceptance. The CBAM model accounts for these differences.

There are those who maintain that in change "storms should be celebrated, as they indicate something is happening," thus suggesting that change is irrevocably fraught with trauma and trials of the first order. The architects of CBAM declare that if individuals are provided support based on their particular Stage of Concerns and Level of Use, the change process can be led and guided in ways that personalizes the experience. When this is done well, the change process does not have to be a negatively challenging experience. If change-facilitating interventions are appropriate, timely, and address the client's particular concerns, the process can be successful for all. As important as the system, organization, and team levels are as units of interventions, without attending to the individual level there is increased likelihood that the change effort will have limited success or will fail. It is truly what happens at the individual level that determines the extent of change success.

BRIDGING THE GAP: EVALUATING IMPLEMENTATION AND THE CONNECTIONS TO OUTCOMES

Change Principle 6, which was introduced in Chapter 1, states: *There will be no change in outcomes until new practices are implemented.* In other words, having a good idea will not make a difference in outcomes until it is implemented by each user. The metaphor of a chasm needing to be bridged was introduced as a way to illustrate the need to support implementation rather than relying on each person making a "giant leap." Unfortunately, with too many change initiatives there is an expectation that changes in practice will come about through giant leaps. For example, the high-stakes testing policies at the federal and state levels assume that as a result of having the pressure of testing, all schools and teachers will change their practices in order to increase test scores. This assumption takes the form of a giant leap when little or no support is provided to assist schools and teachers in making changes in instructional practices. Testing is seen as the impetus for change. There has been little parallel support in policies and funding to facilitate making changes in practices. Without systematically addressing change in instruction in classrooms, it is not realistic to expect that testing mandates alone will lead to steadily increasing scores.

Parallel thinking and work is needed when it comes to evaluating change initiatives. All too frequently, the preponderance of effort is placed on measuring the outcomes, with little examination of the extent to which there were changes in practice. In order to determine if there are any differences in outcomes, one must first determine the extent to which the innovation is implemented by each prospective adopter. Two prior questions must be addressed in conjunction with measuring changes in outcomes:

1. What was done to facilitate implementation?
2. To what extent has the innovation been implemented by each unit of change?

Answering the first question requires examination of interventions and change leadership. The second question requires examination of the innovation-related practices of each implementer. In terms of research, there is a desperate need for longitudinal studies. As Chamblee and Slough (2004) have observed, most CBAM-based studies have focused on the early phases of implementation when Self and Task concerns are high. Studies of the arousal and support for sustaining Impact concerns, higher Levels of Use, and higher fidelity implementation are few. In part this deficit is due to the extended period of time that is needed for most implementers to advance from Self, to Task, and ultimately to Impact concerns. Most change initiatives are not supported for the necessary time. There also is the reality that all change efforts do not steadily advance to full implementation. As was stated in Chapter 1, Change Principle 1: Change is a process, not an event.

Still, there are successful change efforts and related studies that can be used to illustrate how best to address the two prior questions and the bottom-line question of achieving differences in outcomes. Findings from two projects are presented here to illustrate how the same constructs and data can be used as diagnostic information for facilitating change and as summative information for drawing conclusions related to outcomes.

Using Stages of Concern to Introduce a New Product to a National Sales Force

One of the continuing challenges for businesses is the introduction of new products and services. Often, following heavy investment in R&D, there seems to be an assumption that the new product/service will sell itself. This is the "giant leap" approach. Different strategies are used when there is understanding of the need to address the implementation bridge. For marketing purposes, typically features and benefits will be identified and promotional materials developed. But what about preparation of the sales force? An important parallel step is to be thoughtful and thorough in introducing the new product/service to the sales representatives. The following is a true story.

Planning for the New Product Launch. A national company had invested major resources in developing a new product. It was so important that the company's future was dependent on its success in the market place. The CEO and the vice president for marketing and sales were fully aware of the importance of getting the sales force onboard and up to speed. The CEO said more than once, "Our future is dependent on this product selling well." To help with his thinking he had several conversations with the CBAM consultant who was in regular contact with executives in the corporate headquarters and the regional sales offices.

They first used Stages of Concern as a heuristic. They used the SoC definitions (see Figure 7.2) to predict the kinds of concerns that the sale representatives might have. In their phone calls, visits to regional sales offices, and various one-legged interviews, the VP and consultant asked sales reps about their ideas and concerns.

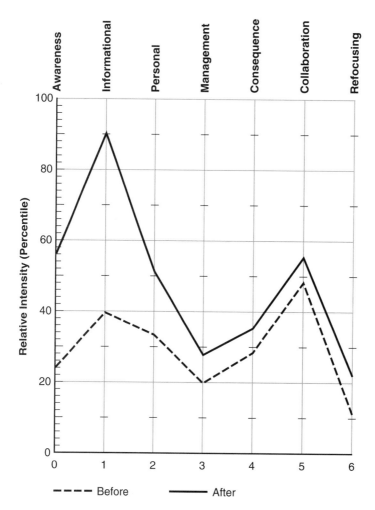

FIGURE 12.2   Stages of Concern Profiles for Sales Representatives Before and After a Three-Day Training about a New Product

They used the Stages of Concern as the rubric to think about what they were hearing from sales representatives and others. Most of the comments seemed to fall into the Self concern area:

- What is the new product like? (Stage 1 Informational)
- When will we get to see it? (Stage 1 Informational)
- How will it look in comparison to what our competitors have come out with? (Stage 1 Informational, maybe some Stage 2 Personal)
- I hear that this is a super product. I am looking forward to seeing it. (Stage 1 Informational, and low Stage 2 Personal)

There were very few comments or questions that could be inferred to be reflective of Task or Impact concerns.

As part of the product launch, one of the key interventions was a three-day training workshop where the entire sales force would be introduced to the new product. As a final step in planning for the training, the vice president and consultant decided to have the sales reps complete a Stages of Concern Questionnaire. Three weeks before the sales rep training meeting, the VP sent out the Stages of Concern Questionnaire (an adapted form for sales reps). He also included an Open-Ended Concerns Statement. He told them that their input would help him in preparing for the three-day training meeting. The dashed line in Figure 12.2 is the SoC profile for the 31 sales reps three weeks before the training.

Cleary, the sales reps as a group had very high Stage 1 Informational concerns about the new product. They wanted to know about it. Their second highest Stage of Concern was Stage 2 Personal. This makes sense by itself, but when combined with the low points on the profile for Stage 3 Management, Stage 4 Consequence, and Stage 6 Refocusing, a sharper picture can be inferred.

The higher Stage 2 Personal concerns had two underlying themes: (1) "I hope that this new product is a good as they say, since my salary depends on it," and (2) "This product better be good or the whole company is in serious trouble, which could mean I lose my job." The third higher than might be expected concerns were on Stage 5 Collaboration. These reflected the long-time emphasis on team building, which was a key component of corporate culture. The Collaboration concerns also reflected the shared sense of responsibility for the success of the new product

The Three-Day National Sales/Training Meeting.   Based on the SoC information, several themes were built into the meeting and careful thought was given to the sequence of presentations. To address Personal concerns, everything was done in positive ways and with enthusiasm for the new product. The company president was the first speaker. He described the major capital investment and the talented team that had worked on product development. Then the product was introduced by the product manager (the beginning of addressing informational concerns). Each sales rep received a notebook that was filled with Information about the product—features and benefits, the results of market testing, an analysis of the competitor's products, and selling tips. Most of the three days was spent in learning about the product and the keys to "helping customers make a buying decision." Also, the sales reps had been trained before in using Stages of Concern to understand "customers' needs" and so key parts of the selling strategies were designed to be concerns based. The three days ended with an afternoon reception and evening at a major league baseball game.

The dotted line in Figure 12.2 represents the profile of concerns at the end of the three days. Clearly, Stage 1 Informational concerns had been addressed. They still wanted more information, but now of a different sort. Personal concerns were still there, but were now related more to "how successful will I be in selling?" The Stage 5 Collaboration concerns were still relatively more intense, which was a reflection of the bonding that took place across the three days.

The Rest of the Story.   This story is a good illustration of how constructs and tools from research and models of change can be used to facilitate a change process. It also illustrates targeting interventions at individuals (the sales reps), the departments (regional sales offices), and the whole organization/system (the whole company). This happens to be a true story with real data. At this time it is satisfying to report that the new product was a huge success. In fact, it dominated the market for the next seven years.

Connecting Extent of Implementation with Outcomes

In most organizations and systems the bottom-line question continues to be: Did the new approach make any difference? Actually, the wording of this question is more open ended than is typical. This wording allows for the possibility that outcomes could be better or worse than expected. The more typical question is: Did the change lead to increases in outcomes? Answering this question requires answering three subquestions:

1. To what extent was the change implemented by each prospective user?
2. What has happened to outcomes?
3. How does the extent of implementation relate to the observed outcomes?

Addressing this set of questions requires the use of change process constructs and measures. The findings from one systematic effort to address these questions in one school district is described next.

A School District Superintendent Wants to Know.   One school system where there is a history of making concerted efforts to improve schooling and to evaluate the results is the U.S. Department of Defense Dependents Schools (DoDDS). This is the system of school districts spread around the world to provide schooling for the children of members of the U.S. military. In one of their school districts in Germany, the superintendent made a concerted effort to support the implementation of a dramatically different approach to teaching mathematics. The curriculum innovation was based on the standards for teaching and learning developed by the National Council for the Teaching of Mathematics (NCTM). The approach required teachers to make a dramatic change in their teaching. Rather than teaching rules for computation, the new teaching strategy was constructivist: Teachers should pose mathematical problems and the students should construct answers using their own approaches. Rather than the teacher explaining the reasoning, students must explain how they got their answers.

This approach represented a major change for many veteran teachers. Understanding this, the superintendent developed an implementation support strategy that was centered on employing three master teachers as districtwide specialists. They designed workshops, presented demonstration lessons, consulted with teachers, and paced the implementation effort. In addition, the superintendent understood that change is a process, not an event (Change Principle 1), so the commitment to having three math specialists was kept in place for three years (Johnson, 2000).

Given the size and serious of the investment plus the political risk, since focusing on mathematics for three years meant that a number of other areas were not as high on the priority list, led the superintendent to ask her question: How can I know if this investment made any difference?

Measuring Implementation (LoU).   The implementation bridge metaphor made sense and the decision was made to assess the extent to which teachers were moving across the bridge. In this study, two constructs and related measures were used: (1) an Innovation Configuration Map (see Chapter 6) was developed and (2) the teachers' Level of Use (See Chapter 8) was assessed. An added dimension to this effort was that the change process researchers and the school district staff collaborated in data collection, data analysis, interpretation of findings, and report writing. It was a true example of action research (Eden & Huxham, 1996), in that the research questions were developed by the district and there was a collaborative effort with the researchers. In addition, the data about implementation were used as diagnostic information for further facilitating implementation, as well as for answering the superintendent's question.

Measuring the extent of implementation was done at the end of the first and second years of the effort. The school district staff, including the superintendent, were trained to research criteria in conducting and rating LoU Interviews. They, along with the researchers, collected data on over 100 teachers representing all schools and across grades K–8 (Thornton & West, 1999).

Findings from the LoU data collection are summarized in Figure 12.3. Three key findings were:

1. Each year all teachers sampled were users at some level of the new approach. No teachers were rated at LoU 0 Nonuse, I Orientation, or II Preparation.
2. The year 2 pattern of an increasing proportion of teachers being at LoU IVA Routine Use or higher was a clear indication that teachers were moving further across the Implementation Bridge (Thornton & West, 1999).
3. Even after two years of systematic support, one-third of the teachers were still at LoU III Mechanical Use.

Measuring Implementation (IC).   The Levels of Use data documented that teachers where engaged with using the innovation, but these data do not inform about the pieces, features, and functions of the innovation that were being used. Answering this question is the purpose of Innovation Configuration mapping. For the math study an IC map was developed. A component of this map was presented as Figure 6.4. The IC map was then used to observe and document classroom practices as well as a guide for targeting teacher training, coaching, and professional development (Alquist & Hendrickson, 1999).

As was described in Chapter 6, in an IC map the key *components* of the innovation are identified. For each component, the different ways it could be made operational, the *variations,* are described. The *a* variation presents a word-picture

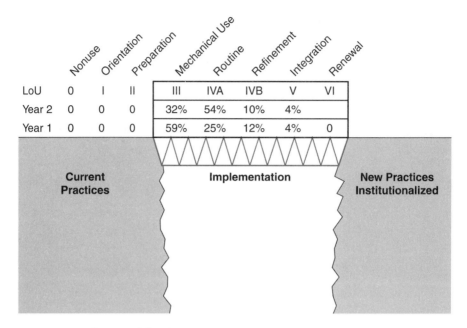

FIGURE 12.3 **Percent of Teachers at Each Level of Use (LoU) of a Standards-Based Mathematics Curriculum**

description of best practice. The *b* variation is slightly less ideal, the *c* is acceptable but not exciting, and the *d, e,* and *f* variations describe practices that are different from what is expected as part of the innovation—in this case, traditional practice. Based on classroom observation and interviewing, the appropriate variation of each component is circled on the IC map.

Computer clustering procedures can be employed to group classrooms according to the extent of fidelity of implementation. IC maps that have more *a* variations circled represent high fidelity, whereas those with many *d, e,* and *f* variations represent use of something other than the innovation. When IC map data are placed on the implementation bridge (see Figure 12.4), those configurations of practice that include more *a* and *b* variations will be placed further across the bridge. These steps were taken in the math study. The analyses revealed a wide range of configurations, including some classrooms that were all *a*s and *b*s, and other classrooms with more *c*s and *d*s. In those classrooms were components where traditional practice was still taking place.

Answering the Bottom-Line Question.   The answer to the superintendent's question is found by relating test scores to the extent to which teachers and classroom practices have moved across the bridge. In this particular study, the findings were that test scores increased for teachers and classrooms that were further across the bridge. This was true for Levels of Use and the Innovation Configuration data. In addition, it was observed

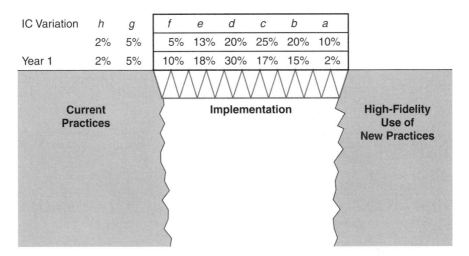

IC Variation	h	g	f	e	d	c	b	a
	2%	5%	5%	13%	20%	25%	20%	10%
Year 1	2%	5%	10%	18%	30%	17%	15%	2%

Current Practices   Implementation   High-Fidelity Use of New Practices

FIGURE 12.4   **Using Innovation Configuration Map Data to Assess Implementation Fidelity**

that students with lower fall test scores seemed to benefit the most from being in "high fidelity" implementation classrooms (George, Hall, & Uchiyama, 2000).

REFLECTIONS ABOUT ORGANIZATION CULTURE: ITS CONSTRUCTION AND PLC

One of the themes carried across the chapters has been the importance of understanding organization culture. Change resistance, implementation success, and the general well-being of an organization and its members are based in the health of the organization's culture. It may actually be that the most critical consideration for all change efforts is reflecting on the extent to which the innovation will be supported by the current culture and the extent to which it will affect changes in the culture. Hill and Crevola (1999) have alluded to this point based on their experiences with disadvantaged schools in Victoria, Australia. In their view (see Figure 12.5), "Beliefs and Understandings" are at the center of school reform. The various programs, processes, and structural innovations in some ways are seen as affecting culture as well as having systemic affects on each other. In addition, efforts to implement each of these initiatives will be affected by the culture.

Understanding the functions, effects, and systemic relationships between leaders, followers, innovations, implementation success, and organization culture is the current cutting edge of research, theory building, and improving practice. In this section we offer some elaborations and emerging hypotheses related to these factors and their interrelationships.

FIGURE 12.5   Placing Beliefs and Understandings (Organization Culture) at the Center of School Reform

Source: Hill, P.W., & Crevola, C.A. (1999). The role of standards in educational reform for the 21st century. In D.D. Marsh (Ed.), *1999 ASCD Yearbook: Preparing Our Schools for the 21st Century.* Alexandria, VA: ASCD. Reprinted by permission.

Relationships between Organization Culture and Leader Succession

As the importance of organization culture has emerged as a key consideration for change success, so has interest in changing culture. In recent years many have assigned a new responsibility to leaders; now they must change organization culture. In our studies and work with leaders it has become quite clear that the shape of an organization's culture is not due solely to what the leader does. In fact, it is a product of the thoughts, talk, and actions of all members of the system; again, *organization culture is a social construction.* In combination, constructs about Change Facilitator Style (Chapter 10), Intervention Mushrooms (Chapter 11), Organization Culture (Chapters 2 and 5), and a number of the Change Principles (Chapter 1) can be used to illustrate the complexity of culture. Even though the shape and dynamics of organization culture is complex, it is central to understanding and facilitating change processes.

Indicators of Organization Culture.   Early analyses, including the works of Schein (1985), focused on identifying the various types of symbols that would be indicators of organization culture. These elements and themes continue to be used to describe and understand culture. The research relied heavily on ethnographic methods. As was stated in Chapter 5, to understand an organization's culture requires that the observer spend extensive intensive time in the organization. Symbolic features of organizations that could be used to characterize the culture were identified, such as:

- *Artifacts:* These are the tangible pieces and features, such as the trophies in the main entrance to the high school, brochures, books, minutes of meetings, and work products.
- *Stories:* Stories are shared descriptions of something that happened in the past. For example, in one school a story was about "the boy who painted the classroom blue." Several years earlier, a boy had literally painted a blue stripe on the walls all the way around a classroom. The story took on a life of its own and was repeated regularly.
- *Myths:* Myths consist of anecdotes and stories that probably are not true but are shared as if they are. In one university a widely shared myth was that the president had not done the work in his doctoral dissertation.
- *Ceremonies:* Each organization has a number of activities and events, such as graduation, marching band at half-time of football games, and a certain rhythm to staff meetings and board meetings. These ceremonies provide continuity and predictability to life in the organization.
- *Metaphors:* Certain elements are represented through shared labels that are indirect. For example, in an organization where the top executives were isolated from the bottom by where their offices were located and also in how they communicated mainly with themselves, the invisible barrier between the top and bottom was referred to as "the thermal layer." This metaphor is a reference to a physical characteristic in oceans where two layers of water with very different temperatures meet. A submarine above or below this layer cannot detect an object on the other side.
- *Humor:* Humor can be used in positive and negative ways. What is the humor about? Who tells the joke and who laughs are clues. Unfortunately, too many high school staffs frequently focus on sick humor about students, colleagues, and the administration. Elementary school staffs share in the funny things young children say and do.

Understanding organization culture does not come about from a simple recording of symbols. The hard work is in ferreting out the interpretations and meanings that organization members ascribe to the symbols.

Organization Culture Is a Social Construction.   In many ways a new organization member is like the ethnographic researcher. Both are observing the symbols and also determining the interpretations and meanings ascribed to each. As information is gathered, the observed themes become the shared norms in the culture. Also, as was described in Chapter 11, some of these become the themes of Intervention Mushrooms. Each person develops his or her own interpretation based on that person's experiences. Individuals also are influenced through the sharing of interpretations with others. In these ways the construction of culture is a social process.

The various constructs introduced in the earlier chapters become important to seeing how particular interpretations are shared. For example, in the Diffusion perspective, opinion leaders, lines of communication, and social networks are mechanisms for spreading a particular interpretation and for developing a shared view. The Stages of Concern offer a way to predict likely topics of discussion and interpretations of events.

There always are new events and new interactions that either add further support to the current interpretations or stimulate the creation of new meanings. This reality means that organization culture is not static. Rather, as Hatch (1993) has described, organization culture is a dynamic phenomenon. This means that, in theory, the shape of culture should be susceptible to efforts to change it. However, direct attempts to influence culture will immediately be filtered through the individual and social interpretation processes. In other words, just because the leader wants to change the culture in certain ways does not necessarily mean that the members of the organization will interpret the intentions in the same way.

The CF Style of Leaders Can Make a Difference in Organization Culture.

Based on fieldwork and a number of consulting projects, Hall (2001) has examined the relationships between Change Facilitator Style and the shape of organization culture. His working hypothesis is that each CF Style is associated with a characteristic culture profile. These different cultures are summarized in Table 12.1 and described briefly below. To assist in seeing the differences in culture types, a set of descriptors is used to describe the *center of action,* the *shared themes,* and the *success criterion for staff.*

TABLE 12.1   Relationships between Leader Change Facilitator Style and Characteristics of Organization Culture

CHANGE FACILITATOR STYLE

	RESPONDER	MANAGER	INITIATOR	CF TEAM
Type of Culture	Balkanized	Highly Organized	Strategic Visioning	Professional Learning Community
Center of Action	Taking care of me	Controlling resources and tasks	Improving outcomes	Viewing problems as opportunities
Theme	Us versus Them	We are very busy.	We are a team.	Collaboration for continuous improvement
Success Criterion for Staff	Who gets what?	*Equality:* All receive the same.	*Equity:* Each receives what he or she needs.	Everyone is productive and learning.

Balkanized Culture.   The organization culture that appears to be associated with Responder CF Style leaders is, in one word, *Balkanized.* Let's use schools as the example. The staff do not work together as whole; instead, a clique of teachers continually works behind the scenes to undercut others and to get what they want. Responders tend to employee strong independent teachers who generally view the school in terms of what is best for *me,* not what will be supportive of others or best for students. This results in a theme of *us versus them.* Those on the outside of the clique see that they are not receiving equal treatment and may complain, but little changes over time. Success is centered on *who gets what* among the adults.

Highly Organized Culture.   Resources, controlling tasks, schedules, and budgets, and treating everyone the same are associated with Manager CF Style leaders. They are skilled at having their organization run efficiently. Procedures will be in place for requesting supplies, resources will be allocated equally, and everyone will be held accountable for not overspending. In simple terms, the center of the action is *controlling resources and tasks.* The leader always wants more resources for the organization. The staff knows what resources they have and the rules/limits for obtaining them. The regularly heard theme is *we are really busy,* "and we can't do more without more resources." The success criterion is having *equality;* everyone gets treated the same in terms of resource allocations and task assignments.

Strategic Visioning Culture.   The Initiator leader is always looking into the future as well as addressing the day-to-day needs of individuals and the organization. The center of the action is *improving outcomes.* Whether it is a school where the bottom-line outcome is student learning, or a company where it is sales and customer satisfaction, the Initiator is leading and expecting all members of the organization to be contributing to improving outcomes. Thus, the theme is *we are a team.* Within this culture success for its members is defined in terms of *equity.* Instead of treating everyone equally by receiving the same supports, there is task-related differentiation with each receiving what is needed to do his or her particular job.

The CF Team.   The optimal arrangement for an organization is to have a leadership team. Although this may sound paradoxical, the strongest and most effective Change Facilitator Teams are led by Initiators. These are the organizations that develop and sustain the characteristics of a professional learning community (PLC). Where others see problems, these organizations see interesting *opportunities.* There is wide collaboration around efforts to *continuously improve.* Perhaps most important is that the criterion for success is to see *everyone learning,* not just students or customers, but all members of the organization learning and growing. These are wonderful places to work and to learn.

Implications of CF Style and Organization Culture for Leader Succession.
Being a successful participant in each of the cultures summarized in Table 12.1 requires emphasizing different themes and focusing on different types of actions. Also,

as was described in Chapter 10, different skills are important to influencing each of the three CF Style leaders. All of these factors become doubly important when there is a change in the leader, which is a time of rapid change in culture. The new leader and the organization will have a very different experience, depending on the departing leader's CF Style and the shape of the culture at the time. The ideas outlined in Table 12.2 can be used to predict some of the changes that will take place with leader succession.

Responder to Initiator.   One of the most challenging changes in CF Style is from a Responder to an Initiator. Unfortunately, this is an all too common transition, as are the predictable events. Assuming that a Balkanized culture was well established, the arrival of an Initiator will mean expectations for rapid change. The Initiator's approach will be strategic, information based, and oriented toward everyone working as a team to make things move ahead. Their aspirations will be to build a professional learning community. An Initiator will not be supportive of a subset of faculty as a clique receiving favorable treatment, which will have been the practice with the previous Responder leader. The Initiator may not even be aware that there was such a clique. While the Initiator is talking about vision, improving outcomes, and setting programmatic directions, members of the clique will be whispering about their loss of personal influence. They will share among themselves about how terrible things have become. They also will likely be busy complaining to central administration and the board about how terrible the new leader is doing.

In terms of the constructs introduced in Chapter 11, the clique will be seeding poisonous intervention mushrooms. The key to what happens next is how the central office executives and board respond. In too many cases we have observed a weak response "Well, I don't know if Jerry is going to make it. I hear things aren't going so well." Rather than coming out strongly in support of the new leader, there is a tendency to avoid direct support, which further empowers the clique and the growth of the poisonous mushrooms.

Other patterns of leader succession carry with them inherent scenarios that may or may not be healthy. In all cases, what happens is not solely the responsibility of the leader and the members of the organization unit. The actions of the supervising executive, whether it is a school district superintendent or corporate CEO, will be critical to how the unit's culture evolves.

A Systemic View of PLC

Across the United States and other countries, the attention to and incidence of the concept and structure of Professional Learning Communities has increased dramatically. One wonders if it is becoming the "innovation du jour." What has become clear is the wide variation in structures, especially in schools, that are claiming to be PLC. This is rather predictable when a relatively new idea hits the press and others see its value and take it on board in hopes of deriving that value. Does it matter whether the

TABLE 12.2   Leader Succession: What Can Happen to Organization Culture with Changes in CF Style

INCOMING LEADER CHANGE FACILITATOR STYLE

	RESPONDER	MANAGER	INITIATOR
Responder	The clique will continue to have extra influence.	Resources will be distributed on an equal basis; supervision will be tightened significantly. Clique members will complain.	All will be expected to produce. Clique members will attempt to undercut and complain to upper levels.
Manager	Initially all will be pleased with increased freedom. In time a clique will emerge and gain influence.	Some changes will occur in procedures and resource allocations. There will be continued stability with close supervision	Less focus will be on resource allocation; increased focus will be on accomplishing outcomes. There will be increased feelings of energy and capacity.
Initiator	There will be immediate feelings of loss of direction. A rapid loss of momentum and initiative will occur.	There will be more forms and procedures with less individual control. A gradual slowing of momentum will occur.	Continued focus will be on improving outcomes; new initiatives are launched; some of the old initiatives may not be supported. A high energy level will develops with many things happening; however, over time the staff may become weary.

structure of a PLC is authentically in place in an organization or not? Maybe yes, maybe no.

If the various structures in an organization contribute to a context and culture that is, for the participants, pleasant and productive and that motivates individuals to do good work that is in accordance with the organization's goals, it probably doesn't matter what their structure, or "way of working," is or how it is defined and described. However, if the leaders of an organization are interested in accessing the outcomes that a PLC typically delivers, then it seems necessary that the attributes or characteristics of the valued PLC are created, or maintained, in one's own organization. Many of the PLCs in schools that are being talked about, written about, and given recognition do not adhere to the characteristics that promise the outcomes noted in Chapter 2.

The Learning of Professionals.   In some cases, little attention is given to the *learning of the professionals* and their discretion about how they will learn. Without this dimension, the staff does not increase its knowledge base, its skills base, or its ability to act more effectively. In this same case, the mission, vision, and goals of the organization (school) are defined and widely communicated; there is much attention given to students' learning and the various ways that different groups of students can be served in their learning, but little focus is on the professionals and how they will develop increased capacity in the long run to assure that students are successful learners.

These descriptions of PLC are highly similar to the typical school improvement process of identifying what students need to learn, bring in a new program to address this gap, and "implement" it with little attention to how well the professional staff is equipped to use it. Nor is the opportunity provided for staff to study thoroughly the conditions of student learning, to determine where the staff is in need of improvement in their instructional effectiveness, to make decisions about what the staff needs to learn in order to become better, and to how they will learn it. In other words, the possibility for the staff to manage its own professionalism has been largely ignored, unfortunately.

Participants in the Community.   Another factor in the wide range of descriptions of PLC is that of who the *community* is. Many writers and speakers refer to grade-level teachers as the learning community; others cite three to four teachers focused on a topic of choice in one section of the school; all claim PLC. Most certainly, there is no requirement for the size of the community. But if the school is striving to identify a major focus for change and improvement, or constructs major goals for the school's achievement, then all teachers and staff need to be on board with this focus or goal. If each of the six or seven grades in an elementary school, or various departments of secondary schools, is targeting disparate goals, then a critical mass cannot form.

What this means in terms of culture is the development of numbers of subcultures, where the focus of attention, the norms of operating, and the particular values and beliefs of the subcultures' members drive them to operate differently. There is no presiding culture that contributes cohesion and collaborative work to the organization. It is easy to see that this multicultural organization is not likely to result in members who care deeply about each other and their work and who share their expertise so that all the professional staff is a community and is a learning one.

POSTMODERNISM: ANOTHER CHANGE PERSPECTIVE

An important perspective that has received limited attention in the change process literature is postmodernism and critical theory. Consideration of this perspective is not without its critics and, for many, feelings of discomfort. However, as Alvesson and Deetz (1996) have observed,

> The increased size of organizations, rapid implementation of communication/information technologies, globalization, changing nature of work, reduction of the working class, less salient class conflicts, professionalization of the work force, stagnant economies, widespread ecological problems and turbulent markets are all part of the contemporary context demanding a research response. (pp. 191–192)

These conditions not only demand research but they also drive and depersonalize change. The postmodernist perspective challenges the desirability of continuing the unquestioning acceptance of these conditions and their consequences for the individuals. There is much to consider in terms of postmodernist perspective for those interested in change, whether they are leaders, participants, or students of the process.

The Foundations of Postmodernism and Critical Theory

Postmodernism represents a very different paradigm, which in many ways is complex and difficult to describe and understand. In part this is due to the different way of thinking. In part, it is due to the number of ideological views that are represented within this general perspective. Interestingly, that these different views do not always agree is inherent to the perspective.

Early Views. The beginning of postmodernism and critical theory can be traced back well over 100 years to works of philosophers and social critics who were concerned about the loss of autonomy for the individual that they believed was a result of the Industrial Revolution and the increasing power of governments. These critics suggested a different way of thinking about knowledge and understanding. The writings of Marx, Neitzsche, Freud, the Frankfurt School, Foucault, and, more recently, Habermas, each in its own way has offered a novel view of individuals and their place in society. For example, they saw a person's reality as being constructed within his or her context, including language and social condition. People working on an assembly line have a different reality than do their bosses. Postmodernists also play close attention to power and its uses especially by authority. In fact, understanding power and its uses are at the value center of this perspective.

The Importance of Critique. The primary analysis method has been critique and critical theory. In practice, this approach is based in examining a situation, such as the place of working in an organization, by identifying different forms of power and control, deconstructing the flow and effects, and identifying ways in which power is distributed and used unequally. In other words, the symbols and actions of people and organizations are "critiqued" in terms of the distribution of power and how people are affected. Power—its form(s), its distribution (especially when it is unequal), and its effects—is the subject of critique.

The Use of Language. The vocabulary used to communicate, for example, carries with it signs of power. Critique is approached with a premise of looking for those who in some way exercise power of others. For example, power is critiqued in terms of *domination.* Those with formal authority due to their position, such as a school principal, are seen in many ways to "dominate" their subordinates in terms of teaching assignments, working conditions, and teaching approaches. The principal, the superintendent, as well as the state and federal governments use positions of authority to dictate curriculum. This "hegemony" results in individual loss of autonomy, freedom, and power to construct one's own reality.

Postmodernism, Critical Theory, and the Change Process

Postmodernists would debate the way change is initiated by various authorities. They would be seen as using their power to achieve their ends. Those who have to make the changes would be seen as powerless and losing identity. There are several ways to consider postmodernism and its implications for the change process.

Change Leaders as "Functionalists." A critical theorist would view most of this book to be about how those in authority can lead change efforts to obtain the outcomes they desire. This critique would apply to our descriptions of organization culture (including PLC) as well as the more "behaviorist" chapters dealing with Levels of Use and Innovation Configurations. The critical theorist would argue that the functionalists treat culture as a variable that can be manipulated by managers. They argue that culture should be understood in terms of its symbols and how these help one understand and control organization life (Smircich, 1983; Martin, 2002).

Critical Theorists as Change Agents. One thing that postmodernists are very good at doing is critique. They are well trained and articulate at examining a situation, identifying the different forms and sources of power, and pointing out how they are being used to achieve someone's agenda. Their reasoning will make sense and be based in fact, as far as it goes. The intentions of those in authority will be questioned, even though most participants trust that they are honorable. Through this strategy the critical theorist gains power over others, although he or she seldom admits this. The role and agenda of the change leaders will be questioned. There is risk in this type of critique when it is not followed by strategies for reconstruction. Critique as an end is not helpful in most of today's change situations.

Critique as a "Tool" for Functionalists.   As difficult as it might be for postmodernists to accept, their perspective and strategies for addressing symbols and issues related to power are very useful "tools" for anyone who is interested in change. The natural tensions that are heightened when there is change have a heavy power component. The leaders of an organization believe that change is necessary. The followers may or may not see the need. Instead of having a dialogue, it is quite easy to have different views turn into polarized debates. When the power of persuasion doesn't work, either side may turn to coercive forms of power: "We will stop work unless you give us . . ." "We will move manufacturing overseas if you don't work more hours for the same pay." "If test scores do not increase, in three years we will reconstitute the school." To use another change construct, Stages of Concern, when raw power is used to force a particular direction, Stage 2 Personal concerns will intensify. As was stated in Chapter 7, when personal concerns are intense, the change process will not move ahead easily. Taking time to consider the different forms of power and how the symbols of power will be perceived and interpreted is important to do before launching a response to apparent resistance. The wrong use of power can lead to less change success.

FINAL REFLECTIONS ABOUT IMPLEMENTING CHANGE

As the writing of this final chapter comes to a close, we offer several notes as points of reflection. Some relate to facilitating change, others to studying change processes, and some hint at current dilemmas of the authors.

Ethical Issues in Facilitating Change

As architects and creators of the CBAM model, and as researchers and writers about professional learning communities and systemic change, we worry about how the constructs, measures, and ideas described in this book will be used by well meaning, and perhaps not so well meaning, persons in the field. Do they understand fully the constructs? Do they have the adequate skills to interpret results from use of the measures, and will their responses—interventions—be valid and appropriate?

Understanding the Constructs.   We have frequent phone calls from individuals who have modest knowledge of Stages of Concern, Levels of Use, and professional learning communities, and who want permission to use the related measures. Obviously, it is worrisome to us that people are trying to use the concepts and measures without a deep and full understanding of what they are measuring. How will they use these measures and their results with people when they are not knowledgeable and skilled? We ask them to do some reading and study, and then talk with us again about their interests in using the ideas for facilitation and for research and evaluation. We encourage participation in training workshops and becoming certified.

Responsible Use. Even more troubling is to receive phone calls of inquiry from people who have administered the Stages of Concern Questionnaire or one of the other measures and don't know how to score it or interpret the results. It is important, we believe, to be sure there is responsible use of various instruments and techniques. But the dark side is not knowing whether the user is a first-time user/novice, or a person with some experience, or a person who has a colleague who is experienced and can assist. On the surface, constructs such as Stages of Concern and PLC appear deceptively simple, but, in truth, they are quite complex. The ethical dilemma for us, and the construct/measure users, is providing assurances that each has sufficient knowledge and skill to use the constructs and measures responsibly.

External versus Internal Impetus for Change. One of the dilemmas of our time is weighing the different potential sources of changes and the impetus for their implementation. There are many sources of change being imposed from outside our organizations. In some cases, the imposition of an external agenda may be necessary. Unfortunately, mandates from outside have become too prevalent today. It could be a school examining its student achievement data or a business studying spreadsheets to explore the "bottom line." When the entire staff is involved in investigating its own performance, it is highly probable that the staff will give more commitment to changes intended to correct distressful situations. An external impetus can be effective in promoting change in an organization, if the leaders of the organization seize the opportunity and bring the external idea home in such a way that makes sense to the organizational members. This means that the organization's leaders must "own" the problem and the change that is intended to correct it. Announcing that "they are making us do it" will not persuade many staff to embrace the change. The use of data (whether statistical or anecdotal) can aid the leader in transferring the need for change into his or her own organization. Addressing staff members' concerns is an obvious key when introducing an external change. At the same time, the various external forces demanding that their changes be implemented need to come to an appreciation of how their agenda affects the targeted organizations.

Support at All Levels of the Organization. Many change efforts fall flat on their face because facilitation and assistance are not provided to all members of the organization, whether they be executive, management, or staff positions. Support must come from the top of the organizational chart to the middle managers. In the case of educational change, this means that principals of the schools that are expected to change will need professional development in order to exercise their facilitation role successfully. All too frequently, principals and other middle managers are left in that space between the executive level that requests change and the staff that will need to implement the change. Frequently, these leaders are without the tools or skills to do the job of supporting and assisting the staff well. Many promoters of change should pay closer attention to the need to develop and support the middle-level managers who are the key to implementation success.

What about the Ethics of Change Agentry?   This is a question that we always raise with our students and clients. One way we phrase it is to ask, "When does change facilitation become manipulation?" After all, we are talking about tools and techniques to get people to change. Unfortunately, little has been said or written about this important issue. Early in our work, we asked Matt Miles (1979) to write a paper and provide us with a seminar on ethics. His thoughts and wise counsel have stayed with us. For example, in reflecting on organization development (OD) consultants, he pointed out critical issues related to the accountability of OD change agents:

> To whom are OD change agents accountable? At one level, as Bermant and Warwick (1978) point out, they are *personally* accountable for their actions, like any person in society. They should not lie, cheat, steal, or engage in similar socially reprehensible actions. And they are *legally* accountable in a very general sense, not only for misdemeanors and felonies, but for items like breach of contract. However, I have never heard of malpractice litigations being threatened against an OD practitioner (though it has occurred for encounter group leaders).
>
> In any case, litigation is a gross tool for insuring ethical behavior by practitioners. The most central form of accountability is that which OD consultants have toward their *sponsors,* who are paying the bill, in several senses. Sponsors can terminate contracts, or at least revise them, if the program is not functioning as intended. . . . Finally, there is *professional accountability* for OD practitioners, for which at present there are no formal structural supports comparable to those in medicine, law, accounting, and psychology. (Miles, 1979, pp. 8–9)

In the concerns-based perspective, "good" and "bad" are primarily defined in terms of what change facilitators do and do not do. It is neither good nor bad for individuals to have certain concerns profiles, Levels of Use, or configurations. What *is* good or bad is the types of interventions that are made. All interventions need to be *concerns-based.* They need to be related to the concerns of the clients, not the change facilitators. As a simple example, consider a teacher with high Stage 2 Personal concerns. We have heard administrators and others say to these individuals something like, "You should be concerned about students, not yourself." This is a wrong intervention from a concerns-based perspective, for its single effect will be to further raise the teacher's personal concerns. "Good" interventions would be to acknowledge the personal concerns, to attempt to provide additional information to increase understanding, to be supportive, to provide stability, and so on. Our point here is that the change facilitator bears major responsibility for whether teachers have implementation success. Just as in the Japanese management models, if an employee is not doing well, the manager has failed. Making concerns-based interventions increases the likelihood of success for the implementers and the facilitators.

SUMMARY

In this book we have presented key concepts about change, especially as they relate to people and how the process unfolds in organizational settings. Many additional ideas, research findings, and stories could be discussed, but it is time for you, the reader, to use what you have learned. Whether you are a potential user of an innovation, a key change facilitator, or a researcher, the constructs and tools presented here should be of help. We offer one brief caveat and one of our favorite phrases in the way of conclusion.

The Caveat

Earlier in this chapter we touched on the ethics of being a change facilitator. We would like to return to this topic here but with a different emphasis. As dramatic as it may sound, the information presented in this book and other similar texts can be used in very inappropriate and inexcusable ways. In fact, the tools and findings from research in the social sciences are in many ways far more dangerous than what the physicists were doing underneath the football stadium at the University of Chicago in 1940, since social scientists are talking about how to change people, organizations, and social systems. In addition, there are no rules of access to the information. Anyone can choose an idea out of this book, some questionnaire, or any other piece of work, and do with it what they please. There are no codes of conduct. There are no security clearances. What happens from here depends on the integrity and professionalism of the users. We ask that you think often about whether you are being responsible in what you do. Fortunately, the first concerns that are aroused when there is change are Self concerns. To a large extent, people begin a change process by protecting themselves. Only when the innovation and change facilitators are perceived to be safe, will people move to implement the change. Your job is to make sure that Self concerns are respected and that the abusive intentions and actions of others are challenged. Change success is achieved when Self and Task concerns are resolved and, ideally, when Impact concerns are aroused.

A Final Phrase

An important perspective to keep in mind as we are engaged in the change process is summarized in one phrase:

The road to success is always under construction.

STAGES OF CONCERN QUESTIONNAIRE

Name _____

Date Completed _____

It is very important for continuity in processing this data that we have a unique number that you can remember. Please use:

Last four digits of your Social Security No. _____ _____ _____ _____

The purpose of this questionnaire is to determine what people who are using or thinking about using various programs are concerned about at various times during the innovation adoption process. The items were developed from typical responses of school and college teachers who ranged from no knowledge at all about various programs to many years experience in using them. Therefore, *a good part of the items on this questionnaire may appear to be of little relevance or irrelevant to you at this time.* For the completely irrelevant items, please circle "0" on the scale. Other items will represent those concerns you *do* have, in varying degrees of intensity, and should be marked higher on the scale, according to the explanation at the top of each of the following pages.

For example:

This statement is very true of me at this time.	0 1 2 3 4 5 6 ⑦
This statement is somewhat true of me now.	0 1 2 3 ④ 5 6 7
This statement is not at all true of me at this time.	0 ① 2 3 4 5 6 7
This statement is irrelevant to me.	⓪ 1 2 3 4 5 6 7

Please respond to the items in terms of *your present concerns,* or how you feel about your involvement or potential involvement with _____. We do not hold to any one definition of this program, so please think of it in terms of *your own perceptions* of what it involves. Since this questionnaire is used for a variety of innovations, the name _____ never appears. However, phrases such as "the innovation," "this approach," and "the new system" all refer to _____. Remember to respond to each item in terms of *your present concerns* about your involvement or potential involvement with _____.

Thank you for taking time to complete this task.

0	1	2	3	4	5	6	7
Irrelevant	Not true of me now		Somewhat true of me now		Very true of me now		

1. I am concerned about students' attitudes toward this innovation.

   0 1 2 3 4 5 6 7

2. I now know of some other approaches that might work better.

   0 1 2 3 4 5 6 7

3. I don't even know what the innovation is.

   0 1 2 3 4 5 6 7

4. I am concerned about not having enough time to organize myself each day.

   0 1 2 3 4 5 6 7

5. I would like to help other faculty in their use of the innovation.

   0 1 2 3 4 5 6 7

6. I have a very limited knowledge about the innovation.

   0 1 2 3 4 5 6 7

7. I would like to know the effect of this reorganization on my professional status.

   0 1 2 3 4 5 6 7

8. I am concerned about conflict between my interests and my responsibilities.

   0 1 2 3 4 5 6 7

9. I am concerned about revising my use of the innovation.

   0 1 2 3 4 5 6 7

10. I would like to develop working relationships with both our faculty and outside faculty using this innovation.

    0 1 2 3 4 5 6 7

11. I am concerned about how the innovation affects students.

    0 1 2 3 4 5 6 7

12. I am not concerned about this innovation.

    0 1 2 3 4 5 6 7

13. I would like to know who will make the decisions in the new system.

    0 1 2 3 4 5 6 7

14. I would like to discuss the possibility of using the innovation.

    0 1 2 3 4 5 6 7

15. I would like to know what resources are available if we decide to adopt this innovation.

    0 1 2 3 4 5 6 7

16. I am concerned about my inability to manage all the innovation requires.

    0 1 2 3 4 5 6 7

17. I would like to know how my teaching or administration is supposed to change.

    0 1 2 3 4 5 6 7

18. I would like to familiarize other departments or persons with the progress of this new approach.

    0 1 2 3 4 5 6 7

0	1	2	3	4	5	6	7
Irrelevant	Not true of me now		Somewhat true of me now		Very true of me now		

19. I am concerned about evaluating my impact on students. 0 1 2 3 4 5 6 7

20. I would like to revise the innovation's instructional approach. 0 1 2 3 4 5 6 7

21. I am completely occupied with other things. 0 1 2 3 4 5 6 7

22. I would like to modify our use of the innovation based on the experiences of our students. 0 1 2 3 4 5 6 7

23. Although I don't know about this innovation, I am concerned about other things in the area. 0 1 2 3 4 5 6 7

24. I would like to excite my students about their part in this approach. 0 1 2 3 4 5 6 7

25. I am concerned about my time spent working with nonacademic problems related to this innovation. 0 1 2 3 4 5 6 7

26. I would like to know what the use of the innovation will require in the immediate future. 0 1 2 3 4 5 6 7

27. I would like to coordinate my efforts with others to maximize the innovation's effects. 0 1 2 3 4 5 6 7

28. I would like to have more information on time and energy commitments required by this innovation. 0 1 2 3 4 5 6 7

29. I would like to know what other faculty are doing in this area. 0 1 2 3 4 5 6 7

30. At this time, I am not interested in learning about the innovation. 0 1 2 3 4 5 6 7

31. I would like to determine how to supplement, enhance, or replace the innovation. 0 1 2 3 4 5 6 7

32. I would like to use feedback from students to change the program. 0 1 2 3 4 5 6 7

33. I would like to know how my role will change when I am using the innovation. 0 1 2 3 4 5 6 7

34. Coordination of tasks and people is taking too much of my time. 0 1 2 3 4 5 6 7

35. I would like to know how this innovation is better than what we have now. 0 1 2 3 4 5 6 7

PLEASE COMPLETE THE FOLLOWING:

36. What other concerns, if any, do you have at this time? (Please describe them using complete sentences.)

37. Briefly describe your job function.

SOCQ QUICK SCORING DEVICE

DIRECTIONS FOR USING THE SOCQ QUICK SCORING DEVICE

The Stages of Concern Questionnaire (SoCQ) contains 35 items. The scoring of the SoCQ requires a series of operations that result in an SoCQ profile. The following steps should be carried out on the Quick Scoring Device:

Step 1 In the box labeled A, fill in the identifying information taken from the cover sheet of the SoC Questionnaire.

Step 2 Copy the numerical values of the circled responses to statements 1 through 35 in the numbered blanks in the Table labeled B. Note that the numbered blanks in Table B are *not* in consecutive order.

Step 3 Box C contains the Raw Scale Total for each stage (0–6) For each of the seven columns (0–6) in Table B, add the numbers within each column, and enter the sum for each column (0–6) in the appropriate blank in Box C. Each of these seven Raw Score Totals is a number between 0 and 35.

Step 4 Table D contains the percentile scores for each Stage of Concern. Find the Raw Scale Score Total for Stage 0 from Box C; locate this number in the left-hand column in Table D, then look in the Stage 0 column to the right in Table D and circle that percentile ranking. Do the same for Stages 1 through 6, only match the left-hand column raw score with the corresponding stage.

Step 5 Transcribe the circled percentile scores for each stage (0–6) from Table D to Box E. Box E now contains seven numbers between 0 and 99.

Step 6 Box F contains the SoC graph. From Box E, take the percentile score for Stage 0 and mark that point with a dot on the Stage 0 vertical line on the SoC graph. Do the same for Stages 1 through 6. Connect the points to form the SoC profile.

For interpretation of the SoC profile, refer to Hall, George, and Rutherford (1979).

SoCQ Quick Scoring Device

A

Date: _____

Site: _____ SS#: _____

Innovation: _____

B

	Stage						
	0	1	2	3	4	5	6
	3__	6__	7__	4__	1__	5__	2__
	12__	14__	13__	8__	11__	10__	9__
	21__	15__	17__	16__	19__	18__	20__
	23__	26__	28__	25__	24__	27__	22__
	30__	35__	33__	34__	32__	29__	31__

C Raw Score Totals __ __ __ __ __ __ __

E Percentile Scores __ __ __ __ __ __ __

F

Relative Intensity (0–100) vs. SoC Stages: AWARENESS (0), INFORMATION (1), PERSONAL (2), MANAGEMENT (3), CONSEQUENCE (4), COLLABORATION (5), REFOCUSING (6)

D

Five Item Raw Scale Score Total	Stage						
	0	1	2	3	4	5	6
0	10	5	5	2	1	1	1
1	23	12	5	5	1	1	2
2	29	16	12	7	1	2	3
3	37	19	14	9	2	3	5
4	46	23	17	11	2	3	6
5	53	27	21	15	3	4	9
6	60	30	25	18	3	5	11
7	66	34	28	23	4	7	14
8	72	37	31	27	5	9	17
9	77	40	35	30	5	10	20
10	81	43	39	34	7	12	22
11	84	45	41	39	8	14	26
12	86	48	45	43	9	16	30
13	89	51	48	47	11	19	34
14	91	54	52	52	13	22	38
15	93	57	55	56	16	25	42
16	94	60	57	60	19	28	47
17	95	63	59	65	21	31	52
18	96	66	63	69	24	36	57
19	97	69	67	73	27	40	60
20	98	72	70	77	30	44	65
21	98	75	72	80	33	48	69
22	99	80	76	83	38	52	73
23	99	84	78	85	43	55	77
24	99	88	80	88	48	59	81
25	99	90	83	90	54	64	84
26	99	91	85	92	59	68	87
27	99	93	87	94	63	72	90
28	99	95	89	95	66	76	92
29	99	96	91	97	71	80	94
30	99	97	92	97	76	84	96
31	99	98	94	98	82	88	97
32	99	99	95	98	86	91	98
33	99	99	96	99	90	93	99
34	99	99	97	99	92	95	99
35	99	99	98	99	96	98	99

Concerns-Based Systems International

The SOCQ Quick Scoring Device was developed by Eddie W. Parker and Teresa H. Griffin.

284

LEVELS OF USE OF THE INNOVATION

CATEGORIES

SCALE POINT DEFINITIONS OF THE LEVELS OF USE OF THE INNOVATION

Levels of Use are distinct states that represent observably different types of behavior and patterns of innovation use as exhibited by individuals and groups. These levels characterize a user's development in acquiring new skills and varying use of the innovation. Each level encompasses a range of behaviors, but is limited by a set of identifiable Decision Points. For descriptive purposes, each level is defined by seven categories.

	KNOWLEDGE	ACQUIRING INFORMATION	SHARING
	That which the user knows about characteristics of the innovation, how to use it, and consequences of its use. This is cognitive knowledge related to using an innovation, not feelings or attitudes.	Solicits information about the innovation in a variety of ways, including questioning resources persons, corresponding with resources agencies, reviewing printed materials, and making visits.	Discusses the innovation with others. Shares plans, ideas, resources, outcomes, and problems related to use of the innovation.
LEVEL 0 NON-USE State in which the user has little or no knowledge of the innovation, no involvement with the innovation, and is doing nothing toward becoming involved.	Knows nothing about this or similar innovations or has only very limited general knowledge of efforts to develop innovations in the area. 0	Takes little or no action to solicit information beyond reviewing descriptive information about this or similar innovations when it happens to come to personal attention. 0	Is not communicating with others about innovation beyond possibly acknowledging that the innovation exists. 0
DECISION POINT A	*Takes action to learn more detailed information about the innovation.*		
LEVEL 1 ORIENTATION: State in which the user has acquired or is acquiring information about the innovation and/or has explored or is exploring its value orientation and its demands upon user and user system.	Knows general information about the innovation such as origin, characteristics, and, implementation requirements. I	Seeks descriptive material about the innovation. Seeks opinions and knowledge of others through discussions, visits or workshops. I	Discusses resources needed in general terms and/or exchanges descriptive information, materials, or ideas about the innovation and possible implications of its use. I
DECISION POINT B	*Makes a decision to use the innovation by establishing a time to begin.*		
LEVEL II PREPARATION State in which the user is preparing for first use of the innovation.	Knows logistical requirements, necessary resources and timing for initial use of the innovation, and details of initial experiences for clients. II	Seeks information and resources specifically related to preparation for use of the innovation in own setting. II	Discusses resources needed for initial use of the innovation. Joins others in pre-use training, and in planning for resources, logistics, schedules, etc., in preparation for first use. II
DECISION POINT C	*Changes, if any, and use are dominated by user needs. Clients may be valued, however management, time, or limited*		
LEVEL III MECHANICAL USE State in which the user focuses most effort on the short-term, day-to-day use of the innovation with little time for reflection. Changes in use are made more to meet user needs than client needs. The user is primarily engaged in a stepwise attempt to master the tasks required to use the innovation, often resulting in disjointed and superficial use.	**KNOWLEDGE** Knows on a day-to-day basis the requirements for using the innovation, is more knowledgeable about short-term activities and effects than long-range activities and effects, of use of the innovation. III	**ACQUIRING INFORMATION** Solicits management information about such things as logistics, scheduling techniques, and ideas for reducing amount of time and work required of user. III	**SHARING** Discusses management and logistical issues related to use of the innovation. Resources and materials are shared for purposes of reducing management, flow and logistical problems related to use of the innovation. III
DECISION POINT D-1	*A routine pattern of use is established. Changes for clients may be made routinely, but there are no recent changes outside*		
LEVEL IV A ROUTINE Use of the innovation is stabilized. Few if any changes are being made in ongoing use. Little preparation or thought is being given to improving innovation use or its consequences.	Knows both short- and long-term requirements for use and how to use the innovation with minimum effort or stress. IVA	Makes no special efforts to seek information as a part of ongoing use of the innovation. IVA	Describes current use of the innovation with little or no reference to ways of changing use. IVA
DECISIONS POINT D-2	*Changes use of the innovation based on formal or informal evaluation in order to increase client outcomes. They must be recent*		
LEVEL IV B REFINEMENT State in which the user varies the use of the innovation to increase the impact on clients within his/her immediate sphere of influence. Variations are based on knowledge of both short- and long-term consequences of client.	Knows cognitive and affective effects of the innovation on clients and ways for increasing impact on clients. IVB	Solicits information and materials that focus specifically on changing use of the innovation to affect client outcomes. IVB	Discusses own methods of modifying use of the innovation to change client outcomes. IVB
DECISION POINT E	*Initiates changes in use of innovation based on input of and in coordination with what colleagues are doing.*		
LEVEL V INTEGRATION State in which the user is combining own efforts to use the innovation with related activities of colleagues to achieve a collective impact on clients within their sphere of influence.	Knows how to coordinate own use of the innovation with colleagues to provide a collective impact on clients. V	Solicits information and opinions for the purpose of collaborating with others in use of the innovation. V	Discusses efforts to increase client impact through collaboration with others on personal use of the innovation. V
DECISION POINT F	*Begins exploring alternatives to or major modifications of the innovation presently in use.*		
LEVEL VI RENEWAL State in which the user reevaluates the quality of use of the innovation, seeks major modifications of or alternatives to present innovation to achieve increased impact on clients, examines new developments in the field, and explores new goals for self and the system.	Knows of alternatives that could be used to change or replace the present innovation that would improve the quality of outcomes of its use. VI	Seeks information and materials about others innovations as alternatives to the present innovation or for making major adaptations in the innovation. VI	Focuses discussions on identification of major alternatives or replacements for the current innovation. VI

Procedures for Adopting Educational Innovations Project. Research and Development Center for Teacher Education, University of Texas at Austin, 1975, N.I.E. Contract No. NIE-74-0087.

CATEGORIES

ASSESSING	PLANNING	STATUS REPORTING	PERFORMING
Examines the potential or actual use of the innovation or some aspect of it. This can be a mental assessment or can involve actual collection and analysis of data.	Designs and outlines short- and/or long-range steps to be taken during process of innovation adoption, i.e., aligns resources, schedules activities, meets with others to organize and/or coordinate use of the innovation.	Describes personal stand at the present time in relation to use of the innovation.	Carries out the actions and activities entailed in operationalizing the innovation.
Takes no action to analyze the innovation, its characteristics, possible use, or consequences of use.	Schedules no time and specifies no steps for the study or use of the innovation.	Reports little or no personal involvement with the innovation.	Takes no discernible action toward learning about or using the innovation. The innovation and/or its accouterments are not present or in use.
0	0	0	0
Analyzes and compares materials, content, requirements for use, evaluation reports, potential outcomes, strengths and weaknesses for purpose of making a decision about use of the innovation.	Plans to gather necessary information and resources as needed to make a decision for or against use of the innovation.	Reports presently orienting self to what the innovation is and is not.	Explores the innovation and requirements for its use by talking to others about it, reviewing descriptive information and sample materials, attending orientation sessions, and observing others using it.
I	I	I	I
Analyzes detailed requirements and available resources for initial use of the innovation.	Identifies steps and procedures entailed in obtaining resources and organizing activities and events or initial use of the innovation.	Reports preparing self for initial use of the innovation.	Studies reference materials in depth, organizes resources and logistics, schedules and receives skill training in preparation for initial use.
II	II	II	II

experimental knowledge dictate what the user does.

ASSESSING	PLANNING	STATUS REPORTING	PERFORMING
Examines own use of the innovation with respect to problems of logistics, management, time schedules, resources and general reactions of clients.	Plans for organizing and managing resources, activities, and events related primarily to immediate ongoing use of the innovation. Planned-for changes address managerial or logistical issues with a short-term perspective.	Reports that logistics, time, management, resource organizations, etc., are the focus of most personal efforts to use the innovation.	Manages innovation with varying degrees of efficiency. Often lacks anticipation of immediate consequences. The flow of actions in the user and clients is often disjointed, uneven and uncertain. When changes are made, they are primarily in response to logistical and organizational problems.
III	III	III	III

the pattern.

ASSESSING	PLANNING	STATUS REPORTING	PERFORMING
Limits evaluation activities to those administratively required, with little attention paid to findings for the purpose of changing use.	Plans intermediate and long-range actions with little projected variation in how the innovation will be used. Planning focuses on routine use of resources, personnel, etc.	Reports that personal use of the innovation is going along satisfactorily with few if any problems.	Uses the innovation smoothly with minimal management problems; over time, there is little variation in pattern of use.
IVA	IVA	IVA	IVA
Assesses use of the innovation for the purpose of changing current practices to improve client outcomes.	Develops intermediate and long-range plans that anticipate possible and needed steps, resources, and events designed to enhance client outcomes.	Reports varying use of the innovation in order to change client outcomes.	Explores and experiments with alternative combinations of the innovation with existing practices to maximize client involvement and to optimize client outcomes.
IVB	IVB	IVB	IVB
Appraises collaborative use of the innovation in terms of client outcomes and strengths and weaknesses of the integrated effort.	Plans specific actions to coordinate own use of the innovation with others to achieve increased impact on clients.	Reports spending time and energy collaborating with others about integrating own use of the innovation.	Collaborates with others in use of the innovation as a means of expanding the innovation's impact on clients. Changes in use are made in coordination with others.
V	V	V	V
Analyzes advantages and disadvantages of major modifications or alternatives to the present innovation.	Plans activities that involve pursuit of alternatives to enhance or replace the innovation.	Reports considering major modifications to present use of the innovation.	Explores other innovations that could be used in combination with or in place of the present innovation in an attempt to develop more effective means of achieving client outcomes.
VI	VI	VI	VI

Reprinted from Hall, G.E., Loucks, S.F., Rutherford, W.L. & Newlove, B.W. Levels of Use of the Innovation: A framework for analyzing innovation adoption. *The Journal of Teacher Education.* 1975. 26(1), 52–56

■ ■ ■ ■ ■

SIX DIMENSIONS OF CHANGE FACILITATOR STYLE

Cluster I: Concern for People

The first cluster of CF Style behaviors deals with how the principal, as the change facilitator, addresses the personal side of change. People have feelings and attitudes about their work and about how a change process is going. They have personal needs, too. Day to day, facilitators can monitor, attend to, and affect these concerns and needs in different ways and with different emphases. For example, it is possible to spend little time directly addressing the feelings of others or to become preoccupied with listening and responding to each concern that is expressed. The emphasis can also be on attending to individual concerns as they are expressed daily or on focusing on the more long-term needs of all staff, with attention to individual concerns on an as-needed basis.

The Concern for People cluster is composed of two dimensions that weigh the degree to which the moment-to-moment and daily behaviors of a facilitator emphasize *social/informal* and *formal/meaningful* interactions with teachers. The Social/Informal dimension addresses the extent to which the facilitator engages in informal social discussions with teachers.

Social/Informal   This dimension addresses the frequency and character of the facilitator's informal social discussions with teachers and other staff. Many of these discussions may not be even remotely related to the work of the school or a specific innovation. Facilitators who emphasize this cluster engage in frequent social inter-actions. They attend to feelings and perceptions by emphasizing listening, understanding, and acknowledging immediate concerns, rather than providing answers or anticipating long-range consequences. There is a personable, friendly, almost chatty tone to the interactions. When concerns are addressed, it is done in ways that are responsive rather than anticipatory.

Formal/Meaningful   This dimension addresses brief, task-oriented interactions that deal with specific aspects of the work and the details of the innovation implementation. Facilitators are centered on school tasks, priorities, and directions. Discussions and interactions are focused on teaching, learning, and other substantive issues directly related to use of the innovation. Interactions are primarily intended to support teachers in their school-related duties, and the facilitator is almost always looking for solutions that are lasting. The interactions and emphases are not overly influenced by superficial and short-lived feelings and needs. Teaching and learning activities and issues directly related to use of the innovation are emphasized.

Cluster II: Organizational Efficiency

The work of the organization can be facilitated with varying degrees of emphasis on obtaining resources, increasing efficiency, and consolidating or sharing responsibilities and authority. Principals can try to do almost everything themselves, or they can delegate responsibility to others. System procedures, role clarity, and work priorities can be made more or less clear, and resources can be organized in ways that increase or decrease availability and effectiveness. In this cluster the principal's administrative focus is examined along two dimensions—*trust in others* and *administrative efficiency.*

Trust in Others.   This dimension examines the extent to which the facilitator assigns others tasks of locating resources, establishing procedures, and managing schedules and time. When there is delay in making decisions, administrative systems and procedures are allowed to evolve in response to needs expressed by staff and to external pressures. The assumption is that teachers know how to accomplish their jobs and that they need a minimum of structuring and monitoring from the principal. As needs for additions or changes in structures, rules, and procedures emerge, they are gradually acknowledged and introduced as suggestions and guidelines rather than being directly established. Formalizing procedural and policy change is left to others and to time.

Administrative Efficiency.   This dimension addresses the extent to which establishing clear and smoothly running procedures and resource systems to help teachers and others do their jobs efficiently is a priority. Administration, scheduling, and production tasks are clearly described, understood, and used by all members of the organization. Emphasis is placed on having a high level of organizational efficiency so teachers can do their jobs better. As needs for new structures and procedures emerge, they are formally established.

Cluster III: Strategic Sense

To varying degrees, principals are aware of the relationship between the long-term goals and their own monthly, weekly, daily, and moment-to-moment activities and those of their school. Some principals are more "now" oriented and treat each event in isolation from its part in the grand scheme, while others think and act with a vivid mental image of how today's actions contribute to accomplishing long-range aspirations. Some reflect about what they are doing and how all of their activities can add up, while others focus on the moment. Principals also vary in the degree to which they encourage or discourage the participation of external facilitators and in how they prescribe their role in the schools. This cluster examines the principal's strategic sense according to two dimensions: *day-to-day* and *vision and planning.*

Day-to-Day.   At the high end of this dimension, there is little anticipation of future developments, needs, successes, or failures. Interventions are made in response to issues and needs as they arise. Knowledge of the details of the innovation is limited, and the amount of intervention with teachers is restricted to responding to questions and gradually completing routine steps. Images of how things could be improved and how more rapid gains could be made are incomplete, limited in scope, and lacking in imagination. There is little anticipation of longer term patterns or consequences. External facilitators come and go as they wish and spend an extraordinary amount of effort advising the principal.

Vision and Planning.   The facilitator with a high emphasis on this dimension has a long-term vision that is integrated with an understanding of the day-to-day activities as the means to achieve the desired end. The facilitating activity is intense, with a high degree of interaction related to the work at hand. There is depth of knowledge about teaching and learning. Teachers and others are pushed to accomplish all that they can. Assertive leadership, continual monitoring, supportive actions, and creative interpretations of policy and use of resources to reach long-term goals are clear indicators of this dimension. Also present is the ability to anticipate the possible systemic effects of interventions and the broader consequences of day-to-day actions. Effects are accurately predicted, and interventions are made in anticipation of likely trends. Moment-to-moment interactions with staff and external facilitators are centered on the present work within a context of the long-range aspirations. The focus is on completing tasks, accomplishing school objectives, and making progress. External facilitators are encouraged to be involved in the school according to the principal's perception of their expertise and value.

For additional information, see G. E. Hall and A. A. George, "The Impact of Principal Change Facilitator Style on School and Classroom Culture," in H. Jerome Freiberg (Ed.), *School Climate: Measuring, Improving and Sustaining Healthy Learning Environments* (Philadelphia and London: Falmer Press, 1999), pp. 165–185.

REFERENCES

Ackoff, R. L., & Emery, F. G. (1972). *On purposeful systems.* Chicago: Aldine-Atherton.

Allen, R. (2003, November). Building school culture in an age of accountability: Principals lead through sharing tasks. *Education Update, 45*(7), 1, 3, 7–8.

Alquist, A., & Hendrickson, M. (1999). Mapping the configurations of mathematics teaching. *Journal of Classroom Interaction, 34*(1), 18–26.

Alvesson, M., & Deetz, S. (1996). Critical theory and postmodernism approaches to organizational studies. In S. R. Clegg, C. Hardy, & W. R. Nord (Eds.), *Handbook of organization studies.* Thousand Oaks, CA: Sage.

Anderson, B. (1993, September). The stages of systemic change. *Educational Leadership, 51*(1), 14–17.

Argyris, C. (1982). *Reasoning, learning, and action: Individual and organizational.* San Francisco: Jossey-Bass.

Argyris, C., & Schon, D. (1978). *Organizational learning.* San Francisco: Jossey-Bass.

Banathy, B. H. (1973). *Developing a system's view of education: A systems models approach.* Palo Alto, CA: Fearon.

Banathy, B. H. (1995). A systems view and systems design in education. In P. M. Jenlink (Ed.), *Systemic change: Touchstones for the future school.* Arlington Heights, IL: Skylight Professional Development.

Banathy, B. H. (1996). *Designing social systems in a changing world.* New York: Plenum.

Bass, B. M. (1990). *Bass & Stogdill's handbook of leadership, a survey of theory, research & managerial applications* (3rd ed.). New York: The Free Press.

Bavelas, A. (1950). Communication patterns in task-oriented groups. *Journal of Accoustical Society of America, 22,* 725–730.

Beckhard, R. (1969). *Organization development: Strategies and models.* Reading, MA: Addison-Wesley.

Bellah, R. N., & Madsen, R. (1985). *Habits of the heart.* New York: Harper and Row.

Blake, R. R., and Mouton, J. S. (1964). *The managerial grid.* Houston: Gulf.

Bobbett, J. J., Ellett, C. D., Teddlie, C., Olivier, D. F., & Rugutt, J. (2002). *School culture and school effectiveness in demonstrably effective and ineffective schools.* Paper presented at the annual meeting of the American Education Research Association, New Orleans.

Bond-Huie, S., Buttram, J. L., Deviney, F. P., Murphy, K. M., & Ramos, M. A. (November 2004). *Alignment in SEDL's Working Systemically Model.* Austin, TX: Southwest Educational Development Laboratory.

Boyd, V. (1992a). Creating a context for change. *Issues . . . About Change, 2*(2), 1–10.

Boyd, V. (1992b). *School context: Bridge or barrier for change.* Austin, TX: Southwest Educational Development Laboratory.

Boyd, V., Fuentes, N., Hord, S. M., Mendez-Morse, S., & Rodriquez, D. (1993). *Leadership for change.* Austin, TX: Southwest Educational Development Laboratory.

Boyd, V., & Hord, S. M. (1994). *Principals and the new paradigm: Schools as learning communities.* Paper presented at the annual meeting of the American Educational Research Association, New Orleans.

291

Bridge, C. A. (1995). *The progress of implementation of the K–3 primary program in Kentucky's elementary schools.* Paper presented at the annual meeting of the American Educational Research Association, San Francisco.

Brown, J., & Isaacs, D. (1996/Jan. 1997). Conversations as a core business process. *The Systems Thinker.* Cambridge, MA: Pegasus Communications.

Caine, R. N., & Caine, G. (1997). *Education on the edge of possibility.* Alexandria, VA: Association for Supervision and Curriculum Development.

Capra, F. (1997, April). *Creativity and leadership in learning communities.* Lecture presented at Mill Valley School District.

Carter, L., Giber, D., & Goldsmith, M. (Eds.). (2001). *Best practices in organization development and change: Culture, leadership, retention, performance and coaching.* San Francisco: Jossey-Bass/Pfeiffer.

Charters, W. W., Jr., & Jones, J. E. (1973). On the risk of appraising nonevents in program evaluation. *Educational Researcher, 2*(11), 5–7.

Chamblee, G. E., & Slough, S. W. (2004). *Using the Concerns-Based Adoption Model to assess changes in technology implementation: A ten-year retrospective.* Presented at the annual conference of the Society for Information Technology and Teacher Education (SITE), 1, 864–871, http://www.aace.org.

Checkland, P. (1981). *Systems thinking: Systems practice.* New York: Wiley.

Chin, R., & Benne, K. D. (1969). General strategies for effecting changes in human systems. In W. G. Bennis, K. D. Benne, & R. Chin (Eds.), *The planning of change* (2nd ed., pp. 32–59). New York: Holt, Rinehart and Winston.

Clune, W. (1993). Systemic educational policy: A conceptual framework In Susan H. Fuhrman (Ed.), *Designing coherent education policy: Improving the system.* New York: Jossey-Bass.

Danek, J., Calbert, R., & Chubin, D. (1994, February). *NSF's programmatic reform: The catalyst for systemic change.* Paper presented at Building the System: Making Science Education Work Conference, Washington, DC.

Darling-Hammond, L. (1996). The quiet revolution: Rethinking teacher development. *Educational Leadership, 53*(6), 4–10.

Deal, T. E., & Kennedy, A. A. (1982). *Corporate cultures: The rites and rituals of corporate life.* New York: Addison-Wesley.

Deal, T. E., & Peterson, K. D. (1990). *The principal's role in shaping school culture.* Washington, DC: U.S. Department of Education.

Dunn, L., & Borchardt, P. *The ESSENTIAL curriculum.* Kansas City, MO: The Teel Institute, 101 East Armour Blvd.

Eden, C., & Huxham, C. (1996). Action research for the study of organizations. In S. R. Clegg, C. Hardy, & W. R. Nord (Eds.), *Handbook of organization studies* (pp. 526–542). Thousand Oaks, CA: Sage.

Entrekin, K. M. (1991). *Principal change facilitator styles and the implementation of consultation-based prereferral child study teams.* Unpublished doctoral dissertation, Temple University.

Fiedler, F. E. (1978). The contingency model and the dynamics of the leadership process. In L. Berkowitz (Ed.), *Advances in experimental and social psychology* (pp. 59–112). New York: Academic Press.

Floden, R., Goertz, M., & O'Day, J. (1995, September). Capacity building in systemic reform. *Phi Delta Kappan, 77*(1), 19–21.

French, W. (1971, August). *A definition and history of organization development: Some comments.* Proceedings of the 31st Annual Meeting of the Academy of Management, Atlanta, GA.

Fullan, M. (1993). Innovation, reform, and restructuring strategies. *Challenges and achievement in American education,* 1993 Yearbook of the Association for Supervision and Curriculum Development, Alexandria, VA.

Fullan, M., Miles, M. B., & Taylor, G. (1980). Organization development in schools: The state of the art. *Review of Educational Research, 50*(1), 121–183.

Fuller, F. F. (1969). Concerns of teachers: A developmental conceptualization. *American Educational Research Journal, 6*(2), 207–226.

Fuller, F. F. (1970). *Personalized education for teachers: An introduction for teacher educators.* The University of Texas at Austin, Research and Development Center for Teacher Education.

Fuller, F. F., & Bown, O. H. (1975). Becoming a teacher. *Teacher Education 1975.* Chicago: The National Society for the Study of Education.

Garmston, R., & Wellman, B. (2000). *The adaptive school: Developing and facilitating collaborative groups.* El Dorado Hills, CA: Four Hats Seminar.

George, A. A., Hall, G. E., & Uchiyama, K. (2000). Extent of implementation of a standards-based approach to teaching mathematics and student outcomes. *Journal of Classroom Interaction, 35*(1), 8–25.

Gonzalez, C. E., Resta, P. E., & De Hoyos, M. L. (2005). *Barriers and facilitators on implementation of policy initiatives to transform higher education teaching-learning process.* Paper submitted for presentation at the annual meeting of the American Educational Research Association, Montreal.

Hall, G. E. (2001). *Principal leadership and the devolution of organization culture.* Paper presented at the annual meeting of the American Educational Research Association, Seattle.

Hall, G. E., & George, A. A. (1999). The impact of principal Change Facilitator Style on school and classroom culture. In H. J. Freiberg (Ed.), *School climate: Measuring, improving and sustaining healthy learning environments.* Philadelphia: Falmer Press.

Hall, G. E., George, A., & Rutherford, W. L. (1979). *Measuring stages of concern about the innovation: A manual for use of the SoC Questionnaire* (Report No. 3032). Austin: The University of Texas at Austin, Research and Development Center for Teacher Education. (ERIC Document Reproduction Service No. ED 147 342).

Hall, G. E., & Hord, S. M. (1984). A framework for analyzing what change facilitators do: The Intervention Taxonomy. *Knowledge: Creation, Diffusion, Utilization, 5*(3), 275–307.

Hall, G. E., & Hord, S. M. (1987). *Change in schools: Facilitating the process.* Albany, NY: SUNY Press.

Hall, G. E., Hord, S. M., & Griffin, T. H. (1980). *Implementation at the school building level: The development and analysis of nine mini-case studies* (Report No. 3098). Austin: The University of Texas at Austin, Research and Development Center for Teacher Education. (ERIC Document Reproduction Service No. ED 207 170).

Hall, G. E., & Loucks, S. F. (1977). A developmental model for determining whether the treatment is actually implemented. *American Education Research Journal, 14*(3), 263–276.

Hall, G. E., Newlove, B. W., George, A. A., Rutherford, W. L., & Hord, S. M. (1991). *Measuring change facilitator stages of concern: A manual for use of the CFSoC Questionnaire.* Greeley: University of Northern Colorado, Center for Research on Teaching and Learning (Available from the Southwest Educational Development Laboratory).

Hall, G. E., & Rutherford, W. L. (1976). Concerns of teachers about implementing team teaching. *Educational Leadership, 34*(3), 227–233.

Hall, G. E., Rutherford, W. L., & Griffin, T. H. (1982). *Three change facilitator styles: Some indicators and a proposed framework.* Austin: The University of Texas at Austin, Research and Development Center for Teacher Education. (ERIC Document Reproduction Service No. ED 220 961).

Hall, G. E., Rutherford, W. L., Hord, S. M., & Huling, L. L. (1984). Effects of three principal styles on school improvement. *Educational Leadership, 41*(5), 22–29.

Hall, G. E., & Shieh, W. H. (1998). Supervision and organizational development. In G. R. Firth & E. F. Pajak (Eds.), *Handbook of research on school supervision.* New York: Simon & Schuster Macmillan.

Hall, G. E., Wallace, R. C., & Dossett, W. A. (1973). *A developmental conceptualization of the adoption process within educational institutions* (Report No. 3006). Austin: The University of Texas at Austin, Research and Development Center for Teacher Education. (ERIC Document Reporduction Service No. ED 095 126).

Hargreaves, A. (1997). Rethinking educational change: Going deeper and wider in the quest for success. In A. Hargreaves (Ed.), *ASCD yearbook: Rethinking educational change with heart and mind* (pp. 1–26). Alexandria, VA: Association for Supervision and Curriculum Development.

Harris, M. (1968). *The rise of anthropological theory.* New York: Crowell.

Hatch, M. J. (1993). The dynamics of organizational culture. *Academic Management Review, 19*(4), 657–693.

Heck, S., Stiegelbauer, S. M., Hall, G. E., & Loucks, S. F. (1981). *Measuring innovation configurations: Procedures and applications* (Report No. 3108). Austin: The University of Texas at Austin, Research and Development Center for Teacher Education. (ERIC Document Reproduction Service No. ED 204 147).

Hersey, P., & Blanchard, K. H. (1988). *Management of organizational behavior: Utilizing human resources.* Englewood Cliffs, NJ: Prentice-Hall.

Hill, P. W., & Crevola, C. A. (1999). The role of standards in educational reform for the 21st century. In D. D. Marsh (Ed.), *1999 ASCD yearbook: Preparing our schools for the 21st century* (pp. 117–142). Alexandria, VA: Association for Supervision and Curriculum Development.

Hord, S. M. (1992). *Facilitative leadership: The imperative for change.* Austin, TX: Southwest Educational Development Laboratory.

Hord, S. M. (1992). *Voices from a place for children.* Austin, TX: Southwest Educational Development Laboratory.

Hord, S. M. (1993). *A place for children: Continuous quest for quality.* Austin, TX: Southwest Educational Development Laboratory.

Hord, S. M. (1997). *Professional learning communities: Communities of continuous inquiry and improvement.* Austin, TX: Southwest Educational Development Laboratory.

Hord, S. M., & Huling-Austin, L. (1986). Effective curriculum implementation: Some promising new insights. *The Elementary School Journal, 87*(1), 97–115.

Hord, S. M., Rutherford, W. L., Huling-Austin, L. L., & Hall, G. E. (1987). *Taking charge of change.* Alexandria, VA: Association for Supervision and Curriculum Development.

Hougen, M. C. (1984). *High school principals: An analysis of their approach to facilitating implementation of microcomputers.* Doctoral dissertation, The University of Texas at Austin.

House, E. R. (1974). *The politics of educational innovation.* Berkeley, CA: McCutchan.

James, L. R., & Jones, A. P. (1974). Organizational climate: A review of theory and research. *Psychological Bulletin, 81*(12), 1096–1112.

Jehue, R. J. (2000). *Development of a measure for assessing military leaders' change facilitator styles.* Unpublished doctoral dissertation, University of Northern Colorado.

Jenlink, P. M. (1995). *Systemic change: Touchstones for the future school.* Arlington Heights, IL: Skylight Professional Development.

Jenlink, P. M., Reigeluth, C. M., Carr, A. A., & Nelson, L. M. (1996, January & February). An expedition for change: Facilitating the systemic change process in school districts. *Tech Trends, 41*(1), 21–30.

Johnson, M. H. (2000). A district-wide agenda to improve teaching and learning in mathematics. *Journal of Classroom Interaction, 35*(1), 1–7.

Joyce, B., Wolf, J., & Calhoun, E. (1993). *The self-renewing school.* Alexandria, VA: Association for Supervision and Curriculum Development.

Kimberly, J. R., & Nielsen, W. R. (1975). Organization development and change in organizational performance. *Administrative Science Quarterly, 20,* 191–206.

Knapp, M. S., Copland, M. A., & Talbert, J. E. (2003, February). *Leading for learning: Reflective tools for school and district leaders.* Seattle: University of Washington, Center for the Study of Teaching and Policy.

Koon, S. L. (1995). *The relationship of implementation of an entrepreneurial development innovation to student outcomes.* Doctoral dissertation, University of Missouri–Kansas City.

Kourilsky, M. L. (1983). *Mini-society: Experiencing real-world economics in the elementary school classroom.* Menlo Park, CA: Addison-Wesley.

Kuhn, T. S. (1970). *The structure of scientific revolutions.* Chicago: University of Chicago Press.

Laszlo, E. (1972). *The systems view of the world.* New York: Braziller.

Lee, V. E., Smith, J. B., & Croninger, R. G. (1995, Fall). Another look at high school restructuring. *Issues in restructuring schools.* Madison: Center on Organization and Restructuring of Schools, School of Education, University of Wisconsin at Madison.

Leithwood, K. A., & Montgomery, D. J. (1982). The role of the elementary school principal in program improvement. *Review of Educational Research, (52)*3, 309–339.

Lieberman, A. (1995). Practices that support teacher development: Transforming conceptions of professional learning. *Phi Delta Kappan, 76*(8), 591–596.

Likert, R. (1967). *The human organization: Its management and value.* New York: McGraw-Hill.

Lippitt, R., Watson, J., & Westley, B. (1958). *The dynamics of planned change.* New York: Harcourt Brace.

Little, J. W. (1982). Norms of collegiality and experimentation: Workplace conditions of school success. *American Educational Research Journal, 19*(3), 325–340.

Little, J. W., & McLaughlin, M. W. (1993). *Teachers' work: Individuals, colleagues and contexts.* New York: Teachers College Press.

Loucks, S. F., Newlove, B. W., & Hall, G. E. (1975). *Measuring levels of use of the innovation: A manual for trainers, interviewers, and raters.* Austin: The University of Texas at Austin, Research and Development Center for Teacher Education.

Lowham, J. (1995). Evolution of intentions: From state policy development to teacher implementation. In D. S. G. Carter & M. H. O'Neill (Eds.), *Case studies of educational change: An international perspective.* Washington, DC: Falmer Press.

Mann, F. C. & Likert, R. (1952, Winter). The need for research on the communication of research results. *Human Oranization,* 15–19.

Martin, J. (2002). *Organizational culture*. Thousand Oaks, CA: Sage.

Matthews, R. J., Marshall, A. K, & Milne, G. R. (April, 2000). *One year on: Report of the notebook evaluation*. Burwood, Victoria, Australia: Deakin University.

McGill, M. E. (1977). *Organization development for operating managers*. New York: AMA-COM.

McGregor, D. (1960). *The human side of management*. New York: McGraw-Hill.

McLaughlin, M. W., & Talbert, J. E. (1993). *Contexts that matter for teaching and learning*. Stanford, CA: Center for Research on the Context of Secondary School Teaching, Stanford University.

Miles, M. B. (Ed.). (1971). *Innovation in education*. New York: Columbia University.

Miles, M. B. (1979). Ethical issues in OD. *OD Practitioner, 11*(3), 1–10.

National Science Foundation. (1993, October). *Presentation on mid-point review,* Washington, DC.

National Staff Development Council. (2001). *National Staff Development Council's standards for staff development, revised*. Oxford, OH: National Staff Development Council.

Newlove, B. W., & Hall, G. E. (1976). *A manual for assessing open-ended statements of concern about the innovation* (Report No. 3029). Austin: The University of Texas at Austin, Research and Development Center for Teacher Education. (ERIC Document Reproduction Service No. ED 144 207).

Novak, A. (1992). *The entrepreneur's Fast Trac II handbook*. Denver, CO: Premier Entrepreneur Programs, PO Box 1236.

Pasmore, W. A., & Woodman, R. W. (Eds.). (2003). *Research in organizational change and development, Vol. 14*. Boston: Elsevier Science.

Persichitte, K. A., & Bauer, J. W. (1996). Diffusion of computer-based technologies: Getting the best start. *Journal of Information Technology for Teacher Education, 5*(1–2), 35–41.

Rogers, E. M. (2003). *Diffusion of innovations* (5th ed.). New York: The Free Press.

Rood, M., & Hinson, R. (2002). *Measuring the effectiveness of collaborative school reform: Implementation and outcomes*. Paper presented at the annual meeting of the American Evaluation Association, Washington, DC.

Rosenholtz, S. (1989). *Teacher's workplace: The social organizations of schools*. New York: Longman.

Rothwell, W. J., Sullivan, R., & McLean, G. N. (1995). *Practicing organization development: A guide for consultants*. San Francisco: Jossey-Bass Pfeiffer.

Roy, P., & Hord, S. (2003). *Moving NSDC's staff development standards into practice: Innovation configurations*. Oxford, OH: National Staff Development Council.

Ryan, B., & Gross, N. C. (1943). The diffusion of hybrid seed corn in two Iowa communities. *Rural Sociology, 8,* 15–24.

Sashkin, M., & Egermeier, J. (1992). *School change models and processes: A review of research and practice*. Paper presented at the annual meeting of the American Educational Research Association, San Francisco.

Schein, E. (1985). *Organizational culture and leadership: A dynamic view*. San Francisco: Jossey-Bass.

Schein, E. (1992). *Organizational culture and leadership: A dynamic view*. (2nd ed.). San Francisco: Jossey-Bass.

Schiller, J. (1991, Winter). Implementing computer education: The role of the primary principal. *Australian Journal of Educational Technology, 7*(1), 48–69.

Schiller, J. (1991). Implementing computer education: The role of the primary principal. *Australian Journal of Educational Technology, 14*(4), 36–39.

Schiller, J. (2002). Interventions by school leaders in effective ICT implementation: Perceptions of Australian principals. Special issue: "Leadership of Information Technology in Education." *Journal for Information Technology for Teacher Education, 11*(3), 289–301.

Schiller, J. (2003, July/August). The elementary school principal as a change facilitator in ICT integration. *The Technology Source,* http://ts.mivu.org.

Schmoker, M. (1997). Setting goals in turbulent times. In A. Hargreaves (Ed.), *ASCD yearbook: Rethinking educational change with heart and mind.* Alexandria, VA: Association for Supervision and Curriculum Development.

Schmuck, R. A. (1987). *Organization development in schools: Contemporary conceptual practices.* Eugene: Center on Organizational Development in Schools, Oregon University. (ERIC Document Reproduction Service No. ED 278 119).

Schmuck, R. A., & Runkel, P. J. (1994). *Handbook of organization development in schools* (4th ed.) Prospect Heights, IL: Waveland Press.

Senge, P. M. (1990). *The fifth discipline: The art and practice of the learning organization.* New York: Doubleday/Currency.

Shieh, W. H. (1996). *Environmental factors, principal's change facilitator style and implementation of the cooperative learning project in selected schools in Taiwan.* Unpublished doctoral dissertation, University of Northern Colorado.

Silberman, M. (1999). *101 ways to make meetings active.* San Francisco: Jossey-Bass Pfeiffer.

Smircich, L. (1983). Organizations as shared meanings. In L. Pondy, P. Frost, G. Morgan, & T. Dandridge (Eds.), *Organizational symbolism* (pp. 55–65). Greenwich, CT: JAI.

Smith, J., & O'Day, J. (1991). *Putting the pieces together: Systemic school reform.* CPRE Policy Brief. New Brunswick, NJ: Eagleton Institute of Politics.

Sparks, D. (2004, May). Set goals for learning with a sense of urgency. *Results.* Oxford, OH: National Staff Development Council.

Spradley, J. P. (1979). *The ethnographic interview.* New York: Holt, Rinehart and Winston.

Staessens, K. (1993). Identification and description of professional culture in innnovating schools. *Qualitative Studies in Education, 6*(2), 111–128.

Stiegelbauer, S. M., Tobia, E. F., Thompson, T. L., & Sturges, K. M. (2004). *Building capacity in low-performing settings: Using research and data-based planning as a tool for system-wide change.* Paper presented at the annual meeting of the American Educational Research Association, New Orleans.

Tarde, G. (1903). *The laws of imitation.* (Trans. Elsie Clews Parson). New York: Holt (reprinted 1969, Chicago: University of Chicago Press).

Thornton, E., & West, C. E. (1999). Extent of teacher use of a mathematics curriculum innovation in one district: Years 1 and 2 Levels of Use (LoU). *Journal of Classroom Interaction, 34*(1), 9–17.

Timar, T., & Kirp, D. (1989, March). Education reform in the 1980s: Lessons from the states. *Phi Delta Kappan, 70*(7), 504–511.

Trice, H. M., & Beyer, J. M. (1993). *The cultures of work organizations.* Englewood Cliffs, NJ: Prentice-Hall.

Trohoski, C. G. (1984). *Principals' interventions in the implementation of a school health program.* Unpublished Ph.D. thesis, University of Pennsylvania.

Van den Berg, R., & Vandenberghe, R. (1981). *Onderwijsinnovatie in verschuivend perspectief.* Amsterdam: Uitgeverij Zwijsen.

Van den Berg, R., & Vandenberghe, R. (1986). *Large-scale change and school improvement: Dilemmas and solutions.* Leuven, Belgium: AACCO.

Vandenberghe, R. (1988). *Development of a questionnaire for assessing principal change facilitator style.* Paper presented at the annual meeting of the American Educational Research Association, New Orleans. (ERIC Document Reproduction Service No. ED 297 463).

Weick, K. E. (1976, March). Educational organizations as loosely coupled systems. *Administrative Science Quarterly, 21*(1), 1–19.

Wheatley, M. J. (1992). *Leadership and the new science: Learning about organization from an orderly universe.* San Francisco: Berrett-Koehler.

Wheatley, M. J., & Kellner-Rogers, M. (1996). A *simpler way.* San Francisco: Berrett-Koehler.

Zmuda, A., Kuklis, R., & Kline, E. (2004). *Transforming schools: Creating a culture* of *continuous improvement.* Alexandria, VA: Association for Supervision and Curriculum Development.

Note: Copies of key papers and reports related to the Concerns Based Adoption Model, and the technical manuals for measuring Stages of Concern, Levels of Use, and Innovation Configurations can be obtained from the Southwest Educational Development Laboratory in Austin, Texas. The authors can be contacted about the various reports and manuals as well as consultation in their use.

INDEX